Lightning War

Blitzkrieg in the West, 1940

RONALD E. POWASKI

John Wiley & Sons, Inc.

Published by John Wiley & Sons, Inc., Hoboken, New Jersey
Published simultaneously in Canada

Maps copyright © 1969, 1988, from *The Collapse of the Third Republic* by William L. Shirer and *Dunkirk: The Patriotic Myth* by Nicholas Harman.

For general information about our other products and services, please contact our Customer Care Department within the United States at (800) 762-2974, outside the United States at (317) 572-3993 or fax (317) 572-4002.

Wiley also publishes its books in a variety of electronic formats. Some content that appears in print may not be available in electronic books.

Library of Congress Cataloging-in-Publication Data:

Powaski, Ronald E.
    Lightning war : Blitzkrieg in the west, 1940 / Ronald Powaski.
      p.   cm.
    Includes bibliographical references and index.
    ISBN 0-471-39431-9
    1. World War, 1939–1945—Campaigns—Western Front. 2. Lightning war.
   3. World War, 1939–1945—Aerial operations, German. I. Title.

D755.2 P69 2003
940.54′21—dc21

2002015344

Credits

Photo Credits

To Olga

Contents

Acknowledgments

In a work of this scope, I am indebted not only to the participants who recorded and recollected the great events that I have attempted to depict in this book, but also to the dozens of historians on whose interpretations of these events I have greatly relied. I have attempted to acknowledge my debt to them in the book's endnotes.

I want to thank my agent, Ed Knappman, who encouraged me to proceed with the project, and my editor, Hana Lane, who guided it to completion. I also want to thank two wonderful research assistants, Meg Fleming and Marian Linsz, working in the Interlibrary Loan Department of Euclid, Ohio, Public Library, who spent hours tracking down and procuring books and articles for this history. Nor can I forget the assistance of Joost Vaesen and Guy Bastiens, who guided me through, and provided information about, Fort Eben Emael.

I owe a special thanks to Lieutenant Colonel David Nichting Jr. (U.S. Army); his wife, Lisa Nichting; Sergeant Karl Van Acken (U.S. Army); and his wife, Zulma Van Acken. Their assistance greatly facilitated our research, and their gracious hospitality while we were in Belgium made our stay in that country an extremely pleasant experience, one we will never forget.

As always, I am most indebted to my best friend and wife, Jo Ann. Her patience, encouragement, wise counsel, and assistance (especially in helping with the research work and reading the manuscript) made the task of writing the book more pleasurable than I could have believed possible.

This book is dedicated to Olga Wojciak. Her compassionate concern for, and assistance to, my mother in her time of need is deeply appreciated by me and my family and will never be forgotten.

Prologue

Europe plunged into war, for the second time in the twentieth century, on September 3, 1939. Two days earlier, Adolf Hitler's *Wehrmacht* (armed forces) had invaded Poland, and Britain and France, Poland's allies, responded by declaring war on Germany.

But hardly anyone in either Britain or France was eager for another conflict with the Germans, considering the horrible bloodletting and destruction of World War I, which had ended only two decades earlier. To be sure, the French mobilized their army and the British sent another expeditionary force to France. But with the exception of a halfhearted invasion of Germany by a very small part of the French army—an invasion that advanced a mere fifteen miles at a time when Germany's western frontier was virtually denuded of military forces—the western Allies did little to help the Poles. Not surprisingly, Poland, which also was invaded by the Soviet army on September 17, was conquered in only three weeks and compelled to surrender on September 25.

With the defeat of Poland, many, if not most, in the west believed there was no good reason to continue the war. This sentiment was evident in the comments of a Frenchman who had made a brilliant record in World War I: "This time I'm going to lie low. I'm not going to get myself killed for Poland." This was a sentiment the Germans did everything to encourage. "Why should war in the West be fought?" Hitler asked in a speech to the German *Reichstag* (parliament) on October 6. "It would be senseless to annihilate millions of men" in order to "reconstruct" Poland.

What followed was one of the strangest intervals in the history of warfare, eight months without meaningful military activity on the western front. Soldiers on both sides watched but did not fire on one another. "Why shoot at the Germans?" was the common sentiment of Allied soldiers. "They would only shoot at us." The Germans called this period the *Sitzkrieg* (sitting war), the French *La Drôle de guerre* (the strange war), and the British the "Phony War."

1

Hitler, however, could not allow the Phony War to continue indefinitely. The conquest of Poland left the Nazi dictator in command of most
of Central Europe. But as long as Britain and France continued in the war,
Hitler's goal of dominating the entire continent would be unfulfilled. In
order to become master of Europe, he would have to eliminate the French
army, which was touted as the strongest in Europe. Hitler was confident
that without France's army, Britain would have to seek a diplomatic way
out of the conflict.

On October 10, Hitler convened a meeting of the *Wehrmacht*'s leaders
and informed them that Germany's war aim was "the final destruction of
the West." He ordered them to prepare an attack on France through neutral Belgium, Holland, and Luxembourg "at as early a date as possible."

But the leadership of the German army, which opposed an all-out war
with France and Britain, because they believed Germany would lose it,
complied only halfheartedly. The war plan drawn up by the Army, *Fall
Gelb* (Plan Yellow), Hitler believed, would not produce a decisive German
victory in the West.

Nevertheless, at first, Hitler had no alternative plan of attack. This
factor, combined with his intense desire to attack in the west while the
Allies were still relatively unprepared, prompted him to stick with the
army's plan. However, repeated attempts to implement it during the fall
and early winter of 1939–1940 were thwarted by bad weather, causing the
Führer to postpone one offensive commencement date after another.

Then, on January 10, 1940, the forced landing of a Luftwaffe plane on
Belgian soil would precipitate a series of events and developments that
together would lead to Hitler's greatest military triumph—and first major
strategic mistake.

CHAPTER ONE

The Reinberger Incident

AN INVITATION TO DISASTER

At ten o'clock in the morning of January 10, 1940, Luftwaffe majors Erich Hoenmanns and Helmuth Reinberger walked across the tarmac of Loddenheide airfield near Münster, Westphalia, and climbed into a waiting Messerschmitt-108 "Typhoon." They quickly took off into a brilliantly blue winter sky.

Hoenmanns, who piloted the plane, was a veteran of World War I. Denied a combat role in the new conflict because of a mild cardiac condition, he had been given command of the airbase at Loddenheide. Reinberger, who sat in the passenger seat behind Hoenmanns, had been in charge of the paratrooper school in Stendal before he was temporarily assigned to the planning staff of General Kurt Student's Seventh Air Division. Unknown to Hoenmanns, in the yellow pigskin briefcase that Reinberger clutched tightly on his lap were the top-secret plans for Hitler's invasion of western Europe.

Hoenmanns and Reinberger had met only the night before in the officers' lounge at the air base. Over a few drinks, Reinberger had explained to Hoenmanns that he was on his way to Cologne, some eighty miles distant, to attend an important meeting at the headquarters of the Second Air Fleet. Coincidentally, Hoenmanns's home was in Cologne. Eager to see his wife, as well as to get in some flying time, Hoenmanns offered to fly Reinberger to the Rhineland city.

Reinberger hesitated before accepting the offer. He realized only too well that members of the planning staff were prohibited from traveling by plane and were liable to severe punishment if they did. The nature of the plans he was carrying only added to the risk of flying. Yet he was equally concerned that train tie-ups, which were now frequent because of the movement of German troops and supplies to the western front, might make him late for his meeting. After weighing the risks briefly, Reinberger concluded that the danger of flying with Hoenmanns was much less than the probability of arriving late in Cologne. He accepted the pilot's offer.

THE CRASH

The flight over the Ruhr Valley went well. The sky formed a deep blue dome; a brilliant coat of white that sparkled in the golden early winter sun covered the landscape below.

But as the two German airmen were enjoying the snow-covered scenery speeding by beneath them, a layer of dark gray mist suddenly appeared on the southern horizon. Within a few minutes, the Messerschmitt was engulfed by the thick vapor. Reinberger glanced anxiously at Hoenmanns, but the pilot did not seem bothered by the changing weather. However, as the mist thickened and visibility dropped to zero, Hoenmanns became increasingly nervous as he realized that he had lost his bearings. After setting a course for the south-southeast, a direction he thought would take them toward the Rhine, Hoenmanns decided to try to get below the cloud deck. As the plane descended, the mist thinned and the snow-covered ground appeared once again, but the Rhine was nowhere in sight.

Now Hoenmanns panicked. He again altered course, trying to find the elusive Rhine. Suddenly, on the white horizon, a black winding ribbon of water was visible. Hoenmanns thought it must be the Rhine. But before he could confirm this assumption, disaster struck. As the pilot raised himself out of his seat to get a better look at the approaching river, he accidentally hit the plane's fuel switch and cut off the engine's gasoline supply. While he feverishly tried to correct his error, the engine coughed, sputtered, and finally stopped altogether. The Messerschmitt dropped rapidly toward the ground, nearly out of control. Narrowly missing two high-tension wires, the plane swept between two poplars, shearing off its wings before the fuselage finally slid to a rest in a snow-covered thicket.

Although badly shaken by the crash, both Hoenmanns and Reinberger managed to free themselves from the plane with only minor cuts and bruises. Still clutching the yellow briefcase, Reinberger for the first time revealed the nature of its contents to his now flabbergasted companion. There was, he exclaimed in desperation, no way he could escape a court-martial. Finally composing himself, he asked Hoenmanns where they were. The pilot responded that they must be somewhere on German soil.

"On German soil!" Reinberger raised his voice in astonishment. "I should hope so!"

Shortly afterward, a wiry old peasant with a weather-beaten and heavily lined face came lumbering toward the two Germans. They immediately asked him where they were. The old man said something in response, but neither airman could understand him—he spoke in French!

Once again, this time in broken French, and more softly, Reinberger asked the peasant where they were. The old man jerked his thumb over his shoulder, in the direction of the river, and replied, "The Meuse."

"The Meuse River!" Reinberger exclaimed. Anguished, he realized that they had crashed in Holland or Belgium. The documents in his briefcase had to be destroyed at once.

After watching the two Germans fumble in their pockets for some matches, the peasant offered them a box of his own. Reinberger snatched them from the old man and disappeared behind a nearby thicket.

THE ARREST

Since the beginning of the war the preceding September, the Belgian border guards near Mechelen-sur-Meuse, some eight miles north of Maastricht, Holland, had experienced little excitement. Neither had their Dutch neighbors across the Maas (as the Meuse is called after it flows from Belgium north into Holland). But suddenly the silence of the winter morning was interrupted by the approaching sound of a sputtering aircraft engine. The noise soon became the whistling shriek of a plane falling from the sky, followed by the jarring sound of a crash. The Belgian guards, four in number, quickly rushed off toward the direction of the crash. They soon came within sight of a German airman—Hoenmanns—standing next to the wreckage of the plane. The German promptly raised his hands above his head as the Belgians approached.

However, the attention of the soldiers quickly shifted from Hoenmanns to a cloud of smoke rising from behind the thicket where Reinberger had scurried to burn the contents of his briefcase. The startled German airman tried to run away from the approaching soldiers, but he froze in his tracks after the Belgians fired warning shots into the air. Two of the soldiers stamped out the flames and then gingerly placed the charred remains of the documents into Reinberger's yellow briefcase. After relieving the Germans of their pistols, the soldiers escorted them back to their guardhouse.

There Reinberger and Hoenmanns were interrogated by a Belgian officer, Captain Arthur Rodrique. He wanted to know what the two Germans
were doing on Belgian soil. Hoenmanns explained that they had lost their
way in the mist and were forced by engine failure to crash land. Reinberger asked the Belgian officer to point out their location on a map and
permit him to make a phone call, but Rodrique replied that he could not
approve either request until he was authorized to do so by his superiors.

Just then, Rodrique's interrogation of the two Germans was abruptly
interrupted by the arrival of the chief of police from the neighboring town
of Eisden, who had come to make a report of the incident. The police chief
examined the partially charred papers in Reinberger's briefcase. He understood little German, but enough to realize that the documents were
important. After completing a preliminary examination, the police chief
left the room.

Rodrique began to pack the partially charred documents as well as the
Messerschmitt's logbook into Reinberger's briefcase. As he was doing this,
Hoenmanns asked if he could go to the toilet. Rodrique nodded and told
a soldier to show the German the way. But as the Belgian officer stepped
back from the table to allow Hoenmanns to pass, Reinberger, who was sitting sullenly in a chair, sprang to his feet, grabbed the charred papers that
were still spread out on the table, and flung them into the potbellied stove
that heated the guardhouse.

Almost as quickly, Rodrique knocked Reinberger aside, shoved his
hand into the flames, and pulled the documents out of the stove. Flinging
them to the floor, he stamped out the flames. His hand badly burned, he
turned toward Reinberger and, cursing, violently pushed him back into
the chair. "It is always the same with you Germans," Rodrique yelled. "We
treat you correctly, and you play a dirty trick like this!"

Rodrique put his revolver on the table while he tried to straighten
out the charred documents. Taking advantage of the opportunity, Reinberger lunged for the pistol. Grabbing Reinberger's arm, Rodrique tore
the gun from his hand and knocked him to the floor. "I did not want to
use the gun on you," Reinberger cried, now becoming hysterical. "I have
committed an unforgivable crime! I wanted your revolver so I could kill
myself!"

Leaning over his comrade, Hoenmann said to Rodrique, "You must
excuse him. . . . It's bad trouble he's in—he's an officer in the regular
army."

Disconsolate, Reinberger returned to his chair and covered his head
with his hands. He offered no further resistance.

CHAPTER TWO

The Dyle Plan

THE DEFENSE OF BELGIUM

Reinberger's partially charred documents, about ten pages in all, were examined and translated by Belgian intelligence personnel during the morning of January 11, 1940. The documents clearly described the elements of a German offensive across neutral Holland, Belgium, and Luxembourg. The Belgians had expected the brunt of any German attack to take place in the north of their country. But the Reinberger documents revealed that the Germans also planned to attack through the Ardennes Forest, in the southeastern part of Belgium, obviously to seize the bridges over the Meuse River between Namur and Dinant.

Belgian intelligence experts debated whether the Reinberger documents were a ruse, one designed to persuade the Belgians to move more of their troops to the south in order to reduce resistance to the German attack in the north. They concluded that the documents were genuine, however, and so informed General Raoul Van Overstraeten, the chief military adviser to King Léopold III.

When the king was informed by Van Overstraeten about the contents of the captured documents later that day, he was startled. As recently as August 26, 1939, six days before the German invasion of Poland, the German ambassador had presented the king a note stating that Germany would continue to respect Belgian neutrality.

❋

The Belgians were in need of such assurances. For centuries, the route of German invaders into France lay through the Belgian plain. Once across the Meuse River, which flows through the western part of the Ardennes

Forest, across eastern Belgium, and then into Holland, an invader would confront no natural obstacles of any significance to impair his advance across Belgium and northern France.

The very vulnerability of the French frontier bordering Belgium had prompted France to obtain international guarantees for the perpetual neutrality of Belgium when that country was created in 1839. But the Germans, arguing military necessity, violated their pledge in August 1914 and invaded Belgium. The German war plan, drawn up by Count Alfred von Schlieffen, chief of the General Staff, emphasized the need to defeat France quickly before the full weight of the more ponderously moving Russian army could be brought to bear against Germany's eastern provinces. Within a matter of days, Belgium's eastern defenses were overwhelmed by the German army, which then moved south into France before it was decisively checked on the Marne River, only a few miles to the northeast of Paris.

In World War I, King Albert, Léopold's father, had rallied his people against the invader, and in the process became a symbol of Belgium's determination to defend her independence. Although the Belgian army was compelled to withdraw to the coast in the face of the far more powerful German juggernaut, it was not destroyed. The Germans had to attack it with troops that, had they been available in the Battle of the Marne, may have enabled them to capture Paris. Albert's courageous resistance was in no small way responsible for the salvation of France. King Albert, however, had been killed in February 1934, the result of a fatal fall while mountain climbing in the Ardennes Forest. His thirty-two-year-old son, Léopold III, had succeeded to the throne.

Intelligent, courageous, and extremely scrupulous, Léopold, like his father, possessed a high-minded conception of a king's mission. He believed that princes should serve their people with complete self-abnegation. The American ambassador to Brussels, J. G. Davies, considered the king among the greatest of European heads of state. But Léopold also was destined to become one of Europe's most controversial leaders.

Like his father, Léopold had hoped to continue Belgium's policy of close collaboration with the Allies. But he was horrified by their passive reaction to Hitler's occupation of the demilitarized Rhineland in 1936. He responded by unilaterally abrogating the Franco-Belgian Treaty of Alliance, which his father had signed in 1920. Henceforth, he informed the Belgian parliament in October 1936, Belgium would pursue a policy he called "solely and exclusively Belgian."

It never seemed to have occurred to Léopold that it might be foolishly naive to bank on German assurances that they would not attack Belgium as they had in 1914. Nevertheless, the king did everything to convince the Germans—and to assure his former allies—that his country was prepared to fight again to defend its neutrality. The king authorized an increase in the Belgian army to 600,000 men, organized in 22 divisions, more than double the size of the British Expeditionary Force (BEF) and five times larger than the army deployed by King Albert in 1914. Yet while the Belgian army contained a fair proportion of armored vehicles, most of its tanks were not only too lightly armored and undergunned, but also were too widely dispersed to counterattack successfully against a German invasion. The Belgian air force possessed only 250 aircraft, most of which were obsolete.

In the event of a German attack, Léopold planned to withdraw the bulk of his army to the so-called Dyle Line, a barrier of steel and concrete fortifications and antitank traps stretching seventy miles from Antwerp on the coast to Namur on the Meuse River. A rearguard force would attempt to stall the German advance before the great fortresses of Eben Emael, Liège, Neufchâteau, Battice, and Pepinster, while the 2nd Cavalry Division and two newly created light infantry divisions, the *Chasseurs Ardennais,* would harass and delay German units trying to move through the Ardennes Forest.

The French, of course, were not pleased by the abrogation of the Belgian alliance. Its termination meant that French forces could not enter Belgium until after Hitler had crossed the Belgian frontier. Although the French had no choice but to release the Belgians from their treaty obligations, their own national security still required them to defend Belgium in the event the Germans attacked. Yet to do so effectively, the French had to know the disposition of Belgium's army, if only to avoid collisions between Belgian and French forces in the heat of battle.

Léopold agreed to provide the French with the information they requested, but he did so clandestinely, in order to avoid provoking a German attack. A secret liaison with General Maurice Gamelin, commander-in-chief of the French army and the supreme Allied commander, was

established in the person of Lieutenant Colonel Auguste Hautcoeur, a
trusted friend of General Van Overstraeten. However, these contacts proved
to be an inadequate substitute for full staff talks. Gamelin communicated
with the Belgians in writing, but Léopold, fearing secrecy might be compromised, insisted that transactions on the Belgian side never be committed to paper.

With respect to the captured Reinberger documents, the king decided
to inform the Allies that there was a strong possibility of an imminent
German attack, but to deprive the Allies of any pretext for intervention in
Belgium before the attack took place, he also decided to refrain from
showing them the captured documents.

At 5:15 P.M. on January 11, 1940, Colonel Hautcouer was summoned to
Léopold's palace by General Van Overstraeten. "We have come into possession of some written information of primary importance concerning the
German war plans," Van Overstraeten informed Hautcouer, that revealed
Germany's aggressive designs. Then, without divulging how the information had been obtained, he gave the French officer a two-page résumé
of the Reinberger documents, and stressed that it was to be given to General Gamelin—"and him alone." The Belgians intended to wait and see
whether the German plan would be implemented before inviting the Allies
to come into their country.

Hautcouer took the résumé of the Reinberger documents and immediately forwarded them to the headquarters of the French General Staff,
which was located in the Château de Vincennes, on the eastern outskirts of
Paris.

General Maurice Gamelin

The Château de Vincennes "seemed to drip with blood," British General
Sir Edward Spears once commented. A former royal residence that had
been transformed into a state prison, with a fort added, the ancient castle
embraced nine centuries of French history. Within its massive gray walls,
England's King Henry V died in 1422, and many of France's enemies,
including the World War I spy Mata Hari, were executed.

Since the outbreak of the war in September 1939, the château had
housed the office of General Maurice Gamelin, who, from an austere, win-
dowless "cell" within the bowels of Vincennes, devised Allied strategy and
gave orders to the French armies in the Alps, Syria, and North Africa. A

small, slightly plump, sandy-haired man who was usually clad in a tight tunic and high-laced boots, Gamelin, now sixty-eight, still possessed a keen mind. In fact, he was considered France's best-educated general. Yet despite his military background, Gamelin preferred to study the liberal arts rather than military science. A senior French diplomat who once dined with the generalissimo was amazed to hear him discuss nothing but philosophy and Italian painting.

Unfortunately, when Gamelin did speak about military affairs, he was often foolishly arrogant. He had predicted, for example, that when war erupted the French army would "go through Germany like a knife through butter." Yet neither the French army nor Gamelin did anything meaningful to help France's Polish ally when Germany attacked her in September 1939. A French offensive against Germany's Saarland, three weeks after the German invasion of Poland, had involved only nine divisions (out of a total of 93 facing the German border). It advanced a mere five miles on a 16-mile front—all at a time when the Germans had only 25 divisions facing the French frontier.

General Franz Halder, the German army's chief of staff, was astounded by the weakness of the French attack. He wrote: "If the French . . . had used the opportunity presented by the engagement of nearly all our forces in Poland, they would have been able to cross the Rhine without our being able to prevent it, and would have threatened the Ruhr, which was decisive for the German conduct of the war."

"If Gamelin could not deal a heavy blow to the German army when nearly all its strength, especially in tanks and planes, was concentrated in Poland," the journalist-historian William Shirer added, "what could he hope to do when the enemy eventually faced him with all its might?"

Gamelin's failure to take advantage of Germany's momentary weakness was a product of excessive caution, rationalized by repeated overestimations of the enemy's strength.

Gamelin had not always been so timid. In World War I, as a young officer, he had displayed considerable courage in keeping a division in action after it had been almost completely surrounded by the Germans. Nor had he lacked imagination when, as an operations officer on the staff of Marshal Joseph Joffre, the supreme Allied commander, he was the first to grasp the opportunity for a counteroffensive against the German advance in front of Paris. The result was the great French victory in the Battle of the Marne.

But having proved his mettle in World War I, Gamelin's enthusiasm for combat, like that of most of the French nation, disappeared. He was content to rest on his laurels. He became an academic, a strategist, a calculator, and in the process seemed to have lost the ability to inspire men to fight. Even Gamelin's political protector, France's premier, Edouard Daladier, admitted his shortcomings. Listening to Gamelin, Daladier said, was "like sand running through your fingers." Daladier's political archrival, Paul Reynaud, said that the generalissimo "might be all right as a prefect or a bishop, but he is no leader of men."

Rather than lead men, Gamelin preferred to plan battles. At Vincennes, according to Colonel Charles de Gaulle, Gamelin "dwelt in an atmosphere very akin to that of a convent, surrounded by only a few officers, working and meditating, completely insulated from current events." Gamelin, de Gaulle added, "gave me the impression of a savant, testing the chemical reactions of his strategy in a laboratory."

Much of the criticism of Gamelin, however, was written from hindsight. In the spring of 1940, Gamelin's voice carried great weight in Paris and London. The British considered him the thinking man's general and referred to him as *"notre* [our] *Gamelin."*

Some modern historians also have taken a more charitable view of Gamelin than did most of his contemporaries. Professor Jeffrey Gunsburg, for example, believes that there is "much to admire in the way Gamelin built a smaller and industrially weaker France into a powerful military machine to oppose Germany." He and his patron, Daladier, not only identified the threat from Nazi Germany; they responded to it with a robust four-year rearmament program. Problems arose, however, when Gamelin determined how to use the new weapons.

Gamelin's preference for strategy over combat was clearly demonstrated by his overhaul of France's command structure in January 1940, only four short months before the German attack. Before then, there had been only one general headquarters, located at Vincennes, and only one staff, all under one roof, which worked under Gamelin's direction. At Vincennes, General Claudel Georges served as Gamelin's deputy and was entrusted with the command of three army groups deployed along the critical northeastern front, which faced the Belgian and German borders. This arrangement provided an essential element in the effective conduct of war: unity of command.

On January 6, 1940, however, Gamelin persuaded the French government to adopt a new, decentralized command structure. Georges was made the commander in chief of the northeastern front, with his headquarters near the small town of La Ferté, some thirty-five miles east of Vincennes. Another deputy, General André Doumenc, whose responsibilities included the supervision of all of France's land forces, was moved to a new headquarters, at Montry, midway between La Ferté and Vincennes.

This cumbersome chain of command was complicated further when, on May 11, 1940, one day after the Battle of France began, Georges, without Gamelin's foreknowledge, appointed General Gaston Billotte the coordinator of Allied forces in the north. The move further diminished the prospects for close Allied cooperation, since neither the Belgians nor the British respected Billotte.

Gamelin also had little influence on the operations of the French air force or navy, both of which were independent branches of the armed forces. Gamelin could submit requests for air support to General Joseph Vuillemin, the air force's commander-in-chief, but Vuillemin did not have to comply. Nor did Admiral Jean Darlan, the chief of the French navy, have to comply with Gamelin's request for naval support. Indeed, because the political and military direction of the war was ostensibly assumed by a "War Committee" of the government, there was no single individual with the ultimate responsibility for the French war effort. As a result, during the most critical hours of the Battle of France, the French armed forces, as one historian put it, "would be literally leaderless, as a result of having too many leaders."

It certainly did not help that Gamelin deeply despised Georges, a tall (six feet, four inches), trim-mustached, but somewhat rotund man of sixty-five who found it easy to return in kind Gamelin's disdain. Intelligent, alert, and—unlike Gamelin—forceful, Georges was considered by many to be France's best general. In fact, Gamelin realized that his rival probably would have been in his place had it not been for the effects of bullet wounds Georges had received while he was standing beside King Alexander of Yugoslavia when he was assassinated during a visit to Marseilles in 1934. After meeting with Georges in June 1939, Britain's military attaché in Paris, Colonel William Fraser, reported that the general was "not a fit man, and that the weight of the responsibility which would be his in war might be too much for him."

It is easy to suspect, as Gamelin's enemies did, that the generalissimo changed the French command structure in order to shift to Georges responsibility for any disaster that might befall France's critical northeastern front. Gamelin admitted to a parliamentary investigating committee after the war that Georges was given the responsibility for the army's operations against Germany but not the authority for planning and organizing them. Georges emphasized this handicap when he defended his wartime actions before the same committee. "History will judge severely," he said, "an organization of command placing in juxtaposition two commanders-in-chief, one of whom held the real powers, while the second had the responsibility for the conduct of operations conceived and defined by the first."

What made Gamelin's task of "supervising" the war effort all the more difficult was the fact that he lacked even the most rudimentary radio communications with the outside world: messages from Vincennes were sent to the various fronts by motorcycle, every hour on the hour. General André Beaufre, then a junior staff officer under Doumenc, recalled that "several cyclists got killed on the way in accidents." Lord only knows what happened to the messages they were carrying. When combat finally did begin on the western front, the delays created by this primitive, and totally inadequate, communication system would prove to be disastrous. Six or more hours would be required for a particular ground unit to obtain air support. The delay involved in moving ground forces could be even longer: a general order issued on May 19 could not be implemented until two days later. After the war, in defense of Vincennes's communications system, Gamelin asked: "What would we, at this level, have done with a [radio] transmitter?" Radio messages were sent from Georges's headquarters at La Ferté. They were not made from Vincennes, he said, "so as not to give our position away."

Though Gamelin occasionally did use the telephone to reach Georges, he did this as little as possible, he said, so as not to disturb Georges. Gamelin's preferred method of communicating with the commander of the northeastern front was to drive to Georges's headquarters in La Ferté. The trip took an hour each way, causing William Shirer to comment, "What a waste of time for the commander-in-chief in the midst of one of the most crucial and decisive battles in the history of France!"

Once the Battle of France began, not only would Gamelin fail to receive information promptly, he often would not get critical information at all. Gamelin's command structure, observed Colonel Jacques Minart, a staff officer at Gamelin's headquarters, was like "a submarine without a periscope."

THE PHONY WAR

In mid-October, after Poland was conquered by the Germans in a quick four-week war, the French troops that Gamelin had sent twenty-five miles into Germany had been abruptly called back into France. Gamelin feared that they would be attacked by German forces being transferred to the French front from defeated Poland. But the Germans did not attack in the fall of 1939, and military activity on Germany's western front virtually came to an end. Only occasional patrols broke the silence of the night, or an infrequent burst of an artillery shell that of the day. Contemporary observers, and historians later, called this period of military inactivity, which lasted until the following spring, the Phony War. To the troops in the field, like the civilians at home, it appeared that no serious fighting would be necessary in this "war."

It was an impression the Germans did everything to reinforce. In a speech in Danzig's Guild Hall on September 19, Adolf Hitler told his audience and the world: "I have no war aims against Great Britain and France." As if mindful of the lack of enthusiasm for war that permeated the French army, he added: "My sympathies are with the French *poilu* [soldier]. What is he fighting for? He does not know." He then called upon the Almighty "to give other peoples comprehension of how useless this war will be . . . and to cause reflection on the blessings of peace." This from the man who had just destroyed Poland.

Along the western front, by loudspeaker and with large signs, the Germans made much of the fact that while one Frenchman in eight was in uniform, the proportion in Britain was only one in forty-eight. The Germans constantly chided French troops about "dying for the British." Their loudspeakers blared: "Don't shoot! We won't, if you don't!" Gamelin obliged by prohibiting his troops from firing on German work parties within full view of the French positions. When asked why he gave this order, he replied, "Open fire on German working parties? They would only do the same to us!"

Under Gamelin's leadership—or lack thereof—the French army's fighting spirit had slowly ebbed as the Phony War extended into weeks, then months. "Our units," General André Laffargue recalled, "were vegetating in a purposeless existence. They settled down to guard duties and killing time until the next leave or relief." Crammed into overcrowded living quarters with civilians, soldiers began to wonder why they had been compelled to leave their homes, their fields, or their factories. Drunkenness became a major problem.

General Alan Brooke, who commanded the BEF's 2nd Corps, was horrified by what passed as a ceremonial parade by French soldiers to commemorate the 1918 armistice: "Men unshaven, horses ungroomed, clothes and saddlery that did not fit, vehicles dirty, and complete lack of pride in themselves or their units. What shook me most, however, was the look in the men's faces, disgruntled and insubordinate, and although ordered to give 'Eyes Left,' hardly a man bothered to do so."

Gamelin's efforts to reverse the deterioration of morale in his army, primarily by requiring incessant reconnaissance patrols, only made matters worse. The cascade of meticulously detailed orders and postoperational reports that were a part of each patrol helped to destroy the fighting edge and initiative of field commanders who, in desperation, attempted to avoid any action that would involve the dreaded mountains of red tape that would result.

Some officers, such as Charles de Gaulle, urged that the idle troops be given intensified training, not only to prepare them for the blitzkrieg tactics that the Germans had used so successfully in Poland but also, by keeping them busy, to raise their morale. Yet the ossified French high command shrank from implementing such an intensive program. "We could allot but one half day a week to training because labor jobs came first," General Edmond Ruby, of the 1st Army, complained. As late as March 1940, only two months before Hitler's invasion of France, General Charles Menu learned that "many infantry units had still not fired a rifle or tried out their antitank and antiaircraft guns." In addition, no effort was made by Gamelin or Georges to hold exercises in divisional strength in order to give officers and men the experience of operating in large units. "Not one of my divisional commanders," said General Claude Grandsard, commander of the ill-fated 10th Corps at Sedan, "ever had his division assembled around him."

THE DEFENSE OF FRANCE

Gamelin, of course, was not entirely responsible for the problems the French army experienced during the Phony War. In many ways, the army was but a reflection of the antiwar sentiment that prevailed in France during the interwar period. One in every ten Frenchmen in uniform—almost one and a half million men—had been killed and another million had been maimed during World War I. Nor could the French people forget the devastation that the nation's ten northern departments had experienced during that conflict. Buildings, factories, mines, communication facilities, and livestock had been destroyed. The population of the region had been decimated. The snows of January 1940 could not conceal the trench furrows and the shell scars on the landscape where French and German soldiers had fought over two decades earlier.

Yet it was not only the memory of the Great War that had crippled the military spirit of the French nation. A host of social, economic, and political problems that had engulfed France during the interwar period were also responsible. Problems related to the industrialization of France, including labor strife resulting from the formation of unions and the drift to the cities of a rural population seeking industrial jobs, were only compounded by the collapse of the French economy during the Great Depression. Added to this was the political instability of the French Third Republic. Between 1932 and the outbreak of World War II in September 1939, 19 different governments had ruled France. It is easy to appreciate why the French people lacked confidence in their leaders.

In addition, old values and beliefs crumbled under the onslaught of new ideas—Dadaism, Marxism, and the theories of Einstein, Freud, and other revolutionary thinkers. Pacifism attacked established notions of nationalism, patriotism, and militarism, and contributed to the widespread revulsion against war. The ideas of peace at any price, rather than victory if provoked, and universal brotherhood, rather than hatred for the enemy, undoubtedly had their effect on the hundreds of thousands of French soldiers who manned the cold fortifications and frozen trenches that faced the German and Belgian frontiers during the winter of 1940.

France also was handicapped by a serious demographic disadvantage. In 1939 there were 300,000 fewer men to defend France than had been available in 1914. Absent were the unborn sons of the soldiers who had been killed in World War I. During the interval between the two wars, France's population had grown by only 2.7 million, to about 43 million, while Germany's had expanded by 10 million, to 60 million. Moreover, Germany's industrial strength was approximately three times as great as France's and was continuing to grow, while the French economy, which had experienced serious decline during the Depression, was still stagnant.

Germany's demographic and economic superiority translated into an impressive military advantage. By May 1940, the Germans had raised 112 divisions, of which ten were armored. By then, the French had mobilized 126 divisions, 101 of which were stationed on the German front. For France, it would have been very difficult to have significantly increased the size of its army beyond this level, since French mobilization had tapped almost all available manpower.

To offset Germany's demographic and economic advantages, France turned to Britain. But it was not until the early months of 1939 that the British had finally decided that they would fight alongside the French. And the British could send only ten divisions to the continent by May 1940, far less than they had contributed to the defense of France in World War I. (During that conflict, the British Empire raised 95 divisions, 74 of which were made up of British troops, while the others were made up of territorial soldiers.) Nor were the British capable of reaching World War I level in the second conflict; their economy simply was not strong enough to support that many divisions (Britain and its empire were able to form only 49 divisions, and that total was reached only in the last year of World War II).

Considering France's disadvantages relative to Germany, it is not surprising that the French high command did not prepare to launch a large-scale offensive against Germany. Instead, they embraced a defensive strategy. As in World War I, they would wait until the German attack was worn down and the Allied side had time to build up, again, they hoped, with American assistance. The idea, explained one of the architects of France's defensive strategy, Marshal Henri Philippe Pétain—a hero in World War I but a man who would play an ignominious role in its sequel—was "first, not to be beaten; then, to beat the enemy."

Without a doubt, the most visible manifestation of France's preference for the defense was the Maginot Line. Constructed during the 1930s and extending from the Swiss border to Longwy, close to the point where the border of France meets the Belgian-Luxembourg frontier, this 87-mile-long barrier of concrete pillboxes and fortifications, subterranean artillery encasements, and underground barracks, all linked together by antitank obstacles and barbed wire, the French were sure, would stop the Germans. Against it, the German Wehrmacht would smash itself to pieces.

But there were serious weaknesses in the Maginot Line. The French failed to extend the fortifications all the way to the English Channel. The Franco-Belgian frontier west of Longwy, facing the Ardennes Forest, remained unfortified. If the Germans broke through here, the Maginot Line would be outflanked.

To prevent this possibility, General Gamelin had insisted that the Allied armies must enter Belgium well before a German invasion began. On October 24, 1939, he had ordered the armies of the northeastern front to be ready to advance to a defensive position along the Escaut (or Scheldt) River, which flows through Belgium from Antwerp to Ghent. While this "Escaut Plan" required the shortest approach march for the Allied armies, the line they would be required to defend would be awkwardly long. And it did not encompass Brussels, the Belgian capital, nor the bulk of the Belgian army, which would be deployed in front of it defending the Albert Canal, unsupported by the Allies.

In an attempt to correct these shortcomings, on November 1, 1939, Gamelin amended the Escaut Plan by extending the Allied advance to the Dyle River—actually, a rather narrow and shallow stream that flows from

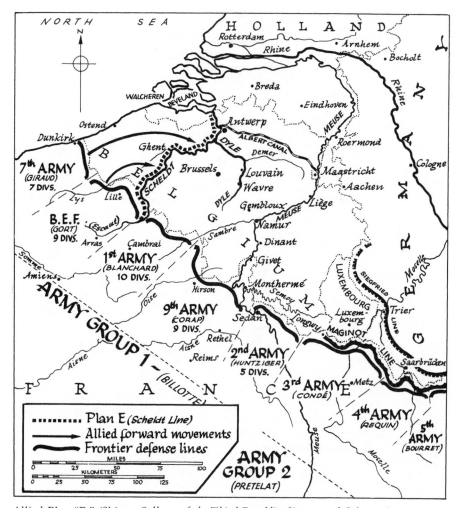

Allied Plan "E." (Shirer, *Collapse of the Third Republic*, Simon and Schuster)

south to north across eastern Belgium. Not only did the Dyle Plan create a shorter line, it promised to protect the Belgian capital as well as give the Allied armies a better chance of linking up with the Belgian army.

The Dyle Plan called for four of the five Anglo-French armies (organized in General Billotte's First Army Group) to advance to the line of the Dyle. On the extreme left flank of this army group, the seven divisions of the French 7th Army (under the overall command of General Henri Giraud) would have to travel the farthest to reach the new line. It would be joined on its right flank by the nine divisions of the British Expeditionary Force, under General John Lord Gort. A tenth British division, the

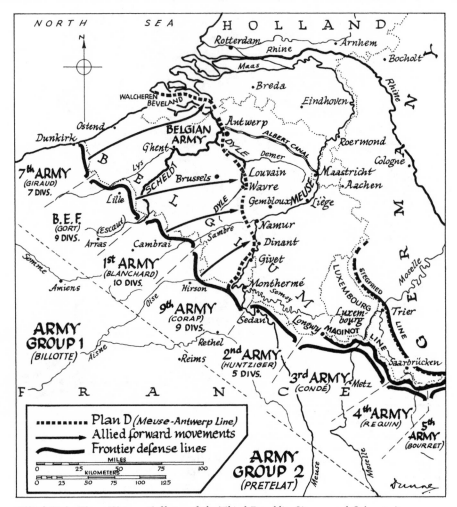

Allied Dyle Plan. (Shirer, *Collapse of the Third Republic*, Simon and Schuster)

51st Highland Division, was attached to the French 3rd Army defending the Maginot Line. The BEF would advance to its position on the Dyle River, just above Wavre.

To the right of the BEF, the French 1st Army, made up of ten divisions under General Jean-Georges Maurice Blanchard, would have the responsibility for blocking a likely German attack through the so-called Gembloux Gap, a 30-mile-wide corridor between the Dyle and Meuse rivers.

On the right flank of the 1st Army, only the left wing of General André Corap's 9th Army (nine divisions in all) would advance into Belgium, marching to a line running along the Meuse River from Namur southward to the French frontier. The right wing of Corap's army would remain fixed on French soil, holding the line of the Meuse from the Belgian border to the town of Sedan.

To the right of the 9th Army, the five divisions of General Charles Huntziger's 2nd French Army would also remain stationary in France. It would have the responsibility for defending the frontier from Sedan to the Maginot Line.

On the right of Billotte's 1st Army Group, the 2nd and 3rd Army Groups would attempt to hold the Maginot Line and the Rhine River defenses, which extended to the Swiss border. All totaled, the three Allied army groups comprised 114 divisions, 104 of which were French and 10 British.

While imposing on paper, the Allied armies were not without serious weaknesses. Recalled General Bernard Montgomery, commander of its 3rd Division, "It must be said to our shame that we sent our Army into that most modern of wars with weapons and equipment that were quite inadequate."

"The British armored forces in the theater of war," Lord Gort complained, "amounted to seven divisional cavalry regiments equipped with light tanks, one regiment of armored cars of an obsolete pattern, and two battalions of infantry tanks, the latter, except for twenty-three Mark II tanks that carried two-pound (37-mm) guns, armed each with one machine gun only." By comparison, one German panzer division alone had almost as much firepower as the entire BEF. When an aide told Gort that the Germans had 10 panzer divisions on the western front, he responded, "In that case, we haven't an earthly chance."

The French army, for its part, suffered from a severe shortage of manpower. For example, Corap's 9th Army was expected to defend a front 65 miles long, bordering Belgium's Ardennes Forest. According to French military doctrine, a division was expected to defend no more than four miles of front. Each of Corap's divisions would have to defend over seven miles. Moreover, at least three days would be necessary to move the troops of Corap's left wing up to the front, since the army was short of the transport needed for the maneuver. Some units would have to march 75 miles, a grueling task for an army on the eve of battle, especially one mostly made up of middle-aged reservists.

The quality of soldiers in Corap's, as well as Huntziger's, armies also left much to be desired. The two generals commanded mostly "B" divisions, which were made up of territorials from North Africa, Indochina, and Madagascar, as well as by "crocodiles"—older family men from France.

Neither army's soldiers had much training, and they had no experience at all in the use of newer equipment, or—and this would prove to be a critical deficiency—in dealing with enemy dive-bomber attacks. The African troops, in particular, suffered severely from the harsh winter conditions during the Phony War. The older men in both armies, who like all *poilus* received only centimes a day in pay, often applied for leave so that they could drive taxis or do other kinds of extra work, to supplement the miserly allowance the government gave their dependents.

The manpower problems of the French army were only compounded by the fact that its commanding generals knew little about mechanized warfare. Corap, for example, had spent almost his entire career with colonial regiments in Africa, while Huntziger had served in Syria, Indochina, China, Brazil, and Madagascar. In none of these places did either man acquire any experience that would prepare him to confront the forces that would emerge from the wooded hills of the Ardennes Forest.

THE "IMPENETRABLE" ARDENNES

Yet Gamelin was not particularly concerned about the weaknesses of Corap's or Huntziger's armies. The generalissimo considered the Ardennes Forest "impenetrable." A German army advancing through the forest, he was fond of pointing out, would have to use narrow, winding roads that threaded through rugged and heavily wooded hills—all of which supposedly were a defender's dream landscape.

But Gamelin overestimated the deterrent value of the Ardennes. The forest was not as thick as he thought it was, and the mountains were in reality nothing more than a series of not-too-steep hills. Moreover, a good road network traversed the Ardennes between Sedan and the German border. Basil Liddell Hart, the noted armored warfare expert, toured the area in both 1929 and 1938, after which he concluded that although the forest was not perfect terrain for tanks, it was not impassable, either. Unfortunately for the Allies, Liddell Hart's thoughts on the "impenetrable" Ardennes, as well as his other writings on armored warfare, were almost totally ignored by the French high command.

So, too, was a report by General André Prételat, who in May and June 1938 conducted a map exercise from which he concluded that 60 hours after crossing the Rhine, the Germans could reach the Meuse with a force of seven infantry divisions (three of them motorized) and an armored division. Further, he predicted, the Luftwaffe would prevent the arrival of French reinforcements after the German attack had begun. Prételat recommended that the 2nd Army be given an additional division, but his request was rejected.

Gamelin argued that even if the Germans were able to traverse the Ardennes, they still would have to cross the Meuse River, which flowed northward from France and then cut through the western extremities of the forest. Along many stretches of that river, especially between Charleville and Givet, the German invaders would have to scale cliffs on the river's far bank. In fact, near Dinant, they would have difficulty just getting to the Meuse. Before they did so, they would encounter twisting, heavily wooded gorges that could easily be blocked by defending forces. Aided by the Ardennes terrain, Gamelin was confident that the cavalry units of the 9th and 2nd Armies would be more than equal to the task of stopping the German Army.

THE BREDA VARIANT

Rather than rethinking French strategy to address the concerns about the Ardennes sector raised by Prételat's report, Gamelin preferred to revise Allied strategy on France's northern front. The Dyle Plan, he argued, would take full advantage of French motorized forces, add the Belgian army to the French side of the scale, and enable the Allies to fight the war away from French soil. Nothing, including Prételat's report, would be allowed to undermine confidence in a plan that offered all of these important advantages.

Gamelin's British allies accepted his reasoning. The decision to adopt the Dyle Plan was approved by the interallied Supreme War Council on November 14, 1939. General Edmund Ironside, the chief of Britain's Imperial General Staff, supported the change primarily because it greatly increased the likelihood of incorporating the Belgian army into the Allied dispositions. British Air Chief Marshal Sir Cyril Newall, on the other hand, wanted the Allies to occupy as much of Belgium as possible in order to prevent the Germans from establishing air bases close to England; the move also would bring the Royal Air Force that much closer to the Ruhr, Germany's industrial heartland. But neither Lord Gort nor his corps commanders liked the idea. However, Gort, who would be commanding only 10 divisions, believed he was in no position to argue with the French high command. "The question of such an advance," Gort subsequently wrote, "was one of high policy, with a political as well as a military aspect; it was therefore not for me to comment on it." The decision to advance to the Dyle Line was ratified by both Allied governments on November 17.

Nevertheless, General Georges, who would command the Allied advance to the Dyle Line, argued vigorously against the new strategy. "We cannot push on . . . to the Antwerp-Namur position," he insisted, "unless the High Command feels . . . it can reach that position *before* the enemy, and organize it *before* the enemy is able to attack it in force." Georges feared that his units would not have time to prepare defensive positions in Belgium before the Germans attacked them.

Georges was even more horrified to learn that on November 23, at a meeting of the 1st Army Group's commanders, which he said he was not invited to attend, Gamelin had requested a "study" on the feasibility of sending the French 7th Army into Holland, at least as far as Breda, in order to forge a link between the Dutch and Belgian defenses. Georges warned that sending his only available reserve army, the 7th, far from the center of the Allied front, which was opposite the Ardennes Forest and where he feared the Germans might send the bulk of their forces, would be disastrous. He wrote: "If . . . the main enemy attack came in our center, on our front between the Meuse and the Moselle, we could be deprived of the necessary means to repel it." On the other hand, if the 7th Army, with six largely motorized crack infantry divisions and one light armored division, were held in reserve along the Meuse-Moselle line, it would be invaluable in checking any German advance coming out of the Ardennes Forest.

But, again, advancing into Belgium presented advantages that Gamelin was not prepared to abandon. Not only would the move add to his combined strength the 22 divisions of the Belgian army, it would also shorten the Allied front by 35 miles. Moreover, Gamelin argued, the move would keep the Germans away from the northern industrial and mining regions of France. These advantages, in Gamelin's mind, outweighed the disadvantages of making the maneuver, including the risk of confronting the Germans in the open field before his troops had time to organize their positions and the difficulty of meshing the Belgian army into his Allied forces because King Léopold refused to allow prior staff talks.

Nor, apparently, did Gamelin coordinate the Breda variant with the Dutch. In the spring of 1940, he learned that the Dutch, partly because of the refusal of the Belgians to cooperate with them and partly because of their own military weakness, had decided to withdraw their scanty forces—only eight divisions in all—from positions south of the Meuse and to concentrate them on defending Fortress Holland, which included the cities of Amsterdam, Rotterdam, and The Hague. The Dutch decision robbed the mission of the French 7th Army of any purpose, since it would have to enter southern Holland, which, denuded of Dutch forces, would have been quickly occupied by the Germans before it could arrive.

As late as April 14, one day before Gamelin made the Breda variant final, Georges begged him to keep the 7th Army in reserve and instead send a corps of two divisions from some other unit into Holland, if the generalissimo still insisted that the Breda operation was necessary. But

Gamelin refused. As a result, Georges would be deprived of any major reserve force with which to repel a German penetration from the Ardennes Forest.

ALLIED INTELLIGENCE

Gamelin's refusal to keep the 7th Army in general reserve is even more mind-boggling when one considers that as early as November 1939, he had begun receiving intelligence reports that indicated the center of gravity of the German attack had shifted farther south. By March 1940, Allied intelligence would locate seven German panzer divisions in positions that would enable them to move between Sedan and Namur, the sector defended by the fragile French 9th Army. This assessment would be reinforced that same month by an intelligence report revealing that German engineers had begun to throw eight pontoon bridges across the middle Rhine River, between Bonn and Bingen. That many bridges so close to Germany's border on the Belgian Ardennes should have alerted Gamelin to the possibility—indeed, probability—that this was going to be the focus of the German attack.

In addition, Colonel Paillole, chief of the German section of French Counterintelligence, would report on March 22 that German military intelligence had begun to study the routes from Sedan to Abbeville, at the mouth of the Somme River on the English Channel, in an attempt to ascertain the weight limits of bridges over intervening rivers, the nature of other water obstacles, the condition of roads, and so on. To Paillole, this information could only mean one thing, as he put it: "an attack through Belgium toward the Channel is imminent."

Paillole's assessment would be supported by Belgian intelligence. On March 8 King Léopold would inform his cabinet ministers that all the intelligence he was receiving pointed to the chief German thrust coming "through the Ardennes, toward Dinant-Saint Quentin, with the object of cutting off the Allied armies in Belgium from Paris and rolling them up in the Pas de Calais" region, along the English Channel. Léopold would instruct his military attaché in Paris to inform General Gamelin about this intelligence assessment.

There is no evidence, however, that Gamelin paid any attention to the Belgian intelligence. He did nothing to strengthen the Sedan sector. His apparent paralysis continued even after he received, on the last day of April, a warning from one of his best intelligence sources, the French military attaché in Berne, Switzerland, who reported that the German attack was set for the period May 8–10 and that Sedan would be "its center of gravity." In fact, so certain was the French military attaché of the validity of his information that he sent his assistant to Georges's headquarters at La Ferté to make sure that both Gamelin and Georges got the message.

The French also possessed the "Enigma" deciphering machine, which was given to them by the Poles. The device enabled the Allies to break and read coded German military messages. However, the flow of German messages would be disrupted from May 12 to 20, the most critical phase of the Battle of France, because the Germans had changed their codes. Although the French decrypters, working night and day, were able to resume reading German military messages on May 20, by then the German panzers had traversed the Ardennes Forest, crossed the Meuse River, and advanced to the English Channel.

But Gamelin does not appear to have been impressed by this intelligence any more than he had been by similar reports. He refused to abandon the Dyle Plan. The only explanation Charles de Gaulle could give for Gamelin's stubborn fixation on the Dyle Plan was that the generalissimo suffered from hardening of the arteries of the brain. Actually, Gamelin was more worried by the possibility of a German attack on the Maginot Line than he was about one through the "impenetrable" Ardennes. He continued to insist that the Germans were holding twice as many troops in Army Group C, opposite the Maginot Line, than French intelligence believed.

Gamelin's blindness—and, for that matter, the blindness of France's other top commanders, Georges and Billotte—lay partly in his belief that the French defenses facing the Ardennes were strong enough to check any German advance through the forest. And it lay partly in the fact that Gamelin had been inundated with much conflicting evidence as well, including repeated warnings that the German offensive was imminent, warnings that had all proved false. As a result, Gamelin's weakest armies, the 9th and 2nd, would be left to their fate on the Meuse River with no organized reserves behind them.

THE UNLEARNED LESSONS
OF THE BLITZKRIEG IN POLAND

There was still another, perhaps more serious flaw in the French strategy. By tying themselves to the static defense, the French had failed to develop the offensive capability they would need to make even their advance into Belgium a success. Although the French had more tanks than the Germans—about 3,000 to about 2,500, respectively—what the French army needed most, but did not have in anywhere near the required numbers, were highly mechanized divisions capable of advancing rapidly into Belgium in sufficient strength to smash the Germans before they could reach the French frontier. Hitler had proved in Poland that the future of ground warfare lay in mechanized divisions. The German spearheads that ripped into Poland were composed of armored and mechanized infantry divisions. The Polish armies, which had few mechanized forces of their own, were quickly surrounded and annihilated.

The strategic lessons of the German blitzkrieg in Poland, however, were not grasped by the French high command. As early as 1921, Marshal Pétain had written that tanks were designed to serve only as auxiliaries to the infantry, not as components of armored divisions that could serve as spearheads for offensives. Pétain's thoughts about the role of tanks still dominated the thinking of the French high command almost two decades later. A memorandum prepared in late 1939 by the French secret service concluded: "The type of warfare used by the Germans in Poland was related to a particular situation: very wide fronts, lack of continuous lines of fortification, superiority in mechanical material, etc. Operations on the western front will be very different." In the west, the report predicted, Hitler's panzers would smash their offensive teeth on the Maginot Line.

But General André Armengaud, who had been in Poland during the fighting and had observed the Wehrmacht in action, came to a much different conclusion. In a report to the French high command, Armengaud warned of Germany's ability to "break through a defensive front that was inadequately manned," and gave a detailed and exact description of the new German mode of mobile warfare, one that not even the Germans could have written better. The German blitzkrieg tactics, he wrote, called for making a breach in the adversary's front with concentrated masses of armor and aircraft, throwing mechanized and motorized columns into the breach, and then enlarging it by moving quickly into the adversary's rear.

Armengaud's report clearly sounded the alarm and, in the strongest possible terms, called for France to shift tactics to meet the new kind of warfare. Knowing that what he had to say was contentious, Armengaud personally presented his conclusions to General Gamelin. But Gamelin considered his observations irrelevant. France's army, air force, and defenses, he responded, were stronger than Poland's had been, and French intelligence would provide adequate warning of the German attack. Afterward, Gamelin shunted Armengaud to the relatively minor post of commander of the Paris air region.

CHARLES DE GAULLE:
PROPHET IN THE WILDERNESS

Among the few in the French army who did appreciate the lessons of the Polish campaign was a tall, gangly young colonel named Charles de Gaulle (who was destined to become a future president of France and the author

of the Fifth Republic's constitution). As early as 1934, de Gaulle had warned
the government that France did not possess the kind of army she would
need in the next conflict. In November 1939 he addressed a memorandum
to the high command in which he stated: "The internal-combustion engine
will upset our military doctrine just as it will overcome our fortifications."
Pointing to the 200-mile unfortified gap between the Maginot Line and
the English Channel, de Gaulle predicted that this would be the avenue of
German invasion. Unless effective countermeasures were taken, he argued,
German armored divisions would be concentrated upon the weakest point
of the French front and, after achieving a breakthrough, would fan out into
the French rear, disrupting the communication and supply networks and
eventually surrounding and annihilating the bulk of the French army. It
would be, de Gaulle warned, a repetition of the Polish tragedy, but on a
much vaster and disastrous scale.

French war matériel, de Gaulle asserted, was excellent. However, if it
were going to be used effectively, it would have to be organized in the
same manner as the Germans organized theirs. What was necessary, he
insisted, was the creation of at least seven armored divisions and the adop-
tion of an offensive strategy by which to use them effectively.

At first, all that de Gaulle would receive in the way of satisfaction was
the government's decision, made in 1938, to create two armored divisions.
The first would not be formed until the winter of 1940; the second would
not appear until the following May. However, in March, Gamelin would
inform de Gaulle that he planned to raise the number of armored divisions
to four. The 3rd Armored Division would be formed in April. He also
would promise de Gaulle the command of the 4th Armored Division,
which, Gamelin said, would be formed after May 15. The new armored
divisions, with only partially trained tank crews, would be too few in
number, and would be deployed far too late, to have much bearing on the
battle's outcome.

While not completely satisfied, de Gaulle nevertheless expressed his
gratitude. "I understand your satisfaction," Gamelin responded. "As for
your misgivings," he said, "I don't believe they are justified. You cannot
hope to achieve real breakthroughs with tanks. The tank is not independent enough. It has to go ahead, but then it must stop, return for fuel and
supplies." Such was the depth of understanding about armored warfare
possessed by the supreme commander of the Allied forces.

A FALSE START

Three days after the Reinberger crash occurred, that is, on January 13,
1940, the Belgian military attaché in Berlin, Colonel Goethals, got off a

coded telegram to Brussels saying he had learned from "a sincere informer" that the Germans intended to attack the following day. According to General Oscar Michiels, who was soon to become chief of the Belgian General Staff, Belgian intelligence knew who the "sincere informer" was: the Dutch military attaché in Berlin, Colonel J. G. Sas.

Since September 1939, Sas had been receiving warnings from an anti-Nazi member of the German intelligence service *(Abwehr)*, Colonel Hans Oster, to the effect that a German invasion of Holland and Belgium was imminent. Oster detested Nazism so much that he was prepared to die a traitor if that was the price he had to pay to hasten the defeat of the Wehrmacht. "Maybe I'll be branded as a traitor," he said, "but I think I am a better German than those who meekly follow Hitler."

Sas, in turn, transmitted Oster's warnings to the Dutch government in The Hague, but the warnings were always discounted by the Dutch military because Sas refused to identify his German informant. However, as a consequence of the captured Reinberger documents, which appeared to validate Sas's warnings, the Belgians were now ready to accept them at face value.

In response to Oster's warning, near midnight on January 13–14 the Belgian army's chief of staff, General Van den Bergen, on his own initiative and without the authorization of General Van Overstraeten or King Léopold, ordered the barriers along the French frontier to be removed. That same evening, the Belgian military attaché in Paris, General Delvoie, informed General Gamelin that a German attack was "almost certain" for the morrow. Gamelin replied, "Are you going to call on us, then?" Delvoie answered that he had not yet received any orders to that effect.

Soon thereafter, shortly after midnight on the morning of January 14, the French and British ambassadors in Brussels were summoned to the office of Belgian Foreign Minister Paul-Henri Spaak, who informed them that the Belgian government considered probable a German attack at dawn. If the Germans did attack, Spaak said, he would ask for the assistance of France and Great Britain. Would the Allies respond positively? What was ironic about Spaak's request was the fact that he had strongly supported King Léopold's decision to abandon Belgium's alliance with France and Britain in 1936. Now, frantically, he was requesting the Allies to come to the aid of his country if the Germans attacked.

Earlier that evening, Léopold had a discussion with Sir Roger Keyes, a 67-year-old admiral in the British Navy who had been a close friend of Léopold's father, King Albert, and now extended that friendship to his son. The intimacy of Keyes's relationship with the Belgian monarchs had prompted Winston Churchill, First Lord of the Admiralty in Prime Minister Neville Chamberlain's government, to ask Keyes to serve as a liaison between the Belgian king and the British prime minister.

For his part, Léopold remembered well how his father had been caught unawares by the sudden German attack in 1914, and had not been able to call upon Britain, France, and Russia in time to deter the German aggression. Léopold was determined that this past mistake would not be repeated. "Do you not think," he asked Keyes, "that the time is right for Great Britain to confirm its readiness to honor its pledge" to defend Belgium? He then added, "Could I ask you to inquire privately of your friend, Churchill, whether it would be wise for my government to make an official request for help?"

Keyes thought the king's suggestion to contact Churchill was an excellent idea. But Churchill misinterpreted the message as a formal request by the Belgian king for British and French intervention, rather than simply a query by Léopold as to whether a formal request should be made at that time. Acting on the basis of Churchill's misinterpretation, on Monday, January 15, the British government gave its reply to Keyes: "We are ready to accept an invitation for British troops to enter Belgium and understand French attitude is the same."

When French Premier Daladier was informed about Léopold's request, he immediately telephoned Gamelin to determine if the French army was ready to respond to the Belgian invitation. Gamelin answered, "I do not believe the Germans are really ready to attack. It is snowing and aviation can do little. Conditions are not favorable for offensive operations by our enemies," but, he added, "we must nevertheless seize the occasion."

Gamelin asked for a quarter-hour to consult with Georges, Admiral Darlan, and General Vuillemin, to see if they were ready for war. He then called Daladier back. He told the French premier that to save time, the order would be given to Allied troops to finish their concentration on the Belgian border that night. The next morning, they would cross into Belgium, that is, as soon as the Belgians authorized the move. This looked like action at last, and Gamelin recalled that "the premier was happy" about the decision.

But a few minutes later, Gamelin experienced what he said was a sense of "disillusionment which wrung my heart." At 4:45 P.M., General Georges telephoned him. He sounded troubled. "I've been thinking it over," Gamelin recalled Georges as saying. "Don't you think it would be better to advise the Belgians not to call on us? We're not entirely ready. Wouldn't it be best to wait until our aviation is stronger and our forces completely reorganized?"

In his memoir, Gamelin recounted that although he was usually the master of his emotions, this time he lost his temper. He snapped back that the decision had already been made. He then calmed down and reviewed the arguments one by one until Georges gave in and agreed that the move into Belgium should be carried out. As a result, Gamelin recorded, "the die was cast—and under favorable conditions." The continuing snowfall, he believed, would actually prevent the Germans from bombing the Allied troops as they streamed into Belgium.

Yet as dawn arrived on the morning of January 15, Gamelin still had not received authorization from the Belgians to cross their border. Impatiently, at 8:30 A.M., he dashed off a message to Daladier. Gamelin said the Allied forces had completed their concentration on the Belgian border. "Now each hour lost can have grave consequences." He urged Daladier to make the Belgian government "face up to its responsibilities. I have already done that," he added, "with their High Command." Daladier responded by saying he would give the Belgian government until 8:00 P.M. to reply. Although Gamelin complained that this might be "very late," he accepted the premier's decision.

Daladier called in the Belgian ambassador and told him that the French army was assembled on the border and was waiting for the call to come into his country. "You must tell us formally, yes or no, if we can enter Belgium. If no, we shall go back to the status quo ante bellum. And let it be understood that, in the case of future danger, we shall be more reserved in our attitude and the nature of our action."

In Brussels, the Belgian cabinet met all day on January 15 without deciding to call in the Allies. It became obvious in Paris that the Belgians were reluctant to take a step that would surely provoke a German attack on their country. They were playing for time, to see if the Germans would in fact attack. Since it was still snowing, the Belgians began to believe that the attack had been at least delayed. This belief was corroborated at 2:30 in the afternoon, when General Van Overstraeten was informed by the Belgian attaché in Berlin that adverse weather conditions had caused the German attack to be postponed. Loss of surprise, which Hitler considered essential, also influenced the German decision.

At 7:30 that evening, General Billotte, commander of the 1st Army Group, telephoned Gamelin with the disappointing news that the Belgians were beginning to put back the barriers on their border. To add insult to injury, the French high command was "informally" advised by the Belgians "that if one of the Allied soldiers stepped into Belgium, he would be regarded as an enemy."

Half an hour later, Daladier telephoned Gamelin to inform him that the Belgians had refused to call in the French army. The Belgian government, Daladier complained, "could not take the responsibility of authorizing us to penetrate preventively into Belgium." Gamelin was stunned. "Once more," he said, "the Belgians have missed their destiny."

Still, while the Belgian refusal to act deeply angered the French, the Belgians were nevertheless comforted by the realization that if the Germans did invade their country, they could count on the help of the Allies.

CHAPTER THREE

The Manstein Plan

A DELAYED OFFENSIVE

While the Reinberger incident stressed relations between the Allies and the Belgians, it threw the German high command into a state of complete upheaval.

At 11:45 on the morning of January 11, 1940, General Alfred Jodl, Adolf Hitler's chief of staff, braced himself before entering the Führer's Reichschancellery office. When he told Hitler about the Reinberger mishap, the Nazi dictator exploded. General Wilhelm Keitel, chief of staff of the Wehrmacht (OKW), recalled that Hitler "went into a trance, frothing at the mouth; he struck the wall with his fists, vowed he would have the guilty parties executed, and roared terrible oaths about incompetence and treachery among the General Staff."

Hitler wanted heads to roll. Reinberger and Hoenmanns were sentenced to death in absentia—a fate they escaped when they were transferred to Canada for the duration of the war. However, their hapless wives, who were in no way connected with their husbands' faux pas, were thrown into prison. General Helmuth Felmy, commander of the 2nd Air Fleet, to which both Reinberger and Hoenmanns were attached, was sacked and replaced by General Albert Kesselring. Hermann Göring, head of the Luftwaffe, got off lightly with a sound berating by the enraged Nazi warlord. Nevertheless, Göring's wife, Ilse, said that "Hermann was beside himself for a number of days."

That evening, Hitler, Göring, and Jodl spent hours going over copies of the operational plans they assumed Reinberger had been carrying. They tried to determine just how much information had fallen into the hands of the Allies. General Ralph Wenninger, the Luftwaffe attaché in Amsterdam, was instructed to fly immediately to Brussels to interview the captured airmen and find out whether they had been able to destroy the documents.

At 10:00 A.M. on January 12, the Belgians permitted General Wenninger to see the two prisoners. The room, Wenninger assumed correctly, was bugged. Nevertheless, his first question to Reinberger and Hoenmanns was, "Did you manage to destroy the documents?" Reinberger replied: "When they were retrieved from the stove, only a few pieces remained, no bigger than the palm of my hand." Immediately after he had talked to the airmen, Wenninger wired Berlin: "Reinberger reports that the courier baggage was burned down to insignificant fragments." The telegram was noted by Jodl for the Führer's attention: "Dispatch case burnt for certain."

But Hitler was not certain. What if Reinberger had not succeeded in destroying the documents? The Allies would be prepared to counter each and every German operation. In the immediate wake of the Reinberger mishap, Hitler was informed, the Belgians and the Dutch had ordered partial mobilization. They could no longer be caught unaware by a surprise attack.

Yet the Führer did not want to postpone the offensive again. Since September, when he had first announced to the Army General Staff (OKH) his intention to attack in the west as soon as possible, the German offensive had been delayed by poor weather sixteen times. The country's railroads were paralyzed by repeated troop movements. The numerous false starts had made the soldiers restless, and Hitler feared that they were losing their fighting edge. At the Nuremberg trials after the war, Keitel revealed that had it not been for the extreme cold on the nights of January 13 and 14, Hitler would have launched the offensive then.

However, Hitler had been assured by Göring's meteorologists that good flying weather could be expected from January 16 to 19. On the evening of January 15, the Führer responded by setting January 17 as the new date for the offensive. But the weather did not improve. Combined with the uncertainty produced by the Reinberger incident and the mobilization of the Dutch and the Belgians, the poor weather compelled the exasperated Nazi warlord to cancel the attack on January 16. The whole operation, he informed the General Staff, would have to be replanned "on a new basis, particularly to be founded on secrecy and surprise." Without realizing it, Hitler's decision may have saved him from the disaster of a premature offensive. Instead, it would result in his greatest triumph.

Hitler and His Generals

Most of the German generals considered Hitler a "facile amateur" when it came to military strategy, tactics, and technology. But they underestimated him. Actually, his understanding of military history and technology was profound. He was a voracious reader and an ardent student of the writings of the great Prussian military strategists, Clausewitz, Moltke, Schlieffen, and Seeckt. But it was Frederick the Great who captured Hitler's unending admiration. The Führer admired Frederick's endurance, determination, and supreme self-confidence. Hitler considered himself another Frederick. He had no doubts about his ability to achieve his ultimate goal, the salvation of Europe from the menace of "Jewish-Bolshevism."

But even the generals were impressed by Hitler's intelligence. He possessed an unusually clever mind and a remarkable memory, particularly for historical data, technical figures, and economic statistics. He continually amazed the generals with his ability to quote relevant passages from things he had read or heard at military conferences. "Six weeks ago you said something quite different," was a favorite, and much dreaded, remark of the Supreme Commander. And no one dared argue with him, for within minutes he would have available the stenographer's record of the conversation in question.

However, what the generals most underestimated was the power of Hitler's will. Even self-confident soldiers, men who had proven their bravery in battle, would surrender to his spell. He was most effective when speaking to small groups. His eyes would shift from one listener to another, always watching to see what effect his words were having on each person present. If he noticed that someone was not succumbing to his powers of persuasion, he would speak directly to the resisting spirit until that listener succumbed. But if Hitler's harangue failed to achieve the anticipated reaction, he would shout, "I haven't convinced that man!" More often than not, "that man" soon would be relieved of his position. The more success Hitler experienced, the less tolerant of opposition he became, particularly from generals who doubted his ability.

One such general was Franz Halder, the army's chief of staff. Halder was immensely relieved by Hitler's indefinite postponement of the western offensive in the wake of the Reinberger mishap. A shrewd, quick-witted, and precisely minded intellectual with a passion for mathematics and botany, Halder's cropped hair, clipped mustache, and pince-nez spectacles gave him the facade of a typical Prussian-born member of the officer corps. But Halder came from an old Catholic family that had provided Bavaria with generals for centuries.

Halder had opposed the western offensive from the time Hitler first announced it on September 27, the day Warsaw surrendered. He was convinced that Germany did not have the resources to fight a long war, the kind of conflict he believed would result from an attack in the west. Moreover, a trip to the front in January had convinced him that the army was not ready for action. The refitting of the panzer divisions that were used in Poland was not complete. The short winter daylight made it virtually impossible to win a tactical decision in the space of a single day, a factor that undoubtedly would deprive the German offensive of the speed it would need to succeed. The bitterly cold weather also made it difficult, if not impossible, for the Wehrmacht to play its two trumps, armor and the Luftwaffe.

Halder had been prepared to go to almost any length to prevent a war with the western powers. He said he had even considered shooting Hitler and actually wept when, after the war, he recounted that he did not. The task would have been relatively easy physically, since Halder was permitted to carry his pistol to meetings with the Führer. But psychologically the act proved impossible for Halder. The idea of cold-blooded murder clashed with his deeply held religious convictions, as well as with the loyalty oath all German soldiers had been compelled to make to the Führer. He also felt duty bound to do all in his power to prevent the army's defeat. Yet he was compelled to plan an operation he felt was morally wrong, professionally questionable, and possibly ruinous for Germany.

During the Munich crisis, in September 1938, Halder had conspired with other conservative generals and politicians to arrest Hitler if and when he went through with his plan to invade Czechoslovakia. The coup, Halder claimed later, had been thwarted by British Prime Minister Neville Chamberlain's capitulation to Hitler's demands. The Führer had gotten all he wanted, without war—the Sudetenland, increased personal prestige, and the humiliation of the German General Staff, which had insisted that Britain and France would fight for Czechoslovakia.

Years later, Halder told Basil Liddell Hart, the English military historian: "It was your prime minister, your Prime Minister Chamberlain, who ruined our hopes by giving in to Hitler!" In fact, neither Halder nor his co-conspirators were ever completely prepared—either logistically or psychologically—to overthrow Hitler. They would act only if they could be absolutely certain that they would succeed, a condition that, of course, could never be met.

For Halder, it seemed, the only way around his moral scruples about killing Hitler was to countenance his assassination by somebody else. Perhaps, a fatal "accident" could be arranged, or a bomb planted on Hitler's train. But Halder would not take the lead in removing Hitler. If mutiny he must, it must be on orders from above, and that meant from his immediate superior, General Walther von Brauchitsch, the commander-in-chief of the army.

The fifty-eight-year-old, Prussian-born Brauchitsch sympathized with Halder's desire to remove Hitler. Like Halder, he detested Nazism and felt that the Führer was leading Germany into a disastrously premature war. However, like his French counterpart, Maurice Gamelin, Brauchitsch was not an aggressive leader, and certainly was not the man to initiate a coup. He abhorred personal confrontations, particularly highly emotional ones with Hitler, with whom, temperamentally, he was no match. Trying after the war to excuse his inaction against his Führer, Brauchitsch said: "Why, in heaven's name, should I, of all men in the world, have taken action against Hitler? The German people had elected him, and . . . were perfectly satisfied with his successful policy." Indeed, Brauchitsch's missing backbone was the very characteristic that had prompted Hitler to appoint him to the high command of the army in the first place. Hitler thought Brauchitsch would prove easier to handle than his deposed predecessor, General Werner von Fritsch. And he did.

On October 27, 1939, Hitler had summoned Brauchitsch and Halder to a meeting at the Reichschancellery, where he informed them that the western offensive would begin on November 12. He ordered them to prepare the plans for the attack.

This was the moment the conspirators had been awaiting. They were sure the generals would act to prevent an all-out conflict with Britain and France. Under increased pressure from Hans Oster and the other conspirators, Halder had agreed to begin a coup on November 5, when the movement of troops to their jump-off points opposite Holland, Belgium, and Luxembourg was to begin. But he insisted that the coup attempt would be made only if Brauchitsch approved.

To obtain Brauchitsch's acquiescence, Halder gave him a report prepared by the army's chief economist, General Georg Thomas, which argued
that a German offensive in the west would prompt the Allies to disrupt
deliveries to Germany of Swedish iron ore, Yugoslavian copper, and Roma-
nian oil. Even if the western offensive should succeed, Thomas warned,
Germany would be forced to defend, at enormous cost, whatever territory
she might gain. And the United States was not likely to remain neutral if
Britain and France were in danger of defeat.

After reading Thomas's report, Brauchitsch finally agreed with Halder
that they had to prevent Hitler from launching the western offensive. They
decided that Brauchitsch would see the Führer on November 5 and hand
him a memorandum containing the findings of a tour of the western front
that both generals were planning to make on November 2–3. Should
Brauchitsch's meeting with Hitler not produce an immediate postponement of the offensive, Halder would launch the coup. Hitler would be
assassinated, after which a new military government would take over and
negotiate an end to the war with the Allies. However, while Brauchitsch
reluctantly agreed to go along with the plot, he stipulated that Halder
should make the necessary arrangements. Halder, in turn, entrusted that
task to Hans Oster, who arranged to supply the would-be assassin, Eric
Kordt, with explosives to murder Hitler. The coup was scheduled to take
place on November 11.

Late in the morning of November 5, Brauchitsch and Halder drove from
Zossen, the army's headquarters, just outside Berlin, to the Reichschancellery. At noon, Halder walked his chief into the anteroom of Hitler's
office and then went back to his car to await Brauchitsch's return. Entering Hitler's office, Brauchitsch saluted and handed the Führer the memorandum containing the views of the frontline generals on the western
offensive. However, instead of summarizing its contents, Brauchitsch began
to bombard Hitler with a variety of arguments designed to persuade him
to postpone the attack.

Hitler would accept none of them. When Brauchitsch pointed out that
the rains of autumn and winter would make a successful offensive impossible, Hitler cynically interjected, "It rains on the enemy too." When
Brauchitsch warned him against underestimating the French, Hitler held
up his hand: "Herr Generaloberst, I would like to interrupt immediately
here, because I hold quite different views. First, I place a low value on the

French army's will to fight. . . . After the first setbacks, it will swiftly crack up."

Realizing that he was getting nowhere, Brauchitsch began to grasp at straws. To convince the Führer that the army was not ready for war, he charged that its soldiers had not demonstrated the same degree of aggressiveness in the Polish campaign that the army had displayed in World War I. Brauchitsch even said there were "mutinies" in some units and displays of drunken indiscipline at the front that invited comparison with the uglier scenes of the army's disintegration in 1918.

With that remark, Hitler blew up. Brauchitsch had rubbed raw the Nazi warlord's pride in everything that National Socialism had done for the Wehrmacht. "In what units have there been cases of lack of discipline?" Hitler demanded to know. "What happened? Where? What counteraction had been taken by the army command?" He stood up and shouted at Brauchitsch, "How many death sentences have been carried out?" He would fly anywhere that very day to investigate Brauchitsch's charges. It was incomprehensible, he yelled, how a commander-in-chief of the army could blacken its reputation. "Not one frontline commander mentioned any lack of attacking spirit to me!" Hitler shouted.

Then the Führer turned his full fury on the army high command. Every insult, every accusation, every manifestation of the hatred and contempt that he held for the generals he spewed forth on Brauchitsch. The General Staff had never been loyal; it had never displayed confidence in his genius. It had consistently sabotaged the German rearmament effort by deliberate, "go-slow" methods. The truth was, Hitler shouted, it was the army high command—and not *his* soldiers—who did not want to fight. He then called in Keitel and, as Brauchitsch fumbled for words, raged to the OKH chief of staff about the defeatist "spirit of Zossen," which he knew all about and would soon destroy.

Brauchitsch, his face chalky white and twisted, tottered back to Halder's car. "When von Brauchitsch reappeared," Halder recalled, "he was so shaken that he could give no account of what had taken place. . . . It was not until later that I picked up one or two details." Hitler, Halder learned, had flung himself at Brauchitsch, seized his papers, tore them up, stamped on them, and pushed him out the door, bellowing, "I have had enough of your doubts. Prepare the troops to attack as soon as possible. I am responsible, not you."

Immediately after pushing Brauchitsch out of his office, Hitler dictated a note dismissing the army commander-in-chief. But Keitel talked him out of taking that step by pointing out how difficult it would be to find a more compliant successor. Still, while Brauchitsch kept his job, Hitler never forgave him for the slurs he had cast upon *his* army—and he never trusted his judgment again.

What shocked Halder the most about Brauchitsch's account of the meeting, however, was Hitler's reference to "knowing all about the spirit of Zossen"—this could only mean that he must know about the planned coup. Halder panicked. He still carried the pistol with which he had planned to kill Hitler. But now he was too paralyzed with fear to act. At any moment the SS* might come and take him away, and along with him the whole upper echelon of the army General Staff. He immediately informed his co-conspirators that the coup was off and ordered them to destroy all evidence that might incriminate them.

While reluctantly agreeing with Keitel's recommendation to keep Brauchitsch in his position, Hitler nevertheless decided to ensure that the general's "defeatist" views would not infect the rest of the army. On November 23, he summoned to the Reichschancellery the top leaders of the Wehrmacht, down to corps commanders and their equivalent ranks in the Luftwaffe and the navy—over 120 officers in all—to listen to a scathing, two-hour-long lecture. He began by reminding his audience that without the Nazi Party the Wehrmacht would never have been rebuilt. He castigated the army high command for failing to appreciate his genius. "No one had ever achieved what I have achieved," he boasted. For the first time in sixty-seven years, since the time of the "Iron Chancellor," Otto von Bismarck, Germany would not have to fight a two-front war, thanks to the nonaggression pact that he had concluded with the Russians the preceding August. But the Russians, he admitted, could not be trusted to remain inactive indefinitely. For this reason, he emphasized, the western powers must be defeated as quickly as possible. The breach of Dutch and Belgian neutrality, he said, was of no importance. "No one will question that when we have won, and we shall not make the breach as idiotically as it was done in 1914."

Then Hitler turned the heat on the leaders of the army. All but accusing them of cowardice, he reminded them that *he* had not created the new

---

*The SS (Schutzstaffel) was originally Hitler's bodyguard, but throughout the war grew into a powerful military force in its own right, comprising several divisions.

Wehrmacht in order to avoid using it. Referring to the charge that Brauchitsch had made on November 5, he declared that he was "infuriated" by any suggestion that *his* troops had been inadequate in Poland. The war in the west would be won, he emphasized, if only the high command would believe in victory. "Everything depends on the military leaders," he insisted. "With the German soldier, I can do anything, provided he is well led."

Hitler, now more calmly, implored the assembled officers to pass on a spirit of determination to their subordinates. "Fate," he said, "demands no more from us than from all the great men of German history. I will shrink from nothing and will destroy everyone who opposes me." Then, prophetically, he continued: "In this struggle, I will stand or fall. I will not survive the defeat of my country." But, he assured his audience, there would be no defeat. "We shall emerge victorious."

The effect of Hitler's harangue on the generals was electrifying. "The reproach turned the brave into cowards," Hans Oster recalled. Brauchitsch, however, tendered his resignation, but Hitler refused to accept it. Brauchitsch, like the ordinary soldier, the Führer reminded him, had a duty to perform. Cowed by Hitler's tirade, both Brauchitsch and Halder turned their attention to drawing up the plans for what now appeared to be inevitable: Hitler's western offensive.

FALL GELB

The original plan for the Western offensive, code-named *Fall Gelb* (Plan Yellow), was drawn up by the General Staff under Halder's direction in October 1939. In some respects it resembled the Schlieffen Plan, whose objectives the German army came within an ace of fulfilling before it was decisively stopped on the Marne River in 1914. Like the Schlieffen Plan, *Fall Gelb* called for the right wing of the German army to deliver the main weight of the attack in the west, through Belgium, and then into northern France.

However, *Fall Gelb*'s objectives were more modest than those of the Schlieffen Plan. The latter had envisaged the German army turning east after passing Paris in order to roll up the mass of the Allied armies facing the Rhine frontier before annihilating them. However, this first version of *Fall Gelb* did not have the annihilation of the Allied armies as its main objective. Instead, it envisioned merely beating back the Allies to the English Channel and then southward to the Somme River. The General Staff was content to simply secure air and naval bases from which the Luftwaffe and the navy could harass the British Isles.

But Lieutenant General Erich von Manstein was not happy with *Fall Gelb*. During World War I, Manstein had served as a staff captain in General von Gallwitz's army, which launched a futile attack on the Allied forces on the left bank of the Meuse River during the battle of Verdun. After examining *Fall Gelb* during October 1939, Manstein, who was now chief of staff of Rundstedt's Army Group A, felt the plan would produce the same result as occurred at Verdun: a futile frontal attack on a strong enemy defensive position. The German army might be successful in pushing the Allies back, Manstein conceded, but sooner or later the attack would falter, leaving the Allied armies intact on a line running from the Channel to Sedan.

Although not deeply concerned about the fate of Belgium—like Hitler, Manstein did not let ethical scruples undermine the demands of military necessity—he did believe that if Germany were going to breach Belgian neutrality for the second time in a generation, the action should produce a decisive victory. Only a successful outcome would thwart an attack by the Russians, whose neutrality could not be counted on indefinitely, especially not if the bulk of the German army was stalemated in the west. A decisive victory, he wrote, could only be achieved by "defeating and annihilating the whole of the enemy forces fighting in Belgium, or north of the Somme River in France, and not only throwing them back frontally."

With this aim in mind, Manstein strongly believed that the *Schwerpunkt*—the offensive's center of gravity—which he emphasized should consist of concentrated masses of panzers, should be shifted farther to the south, where the Allies would least expect it, that is, to the Ardennes Forest, Gamelin's "impenetrable barrier." An attack here, he admitted, was risky. There was always the possibility that the Allies would not advance into Belgium; they might, instead, hold back their armies in northern France until the Germans committed themselves to an invasion of Belgium, and then drive against the German flank near its hinge in the Ardennes. "To prevent this," Manstein wrote, "it was vital to smash any enemy concentrations . . . before they could reach completion." This could be accomplished only if the weight of the German attack fell on the Meuse River. "The cohesion of the enemy front in this area," he wrote, "must be destroyed from the outset with a view to turning the flank of the Maginot Line later."

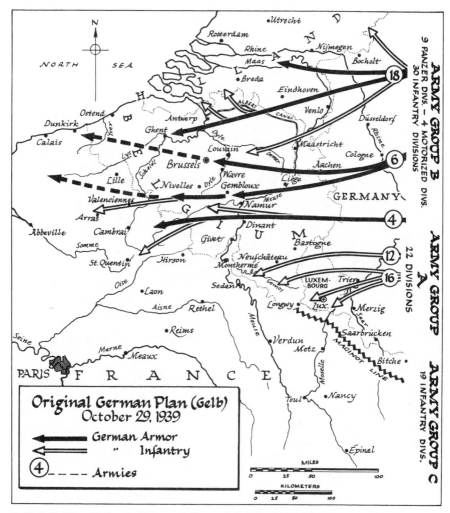

Fall Gelb (Plan Yellow). (Shirer, *Collapse of the Third Republic*, Simon and Schuster)

Manstein's ideas, however, got nowhere with Halder. Like Gamelin, Halder was a member of the old school: tanks were to be used only as accessories to the infantry. The major offensive through the Ardennes, he pointed out to Manstein in October 1939, would pose serious logistical problems that would only increase if a breakout were directed all the way to the English Channel. Moreover, as Manstein was aware, no one was sure that the Allies would advance into Belgium. Halder preferred to keep a large number of divisions in reserve so that they could be sent to either Bock's Army Group B on the northern flank of the German armies invading Belgium, or to Rundstedt's on their southern flank, depending on whether or not

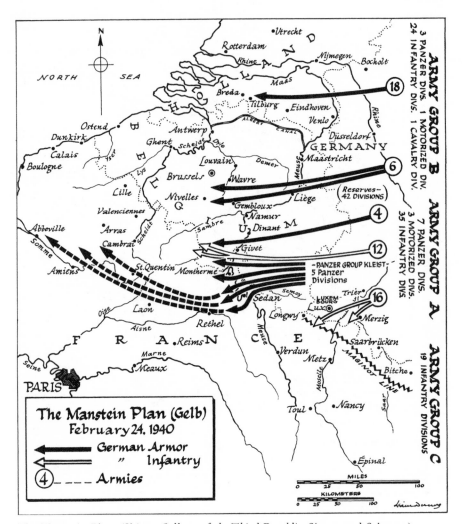

The Manstein Plan. (Shirer, *Collapse of the Third Republic*, Simon and Schuster)

the Allies advanced into Belgium. Halder, in short, was not prepared to endorse Manstein's plan because, while it offered the prospect of total victory, it also carried with it the risk of total defeat.

Halder's views completely exasperated Manstein. "To wait and see which way the cat jumped before deciding where to place one's main effort," he wrote, "was tantamount to abandoning the chance of annihilating the enemy forces in northern Belgium by an outflanking movement from the south." It violated, he argued to Halder, von Moltke's dictum that "an error in the first stages of deployment can never be made good." In other words, once the attack's center of gravity was deployed in northern Belgium, it would be impossible to transfer it to the Meuse in time to take advantage of an Allied counterthrust into central Belgium. It was also von Moltke, Manstein reminded Halder, who emphasized that the military commander must look past the first encounter with the enemy "and keep his eye fixed on the ultimate goal." To Manstein, that goal could be nothing less than total victory on the European mainland.

But Manstein was no expert on armored warfare—at least not in the fall of 1939. Although he would go on to become a field marshal, and probably Germany's greatest strategist during World War II, Manstein was by background an infantry man. He was not sure if panzer divisions could traverse the Ardennes Forest quickly enough to catch the Allies by surprise. Yet there was one general who knew the answer to that question: Heinz Guderian, Germany's leading expert on armored warfare. In November 1939, Manstein invited Guderian to visit him at the headquarters of Army Group A to discuss his plan.

HEINZ GUDERIAN

Guderian came from a family that had provided Prussia with officers for centuries. After serving in World War I as an officer in a telegraph battalion, he was transferred to the Motorized Transportation Department. Like many of his peers, Guderian at that time was faced with the seemingly insurmountable problem of defending a country whose military establishment had been stripped bare by the disarmament provisions of the Treaty of Versailles. The German army was permitted only 100,000 men, the navy only 36 warships. The treaty also prohibited Germany from possessing military aircraft or tanks. Under these conditions, Guderian concluded, Germany could only be defended by creating a highly mobile defense force, one that could be shifted rapidly from the nation's eastern frontier to her western borders, whatever the situation demanded.

To create a mobile defense, Guderian turned to the writings of English strategists and tacticians like Liddell Hart, General J. F. C. Fuller, and Colonel Giffard Martel. All were pioneers in the science of armored warfare. Of the three men, Guderian was most impressed with the ideas of Liddell Hart, primarily because this Englishman emphasized the use of armored vehicles for long-range strikes against the enemy's communications network. In addition, Liddell Hart called for the creation of an armored division that combined both tanks and motorized infantry.

Guderian was so deeply impressed by Liddell Hart's ideas that he tried to adapt them to the German army. In a 1937 book entitled *Achtung*

Panzer!, Guderian discussed what he considered to be the fundamental errors of Allied tank operations in World War I. For one, Allied tanks did not attack in sufficient depth and were never backed up with adequately powerful mobile reserves that would enable them to break through the enemy's front line and then into his rear, where it would have been possible "to knock out his batteries, his reserves, his staffs, all at the same time." In addition, Guderian argued, the full potential of the Allied tanks was sacrificed by yoking them to the much more slowly moving infantry troops and horse-drawn artillery. Moreover, the Allies had used the wrong tanks—thinly armored infantry escort tanks—and had used them in the wrong way, throwing them into battle in "penny packets," rather than in powerful concentrations that would ensure breakthroughs.

Guderian saw the remedy for these errors in the fully mechanized panzer division. Each would contain elements of artillery, infantry, and cavalry, as well as tanks. However, Guderian insisted that its nucleus must be the tank, not the infantry. And the kind of tank that he had in mind was not the slow, short-range, infantry-escort tank that the French were still using in the mid-1930s but rather a medium "breakthrough" tank with "armor sufficient to protect it against the mass of enemy anti-tank weapons." The breakthrough tank, he recommended, should also have "a higher speed and greater cruising range than an infantry-escort tank, and an armament of machine-guns and cannon up to 75 mm."

Guderian also stressed that tank commanders should be trained to work in large armored units, not as individuals attached to infantry units. In this way, the maximum firepower of the panzer division could be concentrated on the weakest point of the enemy line. Motorized infantry units would follow closely behind the tanks. Equipped with anti-tank guns, they would have the job of mopping up enemy units and securing the flanks of the advancing panzers. The unwieldy, horse-drawn artillery of World War I, he felt, should be replaced by self-propelled guns mounted on trucks. In this way, Guderian believed, each element of the panzer division would have the range, speed, and stamina of the tank, and, as a result, would not impair its full offensive potential.

Surprise was another essential element of the panzer thrust. To ensure that it would be achieved, Guderian recommended that *Stuka* dive-bombers should be used whenever possible in place of artillery. The preattack deployment of artillery pieces, he feared, would reveal to the enemy the location and time of the impending attack as well as slow it up. Guderian insisted that the panzers must strike with such great speed that they would break into the enemy's defensive zone before the enemy could bring up anti-tank guns to counterattack. If possible, Guderian felt, the panzers should attack at dawn, when they would present difficult targets to enemy anti-tank gunners.

Yet even more than the anti-tank gun, Guderian regarded the enemy tank as the "most dangerous" threat to the panzer. The only effective counter to the speed, range, and firepower of the panzers was other tanks, provided that they were used in the way that Guderian insisted the panzers must operate. To delay the arrival and concentration of enemy tanks in the path of the advancing panzers, Guderian recommended the use of aerial interdiction and airborne troops, dropped in the enemy's rear.

All in all, Guderian's *Achtung Panzer!* presented the blueprint for the type of warfare, the blitzkrieg, that would give Hitler some of the most outstanding military triumphs in history. However, in the early 1930s the blitzkrieg existed only in the minds of Guderian and a few other strategists. And he had experienced as much trouble selling armored warfare to the German General Staff as Manstein did, or, for that matter, as much as Charles de Gaulle did with the French high command. Infantry was still regarded as the "queen of battle." Moreover, the prohibition against tanks which the Treaty of Versailles had imposed on the German army had made it difficult for Guderian to demonstrate to his colleagues the full offensive potential of the panzer division.

Before the Treaty of Versailles was scrapped by Hitler in 1935, Guderian had tried to get around its restrictions by using sheet-metal wagons as mock tanks. His demonstrations only earned him the scoffing sympathy of the German high command. It was not until Hitler came to power in 1933 that Guderian's ideas received the attention they deserved. In a field exercise attended by Hitler during that year, Guderian was allotted a half-hour to demonstrate the operation of a motorcycle platoon, an anti-tank platoon, a platoon of tanks, and two platoons of armored reconnaissance cars. The Führer was impressed greatly by the speed and precision of Guderian's motorized units. "That's what I need! That's what I want to have!" he said repeatedly as he watched the demonstration.

And that was what Hitler was determined to get. Pressed by the Führer, the army high command reluctantly permitted Guderian to organize the first of three panzer divisions. Each was built around a tank brigade and supported by a motorized infantry brigade as well as by motorized artillery. Between 1936 and 1939, another three panzer divisions were added to the army, each with an authorized strength of 300 tanks. By May

1940, on the eve of Hitler's western offensive, and at a time when France possessed only three armored divisions, Germany had 10.*

Manstein's ideas intrigued Guderian. After studying maps of the Ardennes region and making use of his own memory of the terrain from his experiences during World War I, Guderian assured Manstein that the operation could be carried out. The only condition he attached was that the strongest possible number of armored and motorized divisions must be concentrated in the spearhead of the operation. In Guderian, Manstein had acquired an aggressive and outspoken ally.

HITLER ADOPTS THE MANSTEIN PLAN

On January 12, 1940, the day after the news of the Reinberger crash reached Hitler, Manstein sent his sixth and last memorandum to the General Staff. It was accompanied by a letter to Brauchitsch from Rundstedt, Manstein's superior, requesting the high command to forward it to the Führer. Rundstedt believed that Manstein's ideas were not getting beyond the General Staff. And he was right. Brauchitsch and Halder opposed Manstein's plan for both strategic and tactical reasons. They still were strongly opposed to a western offensive, and they did not want Hitler to see any plan such as Manstein's that he might find attractive. Moreover, Rundstedt's request was a breach of military propriety; only the commander-in-chief of the army, Brauchitsch, and his chief of staff, Halder, were considered competent to make military recommendations to the Führer. Not surprisingly, they turned down Rundstedt's request.

Manstein, however, did not give up. On January 25, he had the opportunity to see Brauchitsch, who was visiting the headquarters of Army Group A in Koblenz. Manstein was amazed to discover that in spite of the now-established fact that the Allies were prepared to move into Belgium

---

*While the Germans had more armored divisions than the Allies, the Allies had more tanks combined than the Germans, about 4,200 to 3,200. Moreover, French tanks, on the whole, were superior to the panzers. The latest French tanks, the Somua S 35 and the heavy Char B, carried twice the armor of the heaviest German tank, the Panzer IV. Moreover, these tanks were equipped with 47mm and 75mm guns respectively, compared to a 37mm for the Panzer III and a 75mm for the Panzer IV. Guderian planned to compensate for these disadvantages by using field artillery and 88mm antiaircraft guns in the forefront of the battle and by outmaneuvering the French tanks, attacking their flanks and getting into their rear areas.

at the onset of the German offensive, Brauchitsch had done nothing to revise *Fall Gelb*. Manstein reacted by repeating all his well-worn arguments against the plan. He concluded by accusing Brauchitsch point-blank of not aiming for a "full decision" in the west. Manstein's audacity was too much for Brauchitsch. A few days later, he was relieved of his position on Rundstedt's staff and reassigned to the command of an infantry corps. In the new position Brauchitsch thought the obstreperous general would be less of a nuisance and much less likely to catch the Führer's ear.

However, Hitler, quite on his own, was already moving toward a more southerly *Schwerpunkt*. As early as October 1939, he had expressed his first misgivings about *Fall Gelb*. After listening to Halder give a presentation of the plan, Hitler commented to Keitel, "That is just the old Schlieffen Plan, with a strong flank along the Atlantic coast; you won't get away with an operation like that twice running." Hitler had quite a different idea, he told Keitel: a vast encirclement of the enemy, spearheaded by armored units thrusting across the Meuse River and then to the coast. This was terrain he had fought on during the Great War, and he knew it was ideal for tanks.

On October 25 Hitler startled Brauchitsch and Halder by asking them whether a main attack on the southern end of the Meuse River might be able to "cut off and annihilate the enemy" as they advanced into Belgium. Then, almost casually, he took a red pencil, sketched a line on a map, and extended it from the Meuse at a point south of Namur to the coast of the English Channel. This was the germ of the plan that was to bring about France's defeat. Yet at first it seemed so bold, staking everything on one card—namely, the ability of the German army to break through the Allied line and advance all the way to the Channel—that Hitler hesitated to order such a radical change of emphasis, particularly since three days before he had provisionally ordered that *Fall Gelb* would begin on November 12. Nevertheless, he asked the army high command to look into his idea and indicated that if necessary to develop this new plan, he would not be averse to postponing the offensive until spring.

Four days later, on October 29, the General Staff produced a revised edition of the plan. As before, the attack's center of gravity remained with Bock's Army Group B, but to include the variant Hitler had presented to Brauchitsch and Halder, it was shifted somewhat to the south, so that the 4th Army, with four panzer divisions, would cross the Meuse both north and south of Namur.

Hitler was not happy with the army's version of his variant. The next day, October 30, he told Jodl that his "new idea" called for a strike with one panzer division and one motorized division through the Ardennes Forest toward Sedan, some fifty miles farther south on the Meuse than Namur. On November 9, Hitler upgraded the size of the striking force to a full corps, consisting of two panzer divisions and one motorized infantry division supplemented by two independent motorized infantry regiments. He gave command of this force, designated 19th Panzer Corps, to Heinz Guderian. His mission would be to gain control of the west bank of the Meuse River near Sedan in order to create favorable conditions for a continued offensive from that position in the event that Bock's panzers became stalled in Belgium. Hitler's conviction that an attack through the Ardennes would succeed was strengthened by the Allies' capture of the Reinberger documents in January, which he believed had convinced the Allies that the main German attack would come through northern Belgium.

Hitler's decision to move the western offensive's center of gravity to the Ardennes was finalized after a meeting he had with Manstein in February 1940. The general finally had been able to get the Führer's ear. In late January, Manstein had the opportunity to discuss his ideas with Colonel Rudolph Schmundt, Hitler's military adjutant. Schmundt was amazed by how closely Manstein's ideas paralleled the Führer's, although, as Schmundt later recalled, in a "significantly more precise form."

Back in Berlin on February 2, Schmundt immediately informed Hitler about his conversation with Manstein. Though not hiding his personal aversion to the general—Hitler incorrectly suspected that Manstein was part Jewish—he expressed his keen interest in Manstein's ideas. He wanted the general brought before him as soon as possible, but in a way that would not arouse the suspicions of Brauchitsch and Halder.

A ruse was devised. On February 17 Manstein appeared at the Reichschancellery along with a number of recently assigned corps commanders to receive his new commission from the Führer. During the luncheon that followed, Hitler, as usual, did most of the talking. But when the meal was finished, he called Manstein aside and invited him into his study. There Hitler asked the general what he thought about *Fall Gelb*. For once, Hitler did most of the listening as Manstein explained his alternative plan in detail.

Manstein's plan called for Army Group A to deliver an overwhelming blow to the French center by driving through the Ardennes Forest, crossing the Meuse on both sides of Sedan and then, after breaking through the French line, speeding across northern France to the Channel coast near Abbeville. In this way, Manstein promised, the Allied armies would be cut off in Belgium. After their destruction, he added, the rest of the French army could be enveloped and destroyed "with a powerful right hook." Hitler nodded his head in approval. "The man," he said of Manstein later, "is not my cup of tea, but he certainly knows what should be done."

The next day, February 18, Brauchitsch and Halder were summoned to the Chancellery. Without any reference to Manstein, Hitler presented his ideas to them, attributing them to his own creative genius. By then, however, both Brauchitsch and Halder also had come around to Manstein's way of thinking, due in no small measure to Guderian's efforts. On February 7, in war games held in Koblenz, Guderian had demonstrated to Halder that his armored spearheads could reach the Meuse at Sedan within three or four days after the commencement of the offensive. They would cross the river on the fifth day and then proceed westward toward the English Channel.

Halder at first disagreed with Guderian on the timing of the Meuse crossing. He wanted Guderian to wait until the ninth day before crossing the river because he feared that unless infantry could be brought up to support the crossing, it would not succeed. Even if it did, Halder insisted, infantry units would be needed to cover the flanks of the panzers as they advanced west of the river.

Guderian disagreed strongly with Halder's assessment. It was essential, Guderian insisted, to use all the available offensive power of the panzers in one surprise blow, at one decisive point, in order "to drive a wedge so deep and wide that we need not worry about our flanks, and then immediately exploit any success gained without bothering to wait for the infantry corps." It was Guderian's line of reasoning that prevailed when Brauchitsch and Halder presented the revised version of *Fall Gelb* to Hitler on February 18.

Hitler had no chance to discuss the new plan with Guderian until March 6, during a full-scale military conference at the Chancellery. Present were General Ewald von Kleist, in whose panzer group Guderian's 19th Panzer Corps would serve, and the leaders of the various armies comprising Rundstedt's Army Group A. Chairing the conference, Hitler asked each of the generals to outline how they intended to carry out their missions. Guderian spoke last: "On zero day," he said, "I shall cross the border of Luxembourg and then head across southern Belgium to Sedan, my corps advancing in three columns. I expect to reach the Belgian frontier on the first day and I shall cross it that night; on the second day, I shall advance to Neufchateau; on the third, I shall reach Bouillon and cross the Semois; on the fourth, I shall get to the Meuse; on the fifth, I shall cross it. By the evening of the fifth day, I expect to have established a bridgehead on the other bank."

"And what will you do next?" Hitler asked.

The Führer, Guderian recalled in his memoir, "was the only one who had thought of asking me this leading question." He replied: "In the absence of orders to the contrary, I expect to continue my westward advance on the following day. It is for the Supreme Command to decide whether my target is to be Amiens or Paris. In my opinion, the correct solution would be to march on Amiens so as to reach the Channel."

Hitler nodded but said nothing.

However, General Ernst Busch, commander of the 16th Army, which would be on Guderian's left flank, objected: "I shall be greatly surprised if you manage to cross the river on the first attempt!"

Hitler, with a tense look on his face, glanced at Guderian to see how he would react.

"You do your own job and leave me to worry about mine," Guderian nonchalantly replied.

Hitler made no comment, but after the conference he formally approved the new version of *Fall Gelb,* based as it was on ideas of Manstein and Guderian.

Later, when Guderian was asked whether he thought Hitler had any talent as a strategist, the panzer leader replied: "Of course! I had the highest opinion of his judgment in military matters, in view of the fact that he adopted my own ideas."

Hitler, however, made two important adjustments in Manstein's plan. First, he decided to add some features of the army's original version of *Fall Gelb.* He directed that three of the ten panzer divisions should be transferred to Bock's army group to support the advance through Holland and Belgium, thereby overruling Guderian's demand that *all* the panzer divisions should be massed in the Sedan sector. One of the panzer divisions would be assigned to General Georg von Kuechler's 18th Army, whose objective was Rotterdam; the other two would be attached to General Walther von Reichenau's 6th Army, whose initial objectives were Maastricht and Liège.

Guderian was not happy with Hitler's decision to transfer the panzer divisions, since it violated his own motto, *"Nicht kleckern, klotzen!"* (Don't disperse, concentrate!) However, Hitler's reasoning behind the move was inspired less by strategic than by psychological considerations. The object of the operation was to encircle and destroy the greater part of the Allied forces as swiftly as possible in order to facilitate the second phase of the battle—the destruction of the remainder of the French army, south of the Somme River. The Manstein Plan would work, he believed, but only if the Allies rushed the bulk of their forces northward into Belgium. But who could be sure that they would? If they did not enter Belgium in strength, they might have sufficient reserves available to thwart the break-through at Sedan. Everything, therefore, must be done, Hitler reasoned, to encourage the Allies to advance as many divisions as possible into Belgium. Assigning three panzer divisions to participate in the advances in the north, he believed, would serve that purpose.

Hitler's second adjustment in the Manstein Plan was inspired by his concern for the ever-lengthening left flank of the panzers as they advanced toward the Channel following their breakthrough at Sedan. It would seem to invite a French counterattack from the south. To guard against this possibility, Manstein had recommended that the motorized infantry divisions advancing westward behind the panzers should constantly attack any French forces along the flank in order to disrupt their ability to launch an effective counterattack. But Hitler preferred a two-part campaign. The first part would culminate in the encirclement and annihilation of the Allied armies in Belgium. The objective of second phase would be the destruction of the remaining Allied forces south of the Somme. Accordingly, he directed that the southern flank of the panzer corridor should be stronger than Manstein believed necessary.

Now that the army had been spared the disastrous consequences of a premature winter offensive and the prospects for a decisive victory in the west began to appear good, planning for the offensive took on a new life. The new plan of attack that was drawn up by the General Staff was aptly christened *Sichelschnitt*—the "Cut of the Sickle." It placed the attack's center of gravity on the Meuse River between Namur and Sedan, as Manstein and Guderian desired. Also in accord with their wishes, the main blow would be delivered by Rundstedt's Army Group A. The spearhead of the attack— no longer merely a diversionary operation—was assigned to Guderian's 19th Panzer Corps, consisting of the 1st, 2nd, and 10th Panzer Divisions, assisted by Hitler's elite *Grossdeutschland* motorized infantry regiment. These units would be supported by General Gustav von Wietersheim's 14th Motorized Infantry Corps and other divisions of General List's 12th Army.

Farther north, the 6th and 8th Panzer Divisions of General Georg-Hans Reinhardt's 51st Panzer Corps would head for Monthermé, a small town downstream from Sedan. The 5th and 7th Panzer Divisions of General Hermann Hoth's 15th Panzer Corps, a part of General Kluge's 4th Army, would provide flank cover for Reinhardt's corps by crossing the Meuse farther north, at Dinant. The five panzer divisions belonging to Guderian and Reinhardt, the spearhead of the attack, were welded together in an integrated armored group under General Ewald von Kleist, a former cavalry man not well disposed to armored warfare, and thus sufficiently cautious to ease Hitler's fears about Guderian's exposed flanks.

While Rundstedt's Army Group A was expected to break through the Allied center, Bock's Army Group B and General Wilhelm Ritter von Leeb's Army Group C would be playing important roles, too. Bock's two armies, the 18th Army, under General Kuechler, and the 6th Army, under General Reichenau, would have to crush Holland as quickly as possible in order to protect the northern flank of Rundstedt's army group. It would also have to advance far enough into Belgium to draw the Allies away from Rundstedt's forces trying to get into their rear. At the same time, Leeb would have to convince the Allies that Germany was prepared to launch a secondary strike against the Maginot Line in order to dissuade the French from shifting divisions in the fortifications northward to counter Rundstedt's crossing of the Meuse.

As winter finally gave way to spring, the Germans were busy taking steps to ensure that the redeployments required by the revised *Fall Gelb* were hidden from the Allies. They hoped that General Gamelin would find no reason to change his plan to send the cream of the Allied armies into northeastern Belgium—and ultimately to their destruction in a carefully planned German trap.

CHAPTER FOUR

The Battle Begins, May 10–14

London: A Change of Government, May 8

Spring finally arrived. It was one of the most beautiful Europeans could remember and was particularly appreciated after one of the severest winters in half a century. Clare Booth, then a budding writer (and later the wife of *Time, Life,* and *Fortune* publisher Henry Luce), found the weather in Paris "insanely beautiful . . . the air sweet . . . the unstartled birds singing in the gardens . . . the flowers at the Madeleine madly colorful."

However, in London, which was bathed in the same beautiful weather that Parisians were enjoying, an air of crisis hung over Parliament. On May 8, the House of Commons convened to debate Prime Minister Neville Chamberlain's handling of the Norwegian campaign. In April, under the very nose of the British fleet, the Germans had succeeded in slipping a small flotilla of troop-carrying ships into the harbors of Norway's leading ports. Within days, Norway was another victim of Hitler's seemingly unbeatable blitzkrieg. Now the opposition was calling the government to task for its failure to defend the important Scandinavian nation.

Chamberlain, in his seventies and looking, as one MP described him, like "a toothbrush in a stiff collar," tried to avoid blame for the Norwegian catastrophe. Instead, he concentrated on the positive aspects of the British war effort, particularly the valor of Britain's soldiers, sailors, and airmen. But the opposition MPs would have none of it. They repeatedly interrupted the prime minister's presentation with catcalls and jeers, yelling "Missed the bus!"—for Chamberlain, a painful replay of the words he had used when he initially had thought British troops had beaten the Germans to Norway.

When Chamberlain finally finished his speech and sat down, members of the opposition parties opened their barrage. Leo Amery scathed Chamberlain for his repeated but ill-founded defense of one failure after another.

"Wars are won," Amery chided the prime minister, "not by explanations after the event, but by foresight, by clear decision, and by swift action." Then Amery turned his burning gaze upon the ashen face of Chamberlain and hurled an admonition gleaned from another parliamentary confrontation of long ago: "This is what Cromwell said to the Long Parliament when he thought it was no longer fit to conduct the affairs of the nation: 'You have sat too long here for any good you have been doing. Depart, I say, and let us have done with you. In the name of God go!'"

Chamberlain's government clearly was doomed. More doubtful was who would succeed him. All eyes turned toward Winston Churchill. Since Hitler had come to power in 1933, until the outbreak of the war six years later, Churchill had been a political outcast for repeatedly warning the nation that the Nazi dictator could not be trusted. Britain, he insisted repeatedly, must prepare for war. But it seemed that no one besides Churchill wanted to risk another war with Germany. Instead, most Britons preferred to support Chamberlain's efforts to avoid another war by appeasing Hitler.

By 1939, however, most Britons had come to realize that appeasement had only whetted Hitler's appetite, as Churchill had predicted it would, and had convinced the Nazi dictator that Britain would not fight to protect non-British interests on the Continent. One of the ultimate consequences of appeasing Hitler had been his invasion of Poland on September 1, a country that Britain and France had belatedly brought under their protection only five months earlier. Two days later, Chamberlain's government, along with the government of France, had reluctantly declared war on Germany.

By the following May, however, Chamberlain's lackluster prosecution of the war, which was accentuated by the Norwegian fiasco, had convinced many MPs on both sides of the aisle that Churchill alone possessed the energy, imagination, and stamina necessary to save the country from the scourge of Nazism. To be sure, Churchill was regarded as impulsive, cocky, and prone to fiascoes himself. Many still remembered his ill-fated effort to capture the Dardanelles from Turkey during World War I. And Churchill, as First Lord of the Admiralty since September 1939, was largely responsible for Britain's tardy, and ultimately unsuccessful, attempt to thwart the German occupation of Norway.

Yet if Churchill was impulsive and overconfident—and he often was—these seemed to be the very qualities that Britain needed in her hour of maximum crisis, qualities that Chamberlain so obviously lacked. However,

Churchill was a member of Chamberlain's government and as such felt a responsibility to defend its war policy. When former prime minister David Lloyd George tried to separate him from the government's responsibility for the Norwegian fiasco, Churchill reacted in a flash. "I take complete responsibility for everything that has been done by the Admiralty, and I take my full share of the burden."

Chamberlain's government was able to survive a vote of confidence that day—281 to 200—but 44 Conservative MPs voted against it, while a number of others abstained. Amid cries of "Resign!" and "In the name of God, go!" Chamberlain rose from his seat, smiled frostily, and left the House. The next day, he decided to surrender the premiership to Churchill.

CRISIS IN THE FRENCH CABINET, MAY 9

The same cloud of crisis that hung over the House of Commons also hovered over the French Foreign Ministry. At 10:30 A.M. on May 9, Paul Reynaud began reading an indictment of General Gamelin's conduct of the war.

Reynaud, a small but athletically trim man of 62, was often called "France's Churchill." Like Churchill, he was extremely energetic, decisive, and innovative, and, like his British counterpart, had spent most of the 1930s in the political wilderness, crying out in vain against the folly of appeasing Hitler. In so doing, Reynaud became a close friend and political collaborator of Charles de Gaulle, another rearmament advocate. Since 1935, Reynaud had backed de Gaulle's efforts to create a corps of French armored divisions to match those that the Germans were building. As minister of finance, he also had pushed for the purchase of war planes and other armaments from the United States. During the first six months of the war, Reynaud had made no secret of his conviction that he could prosecute the war more vigorously and effectively than his archrival, Prime Minister Edouard Daladier.

In March 1940, Reynaud finally got the chance to demonstrate that conviction. When Daladier's government failed to win a vote of confidence in the French Chamber of Deputies, which rebelled against his mishandling of the war, Daladier resigned the premiership. President Albert Lebrun called on Reynaud to form a new government. However, because he was an outsider, Reynaud had difficulty forming a cabinet. He was forced to propitiate his chief antagonist, Daladier, whose Radical Socialist Party controlled the most votes in the Chamber. Reynaud offered him the Foreign Ministry, but Daladier demanded the War Ministry as his price for joining the new government. Reynaud at first demurred. If Daladier retained the War Ministry, it would mean that Gamelin, and the whole stagnant military hierarchy he headed, would also remain in place. Yet Reynaud had no alternative but to pay Daladier's price, and because he did, Charles de Gaulle, who had expected to be appointed secretary of the War Cabinet, angrily refused to join the new government.

※

By May, Reynaud's patience with Gamelin's lackluster prosecution of the war had finally expired. In a cabinet meeting on the morning of May 9, Reynaud fired away at the generalissimo for two hours. Speaking in a hoarse voice caused by a bout with the flu, the premier blamed Gamelin for the Norwegian fiasco and warned that if he continued as commander-in-chief, "we are certain to lose the war." The cabinet, he insisted, must allow him to appoint a new commander-in-chief.

The cabinet reacted with stony silence. No one said a word. It was time, Reynaud finally said, that each member face up to his responsibility. After another period of silence, one minister, Lucien Lamoureux, spoke up in support of the premier. Reynaud, he said, had convinced him "of the impossibility of leaving General Gamelin at the head of the French armies."

But Daladier remained unconvinced. A stockily built, fifty-five-year-old widower and son of a baker, Daladier was a sober but not overimaginative leader who still displayed the very deep patriotism—as well as the manners—of a peasant. The writer James Vincent Sheean described him as "a dirty man with a cigarette stuck to his lower lip, stinking of absinthe, talking with a rough Marseillaise accent." Even General Gamelin, whom Daladier protected, regarded him privately as a weak leader. What France needed in her hour of supreme danger, Gamelin confided to his diary, was another Clemenceau, the "Tiger" of France, the premier who guided the nation through World War I. It was impossible, Gamelin reflected in his diary, "not to sense how much we are missing him now." Yet there was a basic problem Gamelin failed to grasp. The mass of French parliamentarians feared great, dominant personalities. They preferred, instead, machine politicians like Daladier. With Daladier, the historian Sir Denis Brogan observed, the politicians had "succeeded only too well in taking personality out of politics."

With his jaw set, and continually shrugging his shoulders, Daladier sat silently throughout Reynaud's harangue against Gamelin. Then he took the lead in countering the premier's criticism of the generalissimo. The responsibility for the Norwegian fiasco, he asserted, belonged to the British navy, not the French army. Moreover, he reasoned, removing Gamelin would require a housecleaning of the entire General Staff, and who was in the mood for such a fight at this critical point in the war?

(*Left to right*) General Ironside, Winston S. Churchill, General Gamelin, Lord Gort, General Georges (Imperial War Museum F2093)

Paul Reynaud
(AP/Wide World
Photos)

Edouard Daladier (AP/Wide World Photos)

General Georges Blanchard (AP/Wide World Photos)

General Gaston Billotte (*on left*) (AP/Wide World Photos)

General René Prioux (AP/Wide World Photos)

General Maxime Weygand (AP/Wide World Photos)

General Charles de Gaulle (AP/Wide World Photos)

Vice Admiral Jean Marie Abrial (AP/Wide
World Photos)

Marshal Henri Philippe Pétain (AP/Wide
World Photos)

Vice Admiral Bertram Ramsay (Imperial
War Museum A23443)

Generals Sir Harold Alexander (*left*) and Bernard
Montgomery (AP/Wide World Photos)

General Sir Alan Brooke (AP/Wide World Photos)

King Léopold III of Belgium
(AP/Wide World Photos)

Hubert Pierlot (*left*) and Paul-Henri Spaak (AP/Wide World Photos)

Moreover, who would replace Gamelin? General Georges, the most likely alternative, was still physically incapacitated by the bullet wound that he had received during the successful assassination attempt on King Alexander of Yugoslavia in 1934. De Gaulle, Daladier added, was out of the question. Daladier felt that de Gaulle, who was only a lieutenant colonel, lacked "essential experience."

There was, apparently, no alternative to Gamelin, at least not in Daladier's mind. The generalissimo, he added, "possessed all the qualities of a great leader" who "has indisputable prestige and a very good military record. The keenness of his mind was admitted by everybody, and he was much more active than many men of his age." In the end, Daladier's line of reasoning prevailed with the majority of Reynaud's cabinet. Daladier had saved Gamelin's job.

Reynaud was dumbfounded. "In view of such grave opposition," he reacted bitterly, "I shall have to consider the government as having resigned." If Gamelin would not go, Reynaud would.

Later in the day, on learning of Reynaud's decision to resign, Gamelin submitted his own resignation, not wishing, he said, to be the cause of still another governmental crisis. But events would deny both the premier and the generalissmo the opportunity to quit.

THE GERMAN OFFENSIVE BEGINS, MAY 9–10

At noon on that same day, May 9, Adolf Hitler, accompanied by Generals Keitel and Jodl and the staff of the Wehrmacht's supreme command, left Berlin in maximum secrecy. They departed from a small railway station at Gruenewald and headed, as long as daylight lasted, for Hamburg, where the Führer was supposed to arrive the next day. As soon as dusk fell, however, Hitler's train reversed direction and headed for Euskirchen, some thirty miles from Germany's western border, near Aachen, where it arrived at two o'clock in the morning on May 10. Beneath a beautiful canopy of stars, the Führer rode in a long black Mercedes, led and followed by armed motorcyclists, to his command post, *Felsennest* (Eagle's Nest), in the Eifel Mountains.

Earlier, at 9:30 the previous evening, Hitler had transmitted the code word "Danzig" to the commanders of the German armies deployed on the western frontiers of the Reich. His Order of the Day read: "Soldiers of the West Front! With this, the hour has come for you. The battle which is beginning today will decide the fate of the German nation for the next thousand years. Do your duty."

As dawn began to paint the Eifels veridian, Hitler stood looking at the horizon. He heard the gruff rumble of military convoys, the muffled beats of far-off artillery, and then, overhead, the thunder of warplanes heading westward. The great western offensive had finally begun, this time with a plan Hitler was sure would produce total victory in the west.

❋

Returning to his command bunker, Hitler fidgeted nervously as OKW staff officers laid out maps on which he could watch the progress of the offensive. The maps illustrated a front nearly 400 miles in length, from the coast of the North Sea to the junction of the German border with Switzerland and France, near Basel.

On the extreme left of the German front, Hitler's map showed General Wilhelm Ritter von Leeb's 17-division Army Group C, whose major task was to immobilize something like three times its number of French divisions stationed behind the Maginot Line.

On the extreme right, General Fedor von Boch's Army Group B was poised to invade neutral Holland and Belgium. One of Boch's armies, General Georg Kuechler's 18th Army, was assigned the task of overcoming Dutch resistance. Boch's other army, the 6th, with 17 divisions, under General Walter von Reichenau, was deployed north of the Belgian city of Liège, along with General Eric Hoepner's mechanized 16th Corps, consisting of one motorized infantry division and two panzer divisions. They were set to strike across northern Belgium in a southwesterly direction, toward the Channel ports of Ostend and Calais. However, they were not expected to reach those objectives, at least not immediately. If all went according to plan, the Allies would advance northward into Belgium to meet the 6th Army somewhere west of the Meuse River. In so doing, the Allies would be entering a huge trap whose door would be closed by Gerd von Rundstedt's Army Group A, advancing from the Ardennes Forest across France and to the English Channel.

All totaled, Army Group A comprised five armies of 44 divisions, including seven of the 10 available panzer divisions. It was supported in the air by General Hugo Sperrle's 3rd Airfleet with 2,000 fighters and bombers. The most northerly elements of Army Group A, General Guenther Hans Kluge's 4th Army, with nine infantry divisions, and General Hermann Hoth's 15th Panzer Corps, consisting of two panzer divisions, the 7th and 5th Panzers, were to drive across southern Belgium and then across the Meuse River between the Belgian cities of Namur and Dinant. The spearhead of Rundstedt's attack, Kleist's panzer group, consisting of two corps, was deployed opposite the frontier of neutral Luxembourg. Its five panzer and three motorized infantry divisions were prepared to race through the Ardennes Forest and then break through the French lines at Sedan. This armored wedge would be followed by General Siegmund List's 12th Army and General Ernst Busch's 16th Army. Their combined 25 infantry divisions would have to protect the flanks of Kleist's armored group as it advanced westward.

THE FALL OF EBEN EMAEL, MAY 10–11

The initial objective of the huge German onslaught was Belgium's Fort Eben Emael. Located near the juncture of the Maas River and the Albert Canal, three miles south of the Belgian city of Maastricht, the capture of Eben Emael was a vital requirement for the success of *Fall Gelb*. The Germans had to capture the fort as quickly as possible, not only to disrupt the Allied deployment along the Dyle Line, but also to engage the Allies before they could discover and move to counter the knockout punch the Germans were sending through the Ardennes.

The Belgians considered Eben Emael impregnable. Some 900 by 700 yards wide, the fortress was embedded in a hilly plateau whose northeastern flank was a cliff that dropped almost vertically 120 feet to the waters of the Albert Canal. The northwestern side of the fortress was protected by a moat; its southern side was screened by anti-tank trenches and a twenty-foot-high wall. With numerous artillery casements and armored rotating cupolas, equipped with 75mm and 120mm guns, plus antiaircraft, anti-tank, and heavy machine guns, Eben Emael was stronger by far than any fort in the Maginot Line or, for that matter, any other fort in the world.

Eben Emael also commanded the approaches to three bridges that crossed the Albert Canal, which the Germans would have to capture intact if their tanks were to advance swiftly into Belgium. In addition to being protected by the guns of Eben Emael, the bridges were surrounded by pillboxes and armed with demolitions controlled by detonation squads housed in nearby blockhouses. Since the whole defensive complex was some twenty miles from the German frontier, the Belgians believed they would have more than enough time to blow the bridges before German ground forces could reach them.

For months, Hitler had played with the problem of neutralizing Eben Emael and capturing the Meuse bridges intact. In October 1939 he had

Fort Eben Emael *(left)* and Albert Canal (Guy Bastiens)

summoned to Berlin General Kurt Student, at that time the commander of the 7th Airborne Division, the same outfit to which Reinberger was attached.

"I have a job for you," Hitler began his discussion with Student. Pointing to a map on his desk, the Führer said, "The Belgians have a fort here. Do you know it?"

"Yes, mein Führer," Student replied. "I know it well. It is a tremendous fortification."

"I have read something of your work with gliders," Hitler continued. "You have been a glider pilot since the early twenties, I believe. I know you have personally flown the attack glider in tests."

Student nodded affirmatively. He had been the first to appreciate the military potential of the glider. Although frail in comparison with the standard troop transports—the first gliders were merely a steel tube frame that was covered with canvas—Student realized that gliders possessed distinct advantages over transport planes. The glider could carry as many as nine men and land them ready to fight. By contrast, soldiers parachuted from transport planes usually were scattered in patterns 150 to 200 yards long. They obviously could not fight as a unit until they had time to reassemble. If reassembly occurred while the men were under fire, they could expect to suffer heavy losses. The glider possessed another important advantage over the troop transport: it could be released miles from its target and land without detection. Rarely could a parachute operation achieve that degree of surprise.

"I have an idea," Hitler continued. "I think some of your attack gliders could land on top of Fort Eben Emael and your men could storm the works. Is that possible?"

The idea surprised Student. "I'm not sure," he replied. "I must think about it. Give me some time."

Hitler nodded, but he pressed Student for an early answer, without telling him that the action against Eben Emael would be a part of a much larger operation.

The next day, Student returned to Hitler's office. Without delay, he came to the point. "Yes, mein Führer. It is possible under special circumstances."

Hitler looked at Student and asked him in a warm, moderate voice, "What are the circumstances?"

"The landings must be made in daylight, at least in the morning twilight," Student answered, "not before."

"Good!" Hitler responded enthusiastically. "It will be done your way."

"Then may I have your order?" Student replied.

But Hitler ignored the request. Sitting down at his desk and waving Student to a chair, he began explaining how, during World War I, the Germans had taken the Belgian Fort Douaumont, which had stood valiantly against repeated German attacks and did not fall until German siege guns could be brought up against it. The fort was subsequently reduced to rubble. Of course, Hitler admitted, siege guns could not be brought up against Eben Emael without sacrificing the element of surprise, which he demanded.

Yet there was a solution to the problem. To Student, Hitler now revealed that German munitions experts had developed an effective substitute for siege artillery. It was called a *Hohlladung* (a hollow charge), an explosive powerful enough to blow a hole through any known military armament, whether steel or concrete. However, the problem, Hitler added, was getting the hollow charges to the Belgian fortress. Each charge weighed 110 pounds and had to be put into place, fused, and exploded by two or three men. If the weapons could be delivered to the enemy positions, Hitler promised, then nothing, nothing, could withstand their explosive force.

Student was now certain the mission could be accomplished. He again asked Hitler, "Mein Führer, may I have your order?"

"Yes," Hitler replied enthusiastically. "I order you to take Fort Eben Emael."

※

In November 1939 Student assembled, in the utmost secrecy, a detachment of 427 men and 11 officers and placed it under the command of Captain Walter Koch. Koch's men were divided into four combat teams. One, code-named "Granite," with two officers and 83 men under the command of Lieutenant Rudolph Witzig, would be transported in 11 gliders to the top of Eben Emael just four minutes before the bulk of the German forces crossed the Belgian frontier. The other three teams were assigned the task of capturing intact three nearby bridges, over which the German army would cross the Albert Canal. One team, code-named "Concrete," would capture the Vroenhoven Bridge. Another, "Steel," would capture the Veldwezelt Bridge, and the last, "Iron," the bridge at Kanne.

※

Six months later, at 3:30 A.M. on May 10, Koch's men were ready to go. Forty-one Ju-52 transports, each towing a glider carrying seven to eight men, took off at 30-second intervals from two airfields near Cologne, Germany. Once airborne, the planes steered for a point above the green belt to the south of the city, where they met the first of a series of beacons stretching to Aachen. A huge bonfire near Effern was the first. A stationary blue-white beam from a searchlight at Frechen, three miles farther west, served as the second beacon. After exactly 31 minutes of flight, all the Ju-52s and their gliders were at their operational level of 8,500 feet.

Everything was going according to plan. Then, suddenly, a pilot of one of the Ju-52s noticed the blue exhaust of a plane approaching him on a collision course. Instantly he pushed his Ju-52 into a nosedive that enabled him to avoid the approaching plane. While conducting the maneuver, however, the cable to the glider his plane was towing snapped, setting the glider free. Fortunately for its crew, the glider's pilot, Corporal Pilz, was able to steer it back across the Rhine and set it down softly in a meadow. Unfortunately for the Germans, the downed glider also carried Lieutenant Witzig, the man who was supposed to lead the assault on Eben Emael.

Climbing out of the glider, Witzig immediately ordered his men to clear the meadow of trees and fences. While they were doing that, he would try to get another Ju-52 to tow the downed glider. Running to the nearest road, Witzig was able to flag down a car. Within twenty minutes, he arrived at the Cologne-Ostheim airfield, but not a single Ju-52 was left. It was 4:05—only 20 minutes before his men were scheduled to land on Eben Emael.

At 2:10 in the morning of May 10, the telephone rang in the command post of Major Jean Jottrand, commander of the Belgian garrison in Fort Eben Emael. Jottrand was told that the 7th Belgian Infantry Division, holding the Albert Canal sector, had been placed on alert. Jottrand responded by ordering the fort's 780-man garrison to its action stations. For hours nothing happened. To the garrison, it seemed like another in a long series of false alarms. Then, just as the first light of the new day appeared on the eastern horizon, Jottrand heard the sound of concentrated antiaircraft fire coming from the direction of Maastricht, ten miles to the north. A few minutes later, a call came in from a Belgian outpost near Kanne reporting that a large number of planes were approaching overhead from the direction of Maastricht. Hardly had Jottrand hung up the phone when he received a call from another observer: "Airplanes are overhead! Their engines have stopped! They stand almost motionless in the air!" Suddenly, out of the twilight sky, great silent phantoms began swooping down upon the fort. The Belgians feverishly opened fire. But it was too late. At exactly 4:25, German gliders were landing on Eben Emael.

Lieutenant Heiner Lange's glider landed on top of a machine gun emplacement, severing its barrel with one of its wings. Throwing open the glider's door, Lange was astonished to see four terrified Belgians holding their hands up high above their heads. Jumping into the gun emplacement, pistol in hand, Lange landed almost simultaneously with a hand grenade that was tossed in by one of his men, Sergeant Haug. The grenade exploded but, luckily, did not injure either Lange or the Belgians in the gun emplacement. Haug leapt across the emplacement, followed by the rest of the squad.

A number of yards away, another Belgian machine gun opened fire on the Germans. Two of Haug's men charged the position with their own machine guns blazing. One German tossed a grenade over the lip of the emplacement and silenced it.

One hundred yards away, Sergeant Helmut Wenzel's glider landed near another machine-gun emplacement. Wenzel ran directly up to it and flung a two-pound charge through the turret's periscope slit. The subsequent explosion left the Belgian machine guns chattering blindly in every direction. Then Wenzel's men attached a hollow charge onto the emplacement's observation turret. But the explosion failed to penetrate the turret's armor;

it only cracked its skin. Nevertheless, Wenzel's men were able to blow a hole through the turret's embrasure. Entering it, they found only pieces of dead Belgians lying in the wreckage.

※

About the same time, another glider landed on Casement 18. Sergeant Niedermeier, the squad leader, led his men out of the glider and into a hail of Belgian bullets. Some of his men, impatient to get out of the glider, tore through the fabric and crawled out of its side. Niedermeier ran with the top section of a 110-pound hollow charge up a slope to a steel observation cupola. Corporal Drucks ran behind him, carrying the bottom part of the charge.

Inside the observation casement, Belgian Sergeant Marchoul saw mysterious figures enter his field of vision, coming, it seemed, from nowhere. Marchoul shouted down into the gun room below that he could see feet approaching, carrying some large pieces of equipment. Suddenly the hollow charge exploded, killing Marchoul instantly.

Shortly thereafter, two other men in Niedermeier's squad set a 25-pound hollow charge against a small steel door just below the tube of a 75mm gun. Its explosion, Niedermeier recalled, was "absolutely fantastic." It blew the Belgian gun and its gunners against the back wall of the emplacement some 20 feet to the rear. Amid the thick, stagnant smoke that arose from the destroyed casement, wounded men staggered or were dragged down to the casement's lower chamber. Niedermeier and two other Germans quickly leaped through the breach where the gun had been, and fired repeated machine-gun bursts into the shaft leading to the casement's lower chamber. But with the exception of one wounded soldier, all the Belgians had escaped.

In the tunnel below the casement, Sergeant Poncelet ordered the emergency barriers installed to prevent the Germans from penetrating farther into the fortress. Layers of steel beams and two steel doors, with sandbags between them, were quickly put in place. Nevertheless, despite their inability to pursue the Belgians into the bowels of Eben Emael, Niedermeier and his squad had accomplished their mission: they had knocked out the gun casement that they had been ordered to silence.

In fact, within ten minutes after landing on top of Eben Emael, Granite's units had succeeded in knocking out all of the fortress's exterior guns. But the Belgian garrison still held out deep within Eben Emael's interior tunnels. Seeing that there were only some 70 Germans on top of the fortress, Jottrand ordered the Belgian artillery batteries outside Eben Emael to open fire on its surface. Under the intense barrage that followed, the Germans scrambled for cover in the very gun emplacements they had just reduced to ruins.

The battle raged for another three hours. Then a single glider appeared over the fortress and landed atop it. Out jumped Lieutenant Witzig. He had managed to find a Ju-52 and used it to pick up his downed glider. Belatedly taking charge of the German operation against Eben Emael, Witzig spurred his men into action. Reinforced with supplies dropped from Heinkel-111 transport planes, Witzig's men turned their attention toward getting inside the fortress.

In the meantime, Stukas flying in "V" formation buzzed the fort continuously, prepared to bomb any surviving Belgian gun casements and cupolas. But they found none. Every casement was labeled with a swastika, a signal it had fallen to the Germans atop the fort. The Stukas wove patterns high overhead for several minutes before breaking away in search of other targets.

One target was the village of Eben Emael, just outside the fortress. Villagers who had moved into bomb shelters that were dug deeply into a hill near the fort survived the bombing. Many who sought protection in their cellars did not. Thirty civilians were killed and many more were wounded.

Shortly after the first of the Stuka bombs began to fall, Belgian Sergeant Lecron, a commander of one of Eben Emael's gun casements, dashed to his home in the village, only 100 yards away from the fortress. Only three hours before, he had left his wife and children. She had been awakened by the loud thuds of boots hitting pavement as soldiers ran from the nearby barracks. Lecron had tried to assure her that it was just another practice alert, but her fear was not allayed. Lecron quickly dressed, kissed his wife and each of his three children, and rushed to the fort.

Deep within the recesses of Eben Emael when the Stukas attacked, Lecron realized that the bombs were falling near his home. Fearing for his family, he got permission to bring them into the fortress. But as soon as Lecron emerged from the fort, he saw that almost half of the village had vanished. He ran to his home, only to find that it also had been destroyed. Frantically tearing at the rubble, he found the mangled body of his dead wife and those of two his children. Only his youngest daughter survived; she was crying but was miraculously unhurt. Wrapping her in his jacket, Lecron dashed back to the safety of the fort's interior. He took the child to the dispensary, where she remained until the end of the battle, visited by her father whenever he could spare a few minutes away from the battle.

While Witzig's Granite unit was silencing Eben Emael's great guns, teams Concrete and Iron had been successful in capturing intact the bridges over the Albert Canal just north of the fort, at Vroenhoven and Weldwezelt. The operations had been prepared with such unbelievable detail that the Germans were able to overwhelm the Belgian defenders and disarm the explosives on both bridges before they could be detonated. Less than 30 minutes later, German panzers were driving over the bridges on their way into the Belgian heartland.

Some miles to the south, Lieutenant Colonel Mikosch's 51st Engineer Battalion was trying to get through to Witzig's force on the fortress. Their progress was slow. The Belgians had succeeded in blowing the Meuse bridges at Maastricht as well as the one over the Albert Canal at Kanne, the direct link between Maastricht and Eben Emael, before glider force Iron could seize it.

It was not until seven o'clock on the morning of May 11 that Mikosch's engineer battalion could fight its way to Eben Emael. When they arrived before the fortress, Witzig's men greeted them with wild cheers.

Meanwhile, inside Eben Emael, the situation had deteriorated irretrievably for its Belgian defenders. German ground troops were ranging over the vast uncontested surfaces of the fort and in the surrounding area outside its walls. Many of Major Jottrand's men were worn down from combat fatigue, fear, or despair. He informed his superiors in Liège that further resistance would only increase his casualties. They told him to hold out anyway until relief could arrive. But Jottrand did not think he could hold out that long and decided to ask the Germans for surrender terms.

A little over an hour later, at 12:15 in the afternoon, the notes of a trumpet were heard above the now-sporadic gunfire, followed by the appearance of a Belgian officer waving a white flag of truce. Suddenly, before he could walk very far, the officer was shocked to see behind him hundreds of

Belgian soldiers, arms raised above their heads, filing out of the fort. The soldiers had decided not to wait for their officers to negotiate a surrender. As far as they were concerned, the battle was over. Seeing this, Jottrand called Liège to tell his superiors that the fort had surrendered.

In a column almost a mile long, the defeated defenders of Eben Emael marched out to captivity. As the Germans watched the end of the column come into view, they saw a blond head bobbing up and down above the heads of the prisoners. As it drew close, they saw that it was the head of a very young child, riding the shoulders of a broad-shouldered noncommissioned Belgian officer. The girl's hands were clasped tightly around his head. The Germans waved at her, and she waved back. A German officer at that point insisted that Sergeant Lecron must leave his daughter behind. He arranged for the child to be taken to a convent, where she was located by her grandfather after a two-year-long search. Ultimately, after the war, the young girl was reunited with her father.

The fall of Eben Emael stunned the Belgians. Seventy-seven boldly led men, transported in 10 gliders and armed with 56 hollow-charge explosives, had defeated 780 men defending the world's strongest fort.

All totaled, the Belgians suffered 23 killed and 59 wounded in their unsuccessful defense of Eben Emael. Witzig lost 26 men; six were killed and 20 wounded, about a third of his force in something over a day of combat.

Witzig subsequently received orders to report with the other officers of Task Force Koch for special ceremonies presided over by the Führer himself. After a short address commending their achievement, Hitler presented each officer with the Knight's Cross, Germany's highest combat decoration.

One can only wonder what would have been the outcome of the battle of Eben Emael had Hitler launched his western offensive when he had originally intended, during the previous winter. Clearly, a glider attack on Fort Eben Emael would not have been possible at that time, not only because of poor weather but also because there would not have been sufficient time to organize and train Koch's glider force. Postponement of the western offensive was one of those lucky turns of fate that Hitler would experience in the first few years of the war.

WAR COMES TO BELGIUM, MAY 9–10

In Brussels during the evening of May 9, Paul-Henri Spaak, Belgium's foreign minister, had been dining with the Bulgarian ambassador when the telephone rang. Spaak was informed that a loud, unidentifiable noise could be heard the entire length of Belgium's frontier with Germany. This was the worst possible news. Spaak knew instinctively that German columns were on the march. He immediately rushed over to the Foreign Ministry where Premier Hubert Pierlot, Defense Minister General Henri Denis, and King Léopold's private secretary were waiting for him. By the time Spaak arrived, additional, equally ominous news had been received. The skies over Holland were filled with planes. The sounds of moving tanks and trucks were reported all along the entire length of the Dutch frontier with Germany.

However, as the night progressed, nothing happened. At 3:00 A.M. on May 10, the Belgians received word from the Dutch capital that Foreign Minister Eelco van Kleffens had retired for the night. In Luxembourg, the situation was calm. Apparently, the Belgians surmised, it was another false alarm. As a result, the tension in Spaak's office began to subside. Weak smiles broke out, and small jokes were exchanged. Once again, it seemed, the storm had passed.

But the euphoria was short-lived. As the first light of morning brightened the windows of the Foreign Ministry, the calm of the waning night was shattered by the thunder of exploding bombs. The storm had not passed after all. Once again, war had come to Belgium.

Premier Pierlot immediately left the room to call army headquarters. When he returned, his face was pale. "They've captured Eben Emael." No one in the room realized then that the news of the catastrophe was premature. But without wasting another moment, the Belgians decided to appeal to Britain and France for help. When that was done, Pierlot, Denis, and Spaak went to see the king.

Léopold approved the action his ministers had taken, and immediately drove to his military headquarters in the Fortress of Breendock. There he made the following statement: "I have put myself at the head of the Belgian army as my father did in 1914, with the same trust, the same faith."

When Spaak returned to the Foreign Ministry, he found German Ambassador von Buelow-Schwante waiting to see him. The ambassador was attired in formal dress and wore a grave expression on his face. Spaak knew why he had come. However, before the ambassador could read the note that he had drawn from his pocket, Spaak shouted indignantly, "No, me first!" Then, without pausing to catch his breath, the Belgian foreign minister began reading a statement he had prepared for this eventuality. "The German army has just attacked our country," he said in a voice trembling with indignation. "This is the second time in twenty-five years that Germany has criminally, and without provocation, attacked neutral Belgium. The present aggression is, if anything, more vile than in 1914. No ultimatum, no note, no protest has reached the Belgian Government." Then Spaak literally tore the note from von Buelow-Schwante's hand and said, "I'll spare you the rest." With that, the German ambassador bowed and left.

WAR COMES TO HOLLAND, MAY 9–10

Also during the evening of May 9, Colonel Hans Oster called his friend Colonel J. G. Sas, the Dutch military attaché in Berlin. Oster informed Sas that the order for the invasion of the Netherlands had been given. "This is it," Oster said. "That swine [Hitler] has gone to the western front. It's all over now. Let's hope we see each other again, after the war." They never did. Oster was arrested in 1943 and hanged only a few weeks before Germany's surrender.

Sas went to the Dutch embassy in Berlin and informed the Belgian military attaché about Oster's warning. He then called the Dutch War Department in The Hague. After waiting a painful twenty minutes, Sas finally was able to get through: "Tomorrow at dawn. Hold tight." But the chief of the Dutch foreign intelligence was still not convinced. He called Sas back. "We have heard the bad news concerning Mrs. Sas's illness. Have all doctors been consulted?" Very annoyed, Sas replied, "Why bother me again? You know it now. She has to have an operation tomorrow morning," and then hung up.

In The Hague, Foreign Minister Eelco van Kleffens returned home at 9:30 P.M. on May 9. As he entered the house, the telephone rang. It was the headquarters of the Dutch intelligence service reporting the content of Sas's coded message.

Even before Sas's message arrived, the Dutch had noticed great activity on the German side of the border and had placed their frontier forces on alert. However, the troops in Fortress Holland, far from the border, were not alerted. Like the Belgians, the Dutch high command apparently had never heard of airborne landings.

At 1:30 A.M. on May 10, Dutch observers reported numerous planes passing over Holland. By 2:45 A.M., the last of the planes left Dutch territory heading west, toward England. But it was merely a clever German deception, for the planes had turned around over the North Sea and, at 4:00 A.M., began dropping bombs on Dutch airfields. At exactly the same time, German troops started crossing the border.

The battle was already two hours old when the German ambassador, Count Julius von Zech-Burkersroda, asked to see van Kleffens. The count was one of the few remaining German diplomats from an era long past who had been left at his post by the Nazis, the Dutch believed, as window dressing for a despicable regime. Having lived in Holland for seventeen years, von Zech-Burkersroda was overcome with shame at his country's aggression and cried like a baby.

Van Kleffens took the message from his hands and read it. The Dutch government, the note charged, had been guilty of collaborating with England and France. "We inform you of the action of a powerful German force," the note continued. "Resistance is completely senseless." It promised a guarantee for the royal dynasty if the Dutch would not fight, and required the Dutch to make contact with the German military command immediately.

Van Kleffens replied: "You will understand that . . . we must consider ourselves at war with Germany." Still weeping, the ambassador shook hands with Van Kleffens and left.

At 8:00 A.M. on May 10, a communiqué from Queen Wilhelmina was read over the radio. It protested Germany's "flagrant breach of conduct, unusual among civilized nations." The queen asked her people to do their duty. Her address was followed by the playing of the national anthems of Holland, Britain, France, and Belgium.

The Dutch realized how difficult it would be to defend their country. Although Holland is small, its frontier along Germany is over 200 miles long. Considering the small size of the Dutch army—four infantry divisions—it was physically impossible for the Dutch to successfully defend their entire frontier. Instead, they concentrated their defense around "Fortress Holland," the western part of the country. Bordered on the west by the North Sea, Fortress Holland was protected on the south by the

Rhine-Maas estuary, and on the east by the Zuider Zee and an extensive network of dikes and canals. Within this area were Holland's largest cities: Rotterdam, Amsterdam, The Hague, Utrecht, and Leyden.

Fortress Holland, however, was to be the scene of only a last-ditch defense, if one proved necessary. The Dutch hoped to hold the Germans farther east along the so-called Grebbe-Peel Line, a fortified barrier of gun casements, bunkers, and anti-tank obstacles that extended some 80 miles, from the south shore of the Zuider Zee to the Belgian frontier. The Dutch were so confident that the Germans could be held on the Grebbe-Peel Line that they did not bother to alert their forces in Fortress Holland on the evening of May 9. Only the soldiers on the Grebbe-Peel Line were alerted, at 6:45 P.M.

Hitler, however, had no intention of being stalled before the Dutch outer defenses. Holland had to be conquered as quickly as possible, not only to prevent the Allies from occupying the country, but also to release attacking German units for the main action in Belgium. Consequently, Hitler planned to enter Fortress Holland immediately, through, as he put it, "the back door"— across the bridges over the southern branches of the Rhine-Maas estuary.

To open the "back door" to Holland, Hitler again turned to General Kurt Student. His airborne troops would have to capture intact, and hold, a number of key bridges—one over the Holland Deep at Moerdijk, another over the Oude Maas at Dordrecht, and the bridges leading into Rotterdam over the Nieuwe Maas—until Lieutenant General Alfred Ditter von Hubicki's 9th Panzer Division could drive to their relief from the German border, nearly 100 miles distant. Once Rotterdam fell, the rest of Fortress Holland could be occupied quickly.

As the morning of May 10 dawned over Rotterdam, its residents were awakened by the roar of airplane engines passing overhead. Dressed in their nightgowns and pajamas, they streamed into the streets and stared stupefied into a sky filled with seemingly countless white blossoms—the parachutes of German airborne troops.

The Luftwaffe's first heavy blows fell on Holland's airfields, destroying most of the Dutch air force on the ground. The three airfields around The Hague were first bombed, then subjected to German airborne attack. At Ypenburg airport, a vicious firefight broke out when German transport planes attempted to land on its runway. Three waves of transports were shot to pieces by the Dutch defenders; a fourth could not land because the wreckage of the previous three littered the runway. The field was finally taken by German paratroopers who, in turn, were driven off shortly afterward by a strong Dutch counterattack. At Ockenburg airfield, the Germans managed to land twenty transports, but the Dutch were able to hold on. At Valkenburg airfield, the German airborne troops and parachutists took the airstrip in the early morning hours, but by evening it, too, was in Dutch hands.

The successful defense of the three airfields bought some critical time for the Dutch government. Hitler had hoped to capture Queen Wilhelmina by landing airborne troops at the capital's airfields. The queen was to have been given full military honors if she cooperated; if she did not, she was to be shipped back to Germany as a prisoner of war. But by holding onto the airfields, Wilhelmina and her government were able to escape to England.

The Germans were more successful in achieving their objectives on the southern rim of Fortress Holland. The vital bridges over the Holland Deep at Moerdijk, a 1,300-yard-long road viaduct and a 1,400-yard-long railway bridge, were captured by Student's parachutists, who attacked the bridges from both sides of the river while surprised Dutch guards were still trying to put on their uniforms. Because of the great width of the Holland Deep at Moerdijk, the loss of the bridges was an especially severe blow to the Dutch.

The German paratroopers were ordered to hold the bridges until they could be relieved by airborne troops who would be landed at Waalhaven airport, five miles southeast of Rotterdam. Around this airfield, the Dutch defenders, the Queen's Grenadiers, had spent the early morning hours of May 10 shivering in trenches and dugouts manning machine guns, flak guns, and mortars. However, as dawn arrived the morning calm was shattered by the piercing whistle of countless bombs falling through the sky. The bombs smashed into the Dutch trenches and into hangars where, in spite of the alert, a considerate station commander had let his men continue to sleep. The result was catastrophic. The hangars immediately burst into fire and collapsed, burying a great number of the Dutch soldiers in the ruins. Within minutes, the Germans had broken the backbone of Waalhaven's defenses.

No sooner had the bomb explosions subsided than the Dutch defenders were greeted by the sound of triple-engine German transport planes.

"As if by magic," a young officer of the Queen's Grenadiers recalled, "white dots suddenly appeared over the airfield like puffs of cotton wool. First, there were twenty, then fifty, then over a hundred of them! And still they came!" He gave the command, and every machine gun the Dutch still had opened fire on the descending parachutes and at the planes. "With so many targets," the Dutch officer recalled, "the men just did not know where to aim."

The German forces attacking Waalhaven airport belonged to the 3rd Battalion of the 1st Paratroop Regiment, under Captain Karl-Lothar Schultz. Schultz's men had been guided to Waalhaven by clouds of smoke pouring from the burning Dutch hangars. After jumping from their transport planes, the German paratroopers hung helplessly in the air for fifteen to twenty seconds before they finally hit the ground. Most of Schultz's men landed close to the airfield and went immediately on the attack. Others were less fortunate. One Ju-52 dropped its soldiers directly over the flaming hangars; their silk parachutes caught fire long before they reached the ground.

Still another German threat had to be dealt with by the Dutch defenders at Waalhaven. A squadron of Ju-52 transport planes carrying German airborne troops was coming in for a landing on the airstrip. The Dutch immediately turned their guns on this new threat. One of the Ju-52s was hit and destroyed, but the others managed to land. Out of their doors poured a cascade of field gray uniforms, two platoons of soldiers in all, the advance party of a much larger airborne force that was following immediately behind them. Within minutes, the whole of the 3rd Airborne division was on the ground.

"Things went just as expected," recalled its commander, Lieutenant Colonel Dietrich von Choltitz, the man who would make history by surrendering Paris to the Allies four years later instead of obeying Hitler's order to burn the city to the ground. "The sound of conflict was deafening," Choltitz recalled. "The howling of aero-engines and ammunition exploding in the hangars was joined by the crash of mortar fire and the rattle of machine guns plaguing the planes."

"Speed was the thing!" Choltitz realized. The Dutch positions had to be overrun as quickly as possible to prevent their defenders from retreating and reforming in another defensive line around the airport. To that end, the Germans began firing green Very lights, which just happened to be the Dutch signal for a cease-fire! The confused Dutch defenders responded by raising their hands and surrendering. The Germans had captured Waalhaven airport and its defenders much more quickly than they had anticipated it could be done. Now Choltitz's men had to fight their way through the town of Waalhaven and get to the bridges leading into Rotterdam as soon as they could.

THE ALLIES GO TO WAR, MAY 10

At 6:30 that morning, Gamelin called General Georges: "Well, General, is it the Dyle operation?" Georges asked. "Since the Belgians are calling on us," Gamelin replied, "do you see what else we can do?" "Obviously not," Georges answered.

Five minutes later, Georges issued the order setting General Billotte's five armies in motion across the Belgian frontier. General Giraud's 7th Army was to speed into Holland to help the Dutch army. Lord Gort's British Expeditionary Force and General Blanchard's 1st Army were to advance to the Dyle Line, between the Belgian cities of Louvain and Namur. General Corap's 9th Army was to pivot northwest of Sedan and take up positions on the west bank of the Meuse River as far north as Namur. The left flank of General Huntziger's 2nd Army, at the hinge of the great Allied turning movement into Belgium near Sedan, was also alerted. Five mechanized light cavalry divisions belonging to the 9th and 2nd Armies were sent forward into Belgium and Luxembourg in an attempt to stop the Germans in the Ardennes.

Gamelin was extremely confident as his armies went into battle that morning. One headquarters staffer, Captain André Beaufre, saw him shortly after 6:30 A.M. striding up and down the corridors of Vincennes displaying "a martial and satisfied air," the likes of which Beaufre had never seen him display. "He appeared absolutely confident of success in the operations which he himself had conceived and now had launched."

Years later, Gamelin also recalled his feelings that morning: "I confess that I believed in victory. I felt sure we could stop the Germans . . . I had confidence in the army."

On hearing the news of the German offensive, Premier Paul Reynaud quickly realized that it was no time for his government to fall and withdrew his letter of resignation. Nor was it the time to cashier Gamelin. In a brief conciliatory note, he wrote the generalissimo: "The battle has begun. Only one thing counts: to win the victory." Gamelin accepted the premier's offer to set aside their personal differences for the sake of France.

Still, Reynaud's confidence in the Allied commander-in-chief remained shaky. He did not like Gamelin's decision to send the best Allied armies into Belgium. For now, however, he allowed the generalissimo to call the shots. "Gamelin has been saved," he told a confidant that morning. "Now he has got the battle he has been waiting for, indeed hoping for. . . . Well, we'll see what he is worth."

On the other side of the English Channel, the new British prime minister, Winston Churchill, was awakened shortly before six o'clock on the morning of May 10 by the ringing of his bedside telephone. The caller informed him that the Dutch ambassador was on his way to see him. Churchill rose, dressed, and received both the Dutch and Belgian ambassadors. He promised their governments all the assistance Britain could muster.

Shortly afterward, Sir Samuel Hoare found Churchill smoking a cigar and eating fried eggs and bacon, as if nothing serious had happened. In fact, Churchill was exhilarated by the chance—finally—to prove his mettle. "I was conscious," he recalled later, "of a profound sense of relief. At last I had the authority to give directions over the whole scene. I felt as if I were with destiny."

THE ALLIED ADVANCE
TO THE DYLE LINE, MAY 10

While Holland was being overrun by the Germans, the Allied armies were advancing into Belgium. "It was hard to believe that on such a glorious spring day, with all nature looking its best," recalled General Alan Brooke of the BEF's 2nd Corps, "we were taking the first steps toward . . . one of the greatest battles of history."

The British troops were received warmly by the Belgian people. Every man, woman, and child on the road to Brussels poured their affection on the foreign soldiers who, for the second time in 25 years, were coming to the defense of their country. The crowds that lined the roads covered the advancing armies with carnations and roses taken from the vases of floral shops, or with wildflowers hastily gathered from meadows and hedgerows. Beer, cigarettes, and food were given to the troops wherever they stopped. Every village seemed to be flying a Union Jack, alongside the red, yellow, and black of the Belgian tricolor and the red, white, and blue flag of France.

However, the Allies' entry into Belgium was not without mishap. At some points along the border, Belgian obstacles still blocked the roads. One unit of General Bernard Montgomery's 3rd Division was unable to persuade a Belgian officer to remove one of the frontier barriers. The Belgian demanded "a permit to enter Belgium," Montgomery recalled. Finally

Belgian civilians welcome British troops entering Belgium (Imperial War Museum F4345)

the barrier was pushed aside by heavy British trucks and the division finally got under way. Elsewhere, units of the 3rd Division arrived so quickly that Belgian soldiers mistook them for German paratroops and fired at them, seriously wounding a soldier of the Middlesex Regiment.

When the 3rd Division finally did arrive at its predetermined position on the Dyle Line south of Louvain, it found it occupied by the 10th Belgian Infantry Division. General Montgomery asked the Belgian commander to move his men, but he refused, insisting that he would never leave his post without orders from King Léopold. Montgomery finally resolved the problem by placing his division under the command of the Belgian officer. When Alan Brooke asked him what he would do when the German troops arrived, Montgomery replied, "Oh! I then place the Divisional Commander under strict arrest and I take command." Already Montgomery was displaying the spunk and resourcefulness that would make him Britain's most outstanding—and controversial—general in World War II.

By the evening of May 11, the entire BEF was finally in place along the Dyle River. Actually, calling the Dyle a river is an exaggeration; it is not much more than a wide stream that offered the Allied defenders little protection. In fact, as a battle site, the Dyle would be more advantageous to the attacking Germans than the defending British. Its heavily wooded banks would enable the Germans to move up close to the river undetected. This advantage was compounded by the fact that the Dyle was only thinly defended by the Allies. The BEF had been assigned the responsibility for defending a front 17 miles long with only three divisions.

On the extreme left wing of the Allied front, General Giraud's 7th French Army spent May 10 advancing into Holland. Giraud was instructed to move as far north as Breda in order to link up with the Dutch army. On May 11 General Gamelin asked Georges to advise Giraud to be careful. "General Giraud," he said, "must not commit his forces too strongly beyond Breda."

However, by the time Giraud's army reached Breda that day, the Dutch army had already withdrawn to cover Rotterdam. Instead of linking up with the Dutch, Giraud's army encountered the advance elements of Lieutenant General Hubicki's 9th Panzer Division. The French also were attacked by the Luftwaffe. German bombs and machine-gun strafing flattened Giraud's 25th Infantry Division and scattered his 1st French Light Cavalry Division. The next day, Giraud was ordered to withdraw his army from Holland and regroup in Belgium, west of the Escaut River. So much for the French effort to hold the Breda line.

With Giraud's army out of the way, the 9th Panzer Division moved northward across the Moerdijk bridges. They were cheered by the German paratroopers who had captured them and held them until the panzers could arrive. By the evening of May 13, Moerdijk was at last subdued and the first panzers reached the southern end of the Maas bridges at Rotterdam.

"ARE THEY LEADING US INTO A TRAP?"

During the afternoon of Saturday, May 11, before a large map in Paul Reynaud's Foreign Ministry office, his aide, Colonel Paul de Villelume, was explaining the military situation to the premier and a few of his colleagues. De Villelume was dismayed by the lack of German air attacks on the Allied armies moving into Belgium. "Are they leading us into a trap?" he asked. Reynaud was not sure. Everything was going too easily.

The premier voiced his doubts in a telephone conversation with Daladier later that day. "We are laying aside our armor," he said, "by which I mean we are leaving the fortified positions along our frontier and exposing ourselves, at a time when we suffer from an inferiority both in men and material. We are offering our naked bodies to the blows of the German Army."

"What do you want to do?" Daladier replied. "Gamelin is in command and he is putting his plans into operation."

❈

At *Felsennest,* Adolf Hitler was effusive when OKW intelligence informed him that Gamelin had reacted to the German offensive by advancing the Allied armies into central Belgium. "I could have wept for joy," he said. "They'd fallen into the trap! How lovely *Felsennest* was! The birds in the morning, the view over the road up which columns were advancing, the squadrons of planes overhead. There, I was sure everything would go right for me!"

❈

Early on May 12, Gamelin was still confident that his Dyle Plan was the right strategy. Consequently, he was able to turn to other matters, such as giving advice concerning tactical defense against tanks in northern Belgium and warning the defenders in the Maginot Line to guard against the techniques used by the Germans in capturing Eben Emael. These, of course, were military matters, but whether they should have consumed the attention of the Allied commander-in-chief, rather than his subordinates, is another matter.

The matters that should have absorbed Gamelin's attention he ignored. At a conference that day in the Château Casteau, near Mons, which was attended by Daladier, Georges, and representatives of Lord Gort and King Léopold, Gamelin was not present. Without his knowledge or approval, General Billotte was given the responsibility of coordinating the Allied forces. This arrangement was doomed to failure. Billotte was too preoccupied with his own responsibilities to the 1st Army Group to have any time to deal with the other Allied armies. The task of coordinating the northern Allied armies should have been Georges's job. When Gamelin found out about the new arrangement later that day, he accused Georges of abdicating his responsibilities. Yet Gamelin did nothing to change the new command arrangement, with the result that the Allied chain of command was more tangled than ever.

❈

Even more than the chain of command, what should have absorbed Gamelin's attention were the increasingly ominous reports coming from the Ardennes sector. One reported the movement of "numerous" German tanks on the road from Euskirchen to Prüm, and on the Belgian road network to the west of Luxembourg. It also reported German tanks advancing north of Neufchâteau, and motorized infantry forces moving in the direction of Arlon.

Amazingly, even after Allied scouting planes had reported dense columns of German panzers crossing the frontiers of the Low Countries on the morning of May 10, they had not been attacked. At eight o'clock that morning, General Georges limited air activity to pursuit and reconnaissance missions. Not until three hours later, and after many vehement protests, did General François d'Astier de la Vigerie, the commander of the French air force on the 1st Army Group's front, finally get permission to bomb the enemy columns. However, General Joseph Vuillemin, the ineffectual French air force chief, ordered that no towns or cities were to be bombed, an order that severely restricted action against the German invaders. Nor did Vuillemin appreciate the value of close air support of ground units; the skies over the Ardennes were devoid of French fighters on this first critical day of the battle.

THE ATTACK ON THE MAAS BRIDGES, MAY 12

With the fall of Eben Emael, the German army began pouring into the plains of northeastern Belgium. General Reichenau's 6th Army and General Hoepner's 16th Panzer Corps crossed over the Maas River at Maastricht on pontoon bridges erected by German engineers and then traversed the bridges over the Albert Canal at Vroenhoven and Veldwezelt, just west of Maastricht. These German forces attacked the 7th Belgian Infantry Division, which was deployed along the west side of the Albert Canal, and literally knocked it to pieces. By noon on May 11, Hoepner's two panzer divisions, the 3rd and 4th Panzers, were moving on Tongres, seven miles west of Eben Emael. On Hoepner's left, General Alfred Waeger's 27th Infantry Corps was advancing on Liège. During World War I, the German advance into Belgium was held up for eleven days before this great fortress city. However, this time the spearhead of the German drive, Hoepner's panzers, bypassed the city and left it to be invested by Waeger's infantry.

With German tanks and infantry pouring over the Maas bridges, the Maas–Albert Canal defense line was no longer tenable. During the evening of May 11, the Belgian high command ordered a general withdrawal of its forces to the Dyle Line, some fifty miles to the west.

At six o'clock on the morning of Sunday, May 12, General Billotte, commander of the 1st Army Group, finally ordered the French fighter command to fly cover for bombers that would attack the Maas River bridges. Amazingly, however, the French bomber squadrons were still not ready for action. Billotte was compelled to call upon the British air force to perform the mission.

Air Marshal Sir Arthur Barratt, the commander of the RAF in France, knew that the mission against the bridges would be suicidal. By now they were heavily defended by antiaircraft guns and would certainly be screened by German fighters. Barratt asked for volunteers, and he got them. At midday, six two-seater Fairey Battle bombers set out for the bridges in two flights of three aircraft each. Both flights of bombers were protected by a fighter escort of three Hurricanes apiece. One flight of bombers would attack the bridge at Vroenhoven, the other the bridge at Veldwezelt.

Twenty miles from the targets, the British planes were attacked by over 30 German Messerschmitts. The bombers continued on course while the fighters engaged the Germans. "Enemy fighters on our tail!" the rear gunner of one of the bombers shouted. The pilot of the craft took evasive action while the gunner managed to shoot one of the Messerschmitts down. The remaining German fighters sheared off from the attack.

Finally, the bombers arrived over the target. One airman, Sergeant Mansell, recalled the attack: "The big bridge, which was hit by the bombs dropped by the three bombers ahead of us, looked a sorry mess and was sagging in the middle. . . . When we delivered our attack, we were about 6,000 feet up. We dived to 2,000 feet, one aircraft close behind the other, and dropped our bombs. Looking down, we saw that our bridge now matched the other. It sagged in the center and its iron girders looked far from intact. Immediately after we had dropped our bombs, we turned for home, but the antiaircraft barrage was waiting for us. It was even more intense than before, and our aircraft began to show signs of heavy damage. The pilot gave orders to abandon the aircraft."

Mansell bailed out over Liège. As he approached the ground, he saw hundreds of people who were shaking their fists at him. Landing in a small cottage garden, Mansell was unable to unravel his body from his parachute before the crowd grabbed him, shouting, *"Sale Bosche!* [Dirty Germans!]" Mansell yelled back: *"Je suis Anglais!* [I am English!]" But the crowd either did not understand him or did not believe him. He was dragged into the street by the crowd, and while his arms were held behind his back, an old, angry man prepared to shoot him with a pistol. Only the timely intervention of Belgian police saved the British airman.

Out of the five British bombers that had set out for the Maas bridges—the sixth developed engine trouble and was forced to return to base—only one crippled plane managed to get back. To one of the British airmen who was shot down and captured, a German interrogator exclaimed: "You British are mad. We capture the bridge early Friday morning [May 10]. You give us all day Friday and Saturday to get our flak guns up in circles around the bridge and then, on Sunday, when we're ready, you come along with three aircraft and try to blow the thing up."

It was not until midday on May 12 that the French bombers were finally ready for action against the bridges. But they, too, were unable to knock them out. Although the Veldwezelt bridge was temporarily put out of commission, it was not long before German engineers had it repaired, and troops and supplies once again were flowing across it and into the Belgian heartland.

THE BATTLE OF THE GEMBLOUX GAP, MAY 12–15

Between the BEF on the Dyle River and the city of Namur on the Meuse, some 25 miles to the east, there was no river line to block the German advance. This is the location of the Brabant Plain, for centuries the avenue of Germanic invasions into the heartland of France. To fill this so-called "Gembloux Gap," which was named after one of the largest towns in the area, Gamelin had deployed General Jean Georges-Maurice Blanchard's 1st Army. With eight infantry divisions, three of which were mechanized, it was one of the best armies France possessed. Two of its mechanized divisions, the 2nd and 3rd, were under the command of General René Jacques Adolphe Prioux, one of the ablest generals in the French army. The British liaison officer with the 1st Army called him "a magnificent man" who "inspired confidence" in his men.

But Prioux's own confidence was badly shattered by a series of surprises he received when he arrived in Gembloux during the morning of May 11. "First surprise," he recalled, "no defense works around the township . . . no decent trenches, no barbed wire . . . practically nothing at all!" Driving another five miles along the line, Prioux came across a "Cointet" wall—steel anti-tank obstacles over six feet high that the Belgians had constructed as an "impenetrable" tank barrier. However, Prioux discovered large gaps in the barrier, making it almost useless for stopping panzers. Yet behind this "impenetrable barrier," Prioux was expected to check, for at least five days, the advance of an entire German army (General Reichenau's

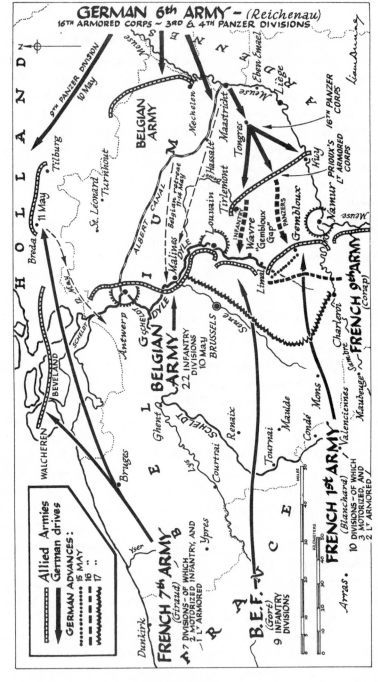

Battle on the Dyle Line, May 12–16. (Shirer, *Collapse of the Third Republic*, Simon and Schuster)

6th Army), one that included two powerful panzer divisions (the 3rd and 4th Panzers of General Hoepner's 16th Panzer Corps). "I am appalled," he reported, "when I think that our army, which counted on finding an organized position here, will first have to . . . dig in. But the enemy won't give us the time."

It was quite obvious to Prioux that it would be impossible for his corps to hold the Gembloux Gap for five days. "The whole [French] plan," he explained later, "rested on two things—the strength of the Gembloux position and the ability of the Belgian Army to delay the enemy." Neither turned out to be as strong as expected. To Prioux, the only solution was to abandon the Gembloux Gap as well as the Dyle River line and withdraw to the more defensible Escaut River, fifty miles to the west.

Prioux's recommendation, however, was rejected by General Billotte. It was too late to change the Dyle operation, Billotte said.* However, he did promise to speed up the advance of the French 1st Army, by night marches if necessary, so that it would be in position along the Dyle Line by May 14, one day earlier than originally planned. "I know that you're going to experience some very tough moments," Billotte told Prioux. "But I have confidence in your corps."

The next day, May 12, General Prioux received more in the way of "tough moments" than Billotte had predicted. The German attack on his position opened in the afternoon with an intense Stuka bombing raid, followed by a heavy barrage from the tanks of the 3rd and 4th Panzer Divisions. It was the beginning of the first big tank battle of the war. The panzers hit the center of Prioux's line at Hannut, but by the end of the day were stopped. Despite the numerical advantage enjoyed by the Germans—824 armored vehicles to Prioux's 520—roughly equal numbers of knocked-out French and German tanks littered the battlefield as the day ended. More importantly, though, the French line had held.

---

*At the Riom trial, which was set up by the Vichy government two years later to investigate the causes of France's defeat, Edouard Daladier said: "If I had known of the advice of General Prioux, I would have summoned a meeting of the War Council to consider it. Since only one third of the French forces had reached the Dyle, it would have been easy to stop the rest at the Escaut. One can only ask if the course of the war might not have been changed if this had been done."

By the evening of the next day, May 13, however, the German advantages began to tell. The Germans slowly pushed the French center backward, causing Prioux to order a retreat to the Perwez-Marchevolette line, a 10-mile-wide Belgian anti-tank obstacle less than nine miles in front of the line (extending from Wavre to Namur) that was being occupied by the French 1st Army. The day had been a tough one for both sides. Prioux's 3rd Cavalry Division had been badly mauled, losing 75 of its 140 Hotchkiss tanks and 30 of its 80 Somuas. But the French division had severely damaged the 4th Panzer Division, which lost 164 German tanks.

On the morning of May 14, the Germans again attacked. This time they were successful in blasting a gap in the Perwez-Marchevolette line. Yet, in the face of stubborn French resistance, they were unable to break through in any strength. Prioux had bought the time the Allied armies needed to get into their positions along the Dyle line. But the price his cavalry corps paid was high. Its two light mechanized divisions were mere shells. Two-thirds of their Hotchkiss tanks were lost, one-third of their Somuas. Some units lost 60 percent of their men. That afternoon, Prioux's entire corps was withdrawn from the battle. It never again returned to the conflict as a cohesive unit. Nevertheless, Prioux had demonstrated what was possible when French divisions were properly led.

The next day, May 15, the Germans again tried to break through the Gembloux Gap, but this time they were stopped by French artillery and by the two divisions that had relieved Prioux's cavalry corps, the 12th Motorized Infantry Division and the 1st North African Division. These divisions, two of the finest in the French army, stood their ground with accurate marksmanship and forced the panzers to withdraw behind Baudeset. The German advance through the Gembloux Gap had been blocked, but only temporarily. The defensive position of the French 1st Army would soon be undermined by other German armies advancing on its northern and southern flanks.

The Battle of the Ardennes Forest, May 10–12

While the Germans were trying, unsuccessfully, to break through the Gembloux Gap, over a hundred miles away to the east, Panzer Group Kleist, the greatest concentration of firepower ever seen in battle—seven panzer divisions, organized in three corps, with 134,000 soldiers, 41,000 motor vehicles, and more than 1,600 tanks and reconnaissance vehicles— was advancing through the Ardennes Forest.

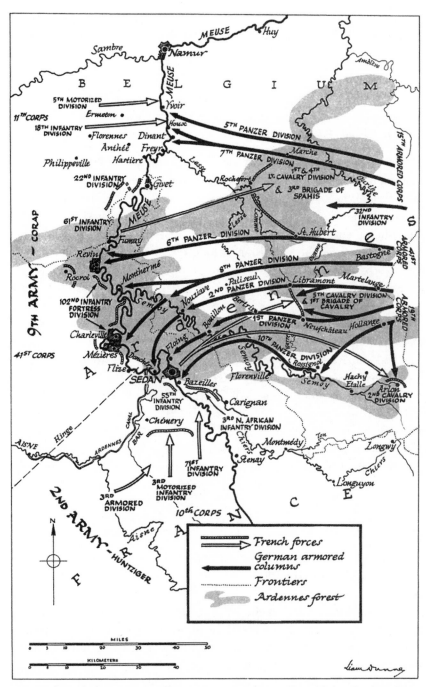

Battle of the Ardennes Forest, May 10–12. (Shirer, *Collapse of the Third Republic,* Simon and Schuster)

On the evening of May 9, while awaiting the order to go, the 7th Panzer Division's commander, General Erwin Rommel, had found a few minutes to write his wife a brief note:

> Dearest Lu,
> We're packing up at last. Let's hope not in vain. You'll get all the news for the next few days from the papers. Don't worry yourself. Everything will go all right.

At the head of Kleist's panzer group was Guderian's 19th Panzer Corps, containing three divisions: the 1st Panzer Division, leading the attack in the center, the 10th Panzer on its left, and the 2nd Panzer on the right. Their destination was the Meuse River at Sedan. Slightly behind them and to their right were the two other panzer divisions—the 6th and 8th Panzers—and a motorized infantry division belonging to General Reinhardt's 41st Panzer Corps. Their target was Mézières, a town on the Meuse ten miles to the west of Sedan. On Reinhardt's northern flank was General Hoth's 15th Panzer Corps, comprising the 5th and 7th Panzer Divisions and the 20th Motorized Division. They were headed for Dinant, farther downstream on the Meuse. Supporting Panzer Group Kleist were the 37 infantry divisions of General von Rundstedt's Army Group A and, behind Rundstedt's forces, the 42 divisions of the German general reserve.

To avoid detection by the Allies, as dusk turned to night the vehicles of Kleist's panzer group had moved toward the Belgian and Luxembourg borders with their lights out. "Like a giant phalanx," remarked General Guenther von Blumentritt, Rundstedt's chief of operations, the German forces "stretched back for a hundred miles, the rear rank lying fifty miles to the *east* of the Rhine."

As the German army crossed the frontier, Hitler was embarking on a daring gamble. He had committed no less than seven-tenths of Germany's total armored strength to the hazardous terrain of the Ardennes Forest, believing that he could catch the Allies before they realized what was happening, and before they had time to bring up reserves to stop his panzers. But the panzers would be traveling on winding roads through the heavily wooded Ardennes, where they would scarcely be capable of engaging in combat and extremely vulnerable to Allied attack. A few well-placed anti-tank guns concealed on the wooded slopes of the Ardennes could wreak havoc with the seemingly endless columns of German vehicles moving bumper to bumper through the forest.

For Hitler, success depended largely on the ability of Kleist's panzer group to push quickly through the Ardennes and cross the Meuse near Sedan. Only then would the panzers have the maneuvering space they needed to prevail against a French counterattack. Only then would they be out of danger.

Guderian's panzer corps encountered only minimal resistance as it crossed Luxembourg on May 10. By 10:00 A.M., the advance elements of the 1st Panzer Division had reached the Belgian frontier near Martelange. There a river bridge destroyed by the retreating Belgian *Chasseurs Ardennais* posed the first serious obstacle the 1st Panzer Division encountered in its advance through the Ardennes Forest. By 4:00 P.M., however, the bridge was repaired by German engineers, and the division's panzers were once again on their way. That evening, Guderian established his headquarters on Belgian soil just west of Martelange.

To the north of Guderian's corps, Rommel's panzer division encountered barricaded roads pockmarked with huge craters from Belgian explosives. But the Belgians had failed to defend the barricades, so Rommel's panzers simply went around them. German engineers dealt with the road craters by placing planks over them. Gamelin's "impenetrable" Ardennes soon proved to be a very penetrable barrier.

What amazed the Germans even more than the timidity of the Belgian defenders was the absence of Allied aircraft in the skies over the Ardennes. What terrific targets the long German armored columns would have made for hostile planes as they moved slowly in close formation through the winding roads of the forest. But not one Allied aircraft appeared over the forest on the first day of battle, not even a reconnaissance plane. The panzer commanders saw only the reassuring black crosses of the Luftwaffe's planes.

The French had planned to delay the movement of the Germans through the Ardennes until at least the fifth day of the battle. Yet on the morning of May 10, cavalry units belonging to General Huntziger's 2nd Army— the 2nd and 5th Cavalry divisions and an independent brigade of cavalry—along with cavalry from General Corap's 9th Army—the 1st and 4th Cavalry divisions and the 3rd Spahi Brigade—advanced to the Bastogne-Arlon line, a short distance from the Luxembourg frontier.

About 11:00 A.M., Corap's advancing cavalry ran into German panzers near Libramont-Neufchâteau. It was a terrifying experience for Corap's soldiers. From the air, wave after wave of Stukas attacked the French tanks, while German panzers and armored cars fired on them from dense woods and open clearings. Suffering heavy losses, Corap's cavalry were forced to pull back to the Meuse River that evening.

Farther south, Huntziger's units experienced the same kind of ordeal. After several hours of intense fighting, they also were forced to withdraw, to the Semois River, a wide stream running through the center of the Ardennes and into the Meuse.

❈

Guderian quickly took advantage of the French withdrawal. During the night of May 11–12, a motorcycle batallion of the 1st Panzer Division crossed the Semois at Mouzaire before the defenders could realize what had happened. This bridgehead, only some five miles from Bouillon, the linchpin of the French defense line, gave the Germans an enormous advantage as dawn broke on May 12. By 6:00 A.M., Guderian's tanks were across the Semois and threatening to collapse Huntziger's left flank.

At Bouillon, Lieutenant Colonel Herman Balck's 1st Rifle Regiment pushed through the steep and densely wooded banks of the Semois until they reached a ford in the river. Soon afterward, lead tanks from the 1st Panzer Division crossed the river at the same ford.

Guderian smiled with satisfaction as he watched Balck's crossing of the river. After engineers completed a bridge over the Semois, the remaining ranks of the 1st Panzer Division crossed the river. Guderian followed the lead tanks as they pushed ahead toward their next objective, Sedan. "But mined roads," Guderian recalled, "compelled me to return to Bouillon."

Once there, Guderian experienced his first enemy attack. A French artillery bombardment attempted to destroy the 1st Panzer Division's bridge over the Semois. Fortunately for the Germans, the bridge was undamaged, but several houses in this picturesque town were set on fire.

No sooner had Guderian set up his headquarters in the town's Hotel Panorama than he was subjected, as he put it, "to a series of explosions in rapid succession." An Allied air attack struck a German engineer supply column, setting fire to the mines and hand grenades it was carrying. "There was," Guderian recalled, "one detonation after another. A boar's head, attached to the wall above my desk, broke loose and missed me by a hair's breadth; the other trophies came tumbling down, and the fine window in front of where I was seated smashed to smithereens, splinters of glass whistled passed my ears." The panzer leader decided it was time to get out of Bouillon. He moved his headquarters back to the small village of Noirefontaine on the Ardennes plateau, three miles north of Bouillon.

The Allied bombardment of the German bridgehead at Bouillon continued throughout the day. The incoming shells came from French long-range 155mm artillery deployed as far away as Torcy, ten miles to the south, near Sedan. Less accurately, RAF Battle bombers, like the ones that had nearly killed Guderian in the Hotel Panorama, made repeated runs up and down the narrow, twisting Semois valley. Despite the intense Allied bombardment, the bridge across the Semois survived, and the Germans were able to pour more and more troops across the river.

By midmorning of the next day, May 12, the tanks of the 1st Panzer Division were racing down the road to Sedan, now only ten miles away. The Germans had broken through Gamelin's "impenetrable barrier," the Ardennes Forest, and were now on French soil. In the distant haze, its soldiers could make out the Frénois Heights where, seventy years earlier, the king of Prussia, Wilhelm I, and his "Iron Chancellor," Otto von Bismarck, had watched German soldiers win the first Battle of Sedan, a victory that brought down the Second French Empire of Napoleon III. Soon, the entire east bank of the Meuse River, from Namur to Sedan, would be under their control. The next day, May 13, they would cross the river.

Early on the morning of May 13, at General Doumenc's headquarters in Montry, Captain Beaufre was marking a map with the latest battle information. He was amazed at what he saw developing on the map. The main axis of the German advance was no longer in northern Belgium, but in the Ardennes. With a bold charcoal arrow, Beaufre marked the new German axis on the map. Beaufre apparently was the first on the Allied side to become aware of the location of the German *Schwerpunkt*.

At his headquarters in Vincennes, Gamelin had decided that the time had come to make a personal appeal to his troops: "We must now stand up to the onslaught of the enemy's mechanized and motorized forces. The hour has come to fight all-out on the positions fixed by the High Command. We no longer have any right to retreat. If the enemy makes fresh local breaches, we must not only plug them, but counterattack and retake them." However, what Gamelin failed to realize—or preferred to ignore—was the fact that the strategic reserve that was required to "plug" the German breaches and "counterattack and retake them," Giraud's 7th Army, had been sent in vain to Holland.

THE BOMBING OF ROTTERDAM, MAY 13–14

Meanwhile, in Holland, Lieutenant Colonel Choltitz's troops were still pinned down by Dutch fire on the southern end of the Willems bridge leading into Rotterdam. German paratroopers were still holding on to the northern end of the bridge, but just barely; his men had just been beaten back by a strong Dutch counterattack. The German high command was becoming anxious. It wanted Holland cleaned up as soon as possible to prevent a British landing on the coast, as well as to free Kuechler's 18th Army for the main thrust through Belgium and into northern France.

Feeling the pressure from above, at 6:45 on the morning of May 13, General Kuechler ordered General Rudolf Schmidt, commander of the 39th Panzer Corps, "to break the resistance at Rotterdam by every means." However, Schmidt also was told "to use all means to prevent unnecessary bloodshed against the Dutch population."

That evening, Schmidt drew up a note demanding Dutch capitulation. Unless resistance was terminated without delay, he wrote to the commander of the Dutch forces in the city, Colonel Scharoo, he would have to use all means at his disposal to break it. "That," he warned, "could result in the complete destruction of the city. I beg you, as a man with a sense of responsibility, to take the necessary steps to prevent this." Simultaneously, Schmidt informed Kuechler's headquarters that he would need air power to support any breakthrough into the city.

The next morning, General Albert Kesselring, commander of the 2nd German Air Force, called Field Marshal Hermann Göring, head of the Luftwaffe, and had, as he put it, "a long telephone discussion which lasted for hours." Kesselring knew Rotterdam might surrender under the threat of aerial bombing, but he did not want a bombardment to occur with German troops entering the city. However, Göring was determined to get a share of the glory for his Luftwaffe; he ordered the air strike for two o'clock in the afternoon. Kesselring accepted the order but at the same time took precautions to call off the attack if Schmidt's negotiations proved successful. It was arranged that in the event that the Dutch agreed to surrender the city, flares would be fired from Vorder Island, in the middle of the river, and the air strike would be canceled.

At 9:40 in the morning, two German soldiers carrying truce flags and Schmidt's ultimatum, Captain Voerst and Lieutenant Plutzar, crossed the Willems bridge. They were taken to the Dutch command post and from there, blindfolded, through the city by zigzag routes to an underground vault. "We had a long and anguishing wait," Plutzar recalled, "well aware that precious time was ticking away." At last, at 11:40, the Dutch commander, Colonel Scharoo, received them. The Germans told him that only the immediate surrender of the city could save it from an imminent air bombardment. Scharoo responded that he did not have the authority to comply, and he asked for a delay until one o'clock to get instructions from The Hague. When informed of Scharoo's response, General Schmidt sent this message to the 2nd German Air Force: "Attack postponed owing to parley."

At 12:50 a Dutch emissary, Captain Bakker, Scharoo's adjutant, appeared on the bridge. There he was met by Generals Schmidt, Choltitz, Student, and Hubicki. The Dutch, the Germans found out, were in no hurry to surrender. They obviously thought they could continue to defend the city indefinitely. General H. G. Winkelman, the Dutch supreme commander, had ordered Scharoo to be as evasive as possible in answering the German ultimatum. Captain Bakker informed General Schmidt that there was an error in the form of the ultimatum delivered that morning. Before the German ultimatum could be considered by the Dutch commander, it must carry the name, rank, and signature of the German commander. The time was 1:15.

At that very minute, 100 German He-111 bombers were approaching the Dutch border on their way to Rotterdam. In the lead aircraft, Colonel Lackner, one of the squadron commanders, was studying a map spread out on his knees. On it were marked the zones of Dutch resistance in Rotterdam and a triangle at the northern end of the Maas bridges. Within this triangle, Lackner's group was to drop its bombs. The Dutch defenders in the triangle were to be immobilized by a short yet intense bombardment that would enable Schmidt's forces to cross the bridges. Every bomber crew was also instructed to avoid hitting the small German bridgehead on the northern end of the river, which was still being held by German paratroops.

However, there was one thing the bomber crews did not know: that surrender negotiations were in progress and that pending their outcome Schmidt had postponed the air attack. The bombers only knew that there was a possibility that their attack on Rotterdam would be canceled. "On our approach to the city," Lackner recalled, "we were to watch for red Very lights on the island in the Maas River. Should they appear, we had orders to attack, not Rotterdam, but the alternative target of two English divisions in Antwerp." But would the lights be visible in the haze and dust raised in five days of fighting?

On the ground, at that moment, General Schmidt was writing out, point by point, the conditions for Rotterdam's surrender. He told the Dutch: "I am compelled to negotiate swiftly, and must therefore insist that your decision is in my hands within three hours, namely at 17:00 hours." Captain Bakker took Schmidt's letter back to the Dutch lines, with Colonel Choltitz escorting him to the Willems bridge. It was now 2:00—the original commencement time for the German air raid.

"The tension was appalling," Choltitz remembered. "Would Rotterdam surrender in time?" At that moment, he heard the sound of approaching planes—the bombers were coming! "Those of us on the spot," he wrote later, "could only hope that the necessary orders had been given, that the communications had not broken down, and that the high command knew what was happening."

But communications had broken down. For a half hour after getting Schmidt's signal, the 2nd Air Force command had been doing its best to contact and recall Lackner's bomber group, but without success. The planes had withdrawn their long-range radio antennas and were now operating on their bomber-to-bomber radio frequencies. In desperation, the 2nd Air Force's operations officer, Lieutenant Colonel Rieckhoff, jumped into a Messerschmidt-109 and raced for Rotterdam, literally hoping to divert the attack in person. He failed.

As the German bombers approached Rotterdam, they divided into two columns. Lieutenant Colonel Otto Hoehne's bomber group turned to approach the target triangle from the southwest, while Lackner's bombers went straight on. "Though there were no clouds in the sky," Lackner recalled, "it was unusually misty. Visibility was so bad that I took my column down to 2,300 feet to be sure of hitting the required target." At 2:05 P.M. Lackner crossed the Maas and reached the city's edge. Dutch flak guns opened up. No evasive action was taken by the bombers; their crews were giving all their attention to the approaching target.

In the middle of Rotterdam, the Nieuwe Maas makes a loop to the north. Just to the west of its vortex, the twin bridges were discernible to the German bombardiers through the mist and smoke hanging above the city. Although the Maas island was clearly visible, they saw no red Very lights. The only thing the crews could make out were small red balls of Dutch flak rising toward them like burning strings.

Yet, on the ground, Choltitz's men were firing Very lights by the dozens. "My God! There's going to be a catastrophe," General Schmidt cried out. General Student was standing next to Schmidt. Both men grabbed and fired Very guns at the bombers as they passed slowly overhead on their way to their targets. But the flares were quickly swallowed up by the smoke that drifted from burning houses and from oily black clouds rising from the still burning passenger steamer *Straatendam.*

Lieutenant Colonel Hoehne concentrated solely on the Maas island, looking for red Very lights, as his bomber approached the city. But he saw nothing. The bombardier called out, "I must let go the bombs now or they'll fall away from the target." Hoehne gave the order to release. Then he immediately caught his breath. Suddenly, and just for a second or two, he had glimpsed "not a barrage but just two paltry little Very lights ascending." He shouted the order to turn back. But the order was too late; the bombs had already been released. The same thing happened with the two bombers following Hoehne's. However, the remaining bombers in the formation, 43 planes in all, received the order in time and were able to peel off from the attack without releasing their bombs.

Nevertheless, 158 500-pound bombs and 1,150 100-pound bombs were dropped on the city, the equivalent of 97 tons of TNT. For years, it was believed that 30,000 people were killed by the raid on Rotterdam. This was an exaggeration. But the real figure was bad enough: 900 people were killed, several thousand were injured, and 78,000 were made homeless.

The world was outraged by what was generally regarded as an atrocity. However, many of the deaths and much of the damage the city suffered was a result of the Dutch firefighters' inability to control the fires ignited by the bombs. Amazingly, Rotterdam, a worldwide trading center of one million people, had only a volunteer fire department. The backbone of the force was a two-wheeled contraption not unlike the one invented by the painter Jan van der Heyden in 1672. In fairness to the Dutch, such equipment had proved adequate for ordinary fires; they never expected Rotterdam to be the target of a massive aerial bombardment.

At four o'clock in the afternoon, barely two hours after the German air raid on Rotterdam, the Dutch commandant, Colonel Scharoo, walked over the Willems bridge and capitulated. Scharoo was bitter. He told General Schmidt that he considered the bombardment of the city before the expiration of the ultimatum a breach of military protocol. Schmidt replied: "Colonel, I understand your bitterness," but he could make no excuse to justify the action of the German air force.

An hour later, the surrender documents were signed. Nevertheless, the fighting within Rotterdam continued. As German tanks and troops moved across the bridges into the city, survivors of the bombardment began to emerge from houses, cellars, and ditches. Student and Choltitz proceeded to Dutch military headquarters, which Student took as his temporary command post.

Outside, several hundred Dutch troops were assembling to surrender their arms. Just then a great roar of tank and truck engines could be heard. Sepp Dietrich's SS motorized regiment *Liebstandarte Adolf Hitler* came racing through the streets of the city, heading for The Hague. Somewhat trigger-happy, the SS men were alarmed to see Dutch soldiers walking in the streets carrying rifles. The Germans immediately opened up on them with machine-gun fire.

As Student and Choltitz ran to the window to see what was going on, Student was hit by a bullet that grazed his head. Bleeding profusely, he fell against Choltitz. His uniform covered with Student's blood, Choltitz rushed out of the building to stop the shooting. The situation was explosive. Choltitz's men were confused by the firing and suspicious that the Dutch had led them into a trap. However, with considerable presence of mind, Choltitz ordered the Dutch soldiers into a nearby church and averted a massacre.

Soon after the Rotterdam disaster, the Dutch city of Utrecht also was threatened with destruction. Another Rotterdam, however, was too much for the Dutch high command to contemplate. At 4:50 P.M. on May 14, General Winkelman ordered his army to stop fighting.

For the greater part of the Netherlands, the war had lasted only five days. The Germans did not intern the Dutch army, but its soldiers were disarmed and demobilized, and Dutch officers had to pledge that they would never again take up arms against Germany. However, most of the Dutch navy, which had not been in home waters when the Germans attacked, continued in the war. But another Axis enemy, the Japanese, would destroy most of Holland's ships in the Java Sea two years later. Few Dutch aircraft escaped destruction at the hands of the Germans, but some planes managed to fly to England.

All totaled, the losses experienced by the Dutch army were relatively slight compared to the losses Belgium and France would suffer in the campaign: only 2,100 dead and 2,700 wounded. Civilian casualties, how-ever, due in large part to the Luftwaffe's bombing of Rotterdam, were

Center of Rotterdam after the debris was cleared (AP/Wide World Photos)

much higher. The number of Germans killed and wounded in Holland was never published. However, the heaviest losses seemed to have been suffered by the Luftwaffe; not fewer than 525 planes were destroyed in the brief campaign against the Dutch. These losses would prove to be critical in the Battle of Britain during the coming summer.

"Blood, Toil, Tears, and Sweat" May 13

While the war was raging on the continent, Winston Churchill appeared before the House of Commons on May 13 to make his first speech as prime minister. In the eerie light of the House, one member of the audience, General Edward Spears, observed, Churchill's face seemed unusually white. But his jaw was set in the pose of fierce determination that had become his trademark.

The new prime minister's first sentences were a short and simple, almost matter-of-fact, introduction. "Then suddenly," Spears recounted, "he was transformed into an inspired leader, the High Priest of a great religion dedicating a nation to measureless sacrifice." The ancient table in the center of the House became the altar before which he spoke. He looked up and above the crowded benches filled with MPs toward the high, narrow, cathedral-like windows that let in broad slits of light, and then said slowly: "I have nothing to offer but blood, toil, tears and sweat."

"A great hush came over the House," Spears noted, "followed by deep murmurs of approval, as if the MPs were responding with a collective Amen. Churchill's words were transforming the House. Each member seemed to be partaking in the anointing of the new leader, and responding with a personal vow of loyalty to his cause. By this time, every sentence Churchill uttered was punctuated with deep-throated cheers."

"You ask," he continued, "what is our policy?" Then, as if he were baring the heart of the nation before heaven, he answered his own question: "It is to wage war, by sea, land, and air, with all our might and with all the strength that God can give us; to wage war against a monstrous tyranny never surpassed in the dark, lamentable catalogue of human crime. That is our policy."

The House, moved to an ever-higher level of emotion, roared its approval.

"You ask, what is our aim? I can answer in one word: it is victory, victory at all costs, victory in spite of terror, victory, however long and hard the road may be."

Spears believed there never had been a more solemn dedication in the history of the world. Churchill had "pledged himself, the Commons, and the people, to follow the path from which there was no turning. Wherever he led, all would follow, however hard the road . . . until victory was achieved."

Generals Walter von Brauchisch and Franz Halder (Imperial War Museum MH13141)

General Erich von Manstein (AP/Wide World Photos)

General Heinz Guderian (Imperial War Museum MH13141)

General Gerd von Rundstedt (Imperial War Museum MH10132)

General Erwin Rommel (Imperial War Museum RML3)

General Kurt Student (Imperial War Museum MH13141)

CHAPTER FIVE

The Battle of the Meuse, May 12–15

THE FRENCH DEFENSES ON THE MEUSE RIVER

The first major obstacle the German panzer juggernaut would encounter as it emerged from the Ardennes Forest was the Meuse River.

One of the great rivers of western Europe, the Meuse rises in France, in the Haute-Marne, and flows quietly northward with increasing twists past the towns of Sedan, Monthermé, and Givet. It then flows into Belgium, past Dinant and into Namur, where it cuts sharply eastward to Liège, and then turns north again before entering Holland (where it becomes the Maas) and finally emptying into the North Sea.

It was behind this great river—specifically along the stretch between Sedan and Namur—that the French intended to stop any German advance through the Ardennes Forest. General Corap's 9th Army would defend the west bank of the river from Namur upstream to Mézières, while Huntziger's 2nd Army was assigned to cover the river from a point just east of Mézières to the western end of the Maginot Line.

General Gamelin thought that Corap had the easier of the two sectors of the Meuse to defend. "The Meuse there," he explained, "is very compressed between rocky, perpendicular cliffs, absolutely unscaleable to tanks, and often very difficult for infantry." However, General André Doumenc, Gamelin's chief of staff, felt the river in Corap's sector favored the attackers "because its wooded banks lend themselves to infiltrations, its winding increases the area of ground to be fought over, and the defending force lacks a wide view and good fields of fire."

Because Gamelin regarded the Ardennes as "impenetrable" and the Meuse as impassable, Corap's army was one of the weakest in the French

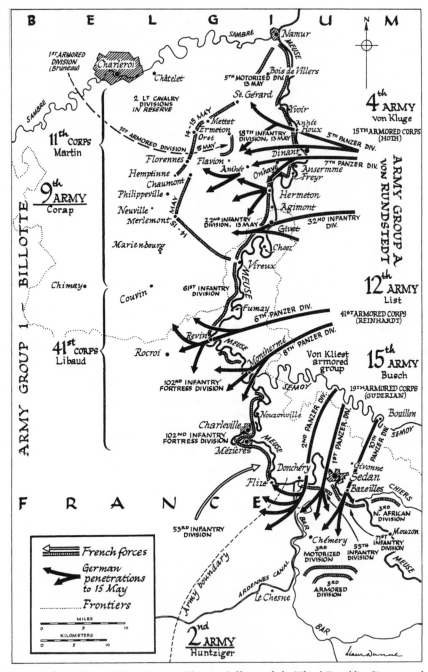

Battle of the Meuse, May 12–15. (Shirer, *Collapse of the Third Republic,* Simon and Schuster)

order of battle. Of its seven infantry divisions, only two—the 5th Motorized and 4th North African—were regular divisions. The others were filled by reservists. Two of the reserve divisions, the 61st and 53rd Infantry, were classified as "Series B" divisions, that is, badly armed, overaged, and undertrained. Unkindly called "crocodiles" by the rest of the army, they were commanded by older-than-average officers, most of whom had been called out of retirement. One of Corap's divisions, the 102nd Infantry, was a fortress division, which, because it had no vehicles to transport its troops, was necessarily confined to defending a fixed position.

At the age of sixty-two, Corap was one of the army's older officers. However, the journalist André Maurois described him as "unmilitary in appearance and running to fat around the middle." "The trouble with old Corap," one officer in the 9th Army told Maurois, was that "he isn't fond enough of banging the drum. . . . An army needs to bang its drums, needs reviews and music—a bit of polish." But there was little drum-banging by Corap. Maurois was struck by the sleepy atmosphere that permeated Corap's headquarters in Vervins. The town's "rough cobblestones," he wrote, "resounded to the unhurried tread of military men walking to their offices with the peaceful punctuality of civil servants."

Daladier had not been enthusiastic about giving Corap the command of the 9th Army. He thought Corap had become mentally slow. However, Gamelin argued that Corap was thoroughly familiar with the terrain the 9th Army would defend and so he was not replaced.

Yet Corap's army had too few weapons to defend that terrain effectively. Only two of its active divisions, the 5th Motorized and the 4th North African, had antiaircraft guns. With the exception of its cavalry corps, which had lost many of its light tanks in the Ardennes, it had no armored units. Corap repeatedly asked the high command for more artillery guns, but he did not get them, at least not in the quantities he wanted or needed. Still, no one expected the 9th Army to do much fighting.

Corap had hoped to get his divisions into place along the Meuse by May 14. But when his cavalry corps was quickly ejected from the Ardennes by the Germans on May 11, he ordered his infantry units to speed up their advance by forced night marches. Yet by the evening of May 12, only half of the 18th Division's infantry battalions had reached the river. By the next morning, only five battalions of the 22nd Infantry Division were in their designated positions. And when Corap's soldiers did arrive on the river, they could find no trace of the fortifications the Belgian high command had promised would be there. Exhausted from three days of long marches, Corap's infantry were too weary to dig in immediately or to make sure that every yard of the river was covered by their guns.

Needless to say, Corap was shocked when he was informed that German troops were sighted near the Meuse on the evening of May 12—well before all of his own units were in place. He was even more alarmed when French reconnaissance aircraft reported that a German mechanized column, some 15 miles long, was winding its way through the Ardennes heading toward Dinant, opposite his army's sector of the Meuse. Corap realized immediately that the German column could only be a panzer division.

Rommel Crosses the Meuse, May 12–15

Corap, of course, was right. The panzer division moving toward Dinant was Erwin Rommel's 7th Panzer Division. Rommel's rapid advance was due partly to his division's favorable tactical march route, which allowed it to skirt the northern edge of the Ardennes, bypassing the forest's densest parts. But the forty-eight-year-old Rommel also had something to prove: that he could command a panzer division. By background an infantryman, he had been a panzer leader for only a short three months. His appointment to lead the 7th Panzer Division had been made by the Führer personally, as a reward for his service commanding Hitler's military bodyguard. In the end, Rommel would prove to be an outstanding panzer leader. During the six weeks his division participated in the western campaign, it would suffer a higher rate of casualties than any other German division—2,594 men killed, wounded, and captured—but it also would capture 97,468 prisoners, shoot down 52 aircraft, and capture a dozen more on the ground.

Rommel's progress through the Ardennes had been so rapid that his corps commander, General Hermann Hoth, had decided to reinforce his division with Colonel Werner's 31st Panzer Regiment, a unit belonging to the 5th Panzer Division, which was lagging far behind Rommel. It was Werner's regiment that the French spotted on the Meuse late in the afternoon of May 12.

Werner's armored cars reached the Meuse just as the last vehicles belonging to Corap's cavalry were crossing the river at Yvoir. One armored car tried to dash across the bridge before the French could destroy it, but a direct hit by a French anti-tank gun stopped it on the center of the bridge. Climbing out of the burning vehicle, its leather-jacketed driver, pliers in hand, ran to the point where he thought the explosives were located, hoping to deactivate them before they blew up. As he did, one of the Belgian defenders, Lieutenant de Wipspelaere, pressed the plunger. Nothing happened. Desperately, Wipspelaere ran out onto the bridge, in an attempt to detonate the charges by hand. He was able to beat the German to the explosives and light the fuse. But just as he stood up to run for cover, a bullet from a German sharpshooter killed him instantly. Seconds later, the bridge erupted in a huge ball of flame, throwing steel, stone, and two German armored cars high into the air and into the river below.

With the bridges at Dinant and Houx destroyed by the retreating French, it seemed as though the Germans would have no alternative but to attempt a perilous crossing with rubber assault boats. But they had one of those great strokes of luck that seemed to keep falling their way. That evening, a German motorcycle reconnaissance patrol discovered an ancient weir near Houx that had not been demolished by the Belgians, for fear that its destruction would drop the water level and make the river fordable. Under cover of darkness, several companies of the motorcyclists scrambled across the weir and found themselves on an island that was connected to the other side of the river by a still intact lock gate. They quickly walked across it, and by dawn on May 13, less than three days after the offensive began, the Germans had made the first breach in the French Meuse defense line.

At Dinant, two miles farther upstream from Houx, Rommel's other units were having a much more difficult time crossing the river. When he arrived there, French fire was destroying the rubber assault rafts of the 6th Rifle Regiment as soon as they hit the water. "The enemy infantry were so well concealed," he recorded, "that they were impossible to locate, even after a long search through glasses." A smokescreen, he thought, was needed to conceal the crossing. But a smoke unit was not available. The problem was solved when Rommel ordered a number of houses along the river set on fire. Under the dense smoke they provided, the German crossing finally got under way.

Rommel seemed to be everywhere that morning. From Dinant, he turned his attention to the bridgehead opposite Houx. Although it was

German troops crossing the Meuse River (Imperial War Museum MH13141)

already some two miles deep and three miles wide, he felt it was still insecure. The Germans had no panzers or close support artillery on the far side of the river, and they were outnumbered and outgunned by the defenders, who also had the support of a few tanks. Nevertheless, Rommel ordered his men to clear the enemy from the cliffs surrounding the bridgehead while he went back and spurred his engineers to complete a pontoon bridge that would enable panzers to cross to the far bank.

Then he drove back to Dinant in a Panzer IV tank, to the point where the 7th Rifle Regiment was trying to cross the river. There the French gunfire was as intense as it was opposite Houx. Again, the German assault rafts were being shot to pieces almost as soon as they entered the water. "The crossing," Rommel recalled, "had now come to a complete standstill, with the officers badly shaken by the casualties which their men had suffered."

Rommel, deciding that the crossing could not be made without panzer and artillery support, drove back to division headquarters to organize it. When the panzers arrived, all hell erupted along the banks of the Meuse. One German tank after another cruised slowly northward along the river bank, spaced 50 yards apart, turrets turned to the left, firing point-blank into the French bunkers and machine-gun nests, barely 100 yards across the river. Under this covering fire, the German crossing finally got under way. Within a short time, the rubber assault boats reached the far bank. In the meantime, engineers started constructing a pontoon bridge to bring over the panzers.

Rommel, now personally taking command of the 2nd Battalion of the 7th Rifle Regiment, got into an assault boat and crossed the river. As soon as he reached the far bank, someone shouted, "Enemy tanks in front!" The Germans had no anti-tank weapons, so Rommel ordered his men to open up on the French tanks with small arms fire and flare guns. Amazingly, this gambit worked; the French tanks withdrew, leaving behind a number of defenders who immediately laid down their arms.

Rommel recrossed the river after the bridgehead seemed secure and drove by panzer northward to the point where the 6th Rifle Regiment was crossing. There he saw German engineers busily engaged in building an eight-ton pontoon bridge across the river. Rommel ordered them to stop; he wanted a 16-ton bridge built, one that would enable at least some of the panzers to get over the river quickly. As soon as the first pontoon bridge was completed, Rommel, now in an eight-wheeled signal truck, led the panzers over to the west bank.

In the meantime, the situation in the Houx bridgehead had become critical: the French had launched a counteroffensive near the small village of Grange.

At 1:00 A.M. on May 13, General Boucher, commander of the 5th French Motorized Infantry Division, learned that Germans had crossed the Meuse and taken the Wastia Heights, opposite Houx. General Martin, commander of the French 11th Corps, did not receive the news until three hours later. Unable to get ahold of Corap, Martin decided to counterattack on his own. But Luftwaffe harassment and poor communications prevented him from getting his forces organized until that evening. Martin had at his disposal the 18th Infantry Division, which had begun arriving on the Meuse the previous evening. But because it had just traveled, in 52 hours of almost continuous marching, some 60 miles from its jumping-off point in France, the men were in no condition for anything but a good night's rest. Consequently, the attack was postponed until the next day.

That evening, however, the 39th Infantry Regiment, supported by a squadron of tanks and three artillery units, was ordered to clear the Surinvaux Wood in the German bridgehead near the Wastia Heights and then drive the Germans into the Meuse. The attack was set for 7:30 P.M., but it was postponed for a half an hour when the commander of the 39th Regiment informed Martin that he was not ready to attack.

Finally, at eight o'clock, the tanks were ready, but the infantry still had not arrived. With darkness fast approaching, the French tank commander decided he could wait no longer. After unleashing a 10-minute bombardment on the German positions, the French tanks entered the woods. They were surprised to find the woods unoccupied. Moving through it, the tanks reached the high ground that dominated the German crossing places. The motorcycle troops holding the crest of the riverbank—without anti-tank guns—were surprised by the French attack; most fled, but eight were captured. The French tanks quickly cleared the crest of the remaining German resistance, but no French infantry were available to hold the reclaimed territory. Fearing a German counterattack in the dark, the tanks withdrew, and the heights were immediately reoccupied by the Germans. Needless to say, the French bungled a golden opportunity to throw the Germans back into the Meuse.

By the next morning, May 14, Rommel had gotten the 25th Panzer Regiment, with 30 tanks under the command of Colonel Rothenburg, across the river. Farther south, Colonel von Bismarck's 7th Rifle Regiment was advancing on Onhaye, a town some two miles west of the river that was being defended by the 4th North African Division. Rommel placed five panzers under Bismarck's command to provide a mobile covering fire for his attacking infantry. Rommel followed closely behind the infantry in a Panzer III.

Suddenly heavy artillery and anti-tank fire erupted from the woods to the west, inundating the German column with shell fire. Two shells hit Rommel's panzer in rapid succession, one striking the upper edge of its turret and the second its periscope. Rommel's right cheek began bleeding profusely from a shell splinter that had glanced off the periscope. The driver immediately hit the throttle and drove the panzer into the nearest bushes. But the vegetation concealed a steep slope, down which the panzer slid, coming to a stop nearly on its side only 500 yards from the French artillery position. The panzer was a sitting duck for the French guns, and Rommel knew it. He ordered the crew to run for cover. And none too soon. As Rommel and his men clambered out of the panzer and up the slope, French shells rained down all around them. It was another close call for the panzer general. Yet Rommel always considered such risks worth taking. He insisted that a panzer leader could not lead from the rear.

Rommel ordered the other panzers in the regiment to attack the French artillery batteries. Within a matter of minutes, the French guns were silenced. By evening, Rommel had succeeded in wresting Onhaye from the 4th North African Division. Following hard on the heels of the retreating French, Colonel Rothenburg's 25th Panzer Regiment had advanced seven miles west of the Meuse, at a total cost that day of three officers, seven noncommissioned officers, and 41 soldiers.

Farther south, the German 32nd Infantry Division, supported by only a few light tanks, was able to cross the Meuse north and south of Givet. After desultory fighting, the commander of the French 22nd Division, General Bézieres-Lafosse, ordered a withdrawal to a new position six miles in the rear, in effect abandoning his whole sector of the riverfront. "Here was another division," one French officer, Colonel Adolphe Goutard, commented bitterly, "that disintegrated at the first blow."

At 7:00 P.M., General Martin also decided to pull back the rest of his battered corps to another "barrier line" running from Oret in the north through Florennes and then southeast to the Meuse at Vireux. The 18th Division, with the remains of the 1st Cavalry Division, would redeploy on the northern flank of the new line, the 4th North African Division would man the center, and the 22nd Division the southern flank. In this new line, Martin hoped to reassemble his retreating infantry and then launch a counterattack the next day.

Martin's order to retreat from the Meuse shocked Corap's headquarters. It already was reeling from the "grave news," as Corap's deputy chief of staff, General Véron, put it, "from the 11th Corps that the 22nd Division was completely broken through and that the 18th can no longer hold." Véron considered Martin's order to pull back "a catastrophe." Yet Corap made no effort to reverse it.

THE COUNTERATTACK OF THE FRENCH
1ST ARMORED DIVISION, MAY 15

By the evening of May 13, the commander-in-chief of the northeast front, General Georges, exhausted by three consecutive nearly sleepless nights, was—finally—alarmed by the successful German crossings of the Meuse at Houx and Dinant. That afternoon, he ordered General Billotte to take strong countermeasures to hurl the Germans back into the Meuse. "The operation," he said, "must be conducted with extreme energy. . . . Failure will not be tolerated."

To add punch to the planned counteroffensive, Georges provided Billotte with General Bruneau's 1st Armored Division. Although it had only 150 tanks, compared to the 225 in Rommel's 7th Panzer Division, Bruneau's division was still one of the most powerful units in the French army. Amazingly, this division still had not seen action, four days after the beginning of the German offensive. It took that long to move it to the front because unlike German panzer divisions, which moved their tanks and wheeled vehicles together, French armored divisions transported their wheeled vehicles by road and their tanks by flat rail cars in order to save wear and tear on tank treads. Had the 1st Armored Division traveled as a unit, as the German panzer divisions did, it easily could have reached its destination in one day, instead of the two that were required. Arriving in Charleroi early on May 13, the 1st Armored Division was only 23 miles from Rommel's bridgehead across the Meuse. Yet it was not until 1:00 P.M. the next day that the division was finally ordered to Florennes, ten miles west of Rommel's lead panzers.

By the evening of May 14, the lead tanks of General Bruneau's 1st Armored Division began arriving in the vicinity of Rommel's Meuse bridgehead. Due to roads cluttered with fleeing troops and civilians, it had taken them seven hours to make the 20-mile trip from Charleroi. Many of the tanks were out of gasoline, but their fuel trucks were still far behind.*

Equally worrisome to Bruneau, there was no trace of any supporting infantry. His tanks stood alone a little north of Flavion, a town about four miles west of the German bridgehead. Bruneau positioned his 28th Battalion facing east, a little north of the village, and his 37th Battalion on the left of the 28th, facing south. Both battalions were partly concealed by woods. Since some of his tanks were out of fuel, while others had only a little, Bruneau could do nothing but await the arrival of his other tank battalions and, above all, the fuel trucks.

---

*French tanks needed frequent refueling because French doctrine called on tanks to be used solely in support of the infantry. Consequently, their fuel tanks were not very large. Rather than relying on fuel trucks, the Germans refueled their tanks with small steel containers (later nicknamed "Jerricans" by British troops) that could be carried on the tanks themselves, thereby enabling the panzers to take their fuel with them as they advanced.

But Rommel would not give Bruneau the time he needed to launch a counterattack. At 8:30 the next morning, Rommel's panzers, supported by swarms of bombers and artillery, fell upon Bruneau's tanks. The Germans concentrated their attack on the two battalions of Bruneau's heavy "B" tanks, which were refueling at the time. Unable to move without fuel, many of the French tanks were set on fire by their own crews before they ran off. Nevertheless, one squadron of French tanks did manage to counterattack and was able to knock out several panzers. The Germans, realizing that their 37mm guns could not penetrate the armor of the French tanks, concluded that the only way to stop them was to shoot off their treads.

Rommel, however, did not allow the rapid advance of his division to be delayed by a French armored division. He simply swung his panzers around Bruneau's flank and continued his westward thrust. Having delivered a devastating initial blow, he left the mopping-up work for Colonel Werner's panzers, which were following behind.

When Werner arrived, he saw that the French armor facing him was made up of heavy tanks, so he withdrew his light panzers and sent in his own heavies, 35 Panzer IIIs and 32 Panzer IVs, supported by artillery. Not realizing that many of Bruneau's tanks were out of gas, Werner was puzzled as to why the French tanks did not move. Nevertheless, his panzers, arrayed in an advancing semicircle, opened fire on Bruneau's 26th Battalion. Bruneau ordered a company of the 37th Battalion, which had completed its refueling, to go to its assistance.

A French gunner recalled that as his tank was advancing to meet Werner's panzers, a shell struck its left side. Fortunately, it bounced off harmlessly. Then the gunner saw red flashes from a low hedge. "I traversed my turret towards the flashes," he recalled, "and shot off five high explosive shells at the hedge, after which nothing moved any longer."

The French tank continued to the edge of a woods, where another tank battle was raging. Suddenly its driver shouted, "A panzer on the edge of the woods in front of us!" Moving the tank's 75mm turret toward the panzer, the gunner fired, and the German tank exploded. Soon afterward, another panzer burst into flames after being struck by the French tank's 75mm gun. Before the panzer was hit, however, it fired a shell at the French tank, knocking out the 75mm gun. Nevertheless, the French tank continued firing with its machine gun. However, when the French tanks started to come under fire from German 105mm guns, the battalion's commander ordered a withdrawal.

Bruneau's 1st Armored Division may have stood a chance—and even may have prevailed—against one panzer division. But against two, the 5th and 7th Panzer Divisions, it really could not have expected to win. Realizing that he was about to be outflanked by Rommel, whose panzers were speeding toward Philippeville, almost 18 miles from the Dinant crossing point, Bruneau ordered his entire division to pull back to the Mettet-Florennes line.

Even though Bruneau's division had knocked out a good many panzers—perhaps as many as 100—it also suffered heavy losses. When the division began its retreat, it had only 50 of the 150 tanks that it had that morning. Of the three companies of "B" tanks in the 37th Battalion, two had been completely wiped out. The 26th Tank Battalion could muster only six light tanks. The 28th Battalion had only three out of its original 36 heavy tanks. Most of them had run out of gas and were destroyed by their crews. Only the 25th Tank Battalion, which had arrived too late to participate in the battle, remained intact. Under cover of night, what was left of the 1st Armored Division withdrew to the French frontier. When Bruneau saw his division the next day, it consisted of only 17 tanks; the remainder had either lost their way or run out of fuel during the night's withdrawal. In effect, the 1st Armored Division ceased to exist as an effective fighting force. It had squandered its tanks in piecemeal engagements with the Germans, rather than using them in massed counterattacks. Three days later, what remained of the division was overrun by the German tidal wave, and its commander, General Bruneau, was captured.

The Germans, for their part, not only had benefited from a superior tactical doctrine, they also had been lucky. Near the end of the battle, Colonel Werner's ammunition reserve was reduced to three shells per gun. Fortunately for him, this proved to be just enough to force the French tanks to withdraw. Moreover, had Werner's panzers not arrived when they did, Rommel would not have been able to disengage from the battle with Bruneau's tanks and continue his advance.

By this time, Rommel's panzers were out in the open, flat country west of the Meuse River, inflicting havoc upon the 9th Army's rear areas. Just short of Philippeville, Rommel's panzer column ran into a body of fully armed French motorcyclists coming from the opposite direction. "Most of them," Rommel recalled, "were so shaken at suddenly finding themselves in a German column, they drove their machines into the ditch and were in no position to put up a fight."

Near Vocedée, three miles east of Philippeville, Rommel had a brief engagement with several French tanks. "The French ceased fire," he remembered, "and were fetched out of their tanks one by one by our men. Some fifteen French tanks fell into our hands, some of them damaged, others completely intact. It being impossible to leave a guard, we took the undamaged tanks along with us in our column, still with their French drivers!"

By midday on May 15, Rommel had occupied Philippeville and was pushing on to Cerfontaine, six miles to the southwest. He had broken through Corap's "intermediate line" even before it could be occupied by French troops. Looking back to the east from the summit of a hill as the sun set, Rommel could see endless pillars of dust rising as far as his eyes could reach—comforting signs that the 7th Panzer Division had broken through the French front. At a cost of just 15 killed that day, he had advanced over 17 miles, taken 450 prisoners, knocked out or captured 75 tanks, and struck a decisive blow against the French 9th Army, ending its ability to launch an effective counterattack.

REINHARDT CROSSES THE MEUSE, MAY 13–14

While Rommel's division was crossing the Meuse at Dinant, General Georg-Hans Reinhardt's 41st Panzer Corps was attempting to cross the river near Monthermé, 45 miles south of Dinant. Reinhardt's two panzer divisions, the 8th and 6th Panzers, had been compelled to travel through the Ardennes behind Guderian's corps and Rommel's division. Consequently, they did not reach the Meuse until the afternoon of May 13, a day later than Rommel.

Monthermé is a typical Meuse village, small, peaceful, and surrounded by breathtaking scenery. But this scenery also included some of the most rugged terrain in the Ardennes, including high mountains that forced the river into a narrow valley covered with thick woods and tangled scrub. Monthermé lies at the base of the valley on a peninsula about half a mile wide formed by a loop in the river. A ridge runs along the spine of the peninsula all the way to the apex of the loop in the river.

Corap deployed two divisions along this stretch of the Meuse. The first, at Monthermé, was the 102nd Fortress Division, one of the few regular divisions in the 9th Army. Farther upstream, Corap deployed the 61st

Division. Made up entirely of reservists, it was one of the weakest divisions in the French Army.

At about three o'clock in the afternoon of May 13, a thin mist hugged the Meuse Valley as the 3rd Battalion of the 4th Panzer Regiment (6th Panzer Division) arrived on the heights overlooking Monthermé. The battalion was ordered to seize a crossing over the river and establish a bridgehead by four o'clock. Surprisingly, there were no French soldiers in sight. The town seemed deserted. Only the sporadic firing of distant French artillery and the rippling flow of the river interrupted the stillness of the beautifully sunny spring afternoon. The German riflemen, weighted down by machine guns, mortars, and ammunition boxes, worked their way down from the heights with difficulty. Many slid and fell on the jagged slopes that dropped abruptly to the river. Finally, the lead soldiers approached to within 50 yards of the riverbank.

Suddenly, as the Germans began putting their first rubber assault boats in the river, devastatingly accurate French machine-gun fire opened up. Several Germans were mowed down. The rest dropped their rubber boats and ran for cover. The second assault team also was badly shot up. With the smoke of the battle filling the air, the Germans had trouble locating the French positions. Finally, a bunker camouflaged by the terrace of a café was pinpointed. Several panzers opened fire on it. Under this covering fire, the next wave of assault boats successfully entered the water. The crews crossed to the other side and made for the crest of the ridge that split the town.

Meanwhile, a little way upstream from Monthermé, the Germans found a metal girder bridge that had been only partially destroyed by the retreating French. After dark, inflatable boats and wooden planks were lashed together and strapped to the buckled girders, enabling infantry to cross without even getting their feet wet. But once across the river and onto the far bank, they were immediately pinned down by French gunfire. Eventually the French bunkers at the river's edge were reduced with flamethrowers, forcing the defenders to pull back to the heights at the base of the Monthermé peninsula. From this seemingly impregnable position, the French artillery continued to pound the German positions.

The town itself was soon a mass of ruins, with flames and smoke rising from once picturesque dwellings. Try as they did, however, the Germans could not capture the heights above the town. Here the 102nd Fortress Division held its ground in spite of everything the Luftwaffe threw at it. Nor, because of the intensity and accuracy of the French artillery fire, could the Germans bring tanks across the river to help with the assault. As a result, as night fell, the Germans were forced to dig in.

At 2:00 A.M. on May 15, General Corap rushed into his office and grabbed the telephone, saying he had to speak to General Billotte at once. Corap told Billotte that as a result of General Martin's decision to withdraw his 11th Corps, he intended to abandon the entire Meuse front. A stormy exchange resulted, with Corap talking so loudly that his deputy chief of staff, General Véron, who was outside his office, could hear him.

At 4:00 A.M., Billotte called General Georges. "The 9th Army," he said, "is in a critical position, the whole front is falling back." Billotte was not exaggerating. The northern flank of the army was completely separated from its center by Rommel's bridgehead opposite Dinant. The remains of its 11th Corps had been pushed back to Florennes, seven miles west of the Meuse. Farther south, its 4th North African Division was withdrawing to Philippeville before it disintegrated that afternoon under Rommel's onslaught. Still farther south, the remnants of the 22nd Infantry Division had been thrown back to within a stone's throw of the French frontier. The line continued to hold at Monthermé, Billotte admitted, but he warned Georges that the divisions that were holding that sector, the 61st and 102nd Divisions, were on the verge of collapse.

With Georges's approval, Billotte ordered a general retreat of the 9th Army to the Marcinelle [south of Charleroi]-Cerfontaine-Rocroi-Signy-L'Abbaye-Omont line. Unfortunately for the 9th Army, the new line was no more than a string of names on an easily recognizable road, with no natural obstacles, no organization, and no garrisons to hold the strong points. Billotte obviously forgot—or preferred to ignore—that the 102nd Fortress Division had no transport and that much of its armament was deployed in fixed positions.

Before hanging up the phone, Billotte also complained to Georges that he was shocked by Corap's spiritless attitude. "It is absolutely necessary to get some life into this wavering army," Billotte concluded. Georges agreed; Corap would have to go. Early in the morning of May 15, he was relieved of his command. General Giraud, whose 7th Army had made the futile dash into Holland just five days earlier, was appointed his successor.

Just before dawn on May 15, General Libaud, commander of the French 41st Corps, was notified that the entire 9th Army had been ordered to withdraw. Libaud was dumbfounded. His two divisions—the 102nd and 61st—were still holding the line of the Meuse around Monthermé. But only barely. During the early hours of that morning, German engineers equipped with flamethrowers and riflemen of the 6th Panzer Division crept up to within a few yards of the French bunkers. At 3:30 A.M., they attacked under the cover of a powerful artillery barrage, supplemented after dawn by Stuka dive-bombers. By 8:30 A.M., the Germans had broken through the first French defense line and then overrun their reserve positions. Soon afterward, the tanks of the 6th Panzer Division began to swarm over a pontoon bridge that had been constructed across the Meuse.

As a fortress division, the 102nd stood a chance of surviving in a fixed position, like the one it was defending on the heights overlooking Monthermé. But once it was ordered to withdraw, its soldiers—without motor transport and compelled to abandon their machine guns, mortars, and antitank guns—were at the mercy of the mechanized might of Reinhardt's panzers. The withdrawal soon turned into a rout. The majority of the division's exhausted soldiers quickly surrendered, simply throwing their weapons into the ditches that lined the roads.

Breaking out of the Monthermé bridgehead, the motorcyclists of the 6th Panzer Division roared past a French munitions dump and past numerous abandoned guns. Riding with the advancing panzers, one soldier, Karl von Stackelberg, described the evidence of the French rout: "All along the side of the road lay dead horses, abandoned baggage wagons, . . . rifles thrown away, steel helmets, saddles, and all kinds of other pieces of equipment. I saw dead Frenchmen lying in the ditches." Later, Stackelberg was astonished to meet a column of French soldiers marching in the opposite direction, in perfect order and led by their own officer. "They had no weapons and did not keep their heads up," he recorded. "They were marching, willingly, without any guard into imprisonment. . . . 20,000 men . . . heading backwards as prisoners."

How was it possible, the historian Alistair Horne has asked, that these French soldiers could allow themselves to go, more or less voluntarily, into imprisonment? French prisoners interrogated by Stackelberg provided the answer: They simply were surprised and overwhelmed by the speed of the panzer advance.

The following day, General Portzert, along with what remained of his 102nd Fortress Division, was captured. The division, which once numbered over 10,000 soldiers, had been reduced to only 1,200 men. It no longer was a fighting unit. Its sister division, the 61st, also was eliminated that day. Its fleeing transport vehicles were easily overrun by Reinhardt's panzers. At 9th Army headquarters, General Vauthier, the commander of the 61st Division, reported that he was the only one remaining from his division, although the next day some 700 to 800 additional men straggled in.

THE FRENCH 2ND ARMORED DIVISION DISSOLVES, MAY 14–16

The only force with any chance of preventing Reinhardt's panzers from pushing unimpeded into the interior of France was the 2nd Armored Division, one of the most formidable units in the French army. But the division had experienced a tough time assembling for combat. Conforming to French practice, its tanks had been loaded onto trains and separated from the division's wheeled elements, some 1,200 vehicles. On the morning of May 14, its commander, General A. C. Bruché, was not sure where all his division's components were located.

The next day, Bruché's division was ordered to Signy, about ten miles west of the Meuse at Charleville-Mézières. However, before its tanks could complete their detraining at the Hirson railway station, the 6th Panzer Division attacked them. Reacting to the sight of the advancing panzers, the train's engineer threw the locomotive into reverse and, traveling at full speed, did not stop until he reached Niort, several hundred miles to the west. The German panzers attacked the 2nd Armored's other tanks as they assembled, scattering those they did not destroy. By the morning of the following day, May 16, the 2nd Armored Division was all over the countryside, out of supplies, and without a communications link with the French high command.

Meanwhile, Reinhardt's panzer columns continued their westward drive. By nightfall on May 15, they had captured Montcornet, thirty-seven miles from the Meuse, and had come within a half-hour's drive of the 9th Army's headquarters at Vervins, some 12 miles to the northwest. Even Reinhardt was surprised by the speed of his panzer corps' advance. It had not only broken through the 9th Army's lines, it was now deep into the French rear defense zone. In fact, by the end of the day, there was very little left of the 9th Army. Its disappearance had created a gap in the French front some 60 miles wide. Through it, the panzers of Hoth's and Reinhardt's panzer corps were pouring, virtually unopposed, into the heartland of France.

THE DEFENSE OF SEDAN

While Corap's army was disintegrating, Huntziger's 2nd Army, farther upstream on the Meuse, was bracing itself for an even more powerful enemy: Kleist's panzer group.

The section of the Meuse alotted to Huntziger's army was in some ways more difficult to defend than Corap's front. Although the river is about 60 yards wide at Sedan, it is less enclosed than farther downriver. In some places, the river's southern bank rises sharply enough to expose defenders to forces attacking from the slopes above the northern banks, but it is also so narrow that it prevents defending infantry from deploying in adequate depth. In addition, enemy troops moving toward the river would find good protection in villages on the north bank such as Donchéry, Bazeilles, and Sedan.

Another major concern of the French defenders was the peninsula formed by the bend in the river just southwest of Sedan. Defending this salient—aptly called the "mushroom of Glaire," not only for its shape but also because Glaire is the largest town on the peninsula—was risky because it would expose French defenders to German fire from three sides. To avoid this problem, the 2nd Army's planners considered, but then quickly abandoned, the idea of moving the defensive line farther south of the river. They concluded that leaving the peninsula undefended would amount to simply giving the Germans a bridgehead on the southern side of the river.

Yet the Sedan sector did offer the defenders important advantages. For one, from the heights of the Marfée Woods, just south of the city, French artillery commanded the entire forward combat zone as far as the Ardennes Forest, some six miles to the north. From this position, French artillery could easily shell German tanks traveling down the narrow, unwooded roads that descended from the forest to the river.

Huntziger, however, hoped to delay the advance of the Germans farther to the north, near the edge of the Ardennes Forest. There the French had erected a forward line of pillboxes that the Germans would have to pass before moving on to Sedan. Each pillbox was held by five or six men who were supposed to set off demolition charges and spray the Germans with small arms fire as they approached. Unfortunately for Sedan's defenders, however, the pillbox garrisons disappeared as soon as they caught sight of the advancing Germans. As a result, the primary French defense line along the southern bank of the Meuse was the only remaining barrier against the advancing Germans.

The French line had been reinforced with barbed wire, trenches, and eight concrete pillboxes deployed roughly every 200 yards along the front,

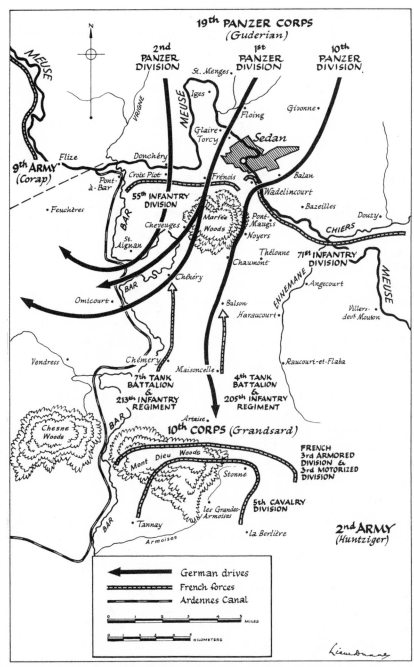

Battle of Sedan, May 13–16. (Shirer, *Collapse of the Third Republic,* Simon and Schuster)

each armed with an anti-tank gun and machine guns. Yet despite what appeared to be a formidable defensive position, the constituent elements of the Sedan front had not been completed before the Germans put them to the test.

The preceding March, a parliamentary report drafted by Pierre Tait-tinger and another deputy, M. Frammond, revealed glaring weaknesses in Sedan's defenses. In some of the defensive works, the report stated, "only the base is finished and the concrete has not even settled. In others, the embrasures, iron doors, anti-gas apparatus, and part of the armament are lacking." For an effective defense to be made on the southern bank of the Meuse, the report concluded, "there remains much to be done."

Gamelin responded to the report by ordering the construction of addi-tional blockhouses midway between the Belgian frontier and the right bank of the Meuse, but they were far from completed when the Germans arrived on the Meuse during the afternoon of May 12. Only 54 of the planned 100 bunkers had been finished, and most of these still had not received their steel doors or the armored shields, which were designed to protect the weapons' embrasures. On the vital Marfée Heights behind Sedan, only one casement, mounting two 75mm guns, was ready when the Germans arrived.

The real weakness in Sedan's defenses, however, lay in its defenders, not in its fortifications. Two of Huntziger's divisions, the 55th and the 71st, were "B" divisions. Most of their men, observed General Claude Grandsard, the commander of the 10th Corps, of which these two divisions and the 3rd North African Division were a part, were "fat and flabby men in their thir-ties who had to be retrained." Their "ardor for work, for training, and their desire to fight," he said, was nonexistent. Their officers were not much better. Only 20 of the 71st Division's 450 officers were "active"; the rest were reservists. And reserve officers made poor leaders. They were reluc-tant to give orders, and what little they did know about soldiering was badly dated. They were, as one junior officer described them, "too old." Like the high command, they tended to think in terms of the last war.

The same thing could not be said of the 2nd Army's commander, Gen-eral Charles Huntziger. Slim, erect, and distinguished-looking, Huntziger was also one of France's more intelligent generals. His officers admired his sharp, incisive mind, infallible memory, and powers of leadership. But most of Huntziger's experience lay in the staff and diplomatic spheres; he knew nothing about mechanized warfare. His main weakness, however, was overconfidence. Three weeks before the German offensive, he was asked by Pierre Jacomet, the Controller General of the Army, "In your opinion, are the Germans going to attack?" Huntziger replied, "Certainly not. On the contrary, they are frightened that we are going to do so!"

Yet Huntziger did become concerned about what was happening in the Ardennes. At 3:30 P.M. on May 12, he sent what was described as an "alarming" telegram to General Georges's headquarters, the gist of which was that his cavalry corps had suffered severe losses in the Ardennes. He asked Georges for additional divisions, including an armored division, and more air support. Because Georges was away from his headquarters, Huntziger's telegram was received by General Roton, Georges's chief of staff. Roton immediately reacted by ordering the 3rd Armored Division and the 3rd Motorized Divisions to head toward Sedan as quickly as possible. In addition, Roton directed General de Lattre de Tassigny's crack 14th Infantry Division, which was far to the east, behind the Maginot Line, to move to Sedan by rail.

By 5:00 P.M., however, Huntziger felt his front was once again "calm," so he advised Roton that there was no urgency in sending the reinforcements. Huntziger believed he had more than enough time, and forces, to prepare for the German attack. The daily report from the operations section of the 2nd Army, which was signed by Huntziger himself, stated that "in spite of pressure from the enemy and the presence of tanks, our front has not been ruptured at any point, and the delaying action occurred under satisfactory conditions."

General Grandsard was also feeling better about the condition of his front. On May 10 he was informed by Huntziger that the 71st Division, which had been held in reserve, was being put at his disposal and should be put into line over the next two nights. Grandsard decided to squeeze it into the front between the 55th and the 3rd North African Divisions. When the commander of the 71st Division, General Baudet, said he would not have enough time to redeploy his division before the Germans arrived, Grandsard tried to reassure him: "The enemy cannot possibly attack today with forces of any size. If he attacks, he will be repelled, and therefore forced to regroup, which will give the 71st time to complete its preparations." However, the 71st Division, still far behind the front at the outbreak of hostilities, did not arrive on the Meuse until late during the night of May 12. Weary after two nights of marching, its soldiers would have to face the Germans the next morning.

Grandsard's confidence was severely jolted as he watched the Germans emerge from the Ardennes Forest during the afternoon of May 12. There was, he recalled, "an almost uninterrupted descent of infantry, armored vehicles, and motorized infantry, . . . at least 200 tanks in the St. Menges area [two miles north of Sedan], . . . another 200 in the outskirts . . . of Sedan." What Grandsard witnessed was the approach of the most formidable concentration of mechanized firepower ever assembled in warfare—Guderian's 1st and 10th Panzer Divisions (the 2nd Panzer was still lagging far behind in the Ardennes Forest).

From the heights above the northern bank of the Meuse, Guderian also was watching as his divisions moved out of the forest and down the slopes leading to the river. Tanks, half-tracks, and mechanized artillery crammed every road and gully. The noise from their engines filled the valley for miles.

One officer, General Charles Menu, wrote later that if the artillery had mounted a full-scale, concerted blow at this assemblage, Guderian's panzers might have been broken up before they even attempted the Meuse crossing. "What a chance," Menu observed, "for the artillery to strike hammer blows" and turn these armored units "into scraps of burnt and twisted metal." But, amazingly, the French artillery did not open up with everything they had. Grandsard later explained that "as a counterattack would have to be launched with as much weight as possible against the Germans massing for the assault, our artillery was very sparing with its ammunition."

Nor was the French air force called in to strike at the concentrated masses of German tanks. The headquarters of the 2nd Army informed the air force that bombers were not needed because there was more than enough artillery on hand to deal with the Germans.

GUDERIAN'S PLAN OF ATTACK, MAY 12

At six o'clock in the evening of May 12, a Fieseler Storch landed near Guderian's command post. The plane would fly him to a meeting with General Kleist at the panzer group's headquarters in Ebly. At that meeting, Kleist emphasized that time was now the critical element in the success of the operation. Not wanting to lose the element of surprise, he directed Guderian to cross the Meuse at 3:00 P.M. the following day.

Guderian at first did not think that Kleist's timetable was realistic. While he was sure the 1st and 10th Panzer Divisions would be in attack positions by 3:00 P.M. the next day, the 2nd Panzer Division, which had run into difficulties along the Semois, would not arrive until later. Without the 2nd Panzer and the corps's artillery, which were also trailing far behind, Guderian feared the attack would not be strong enough to break through the French defenses. He asked Kleist to postpone the crossing one day.

Kleist was one of the more soft-spoken of the senior German commanders. This quality was not, however, what had prompted General Halder to give him the command of the panzer group. Halder had wanted someone who was strong enough to control Guderian's enthusiasm, yet not so cautious that he would hinder the offensive unnecessarily. Kleist fit this role admirably. This time, however, it was Kleist who wanted to strike while the iron was hot, not Guderian. When Guderian continued to object, Kleist cut him short and told him to obey his order to attack the next day, with or without the 2nd Panzer Division and the corps' artillery. Later, Guderian recalled that he had been "obliged to admit that there were probably advantages in thrusting forward immediately without waiting for all our troops to be ready."

Yet there was another part of Kleist's plan that Guderian disliked strongly. Earlier that day, Kleist informed Guderian that he and General Hugo Sperrle, 3rd Air Corps commander, had agreed on a massive, once-and-for-all aerial bombardment of the French positions, one that would be coordinated with the beginning of the artillery barrage. Kleist did not know that Guderian, in early May, had already told General Bruno Loerzer, commander of the 2nd Air Corps, that he wanted "continuous support" of the crossing—not the concentrated bombardment preferred by Kleist—because he believed that this was the best way to keep down the heads of the French defenders while his men were crossing the river. Furthermore, Guderian emphasized to Kleist, the panzer group's artillery assets could not be brought forward in time to support the crossing. Again, Kleist refused to change his mind. The air attack would be massive but relatively short, he told Guderian. With that, Guderian recalled, "the whole attack plan was placed in jeopardy."

Flying back to his headquarters at Bouillon, Guderian's life was also placed in jeopardy. In the waning light of the day, his inexperienced pilot had trouble finding the corps's landing strip. "The next thing I knew," Guderian remembered, "we were on the other side of the Meuse, flying in a slow and unarmed plane over the French positions. An unpleasant moment, I gave my pilot emphatic orders to turn north . . . we just made it."

Safely back at corps headquarters, Guderian drew up the battle plan for the next day. "In view of the very short time at our disposal," he recalled, "we were forced to take the orders used in the war games at Koblenz from our files and, after changing the dates and times, issue these orders for the attack. They were perfectly fitted to the reality of the situation. The only change that had to be made was that, at Koblenz, we had imagined the attack going in at 0900 instead of 1500 hours."

Guderian planned a three-pronged attack. The 1st Panzer Division, in the center, would cross the Meuse at Glaire, a half-mile downstream from Sedan. After scaling the heights of the Marfée Woods, it then would push southward to a line running from the villages of Chéhéry to Chaumont, some two miles south of Sedan. If the 2nd Panzer Division arrived in time, it would lead the attack on Guderian's right flank, crossing the Meuse at Donchéry, two miles west of Sedan. It then would occupy the heights of the Croix-Piot, just south of the river. The 10th Panzer Division, on the corps's left flank, would cross the Meuse just to the southeast of Sedan, near Bazeilles, across from the village of Wadelincourt, and then occupy the heights to the south of the river.

The brunt of the attack, and its success or failure, would rest on the shoulders of a much smaller force: the three rifle battalions of Lieutenant Colonel Hermann Balck's 1st Rifle Regiment, the four battalions of Lieutenant Colonel Graf von Schwerin's *Grossdeutschland* Regiment, and a number of assault engineer companies. It would be their responsibility to cross the river, establish a bridgehead on the far bank, and hold it until the engineers could build a bridge over which the panzers could cross the river.

Once established across the Meuse, Guderian planned on pivoting to the west and then plunging into the French rear. To protect the southern flank of his corps while his panzers advanced westward, he planned on using the *Grossdeutschland* Regiment or the 10th Panzer Division, or both units, if necessary, to occupy the heights around the Mont Dieu Woods and the nearby town of Stonne, ten miles south of Sedan. Obviously, he preferred to have the 10th Panzer Division accompany his other two panzer divisions, since he believed that this would ensure sufficient strength to move deeply into the French defenses. But he also realized that his flank would have to be protected as he drove westward. Ultimately, the size of the forces he could take with him depended on how rapidly the Germans could push infantry units across the Meuse to protect his flank, as well as on how many reinforcements the French could bring into the Sedan area to threaten it.

THE ATTACK BEGINS, MAY 13

The aerial bombardment of the French positions began at 10:00 A.M. on May 13. For four straight hours, in increasing intensity, 200 Stuka dive-bombers and 310 Dornier 17 level bombers, escorted by 200 fighters, pounded the French positions.

The scene was vividly described by a soldier of the 1st Panzer Division, Sergeant Pruemers: "Squadron upon squadron rise to a great height, break into line ahead and there, there the first machines hurtle perpendicularly down, . . . like some bird of prey, they fall upon their victims and then release their load of bombs on target. Each time the explosion is overwhelming, the noise deafening." The Stukas operated in three waves, each with about 40 planes. The first wave came in at about 5,000 feet, attacking with two or three planes at a time, while the second wave hovered above at about 12,000 feet. After the second wave had expended its bombs, the third wave would begin its attack. When the Stukas were finished, the Dorniers resumed their work; then more Stukas followed. Around them fighters buzzed, prepared to pounce on any French fighters that might attempt to interfere with the bombers—few of them appeared that day.

Guderian sighed with relief as he watched the aerial bombardment. Obviously, Kleist's orders for a massive, once-and-for-all bombardment were not being followed. Instead, the Luftwaffe was conducting the sustained attack of several hours' duration that Guderian requested, one designed not only to destroy the French batteries but, even more importantly, to keep the French gunners pinned down as his troops crossed the river.

That was exactly what happened. "The gunners stopped firing and went to the ground," General Edmond Ruby recalled. "Their only concern was to keep their heads well down. They did not dare move. Five hours of this torture was enough to shatter their nerves. They became incapable of reacting to the approaching enemy infantry."

Later that day, Guderian asked General Loerzer what had caused the change in Kleist's plan. Shrugging his shoulders, Loerzer replied that Kleist's orders had arrived "well, let's say, too late. They would have muddled the air fleet. So I didn't pass them on."

What was particularly demoralizing to the French soldiers was the almost total absence of their own fighters over Sedan. Why, they asked, were they being bombed with impunity? Where was the fighter protection they had been promised?

On the night of May 11, about the time Guderian's panzer corps had reached the Semois River, General Billotte, the commander of Army Group 1, had given priority for the use of aircraft to the 1st and 7th Armies and the BEF in northern Belgium. It was not until 4:00 P.M. on May 12 that General Georges ordered first priority to go to the 2nd Army and the second to the 1st Army. But Billotte ignored this order and directed two-thirds of the aerial support to the 1st Army and only one-third to the 2nd Army. Not until the morning of May 13, after aerial reconnaissance the previous night had confirmed the presence of German armor approaching Sedan, did Billotte give first priority to the 2nd Army.

As for the RAF, it spent the day licking its wounds from three cruel days of combat in northern Belgium. On May 10, the RAF lost 40 percent of all its sorties. It lost 100 percent the following day and 62 percent on May 12. By evening of that day, the British had only 72 serviceable bombers available in France. That evening Air Marshal Barratt received a communication from the Chief of the Air Staff in London: "We cannot continue indefinitely at this rate of intensity. . . . If we expend all our efforts in the early stages of the battle, we shall not be able to operate effectively when the critical phases come." Yet *this* was the critical phase of the battle. Beyond the Meuse, virtually nothing stood between the Germans and the English Channel. Nevertheless, Barratt did nothing to help the defenders at Sedan. The British Blenheims and Battles were sent off to bomb crossroads near Breda in Holland.

The Luftwaffe's attacks on the Sedan sector began to intensify after 2:00 P.M., culminating an hour later with a massed raid of 900 to 1,000 aircraft. At 3:30 P.M., Guderian's artillery, having finally arrived at the front just in the nick of time, joined the Luftwaffe in a combined one-half-hour, concentrated bombardment in preparation for the river assault. Then, almost precisely at four o'clock, the inferno eased. From the German side of the river, the entire Meuse Valley seemed to be a thick blanket of smoke. Taking advantage of the cover this offered, the Germans moved their weapons—20mm and 37mm automatic cannons, along with the new 88mm antiaircraft guns—out of cover and down to the very edge of the river. These guns fired point-blank into the French bunkers and gun emplacements barely 100 yards away. One by one, the guns in the French bunkers were smashed, their crews blinded by splinters or horribly mutilated by shells exploding within the bunkers' restricted interiors. Many of the defenders fled in panic. Yet many remained to fight.

While the bombardment was still in progress, German infantry—soldiers from the *Grossdeutschland* Regiment, the 1st Infantry Regiment, and the 1st Motorcycle Battalion—began crossing the Meuse on rubber boats only partially concealed by the smoke and dust of the bombardment.

Because the *Grossdeutschland* was a crack unit specializing in tough operations, Guderian had earmarked it for the role of smashing a hole in the French lines, one through which the tanks of the 1st Panzer Division could pour. Lieutenant Colonel Graf von Schwerin, the regiment's commander, had more than pride and his reputation at stake in the task that lay before him. Guderian, a few months before, had expressed dismay at the way, it seemed to him, that infantry units were prone to sleep rather than march at night. Schwerin bet him a bottle of champagne that this would not be said about the *Grossdeutschland*. Throughout April, he ran his troops through a series of rugged toughening-up exercises that included marching on short rations, crossing the Mosel River in rubber rafts, and night attacks.

At noon on May 13, Schwerin arrived in Floing, less than a mile from where his regiment was to cross the river. Jauntily carrying a stick, he inspected his men as they packed their weapons and readied their equipment. His men had been issued their rations, their field flasks had been filled with coffee, and their weapons had been loaded. Schwerin was confident his men would not fail.

Some of the men were uneasy about the unnatural stillness of Floing. Senior Lieutenant von Courbiere, commander of the 6th Company, 2nd Battalion, wondered whether the French had been hit so hard by the aerial bombardment that they could not react to the infantry buildup, or whether they were just waiting for the Germans to enter the river, when they would be most vulnerable.

Courbiere soon found out. As the first raft entered the water, between Torcy and Glaire, the French guns opened up, shooting it to pieces and killing all of its occupants. The second raft met the same fate. At this point, a German half-track, carrying a 37mm flak gun, opened up on the French bunkers, but the third boat also was shot up. Only after two 75mm armored assault guns were brought up and fired several rounds of ammunition were most of the French bunkers finally silenced.

At 4:50 P.M., the *Grossdeutschland*'s 2nd Battalion crossed the river. The men quickly got out of their rubber rafts and spread out through the village of Glaire, with its vegetable gardens, ramshackle tool sheds, and barns. Most of the French infantry were stunned, shocked, and deafened by the German bombardment, and most of their guns were clogged with dirt and debris. Through the turmoil of swirling dust and smoke, the German infantry suddenly appeared and rushed forward before the French defenders had a chance to recover.

The German infantry made short work of the French bunkers. One was knocked out with hand grenades, its defenders emerging with hands above their heads and their faces etched by the strain of the tortuous bombardment. In another bunker, a barn that had concealed a French anti-tank gun, Lieutenant Courbiere's men were delighted to discover a cache of soda water bottles. They were emptied quickly as the Germans slaked the ravenous thirst they acquired fighting their way from the river's edge.

In the distance, some two miles away, Courbiere could clearly make out his company's primary objective, Hill 247, which was located between the towns of Frénois and Wadelincourt, on the edge of the slope leading up to the Marfée Woods. But their advance to the hill was stymied by French gunfire from the neighboring towns of Torcy and Les Forges. The shelling from Torcy was soon ended by soldiers from the *Grossdeutschland*'s 3rd Company, while the resistance in Les Forges was broken by soldiers of the 1st Infantry Regiment, which had crossed the Meuse just to the east of the *Grossdeutschland*.

The 1st Infantry Regiment Crosses, May 13

The 1st Infantry Regiment was led by one of the most capable members of Germany's officer corps, Lieutenant Colonel Hermann Balck. A highly decorated veteran of World War I, Balck was described as "a notorious optimist with a reputation for ruthless aggression," qualities that would help him rise through the ranks from lieutenant colonel to the command of an army group by the end of the war. It was the great misfortune of the 55th French Infantry Division that it had to face a regiment commanded by Balck.

Accompanying his soldiers to the Meuse's edge at 3:00 P.M., Balck discovered that his regiment's transportation column had delivered rubber assault rafts for the river crossing, all right, but their operators were nowhere in sight. Apparently someone had forgotten to tell the engineers where to go. Balck tried to get the *Grossdeutschland*'s engineers to operate his rafts, but their commander refused, telling Balck that his soldiers were assault engineers, not boat pilots. Fortunately for Balck, he had trained his soldiers to use the rubber rafts, so he decided to let them do it. Balck led the first wave across the river.

Balck's regiment had a much easier time crossing the Meuse than did the *Grossdeutschland*. Ordinarily, the French artillery and machine-gun fire would have decimated the assault boats. But the French pillboxes and artillery positions had either been silenced, or their crews remained pinned down, by the intense German aerial and ground bombardment. The bunker defenders who survived the bombardment were too stunned to offer effective resistance. And, again, many of their weapons were too clogged with dust to fire. Even if the French defenders had been able to fire their guns, the smoke that filled the valley made it hard for them to see the German assault rafts crossing the river.

Yet one French sergeant, who was in charge of the bunker in Glaire, was able to see "large numbers" of German rubber rafts crossing the river. However, when he moved forward to fire at them, his machine gun jammed. He had no more luck with the artillery barrage he tried to arrange; he could not get through to the artillery units. The phone wires, which the French had failed to bury underground, had been broken by the German bombardment. Nevertheless, some of the French positions were able to fire their machine guns on the approaching German boats, and some of them were shot up. But most of the rafts managed to get across the river, with what Guderian described later as relatively light losses.

Leaping from their rubber boats, Balck's men dashed for the French forward bunkers and attacked them with machine guns, flamethrowers, and powder charges. The bunkers were soon silenced. Balck's men then began advancing toward their next objective, the second line of French bunkers, which extended from the northwestern slope of Hill 247 through the town of Frénois and then to the road junction at Bellevue.

About six o'clock, after watching the attack from the northern heights overlooking the Meuse, Guderian became impatient. He wanted to be a part of the action. He went down to the river, crossed it, and joined Balck's regiment. On the far bank, he was greeted by the regiment's commander with the words: "Joyriding in canoes on the Meuse is forbidden!" This was the same expression Guderian had used in one of the precombat exercises months before to dampen what he thought was the "lighthearted" attitude of the division's younger officers. "I now relaxed," Guderian admitted. Those seemingly nonchalant officers "had judged the situation correctly. The attack was developing as though it were being carried out on maneuvers."

THE COLLAPSE OF THE FRÉNOIS LINE, MAY 13

Meanwhile, the French sergeant in charge of the bunker at Glaire ordered his men to pull back to the next defensive line, the blockhouse near Frénois, a half-mile to the south. Balck's men immediately came after them, destroying some bunkers as they moved but leaving others behind for follow-on troops to destroy. To the surprise of the Germans, they found many of the bunkers abandoned. Their French defenders apparently had fled without fighting.

Near the Château de Bellevue, on the second French defensive line, just west of Frénois, two blockhouses (numbers 103 and 104), under the command of Second Lieutenant Verron, were still resisting the advancing Germans. However, both blockhouses were isolated, not only from one another but also from their division's headquarters. The only communication link they had were foot runners. Since the battle erupted on May 10, their only contact with the outside had been a delivery of soup.

More critical to the defense of the French blockhouses than communications, however, was infantry support. This was especially true for Blockhouse 103, which Lieutenant Verron occupied, than it was for its neighbor, Blockhouse 104. Much of the terrain surrounding Blockhouse 103 could not be covered by its guns. To the north, the movement of advancing Germans could be concealed by a slope that rose from a nearby stream. The blockhouse's line of sight also was obstructed by a neighboring orchard. Infantry were needed to cover these positions to prevent the Germans from attacking the blockhouse from its blind sides. Earlier that morning, however, Verron had watched a mass of French soldiers fleeing to the rear without their weapons. One of the soldiers told him that there was no one left to defend the bunkers to the north.

Nevertheless, even without infantry support, both of the blockhouses under Verron's command were resisting. However, just before six o'clock that evening, they were attacked by German dive-bombers and the infantry of the *Grossdeutschland* Regiment, including Lieutenant Courbiere's 6th Company, which by this time had advanced up from the river. Although Verron's blockhouse received a direct hit by a Stuka-delivered bomb, it was not heavily damaged. But the explosion did injure some of its defenders. Soon afterward, however, a grenade exploded in the blockhouse's air vent. In furious close-in fighting with the German attackers, the defenders' machine gun was put out of action. Verron had no choice but to surrender. After he and his men filed out of the blockhouse, they watched helplessly as the Germans attacked Blockhouse 104, about a half-mile to the east.

Unlike Verron's blockhouse, number 104 could fire in all directions, preventing the Germans from moving large numbers of troops forward.

Nevertheless, this blockhouse fell an hour later, after firing more than 10,000 cartridges and losing more than half of its defenders, killed or wounded. Its surrender gave the Germans control of the road leading south from Bellevue, meaning that they had not only broken through the second line of Sedan's defenses, they also had shut off the covering fire this position had rained upon the 2nd Panzer Division, holding up its crossing at Donchéry.

Shortly after his capture, Lieutenant Verron was taken before an unidentified German general. The officer looked over Verron for a short while and then ordered him to be returned to his men. Verron never could figure out why a German general would want to see a captured French officer but not interrogate him.

What is significant about this episode, however, is the fact that the German general was located only a few hundred yards from the decisive action that was taking place around Frénois. In contrast, the French generals remained far to the rear, where French military doctrine held that they could best oversee and direct the entire battle. But rooted in their distant command posts, French generals could not really know what was going on at the front, nor could they make the quick decisions that were often necessary to win a battle. Moreover, from the rear of the battle zone, it was difficult to inspire soldiers fighting on the front to make the sacrifices that were required of them.

As early evening gave way to dusk, Balck's men were exhausted. But he would not let them rest. He kept pressing them to continue the attack, to carry the bridgehead as far forward as possible. With French resistance at this point almost nonexistent, Balck did not want to pay a higher price the next day for territory that was available so cheaply now. By midnight, his soldiers had advanced to a point just south of Cheveuges, near the southern edge of the Marfée Woods, almost five miles from the spot where they had crossed the Meuse only eight hours earlier.

By 3:30 A.M. on May 14, Balck's 2nd Battalion had advanced another two miles, to Chéhéry, while his 1st Battalion secured nearby La Boulette and the 3rd Battalion encamped for the night near the St. Quentin farm, about a mile and a half northwest of the town of Bulson. By occupying these positions, Balck's battalions protected the vulnerable flanks of the 1st Panzer Division's bridgehead. However, by advancing as deeply as it did, some five miles from the river, Balck's Regiment resembled an extended and exposed neck that could have been severed by an aggressive French counterattack. And in this early stage of the crossing, Guderian had no tanks on the southern bank of the river to protect them. Fortunately for Balck, the *Grossdeutschland* Regiment was advancing on his left, toward Bulson and Maisoncelle. After reaching these positions, the two regiments would be in line, adding greater strength to the shoulders of the bridgehead.

The Crossing of the 10th Panzer Division, May 13

The 10th Panzer Division had a much tougher time crossing the Meuse than did its neighbor, the 1st Panzer. Before reaching the river, at Bazeilles, about a half-mile upstream from Sedan, its infantry had to traverse flat, open terrain leading to the water's edge. While doing this, they were within the sights of French machine gunners nestled in bunkers across the river. These bunkers, which were largely missed by the German bombers and artillery, saturated the assault forces with devastatingly accurate fire and pinned down most of the assault troops before they could get to the river. Those that were able to enter the water were quickly shot up: only two of the first 50 rafts that entered the river managed to survive the crossing.

Unfortunately for the French, however, a few German soldiers did manage to get across about 7:30 P.M. They were led by Sergeant Rubarth, who was attached to the 48th Engineer Battalion. Rubarth's men entered the river in a hail of French machine-gun fire. Because there were only two rubber rafts available, Rubarth had to squeeze four men into each raft instead of the usual three they carried. However, the extra weight from the additional man, plus the weight of the heavy equipment they were carrying—wire cutters, grenades, and hollow charges—brought the water perilously close to the tops of the rubber rafts. Rubarth ordered his men to throw out all unnecessary ballast, including entrenching tools. "No digging in for us," he said, "either we get through, or that's the end."

To the Germans, the 60-yard-wide river seemed like 60 miles of hell, with bullets whizzing all around them. To throw off the aim of the French gunners, Rubarth ordered one of his men to fire a machine gun into the weapon slits of a particularly menacing bunker straight ahead of them. The gunner used another man's shoulder to steady his aim in the wildly unstable raft.

The Germans got across, blazing away at the bunker's gun slits with their machine guns, as they ran toward it from the river's edge. Within minutes, the bunker was silenced. The Germans then moved on to the next bunker, where they used a hollow charge followed by grenades to blast out the defenders. After a brief fight, the surviving French soldiers emerged with white flags. A few seconds later, a swastika was flying over the bunker. "From the other bank," Rubarth recalled, we heard "the sound of loud cheers from our comrades."

Rubarth's men continued advancing. After wading through a swamp, where they were often up to their thighs in water, they knocked out two more bunkers. In a matter of minutes, Rubarth's engineers had punched a gap in the first French defense line over 100 yards wide. They then pushed onto a railway embankment about 100 yards from the river's edge before they were stopped by French machine-gun fire. For Rubarth, the situation was now critical. With only a few men on the French side of the Meuse, his ammunition was almost exhausted. The time was ideal for a French counterattack, and one began just then. Fortunately for the Germans, they were able to beat it off before their ammunition expired.

Even more fortunate was the timely arrival of a fresh detachment of German assault engineers, who had just crossed the river. Gradually, more and more German infantry came over. With these reinforcements, Rubarth blasted a gap in the second line of French bunkers. By nightfall, exhausted and having lost six dead and three wounded out of his original 11-man squad, Rubarth reached his primary objective, the heights above Wadelincourt. All totaled, Rubarth's men had destroyed four French bunkers along the Meuse and three more behind the river, making it possible for the 10th Panzer Division to get a bridgehead on the south side of the river. For his remarkable actions this day, Rubarth was awarded the Iron Cross and a lieutenant's commission.

By midnight, the infantry of the 10th Panzer Division were advancing up the eastern slope of the Marfée Woods. They spent the whole night cleaning out French artillery batteries and machine-gun nests in the vicinity of the woods. Even though Sergeant Major Schulze's company had lost half of its men, its commander called on them to make one more effort. "Men," he cried, "this will be the last! We must pursue at once, the main job has been done, and the enemy is fleeing!"

"With our last bit of strength," Schulze recounted, "we combed Thélonne. We met only feeble resistance in the village proper, and this we broke with carbines and hand grenades." But the company was completely worn down by its "last effort." "The men, exhausted, dropped into the grass," Schulze's account continued. "The troops that had not yet seen action climbed down from their vehicles and took up the pursuit."

The "last effort" of Schulze's men was duplicated in platoon after platoon and company after company in the 10th Panzer Division. It explains why the French quickly lost any chance to destroy the bridgehead at Sedan. The Germans threw wave after wave of fresh troops and weapons into the breaches so quickly that the French never had time to react. This continued all through the night. And even though the first and second waves of attackers suffered heavy casualties—as much as 50 percent in the first assaults made by the 10th Panzer Division—reinforcements were almost immediately sent in to replace the men who were lost. There was never a letup in the German advance.

THE 2ND PANZER DIVISION CROSSES, MAY 13

Of the three divisions in Guderian's 19th Panzer Corps, the 2nd Panzer Division experienced the greatest difficulty getting across the Meuse River. The division's slow advance through the Ardennes—largely because of the poor roads it was assigned—had delayed its arrival on the Meuse. It finally approached the river late in the afternoon of May 13, at Donchéry, about two miles west of Sedan. However, only the division's advance elements, the reconnaissance battalion and the motorcycle battalion, together with the division's heavy artillery, were available for the crossing. In fact, even these elements had trouble getting to the river. They were stopped cold in front of Donchéry by deadly accurate flanking fire from French guns deployed across the river in Bellevue, Glaire, and Villette. Finally, some panzers were brought up and began firing at the French positions. The ensuing fight was described by the French commander at Donchéry.

> Our artillery and mortars fired . . . very effectively. But the enemy did not stop bringing tanks—about 60 came . . . between 13.00 and 14.30 hours—and placed his armored vehicles under the protection of the railway embankment so well that at 15.00 hours he . . . was able to fire simultaneously at our blockhouses with 60 tanks at a time. . . . Having thus "treated" each blockhouse, he continued his fire on the other machine gun and submachine gun emplacements.

The systematic shelling of the French bunkers finally enabled the 2nd Panzer's advance units to move up to the railway embankment in front of the river. But it did not stop the French flanking fire coming from across the river. In fact, exposed to this intense French artillery fire, the division's assault engineers were unable to even enter the river, let alone cross it. Even after panzers were enlisted to carry the engineers and their boats to the very edge of the river, the Germans were forced back by the French bunker fire. The panzers desperately tried to knock out the bunkers, but with the late-afternoon sun glistening brilliantly on the hills lining the southern side of the Meuse, they found it extremely difficult to pinpoint the French positions.

The battle raged for hours, with tracer shells whizzing back and forth across the river like a fireworks show. "We fired off shell after shell, always at the recognized bunkers to try to silence them," Sergeant Major Keddig remembered. "It became unbearably hot inside the panzer's turret, which was filled with powder smoke. A beautiful summer evening lay across the countryside. But the firing of the French artillery continued with undiminished violence. We couldn't dream of opening any of the panzers' hatches."

Finally, about 10:00 P.M., one of the German assault rafts made it across the river, followed by more throughout the night. The crossing was made possible only because soldiers belonging to Balck's 1st Infantry Regiment moved westward along the southern bank of the river and knocked out the bunkers that had been firing on the 2nd Panzer Division. By the next morning, May 14, the 2nd Panzer finally was able to establish a toehold on the southern bank of the Meuse.

THE PANIC OF THE FRENCH 55TH INFANTRY DIVISION, MAY 13

At 6:00 P.M. on May 13, about three hours after the German crossing of the Meuse started, General Lafontaine, commander of the French 55th Infantry Division, was analyzing the situation from his command post at Fond-Dagot, five miles south of Sedan. The situation seemed to be improving. The German aerial bombardment had stopped, and he had succeeded in establishing liaison with Corap's 53rd Infantry Division on his left flank. Moreover, the battalion he had dispatched to reinforce the position in the Marfée Woods appeared to have checked the German advance in that sector.

Suddenly, however, a wave of terrified soldiers, in trucks and on foot, many firing their weapons madly in the air, swept down the road from Bulson. "The tanks are at Bulson!" they shouted. It gradually became apparent that most of the men were from the 285th Infantry Regiment and the 147th Fortress Regiment, the garrison that was charged with the defenses at Frénois.

Lafontaine, with a number of his officers, ran out in front of this rampaging mob, firing his revolver in vain to stop it. Then he ordered trucks placed across the road in an attempt to block the way south, but the panicked soldiers simply poured around them. The mad flight continued throughout the night and did not stop for most of the fugitives until they reached Reims, 60 miles away. In their wake, the fleeing soldiers left behind ration and ammunition wagons, infantry weapon carriers, horses, motor vehicles, and, most importantly, their artillery.

General Lafontaine later blamed the panic on the fact that the division was composed primarily of reservists. "Without combat experience," he said, "they were surprised by the violence of the gun fire and . . . numerous units abandoned their positions in disorder under the threat of approaching tanks." Many of the men who fled, however, believed they had been abandoned by the French high command. They saw little or no effort by the French air force to defend them during the long and tortuous German aerial and ground bombardment.

They also were unsettled by news that General Lafontaine had decided (around 6:00 P.M.) to move his command post from Fond-Dagot to Chémery. Although the move was made ostensibly to enable him to direct a counterattack more effectively, the haste with which the command post moved out, leaving vehicles, equipment, and disrupted communications in its wake, obviously increased the fear of soldiers whose nerves were already frayed raw by the terrible bombardment they had experienced that day. "Our officers have abandoned us" were words that spread like wildfire.

Regardless of the reasons for the panic, its effects were catastrophic. In an army that had indoctrinated its soldiers with the importance of artillery support, the loss of almost all the division's artillery was a staggering blow. As a result, instead of blanketing the enemy's crossing sites with massive amounts of artillery, the division did little more than disturb the German soldiers in their vulnerable bridgehead.

THE FRENCH HIGH COMMAND AWAKENS, MAY 13

The news from Sedan slowly filtered into the headquarters of Georges and Gamelin. At 9:25 P.M. Georges passed on to Gamelin a report filed at 5:00 P.M. by General Huntziger, stating that a "small slice had been bitten off south of Sedan." Huntziger added that he was calling up the 3rd Armored Division to attack it. At 11:45 P.M. Georges sent Gamelin another report from Huntziger that stated: "Our units are fighting in the Marfée Woods. . . . We are calm here." But Huntziger's latest report was misleading because French units were no longer fighting in the Marfée Woods. In fact, they were in flight considerably south of the woods. Nor did Huntziger make any mention of the disaster that had befallen the 55th Division. More importantly, three panzer divisions had gained a substantial bridgehead south of the Meuse, roughly five miles deep and five miles wide.

BRIDGING THE MEUSE, MAY 13–14

While the Germans had succeeded in crossing the Meuse, their hold on the south side of the river was still extremely precarious. Guderian still had no panzers and little artillery on the far side of the river as dusk arrived on May 13. Like Rommel to the north, he worried that the French might launch a counterattack and crush his unprotected infantry before the first panzers could be brought across the river.

At Gaulier, opposite Glaire, Guderian spent an anxious evening watching his engineers build a 16-ton bridge over the river. Senior Lieutenant Grubnau, the engineers' commander, recalled how he was astonished at "how easily heavy bridge-building could be carried out" that day. It seemed "that the French were expecting our bridge to be built at another place." Although French shells fell within 50 yards of the bridge, the village of Glaire blocked direct observation of it from the French side of the river.

Grubnau's engineers were fortunate in another way. They had arrived on the Meuse with only 70 meters of bridging material; the rest had been used up in building the bridge over the Semois the previous day. As luck would have it, the engineers found a section of the river just under 70 meters in width. If the French air force or artillery had destroyed only one section of this bridge, it could not have been completed, certainly not as quickly as it was. This bridge became operational at two o'clock in the morning.

Farther upstream, on the southeastern edge of Sedan, the engineers of the 10th Panzer Division also were building a bridge across the river. It was not completed, however, until 5:45 on the morning of May 14. The engineers of the 2nd Panzer Division did not begin their bridge near Donchéry until eight o'clock that morning. Continued French artillery fire was responsible for the delay. The bridge was not completed until 4:00 A.M. on May 15, almost thirty hours after the division's first assault rafts began crossing the river.

Guderian was very pleased that at least some of his panzers were getting across the Meuse. He returned to his headquarters to prepare the operational orders for the new day, which, he felt, would "bring a decision." At the same time, he could not resist sending a telegram to General Ernst Busch, the commander of the 16th Army who, at that meeting with Hitler the previous March, had bet him a bottle of champagne that he would never get across the Meuse, let alone during the fourth day of the campaign. Busch responded with a congratulatory telegram—and a bottle of champagne.

By the time Guderian returned to his headquarters, his chief of staff, Colonel Walther Nehring, had begun planning the day's moves. His operational order for May 14 reflected the intelligence estimate that French armored forces would reach the corps's forward positions sometime during the morning. Nehring's plan called for the 1st Panzer Division to continue its advance toward Bulson and then turn due west toward Rethel, with its left flank perpendicular to the Aisne River. The 2nd Panzer Division would also turn west and advance toward Poix-Terron, then head southwest toward Rethel. The 10th Panzer Division would be left behind to protect the corps's left flank by advancing south, directly east of Bulson and on toward Stonne. Nehring, recognizing the extreme vulnerability of the bridge at Gaulier, also ordered all available flak guns concentrated around the crossing site. The bridge had to be protected at all costs, since it carried not only panzers but also the vitally important supplies required to sustain the advance.

At the same time, at the headquarters of the 1st Army Group, its commander, General Billotte, was doing all he could to make sure the Gaulier bridge was destroyed. At 10:00 P.M. on May 13, he had called General d'Astier, commander of the French air force on the 1st Army Group's front, to inform him that the situation at Sedan was becoming "more grave." Billotte insisted that the air force must destroy the Sedan bridges "as soon as possible"—that night, if they could. When d'Astier pointed out that it was "practically impossible" to bomb a bridge in darkness, Billotte asked him to try anyway: "Victory or defeat," he said, "hangs on those bridges."

French as well as British fliers responded the next day, May 14, by carrying out suicidal attacks on the Gaulier bridge. Protected by French fighters, 170 French and British bombers, of which about 100 were Blenheims, swept over the Sedan valley trying to cut the vital artery of Guderian's panzer corps. To protect the bridge, the Germans concentrated all their available aircraft over Gaulier and surrounded the bridge with some 200 antiaircraft guns.

Major Johann Adolf Kielmansegg described the Allied air attacks on the Gaulier bridge:

> The summer landscape with the quietly flowing river, the light green of the meadows bordered by the darker summits of the more distant heights, spanned by a brilliantly blue sky, is filled with the racket of war. For hours at a time, the dull explosions of the bombs, the quick tack-tack of

the machine guns, . . . mingles with the droning of the aircraft motors and the roar of the division passing over the bridge unimpeded. . . . Again and again, an enemy aircraft crashes out of the sky, dragging a long black plume of smoke behind it. . . . Occasionally, from the falling planes, one or two white parachutes release themselves and float slowly to earth. . . . In the short time that I am at the bridge, barely an hour, eleven planes alone were brought down.

In fact, by the end of the day the British had lost 45 of the bombers they had committed, while the French lost five. Yet the Gaulier bridge remained intact. Had it been damaged, even slightly, the German bridgehead on the south side of the Meuse would have become precarious; most of the Germans' bridging equipment had been used up in traversing the Ardennes Forest. It would have taken hours to bring additional materials forward.

Toward midday, to Guderian's delight, General Gerd von Rundstedt, the commander of Army Group A, arrived to have a look at the crossing. Guderian talked with him right in the middle of the Gaulier bridge while an air attack was in progress.

Rundstedt asked dryly: "Is it always like this here?"

Guderian could only reply, Yes, it was.

Rundstedt then expressed his deep appreciation for the achievements of Guderian and his soldiers.

Lafontaine's Counterattack, May 14

A dozen miles to the south of Bulson, two agitated French officers arrived at Senuc about 9:00 P.M. on May 13 demanding to see General Huntziger. They told him that they had seen German tanks at Vendresse, ten miles southwest of Sedan. Huntziger was furious; he berated the two officers and called them liars. What they had seen were not German panzers, he said, but tanks belonging to the 10th Corps's 7th Tank Battalion.

Earlier that day, General Grandsard had ordered these French tank battalions to counterattack the German bridgehead. Along with the 213th Infantry Regiment, the 7th Battalion was to move from Chémery north toward Cheveuges. They would be supported on their right flank by the 4th Tank Battalion and the 205th Infantry Regiment, which were directed to move from Maisoncelle toward Bulson and then on toward the German positions near the Meuse. Grandsard had ordered the counterattack, which was placed under the overall command of General Lafontaine, to start at 3:00 P.M., an hour before the German assault began. But the slowness of the participating units in moving up to the front, and their fear of German bombing once they did, forced Grandsard to delay the counterattack's starting time until after nightfall. In fact, it would not begin until the next morning, May 14.

In the meantime, at Chémery, where General Lafontaine had retreated with his staff after the 55th Division's panic at Fond-Dagot, pandemonium still reigned. In his makeshift command post, with hardly any communications or headquarters facilities, the harassed general sat down to plan the counterattack Grandsard had ordered. Outside in the darkness, fugitives were still swarming southward. Lafontaine had no idea which units he could count on for the counterattack.

Toward midnight on May 14, he sent out three officers to different locations to find out. The first officer failed to return, the second could not get through, and the third—who had been ordered to rendezvous with the 7th Tank Battalion—arrived to find its tanks engulfed by waves of fleeing troops. In the confusion, Lafontaine realized that the counterattack would have to be delayed. About 1:00 A.M., he decided to drive to Grandsard's headquarters at La Berlière. But the roads were choked with traffic, so he returned to Chémery, where Lieutenant Colonel Pierre Labarthe, the commander of the 213th Infantry Regiment, was waiting for him.

Labarthe, whose troops were to participate in the counterattack, expressed his strong misgivings about the planned operation. Although he was regarded as the best regimental commander in the division, the sight of fleeing soldiers, the continued reports of "tanks at Bulson," and the disorganization that still prevailed in the panic's wake apparently unnerved him. He could not assure Lafontaine that his men would not also bolt for the rear. "Whatever happens," he implored Lafontaine, "no counterattack!" But just then Lieutenant Colonel Cachou, Grandsard's deputy chief of staff, arrived with an order to begin the counterattack at dawn. Angry as he left, Labarthe told Lafontaine: "General, you're sending my regiment on a mission of sacrifice."

At 2:00 A.M. on May 14, General Georges called Captain Beaufre at General Headquarters Montry. "Ask General Doumenc to come immediately,"

Georges said. Within a half an hour, Doumenc and Beaufre arrived at Georges's headquarters at Le Ferté. The atmosphere in Georges's office was, Beaufre remembered, like a "watch over the dead." The lights were dim; a staff officer was on the phone, repeating in a low voice the information he was receiving. The others were silent. General Roton, Georges's chief of staff, was slumped dejectedly in a chair.

As Doumenc entered the room, Georges quickly jumped to his feet and approached him. "Our Sedan front is broken!" he said, his face white with panic. "There's been a collapse." He then fell back into his chair, stifling a sob.

Doumenc was flabbergasted. Reacting swiftly, he said, "General, this is war. In war there are always incidents like these." Georges countered by describing the rout of the 55th Division and by repeating the rumor that there were German tanks in Bulson. He then broke into sobs.

For a moment, everyone was too overcome to speak. "Come, General," Doumenc finally said. "Every war has seen its routs. Come over to the map. We'll see what can be done." Walking over to the wall map, Doumenc confidently sketched out a plan. It was essential, he said, to plug the gap. The 1st Armored Division, then still at Charleroi, could be sent to reinforce Corap. The 3rd Armored Division, just south of Sedan, could counterattack toward the north. The 2nd Armored Division, en route to the Dyle Line, could be transferred to Vervins and also put into the counterattack. These three divisions, comprising 600 tanks, could attack the German bridgehead and hurl the Germans back into the Meuse. The 3rd Armored could begin the counterattack that morning.

Doumenc's forceful handling of the crisis had a calming effect on Georges's shattered staff. Georges quickly ratified all of Doumenc's proposals. Beaufre turned up the lights and roused the mess cook to make coffee. Soon afterward, Doumenc and Beaufre returned to Montry, confident that the night's "evil spell" had been banished from Georges's headquarters.

※

Lafontaine's counterattack did not get going until seven o'clock on the morning of May 14. On the left, the 213th Infantry Regiment, led by the 7th Tank Battalion, began advancing north from Chémery toward Chéhéry. On its right, the 71st Division's 205th Infantry Regiment, with the 4th Tank Battalion in the vanguard, began moving north from Maisoncelle toward Bulson at 7:45 A.M. Fifteen minutes earlier, Georges incorrectly informed Gamelin that the "breach at Sedan has been contained and that the counterattack with strong formations was carried out at 4:30 A.M." In fact, the "strong" French counterattack ran smack into the 1st Panzer Division's 2nd Panzer Regiment.

The 2nd Panzer Regiment was the first German armored unit across the Meuse. Although its lead panzers began crossing the bridge at Gaulier at two o'clock that morning, it took until 8:00 A.M. to get the regiment's 1st Battalion across the river. Had the French counterattack gone in as planned, at 4:00 A.M., Balck's infantry, just south of Chéhéry, probably would have been overrun.

Guderian, as usual, left his command post at 6:30 that morning and drove directly to the front. German air reconnaissance had told him that enemy motorized and tank columns were heading toward his 1st Panzer Division. He ordered the immediate dispatch of all available tanks and anti-tank units to meet them. If the French counterattack were successful, Guderian believed, the entire campaign could be lost.

The 2nd Panzer Regiment's 1st Battalion was sent toward Bulson. Its 2nd Battalion was directed toward Chémery. By 8:30 the tanks of the 2nd Battalion were engaged in heavy combat with the French near Connage, on the Bar River midway between Chémery and Chéhéry. At about the same time, the 1st Battalion's panzers collided with French forces around Bulson. To the great relief of the German infantry holding the southern end of the Meuse bridgehead, including Balck's 1st Infantry Regiment near Chémery, the panzers arrived in the nick of time, only minutes before the French 213th Regiment and 7th Tank Battalion began their counterattack.

THE PANZERS ATTACK, MAY 14

Just behind the 2nd Panzer Regiment, the tanks of the 1st Panzer Regiment crossed the Meuse and also moved toward the French positions. Just as its panzers were approaching Bulson, eight French tanks appeared south of the town. Seven of them were quickly destroyed by the panzers' guns. The survivors began pulling back from Bulson, pursued by the 2nd Panzer Regiment. The commander of one of its panzer companies described the ensuing battle:

> Close to the Chémery road, east of Maisoncelle, . . . ten French tanks, grouped together closely in a column, appeared. In a flash, the panzer company opened fire with every gun barrel. The enemy was completely surprised. He did not fire a single round. Three vehicles turned toward the south and, although hit, managed to escape. Four tanks remained in place, one of them burning in a fiery blaze. Although the other three vehicles could turn and drive back into the village, they were nevertheless so badly damaged that their crews abandoned them.

By 9:00 A.M. on May 14, the counterattack of the French 4th Tank Battalion was over. Although the battalion had fought bravely, it attacked in piecemeal fashion without coordinating its movement with the 7th Battalion of tanks on its left, and as a result was quickly decimated by the German panzers, losing three-quarters of its tanks in the battle around Maisoncelle alone. Its supporting infantry regiment, the 205th Regiment, also fell back in disorder.

The western wing of the French counterattack, comprising the 7th Tank Battalion and the 213th Infantry Regiment, also was repulsed by the Germans, south of Chémery. But here the French tanks were stopped primarily by German anti-tank guns rather than by panzers. About eight o'clock that morning, the 14th Antitank Company of the *Grossdeutschland* Regiment destroyed an approaching French tank. Seconds later, more French tanks arrived from the south and southwest of Chémery. The German anti-tank guns began firing at them, but could only penetrate their armor when several shells hit the same point. A few of the French tanks came within 200 meters of the German guns before they were knocked out.

The arrival of the 2nd Panzer Regiment, about 8:30, provided much-needed relief for the hard-pressed anti-tank gunners. Its panzers moved to the front of the anti-tank company and attacked southward toward Chémery. The guns of the anti-tank company followed behind, providing fire support for the advancing panzers. When the German units entered Chémery, according to the daily log of the 1st Panzer Division, "both sides fought tenaciously."

Despite the stout resistance of the French defenders in Chémery, however, the Germans drove them out of the village by 11:00 A.M. The panzers then hooked to their left and attacked the exposed flank of Colonel Labarthe's 213th Infantry Regiment. Labarthe was wounded and then captured, along with his entire staff, and the broken remnants of his regiment fell back to the Mont Dieu Woods, two miles farther south, ending what he had earlier predicted would be a "mission of sacrifice." In only a few minutes of fighting, the 7th Tank Battalion lost 50 percent of its personnel and 70 percent of its vehicles.

Although the panzers provided much of the firepower in smashing the French counterattack, it is quite probable that the German infantry would have been overrun before the panzers arrived had it not been for the guns of the 14th Antitank Company. The company reported later that it had destroyed 44 French tanks in the fighting around Chémery and had not lost a single soldier. While the report probably exaggerated the results, the importance of the anti-tank company's role in checking the French advance at Chémery would be difficult to overestimate.

THE FRENCH 71ST DIVISION PANICS, MAY 14

As dawn broke on May 14, the French 71st Infantry Division was still effectively blocking the advance of the 10th Panzer Division out of its Meuse bridgehead. But about 6:30 A.M., its commander, General Baudet, received an urgent telephone call from General Grandsard's 10th Corps headquarters reporting that enemy tanks had reached Chaumont, about two miles north of Bulson. To avoid being outflanked, Baudet was directed to form a defensive loop facing west and to prepare to counterattack with an infantry regiment and a tank battalion. But only 10 minutes later, Grandsard's headquarters called again, reporting that the panzers were already in Bulson and that General Lafontaine, the commander of the 55th Division, was evacuating his command post.

Baudet decided to move his command post as well, seven miles farther to the rear. As with the 55th Division the day before, news that the 71st Division's command post was retreating spread quickly through its artillery units. Soon the cry "German tanks are in Bulson" swept the division's artillery positions. The result was another panic-driven flight. "Riflemen and machine-gunners got up and fled," General Menu recalled. "By 14.00 hours [2:00 P.M.] there was no one any longer in position."

One officer tried to persuade the soldiers to return to their positions: "Look here, men," he said. "We've got plenty of guns and ammunition. Let's go back to the fighting."

"Colonel," a soldier replied, "we want to go home, back to our little jobs. There's no use trying to fight. There's nothing we can do. We're lost! We've been betrayed!" They resumed their flight.

By the end of the day, the guts of the 71st Division, like the 55th Division to its west, had been torn out. By the following day, little remained of either division.

Much the same thing happened to the rest of General Grandsard's 10th Corps. By nightfall on May 14, all that remained of his corps's artillery was one 105mm and one 155mm gun, and both were in the repair shop. His only intact division, the 3rd North African, had been transferred by Huntziger to the 18th Corps, which was deployed to the east of Grandsard's corps. The remnants of Grandsard's corps were transferred to General J. A. Flavigny, the commander of the newly constituted 21st Corps, which, with the 3rd Armored and 3rd Motorized Divisions, was preparing to launch another counterattack against the German bridgehead at Sedan.

GUDERIAN TURNS WEST, MAY 14

By early afternoon on May 14, following the collapse of Lafontaine's counterattack, it was obvious to Guderian that the whole French Sedan front was crumbling. The panzer leader drove to the headquarters of the 1st Panzer Division and asked its commander, General Friedrich Kirchner, "whether his entire division could be turned westwards or whether a flank guard should be left facing south on the east bank of the Ardennes Canal." Overhearing the question, another officer, Major Wenck, quickly responded, using one of Guderian's own catchphrases, *"Klotzen, nicht Kleckern!"* ("You should strike as a whole and not disperse the effort!")

Wenck's reaction settled any doubts in Guderian's mind. He immediately issued orders for his entire panzer corps to head west, with their objective Rethel, a town on the Aisne River, 32 miles southwest of Sedan. Its capture would complete the rupture of the link between the French 2nd and 9th Armies and would open the way to Paris, little more than 100 miles away, or to the English Channel, 50 miles farther west.

Later in the afternoon, the 1st and 2nd Panzer Divisions crossed the Bar River and Ardennes Canal, and then turned slightly to the southwest. However, after German intelligence warned Guderian that additional French tanks were moving toward Stonne, a village just southeast of the Mont Dieu Woods, he decided to keep behind the 10th Panzer Division and the *Grossdeutschland* Regiment to defend his southern flank until additional infantry could be brought up. However, the *Grossdeutschland* had already suffered heavy losses, and the 10th Panzer Division would need more time to bring all of its tanks up to Stonne. It was, in short, an ideal time for a French counterattack.

And Guderian knew it. All that day he worried about his weak southern flank. But his immediate superior, General Kleist, worried even more. Kleist could not forget the Battle of the Marne, when the German army turned prematurely in front of Paris and exposed its flank to a decisive French counterattack out of the capital city. To avoid the same kind of error, at 10:30 that evening Kleist ordered Guderian to halt the advance of the 1st and 2nd Panzers until their flank could be protected by the 14th Motorized Infantry Corps, moving up in support of the 10th Panzer Division.

Guderian exploded when he received Kleist's halt order. "I neither would, nor could, agree to these orders, which involved the sacrifice of the element of surprise we had gained and of the whole initial success that we had achieved." After a lengthy and heated argument, Kleist reluctantly agreed to let Guderian continue his advance for another 24 hours, in order to gain sufficient maneuvering space for the infantry divisions that were following in his wake.

THE FRENCH 3RD ARMORED DIVISION'S "COUNTERATTACK," MAY 14–15

As early as 6:00 P.M. on May 13, General Huntziger had ordered the French counterattack that Guderian and Kleist feared might happen. He directed the French 21st Corps to prepare to attack with the 3rd Motorized, 3rd Armored, and 5th Light Cavalry divisions, all under the command of General Flavigny.

Of all the French generals, none, apparently, was more qualified to lead an attack against the vulnerable flank of the German salient than Flavigny. No other French general had as much experience with armored operations. As director of the Department of Cavalry in 1933, he was the first to propose the formation of a mechanized cavalry division, and when the 1st Light Mechanized Division was formed in 1935, Flavigny was named its first commander. He also helped develop the Somua 35, the best tank in the French inventory. Hard-nosed, decisive, and experienced, he was the closest equivalent to a "French Guderian." General Huntziger must have been relieved to have a man of his ability and experience available at such a critical moment.

Late in the evening of May 13, Flavigny arrived at Huntziger's headquarters, where he received a briefing on his mission. He was to move to the southern edge of the Mont Dieu Woods near Stonne and attack toward Sedan at noon the next day. This would enable Flavigny's corps to take advantage of any gains made by Lafontaine's counterattack, which was scheduled to begin earlier that morning. Two major French counterattacks in rapid succession, Huntziger and Flavigny assured one another, would wipe out the German bridgehead.

However, all of Flavigny's mechanized divisions were not yet ready. Only the 3rd Motorized Infantry Division was fully up to combat standards. The 5th Light Cavalry Division, on the other hand, had suffered significant losses in men and matériel fighting in the Ardennes. But the key object of Flavigny's concern was the 3rd Armored Division, which was to spearhead the counterattack. It had been formed only six weeks earlier. Not only did it lack essential equipment—including anti-tank guns, individual tank radios, and supporting artillery—its soldiers had not completed their training when they were ordered to rush to the Sedan sector during the afternoon of May 12. Nevertheless, the 3rd Armored Division was still a powerful unit, equal, if not superior, to a German panzer division.

At 6:00 A.M. on May 14, the tanks of the 3rd Armored Division finally began to arrive in Le Chesne, some nine miles from the front, apparently eager to take on the Germans. But many of its tanks were out of gas, and because there was no fuel for them on hand, they had to await the arrival of their own fuel trucks. Nevertheless, Flavigny ordered the division's commander, General Antoine Brocard, to attack "as soon as possible," coordinating his attack with that of the 3rd Motorized Division. The beginning of the counterattack was rescheduled for 4:00 P.M.

However, at 3:30 P.M.—one half-hour after the 1st and 2nd Panzer Divisions had begun their turn to the west—he postponed it until the next day. Apparently Flavigny thought that it was not a propitious time to launch a counterattack after all. His divisions were now being engulfed by the panic-driven soldiers of the 55th Division, and in the resulting pandemonium, it was impossible to establish communications with the front. Accordingly, Flavigny decided that he would implement the principle of "containment first" before attacking the next day. "The most important thing," he said later, "was to ensure the safety of the [2nd Army's] second defensive line, which extended in front of the Mont Dieu Woods."

To achieve this objective, Flavigny ordered the 3rd Armored Division to disperse its tanks over a 12-mile front and block every road down which German armor might come. In so doing, of course, he destroyed any possibility of conducting an effective counterattack the next day. Its units hopelessly scattered over a wide front, the 3rd Armored Division would not be able to reassemble quickly enough to smash the vulnerable flank of Guderian's panzer corps before it could be reinforced with mechanized infantry. By the end of May 14, Colonel Goutard lamented, "there was a line, a few tanks, but no 3rd Armored Division. The steel lance was buried forever, and so was the counterattack."

At 7:30 that evening, General Huntziger personally phoned General Georges and told him: "The enemy advance has been stopped and sealed off between the Ardennes Canal and the Meuse by the Flavigny Group." In fact, two of the German panzer divisions, the 1st and 2nd Panzers, were already driving west of that canal and a third, the 10th Panzer Division, was advancing on Stonne, the scene of heavy fighting during the next two days.

Georges was not at all happy with the news. "The 3rd Armored Division," he told Huntziger, "was put at your disposal to counterattack toward

Sedan. Therefore, tomorrow, you must energetically pursue the operation started so well today by pushing on, without letup and as far as possible, toward the Meuse. It is the only way to regain the initiative from the enemy and to paralyze any advance toward the west or south from the enemy pocket."

Georges's order, however, proved impossible to implement. The next morning, the tanks of the 3rd Armored Division were still dispersed over a wide front, and its commander, General Brocard, reported that they could not be reassembled before 3:00 P.M. Flavigny, therefore, decided that the counterattack would begin at that hour. However, he changed the nature of the counterattack in a significant way. The French tanks would not be massed for a concentrated attack, as the Germans were employing them, but would be deployed as they were in World War I, that is, to "accompany the infantry." This, Flavigny explained later, "was the kind of tactics we all understood." Furthermore, to ensure that the traditional tactical doctrine would be followed, Flavigny placed Brocard's 3rd Armored Division under the command of an infantry man, General Bertin-Bossu, the commander of the 3rd Motorized Infantry Division. Flavigny already had given him command of all of Brocard's artillery and infantry.

Before the French counterattack could begin, however, General Bertin-Bossu informed Flavigny that all of the tanks still were not ready to attack. Some were still being assembled and refueled. Bowing to this state of affairs, Flavigny postponed the counterattack once again, until 5:30 P.M. Then, according to Bertin-Bossu, at 5:15 he canceled it altogether.

Flavigny later denied that he had canceled the attack. On the contrary, he asserted, after a reconnaissance plane reported seeing French tanks fighting north of the Mont Dieu Woods, he telephoned 2nd Army headquarters to report that the counterattack indeed had begun. Later, he admitted, he learned that the reconnaissance report had been wrong. "In fact," he said, "the tanks had moved barely a hundred meters and the infantry had not followed."

For whatever reasons, Flavigny's counterattack never got under way. Except for a limited attack by the 1st Colonial Infantry Division and the 2nd Light Cavalry Division, which were deployed to the east of Mont Dieu and near Stonne, the French 21st Corps let pass the opportunity to attack the vulnerable flank of Guderian's 19th Panzer Corps.

While Flavigny was pressuring Bertin-Bossu to get the tanks of the 3rd Armored Division to counterattack the German flank, the division was engaged in bitter fighting around Stonne. In fact, control of the village changed hands a number of times during the next two days until the Germans finally captured it. Even though the French ultimately lost Stonne, General Bertin-Bossu's 3rd Motorized Division performed extremely well in trying to hold the village. One can only wonder what the outcome would have been had the 3rd Armored Division been available to support it.

General Huntziger, by this time safely back at his new headquarters in Verdun, almost 40 miles south of Sedan, waited until the morning of May 16 before notifying General Georges that Flavigny's counterattack had not taken place. Huntziger said it was "because of unfavorable technical conditions and also, it seems, because of mechanical breakdowns." He blamed Flavigny for these problems.

Flavigny, in turn, blamed General Brocard, the commander of the 3rd Armored Division. He ordered Brocard to explain why "most of his heavy B tanks were not ready to take part in the counterattack ordered for 3:00 P.M., May 15"—this from the man who had ordered the dispersal of Brocard's tanks in the first place. Brocard dutifully replied that it had been impossible to reassemble in time for the counterattack a whole armored division that he had been ordered to disperse the previous day. Huntziger nevertheless accepted Flavigny's convenient scapegoating of Brocard and relieved him of the command of the 3rd Armored Division.

General Georges, however, was not fooled by either Huntziger's or Flavigny's attempts to avoid responsibility for the fiasco. "In reality," he later told a parliamentary investigating committee, "the 3rd Armored Division had been so widely dispersed over a broad front, in order to cover every road and path in the woods, that its regroupment for the counterattack was impossible. This division . . . was not properly used." It is difficult to avoid the conclusion that the man who had ordered the armored division dispersed in the first place—namely General Flavigny—was the man most responsible for its misuse.

What is really significant about the failure of the French counteroffensive at Stonne, however, is the differences it demonstrated in the French and German tank tactics, doctrines, and personnel. The German tactics of striking unexpectedly from all directions, massing the overwhelming firepower of the panzers, and supporting them with the shock effect of dive-bombers had such a demoralizing impact on the French soldiers that they could not defend themselves effectively, let alone launch a successful counterattack.

In addition, one can only wonder why General Flavigny did not personally assume control of the counterattack, considering that Bertin-Bossu was preoccupied with holding Stonne against a German attack. As with other French commanders, and in sharp contrast to the command style of German generals, Flavigny remained insulated from the decisive point of the battle.

Guderian, by contrast, took advantage of the extra 24 hours that Kleist had given him by spurring his panzer divisions to advance as far west as they could. And, in marked contrast to the French commanders, he arrived at the front at the psychologically critical moment—at dawn on May 16—when the French were withdrawing and his own soldiers were exhausted and longing for a rest. It was at times such as this that Guderian was at his best, observed Paul Diedrichs, who often accompanied him: "He speaks with enthusiasm to put over his intense desire to advance." And advance they did. In short, during the breakthrough at Sedan, German generalship, experience, training, and doctrine proved to be far superior to that of the French army.

Flavigny's sabotage of the French 21st Corps's counterattack was compounded by an even more significant error that was committed by General Huntziger. Concluding that Guderian's thrust was aimed principally at outflanking the Maginot Line and then rolling it up from the west, Huntziger decided to meet this perceived threat by pulling back his army from its position astride the Meuse. In so doing, he permitted the five-mile-wide German bridgehead to expand to one more than 15 miles across, one that could hardly be closed by the French counterattack that was supposed to have been conducted by Flavigny's corps. Even worse, Huntziger's decision to withdraw from the Meuse line would leave an even wider breach between his army and that of Corap's on his left, and thus a larger gap in the French front through which Guderian's panzer corps was already lunging.

GUDERIAN DESTROYS CORAP'S RIGHT WING, MAY 15

While the westward advance of Guderian's two panzer divisions eased the pressure on Huntziger's front, it seriously endangered Corap's right wing. However, unlike Huntziger, Corap had no armored divisions to bolster his front. Instead, he had to rely on a "B" division, the 53rd Infantry, and the

3rd Spahi Brigade, seriously weakened by combat in the Ardennes, to defend the gap created by the withdrawal of Huntziger's left flank.

The Spahi Brigade had established itself in a strong defensive position around the village of La Horgne, five miles west of the Ardennes Canal. Early on May 15, it was attacked by Hermann Balck's 1st Panzer Regiment. Proving that French soldiers could fight ferociously, the brigade deprived Balck of an easy victory and held up the German advance for several hours.

Balck's first attempt to overcome the Spahis was a frontal attack by his 3rd Battalion, but the attack failed to roll up the French position. Trying to outflank the Spahis, Balck ordered his 2nd Battalion to maneuver through the dense forest on the northern side of the village. While making their way through the forest, the German battalion surprised the staff of the Spahi's 2nd Regiment, killed its commander, and forced the survivors to surrender. After crossing through the forest, Balck then ordered a combined frontal and flank assault on La Horgne. The attack, with tanks and infantry, finally broke the back of the French resistance by 6:00 P.M. By the end of the day, 27 Spahi officers and 610 of its soldiers had been killed; the remainder were either wounded or scattered. The Spahi Brigade, in effect, had ceased to exist.

Having destroyed the Spahis, Balck's 1st Infantry Regiment continued its westward advance toward Bouvellemont. Reaching that town as twilight fell, Balck's men collided with elements of the French 14th Infantry Division, a unit commanded by a future marshal of France, General Jean de Lattre de Tassigny. Balck was fully aware of the significance of capturing Bouvellemont. Not only would it cut off the French forces in the neighboring village of Chagny, it would shatter the last line of French defenses behind the Meuse.

But Balck's men were exhausted. And they were extremely dispirited by the huge losses they had suffered in five days of almost continuous combat. More than half of their officers were either dead or wounded, and many of the regiment's companies were barely above half-strength. In addition, the men had received hardly anything to eat or drink all this very hot day. For the first time since leaving Germany, Balck's officers were reluctant to carry out his order to attack. They pleaded with him to give the men a night's rest before making them attack the town. But Balck rejected their pleas. He argued that the capture of Bouvellemont would complete the stupendous task that they had begun five days earlier: punching completely through the French front. Yet Balck's officers still refused to carry out his order.

"In that case," Balck finally reacted, "I'll take the place on my own."
He then walked off, alone, in the direction of the French position. He
advanced no farther than 100 meters before his officers and men, realizing
that he was serious, jumped up and joined him. With support from the
regiment's artillery battalion, they stormed the village and, after vigorous
house-to-house fighting, captured it.

Amid the burning ruins of Bouvellemont the next day, Balck related
to Guderian how he had persuaded his men to overcome this last link in
the French defensive chain. "His dirty face and his red-rimmed eyes,"
Guderian recounted, "showed that he had spent a hard day and a sleepless
night." Balck received the Knight's Cross for his actions at Bouvellemont.

During that night, the French soldiers in nearby Chagny, recognizing the
hopelessness of their situation now that Bouvellemont had fallen, withdrew toward Rethel. Though they claimed to have destroyed some 20 German tanks, they also had lost all of their anti-tank guns and a third of
their comrades. Their retreat that night signaled the collapse of the last
organized French resistance in the Meuse breakout sector.

Meanwhile, to the north, the 2nd Panzer Division had smashed through
Corap's 53rd Infantry Division without much difficulty. By the close of the
day, its reconnaissance detachments were already making contact with
Reinhardt's panzers at Montcornet, some forty miles west of Sedan. Only
24 hours earlier, the German bridgeheads across the Meuse had consisted
of three isolated bulges; now they formed one continuous pocket 62 miles
wide and with no bottom. For the panzers, the way westward lay open,
with virtually no obstacles between them and the English Channel.

CHAPTER SIX

The German Drive to the English Channel, May 15–20

"We Have Been Defeated!"

At 7:30 on the morning of May 15, Prime Minster Winston Churchill was awakened from a deep sleep by the ringing of his bedside telephone. It was Paul Reynaud.

"We have been defeated!" the French premier exclaimed. "We have lost the battle!" Churchill, only half awake, could not quite grasp the meaning of Reynaud's words and said nothing. Reynaud repeated them. "We have been beaten. We have lost the battle!"

"Impossible!" Churchill finally replied. "Surely it can't have happened so soon."

"The front is broken near Sedan," Reynaud responded. "They are pouring through in great numbers with tanks and armored cars."

Churchill tried to settle Reynaud down: "All experience shows that the offensive will come to an end after a while. . . . After five or six days they have to halt for supplies, and the opportunity for counterattack is presented. I learned all this . . . from the lips of Marshal Foch himself."

"All that has changed," Reynaud replied. "We're faced with a torrent of tanks." The French premier then talked "of giving up the struggle."

Churchill replied that he must not be misled by panic-stricken messages of this kind, that only a "small proportion of the French army was engaged," and that the Germans who had broken through would be in a "vulnerable position." The German penetration was on a "narrow front" and could not possibly be "rapidly exploited in strength."

Reynaud then pointed to what he called "the small number of British troops in France" and "begged for assistance."

159

Britain could not send troops to France, Churchill replied, "quicker than the schedule to which we were working, and in any case nothing could arrive in time to influence the present battle." He added that while he would do everything possible to aid France, he could not denude England of her essential defenses. Churchill also pointed out to Reynaud "that whatever the French might do," Britain would "continue the fight, if necessary, alone."

Reynaud finally pulled himself together. France, he said, also would fight to the end.

Churchill concluded the conversation by saying that he would be glad to come over to Paris the following day "and have a talk."

The prime minister then phoned General Georges, an old personal friend. The general, he recalled, "seemed quite cool, and reported that the breach at Sedan was being plugged."

GAMELIN'S EYES ARE FINALLY OPENED, MAY 15

Later that day, Churchill also received a telegram from General Gamelin. It informed him that although the position between Namur and Sedan was "serious, he viewed the situation with calm."

However, Gamelin really did not know what was going on at the Meuse front. That morning, he sent out an aide, Colonel Guillaut, to find out what had happened to the 9th Army. "It was the first time," Gamelin noted, "that I had sent out a personal liaison officer to an army," insisting, until then, on following the French chain of command. That night, however, Colonel Guillaut returned to Vincennes and reported that the situation of the 9th Army was "truly critical." The troops were in disorder, "devoid of any taste for the fight." In fact, he concluded, "from the moment the Germans appeared, everyone had run away." The next day, Gamelin ordered General Georges to use the *gardes mobiles*—the military police—to stop the fleeing troops, regroup them, and "advance toward the front."

That evening, U.S. Ambassador William Bullitt happened to be in Daladier's office when Gamelin called. Bullitt could not hear Gamelin's words, but the defense minister, he recalled, sat listening "totally incredulous and stupefied." Finally, Daladier exclaimed: "No! What you tell me is not possible! You must be wrong! It's impossible!" Gamelin explained that a column of German tanks had broken through the French front and was advancing on Rethel and Laon.

"Then you must counterattack at once!" Daladier roared.

"What with?" Gamelin asked. "I don't have the reserves."

Bullitt remembered that Daladier's face fell and became more and more contorted. "So it means the destruction of the French Army?" Daladier ended the discussion.

"Yes, it means the destruction of the French Army!" Gamelin replied. "It's finished."

Late that night, a meeting was convened by Reynaud at the Ministry of the Interior in Paris. Daladier, General Pierre Héring, the military governor of Paris, and Colonel Guillaut, representing Gamelin, were present. In an atmosphere etched with panic, they discussed measures for defending Paris, and even for evacuating the government from the capital.

"It seems obvious," Bullitt cabled President Franklin Roosevelt the next day, "that unless God grants a miracle, as at the time of the Battle of the Marne, the French Army will be crushed utterly."

In addition to Bullitt, Roosevelt was also being urged by his ambassador in London, Joseph Kennedy (father of the future president), to take action. However, whereas Bullitt wanted as much immediate U.S. assistance to the Allies as possible, Kennedy wanted Roosevelt to help the Allies throw in the towel. The next day, May 16, Kennedy informed the State Department that "nothing can save [the Allies] from absolute defeat unless the president, with some touch of genius and God's blessing, can do it."

Churchill also cabled Roosevelt on May 15. In fact, he had been corresponding with the president secretly since assuming office as First Lord of the Admiralty in September 1939. Yet even as late as mid-May 1940, Roosevelt was still uncertain about Churchill's leadership cabilities. On May 11, one day after Churchill became prime minister, Roosevelt asked his cabinet "what kind of man" was the new British leader. Secretary of the Interior Harold Ickes replied that "apparently, Churchill is very unreliable under the influence of drink." And he was "too old." After other cabinet members expressed much the same view, Roosevelt said that nevertheless "Churchill still was the best man England had."

Churchill's telegram to Roosevelt painted an alarming picture of the Allies' plight. It emphasized the demoralizing effects on the French army of the German blitzkrieg. Still, the prime minister cautioned, "the battle has only begun. I am waiting to see the full strength of the forces thrown in." Nevertheless, even at this early date, only five days into the battle, Churchill raised the possibility that Britain might have to continue the struggle alone. It was now time, he emphasized to Roosevelt, for the United States to bring its material strength into the struggle if Europe was not shortly to become "Nazified." He asked the president to proclaim a state of "nonbelligerency," which would permit the United States to supply all kinds of aid but not engage in armed action. Specifically, he requested U.S. destroyers, which would enable Britain to protect the convoys from the New World from German submarine attacks. "I trust you realize, Mr. President," Churchill concluded, "that the voice and the force of the United States may count for nothing if they are withheld too long."

At this time, however, there was very little that Roosevelt could do for the Allies. Both U.S. public opinion and the Congress were rigidly isolationist, and Roosevelt's desire to assist the Allies, at least materially, was severely hampered by a number of neutrality laws that Congress had enacted in the 1930s, with his approval, to keep the United States out of war.

Privately, Roosevelt had told intimates that he would not run for reelection that fall, that is, "unless . . . things got very, very much worse in Europe." Obviously, it would have been very difficult, if not impossible, for Roosevelt's successor, not having his experience and prestige, to get Congress to approve U.S. assistance to the Allies, let alone declare war on Germany. Indeed, it ultimately required Hitler's declaration of war on the United States, four days after the Japanese attack on Pearl Harbor on December 7, 1941, to bring America into the war against the Axis powers. But all of this was still more than a year and a half in the future. In mid-May 1940, as one presidential intimate astutely observed, "The question of whether Roosevelt would run" was being settled "somewhere on the banks of the Meuse River."

In his reply to Churchill, Roosevelt suggested a way around the Neutrality Act, that is, "utilizing reserve civil transport planes and private-owner planes for Allied transport and light bombing purposes." That evening, Secretary of the Treasury Henry Morgenthau arranged for the delivery of 35 such aircraft to Allied purchasers over the next three months. Needless to say, this very limited amount of assistance that late would not be very significant in staving off Allied defeat. But this was as far as Roosevelt was prepared to go. Indeed, at that time, he had been advised, U.S. military aircraft numbered only 150 pursuit planes and 144 bombers.

While American opinion may have been moving in the direction Roosevelt wanted it to go, that is, toward aiding the Allies, he did not want to get too far ahead of the people. The isolationists were watching his every move and were ready to pounce on any presidential effort they feared might drag the United States into the European war.

Churchill in Paris, May 16

In an attempt to counter the panic that was gripping Paris, Churchill decided to fly to the French capital. He arrived at Le Bourget airport at 4:00 P.M. on May 16. "From the moment we got out of [his plane] the *Flamingo,*" Churchill recorded, "it was obvious that the situation was incomparably worse than we had imagined. . . . the Germans were expected in Paris in a few days at most." Deputy Secretary of the War Cabinet General Hastings Ismay was "flabbergasted" at the scenes he saw while driving with Churchill to Reynaud's office: "The people seemed listless and resigned. . . . There were no cheers for Churchill."

The British prime minister and his entourage immediately drove to the Foreign Ministry, where Reynaud, Daladier, and Gamelin were awaiting his arrival. "Everybody was standing," Churchill remembered, "at no time did we sit around a table. . . . Utter dejection was written on every face. In front of Gamelin, on a student's easel was a map, about two yards square, with a black line purporting to show the Allied front. In this line there was drawn a small but sinister bulge at Sedan." Poking at it to show where the Germans had broken through, Gamelin "lectured as though he were giving a lesson in military strategy." North and south of Sedan, on a front of 50 or 60 miles, the generalissimo explained, the Germans had broken through. The French army in front of them was destroyed or scattered. A heavy onrush of armored vehicles was advancing, Gamelin said, with unheard-of speed toward Amiens and Arras, with the intention, apparently, of reaching the coast at Abbeville. Or they might make for Paris.

At this point, Reynaud, who was standing stiffly next to Gamelin, remarked that German tanks, followed by trucks carrying infantry, had been thrown into this breach and were now fanning out in three directions toward Paris.

When Gamelin had finished, there was a long silence, and finally Churchill asked: "And where is the strategic reserve?" Slipping into French, he repeated his question: *"Ou est la masse de manoeuvre?"*

"General Gamelin turned to me," Churchill recalled, "and with a shake of the head and a shrug said: *'Aucune.'* [There is none]."

"I was dumbfounded," Churchill remembered. It did not seem possible "that any commanders, having to defend five-hundred miles of engaged front, would have left themselves unprovided with a mass of maneuver. . . . I admit this was one of the greatest surprises I have had in my life." He could only mourn, belatedly, that the British government had not insisted on knowing the dispositions of the French army before the battle began.

Churchill got up and walked over to the window. Curling wreaths of smoke were ascending from bonfires burning in the garden below. One after another, wheelbarrows full of papers—government documents—were brought before the pyres and then emptied into the flames.

Returning to the conversation, Churchill asked Gamelin when and where he proposed to counterattack the flanks of the German bulge. He received another devastating reply: "Inferiority of numbers, inferiority of equipment, inferiority of method," followed by a hopeless shrug of Gamelin's shoulders.

While this exchange was going on, Daladier sat in a corner of the room, his face red and drawn, looking, according to Reynaud's aide, Paul Baudouin, "like a school-boy in disgrace." Calling Baudouin over to him, Daladier whispered: "The mistake, the unpardonable mistake, was to send so many men into Belgium." Then Daladier responded to Churchill's call for a counterattack. "The French Army has nothing left to cover Paris. We must withdraw the troops in the north."

"On the contrary," Churchill replied, "they should dig in where they are." The primary reason for sending the Allied armies into Belgium in the first place, he argued, was "that by doing so, we would shorten our front and economize twenty divisions. Now we had got there, why should we retire? Let us fight on that line."

Churchill simply refused to believe that the thrust of the German armor represented a serious menace. "Unless the tanks are supported by infantry," he argued, "they represent a limited force. They will not be able to maintain themselves. They will have to be refueled, resupplied. . . . I refuse to see in this spectacular raid of the German tanks a real invasion." He urged Gamelin to launch a counterattack against the flanks of the advancing panzers.

But Gamelin replied that the French armored divisions were "very exhausted" and incapable of counterattacking. A third of the heavy tanks, and two-thirds of the light tanks, he said, were now out of action. What was essential to stop the panzers, attack the Meuse bridges, and "protect the infantry," Gamelin now insisted, were more fighters. He demanded—a demand that was strongly seconded by Reynaud and Daladier—that the British throw in more planes: six more fighter squadrons, in addition to the four already in France and the four that Britain had promised to send only the previous day.

"No," Churchill responded, "it is the business of the artillery to stop the tanks. It is the business of the fighters to cleanse the skies over the battle." France, he pointed out, had an almost unlimited supply of 75mm guns left over from the first war. Why were they not being used to stop the panzers? Furthermore, he did not think six more aircraft squadrons "would make any difference" in the outcome of the battle.

"The French believed the contrary," Daladier interjected. If the French infantry could feel that fighters were above, protecting them, "they would be given confidence, and would not be taking cover when the tanks came along."

Churchill then argued that Britain had to keep a certain minimal number of fighters in England to protect her factories and other facilities against Hitler's bombers. Britain now had only 39 squadrons in England, compared to the 50 that the British chiefs of staff considered the minimal amount. These, he emphasized, had to be conserved. He then pointed out that the RAF had sent four squadrons to attack Sedan: "We had taken great risks in order to destroy the bridges over the Meuse and had lost 36 aircraft in doing so. You can replace bridges," Churchill said, "but not fighters."

In fact, by the end of the previous day, May 15, the RAF had lost nearly 250 aircraft—nearly one-quarter of Britain's air power—either destroyed or damaged beyond immediate repair. This could not go on, insisted Air Chief Marshal Sir Hugh Dowding, the commander-in-chief of RAF fighter command. To retain a sufficient force to defend the whole of Britain, he had to keep his fighters out of a battle—the battle of France—that he believed was already lost. The War Cabinet agreed with Dowding's line of reasoning and canceled any orders to send more Hurricanes to the Continent.

But the French had even less surviving aircraft than the British. The next day, General François d'Astier de la Vigerie, commander of the French air force on the front of the 1st Army Group, would report that he had only 149 fighters in operation, plus 24 modern and 30 old bombers. The rest of France's aircraft had been destroyed on the ground or in battle, or were deployed on other fronts.

Reynaud politely told Churchill that the British government would have to choose between "two big risks": either they must leave the English factories without fighter protection—"like the French factories"—or they must be prepared "to see the German armies continue their advance toward Paris."

Realizing that he was not dampening the French calls for additional British fighters, at 9:00 P.M. Churchill telegraphed the War Cabinet in London to explain a "situation grave in the last degree," with the Germans having driven a 50-kilometer "bulge" into the French front line. Unless this battle of the bulge were won, Churchill warned, "French resistance may be broken up as rapidly as that of Poland." He wanted the War Cabinet to approve the French request for six additional RAF squadrons. "It would not be good historically," he added, "if their requests were denied and their ruin resulted." He concluded by saying that he must have an answer by midnight, "in order to encourage the French."

Just before midnight, Churchill received the War Cabinet's approval for the air reinforcements. He immediately hurried to Reynaud's apartment to give him "a pearl beyond price," as he put it, and he wanted to watch the premier's face when he received the good news. He found Reynaud's apartment more or less in darkness, the only sign of life in the sitting room a lady's fur coat—it belonged, no doubt, to Reynaud's mistress, Countess Hélène de Portes.

Reynaud emerged from his bedroom in a dressing gown. Churchill insisted on reading out loud, with great emphasis, the telegram he had sent to London requesting the additional aircraft. Reynaud thought it was "admirable." Then "I told him," Churchill recalled, "the favorable news: Ten fighter squadrons!" The prime minister then urged Reynaud to send for Daladier, so he could give him the great news, too. Reynaud only reluctantly agreed to summon his archrival. When Daladier arrived, Churchill again read his telegram to the War Cabinet and repeated its reply. "Daladier," Churchill remembered, "never spoke a word. He rose slowly from his chair and wrung my hand."

Churchill now launched into what Reynaud described as "a forthright harangue on carrying the war to the enemy." Daladier stood silently, "crushed, bowed down with grief." Reynaud also was silent, but stood with his head erect, "like some small broken piece of machinery," as General Ismay, who accompanied Churchill, put it. The prime minister, Ismay recounted, paced back and forth, "crowned like a volcano by the smoke of his cigars," exhorting them: "You must not lose heart! Did you ever suppose we should achieve victory except after dire setbacks?" Warming to his subject with true Churchillian vehemence, he declared that "even if France were invaded and vanquished, England would go on fighting." He envisaged himself in the heart of Canada directing the New World's war against an Old World dominated by Germany. "We will starve Germany out. We will destroy her towns. We will burn her crops and her forests."

Reynaud was greatly impressed; Churchill apparently had renewed his confidence in ultimate victory. Returning to the British Embassy about two in the morning, Churchill recorded that he "slept well, though the cannon fire" and "petty aeroplane raids" caused him to "roll over from time to time."

Yet while the promise of additional British fighters temporarily boosted the morale of the French leaders, in the end, the actual size of the reinforcements was considerably less than Churchill had suggested. When, the next day, Air Staff Chief Sir Cyril Newall warned the War Cabinet that there were only six complete Hurricane squadrons remaining in the United Kingdom, its members decided only six additional fighter squadrons would be sent to help the French, not the 10 Churchill had promised. Moreover, they would remain based in England. Three of the squadrons would work in France from dawn until noon and then return to England, where they would be relieved by the other three squadrons, which would operate over France in the afternoon. Considering the short maximum range of the fighters, about 300 miles for a Hurricane, there was no way the additional squadrons, based in England, could "dominate the air above the bulge for the next two or three days," as Churchill had promised Reynaud and Daladier. It was this kind of hedging on the part of the British that would soon severely strain their relationship with the French.

CHURCHILL AND ROOSEVELT, MAY 17

After Churchill flew back to London early in the morning of May 17, the impact of the German onslaught finally hit him. At 10:00 A.M., he met with the War Cabinet to report on his trip to Paris. "It was now plain," he said, "why the Allied troops had not been bombed during their advance into Belgium: the Germans had wanted to get us into forward positions in order to affect a break through and turn our flanks." Now he understood the great design of Hitler's war plan, in fact, much better than the French generals, who had spent their entire careers preparing for this battle.

Yet Churchill's ability to see the German design also darkened his spirits. "Winston is depressed," his secretary, John Colville, noted in his diary. "He says the French are crumpling up as completely as did the Poles, and that our forces in Belgium will inevitably have to withdraw in order to maintain contact with the French." According to Colville, Churchill feared that the British Expeditionary Force "will be cut off if the French do not rally in time." This gloomy prognosis seemed confirmed by General Ismay's remark to Colville that the French were not merely retreating, they "were routed." "Their nerves," Ismay explained, "were shattered by this armored warfare and by the German air mastery."

To make matters even worse, if that were possible, Ambassador Kennedy arrived at 10 Downing Street to personally deliver Roosevelt's reply to Churchill's plea for additional American aid. The president's message stated "that the loan or gift of forty or fifty older destroyers" would require the authorization of Congress. He was "not certain that it would be wise for that suggestion to be made to the Congress at this moment." It also seemed doubtful, "from the standpoint of our own defense requirements," including American obligations in the Pacific, "whether we could dispose even temporarily of these destroyers." Roosevelt added, however, that he was doing all in his power to make it possible for the Allied governments "to obtain the latest types of aircraft in the United States," and to discuss the possible purchase by the Allies of U.S. antiaircraft equipment, ammunition, and steel. In effect, according to Alexander Cadogan, the British permanent undersecretary for foreign affairs, the president "will do all he can, but he can't go ahead of his public." And even then, Cadogan added, "what can they [the Americans] do to affect *this* battle?"

In Washington that evening, Roosevelt had a long conversation with Lord Lothian, the British ambassador. Deeply moved by the dramatic turn of events during the previous few days, the president expressed anxiety about the fate of the Royal Navy in the event of Britain's defeat. If that should happen, Roosevelt said, he wanted "His Majesty's Government to place its fleet in the shelter of American ports."

Shocked by Roosevelt's intimation that Britain might be defeated, Lothian lost no time in reporting the president's concern to Churchill. In a telegram to Roosevelt the next day, Churchill declared: "We are determined to persevere to the very end, whatever the result of the great battle raging in France may be. We must expect in any case to be attacked here, on the Dutch model, before very long, and we hope to give a good account of ourselves." But, Churchill added, "if American assistance is to play any part, it must be available soon."

Beneath all the outward concern, however, Churchill was convinced that sooner or later, the United States would enter the war and once again save Britain, as America had done in World War I. Randolph Churchill recorded how his father revealed this conviction to him earlier that day:

> I went up to my father's bedroom. He was standing in front of his basin and was shaving with his old-fashioned Valet razor. He had a tough beard and, as usual, he was hacking away.
>
> "Sit down, dear boy, and read the papers while I finish shaving."
>
> I did as told.
>
> After two or three minutes of hacking away, he half turned and said:
> "I think I can see my way through." He resumed his shaving.

I was astounded, and said: "Do you mean that we can avoid defeat? (which seemed credible) or beat the bastards (which seemed incredible)."

He flung his Valet razor in to the basin, swung around, and said: "Of course I mean we can beat them."

I said, "Well, I'm all for it, but I don't see how you can do it."

By this time he had dried and sponged his face and, turning round to me, said with great intensity: "I shall drag the United States in."

King Léopold Decides to Stay in Belgium, May 15–18w

On the morning of May 15, shortly after Winston Churchill was shocked by Reynaud's phone call proclaiming the French army's defeat, King Léopold of Belgium was coming to much the same conclusion. He had just learned that between the German breakthrough at Sedan and the English Channel, the French had no fortified line, no reserves, nor indeed any means of preventing the onrushing German armor from reaching the sea. The king also was told by General Oscar Michiels, the Belgian army's chief of staff, that "it looks as though the French 1st Army has been broken up in the northern and southern outskirts of Namur."

Léopold reacted to this news by calling his chief ministers to his military headquarters at Breendock to discuss the deteriorating situation. He began by showing the ministers a map on which were marked the German breaches in the French line; they extended north and south of Namur and all the way to Sedan. Pointing to the English Channel, between Dieppe and Abbeville, the king said: "They will be there in less than eight days." In fact, the panzers would reach the coast in five days. Obviously, this would leave most of the Allied armies in Belgium cut off from the other French armies to the south. Léopold then asked the ministers what they proposed to do. Before they could answer, however, he expressed his opinion that the government must remain in Belgium at all costs, in order to prevent its separation from the king and the army.

Prime Minister Hubert Pierlot agreed that the separation of the king, the army, and the government must be avoided at all costs. To prevent this, he said, "We must manoeuvre in such a way as to lead our army towards France and not towards the North Sea." This, he explained, would enable the army "to conserve its liberty of movement and remain in contact with the Allied armies."

"No," Léopold replied. "Not toward the west. Toward the north." He wanted to establish a "redoubt" on the coast, much as his father had held on to a small stretch of Belgian territory during World War I.

Pierlot protested that a withdrawal to the north would mean "certain capitulation." Not wanting to press the issue, Léopold replied that the army's maneuvers ultimately would be governed by the military situation. Nevertheless, for the first time, Pierlot began to suspect that the king might be considering a separate peace.

This suspicion was reinforced by Léopold's insistence that Belgium must not join the Anglo-French alliance. Neither Britain nor France, he pointed out, were disposed to guarantee the future independence of Belgium or its continued possession of the Congo, its African colony. In giving this advice to his ministers, as the journalist William Shirer pointed out, it did not seem to have occurred to Léopold that if Belgium were overrun by the Germans, as now seemed probable, its only hope of eventually having its independence restored lay in the ultimate victory of the Allies.

Paul Reynaud obviously thought so. When Belgian Foreign Minister Paul-Henri Spaak appeared in Paris on May 15—of all times, the same day the French government was considering evacuating its capital—to demand that France give Belgium the desired guarantees of its future status, the French premier exploded. Reynaud fiercely upbraided the Belgians for terminating the alliance with Britain and France in 1936 and for refusing to allow the Allied armies to enter Belgium before she was attacked. He argued that France and Britain were fighting for Belgium's future as much as they were their own. Even after being invaded by the Nazi armies, Reynaud complained, the Belgian king was still trying to maintain the neutrality of his country. "It is in the name of this principle"—neutrality—he commented sarcastically, "that the Belgian army saw eight thousand of its men fall in vain on the battlefield."

The next day, May 16, Léopold again summoned Pierlot, Spaak, and General Denis to his headquarters. He informed them that the collapse of the French 9th Army had obliged General Billotte to order the French 1st Army Group, the Belgian army, and the BEF to make a phased retreat from the Dyle line to the Escaut (or Scheldt) River. That night, they would retreat to the River Senne; on the following night, to the Dendre, and, finally, on May 18, to the front envisioned in Gamelin's old, never implemented "Plan E." If the three armies were encircled, as Léopold believed they would be, the only hope for the Belgian army would be to take up a position on the coast, "if possible, in concert with the British and French forces." On a map, he drew a rough semicircle around the town of Zeebrugge. This, he said, would be the area of the "national redoubt."

After the king finished his presentation, his ministers again insisted that everything must be done to prevent the Belgian army from being hemmed in on its own territory and cut off from the Allied forces. Such a move would compel the army to surrender, an outcome that would be disastrous to Belgium both politically and morally. They insisted that at the very least the government and a few soldiers should remain free so the country could continue in the war and participate in the peace conference once Germany was defeated.

Léopold, however, rejected his minister's advice that he and the army withdraw to France. He argued, as he put it, that "once I am in foreign territory, I will have to submit to the laws of that country, as will the army. Consequently, the Belgian command will no longer be free." However, Pierlot and Spaak did not buy Léopold's reasoning. They said that the king, as commander-in-chief of the army, could always refuse to accept any untenable orders the Allies might attempt to impose upon him. They pointed out that the queen of the Netherlands, Wilhelmina, had gone to London when Holland was overrun by the Germans. However, Léopold only replied: "Was she right in leaving?"

Two days later, on May 18, the Belgian government, including 13 of the 17 chief ministers, would also leave the country and seek sanctuary in France. Only Pierlot, Spaak, and Denis remained on Belgian soil, and they did so only because the king had insisted they stay.

That morning Léopold read a letter, which was drafted by Pierlot and approved by the Council of Ministers the previous day, which stated: "If the army cannot avoid encirclement, the unanimous view is that the king must, at all costs, escape in time from the danger of being made a prisoner." Léopold, however, remained unbudged in his determination to remain with his troops, no matter what.

Lord Gort's Growing Dismay, May 15–16

Like King Léopold, the commander-in-chief of the British Expeditionary Force, John Standish Surtees Prendergast Vereker, the sixth Viscount Gort, was increasingly alarmed by the French high command's handling of the war. He was not told about the French decision to withdraw from the Dyle line, which was made during the evening of May 15, until the next morning. Although Gort appreciated the necessity for an Allied withdrawal from the Dyle, he was not happy with the orders he received from Billotte.

Worn-out Belgian troops retreating. (Imperial War Museum F4483)

They were not only late in arriving, in Gort's opinion, they were only half-measures, which resulted in the retreat being carried out too slowly to meet the rapidly changing conditions.

Gort had never liked the idea of advancing into Belgium in the first place. It just did not make any sense to him to abandon a defense line in France, which, after a lot of hard work during the previous winter, had been effectively strengthened, in order to risk battle in the open Belgian plain against numerous German panzers. Yet, in the interest of Allied unity, and considering the pitifully small British contribution to the land war, Gort did not object when Gamelin had explained the Dyle Plan to them at a meeting in Vincennes the previous November 9.

In retrospect, Gort was roundly criticized—and was even accused of dereliction of duty—for acquiescing to what, in hindsight, almost everyone viewed as an extremely risky plan. Gort defended himself by saying the decision to advance into Belgium "was one of high policy, with a political as well as a military aspect; it was therefore not for me to comment on it." Nor, once the battle had begun, did he see much sense in berating the

French for their failures. Whatever doubts he had about the Dyle Plan, he believed that once the battle had begun, it served no good purpose to express them. More important to Gort was the morale of his troops. He was well aware that defeatism at the top could spread downward through an army as rapidly as any physical infection.

More than a few of Gort's own officers felt that his own mode of command left much to be desired. General Bernard Montgomery, the brash and flamboyant commander of the 3rd Infantry Division, described the command of the French and British armies as "a complete eggs breakfast"—a mess—for which he blamed Gort as much as he did Gamelin. "Gort," Montgomery wrote, "was unfitted for the job—and we senior officers all knew it. He was not clever, and he did not bother about administration." In fact, Montgomery was so incensed by Gort's alleged mismanagement of the BEF that he went straight to the War Office at the end of the campaign and told the new chief of the Imperial General Staff, General Sir John Dill, that "the events of the past few weeks had proved that certain officers [meaning Gort and his chief of staff, General Sir Henry Pownall] were unfit to be employed again, and should be retired."

General Alan Brooke was one of the officers who shared Montgomery's assessment of Gort. "Unfortunately," Brooke charged, "Gort's brain was geared to detail all the time. The important points . . . he left entirely to his staff, while he dealt with details such as platoon log-books, carrying of sandbags, booby traps. . . . He took practically no part in the [important] discussions. . . . As the time passed, these failings became more and more disconcerting."

Even Gort's faithful lieutenant, General Pownall, complained—albeit privately—about his chief's shortcomings. In his diary entry of May 14, Pownall wrote that Gort preferred to be a field commander of a division than the commander-in-chief of an entire army. That day, Pownall recorded, Gort was away from his headquarters for eight hours, "too long, at difficult times."

Yet, in spite of Gort's deficiencies as a commander-in-chief, nobody—including Montgomery—questioned his courage. As a young officer in World War I, during which he was twice badly wounded, Gort won one distinction after another: the Victoria Cross, three Distinguished Service Orders, and the Military Cross. As a soldier, his lifestyle was austere and self-denying. Indeed, he seemed to delight in personal privations and expected others to do the same. On hearing about Gort's appointment to the Army Staff College in 1936, one colonel predicted: "He will have all the beds made of concrete and hosed down with cold water nightly."

The following year, Gort was appointed military secretary at the War Office and, shortly afterward, chief of the Imperial General Staff, the youngest officer ever to hold that position. In promoting Gort to the highest position in the army, the secretary for war, Sir Leslie Hore-Belisha, expected Gort's reputation as a tough, no-nonsense war hero to appeal to the troops as well as enhance the army's standing with the public. But more than a few—including even Winston Churchill—felt that Gort's wartime exploits were not sufficient qualification for giving him the leadership of the army. In 1930 Churchill criticized officers like Gort: "I am doubtful whether the fact that a man has gained the Victoria Cross for bravery as a young officer fits him to command an army twenty or thirty years later. . . . Age, easy living, heaviness of body, many years of promotion, and success in time of peace, dissipate the vital forces indispensable to intense action."

In the opinion of many of his contemporaries, apparently, Gort was regarded as an ideal man to command a division, not an entire army.

The Allied Retreat Begins, May 16

When Gort ordered his soldiers to pull back from the Dyle line to the Escaut River, most of them were caught by surprise. Less than a week before, they had advanced 60 miles into Belgium to meet the enemy. They had met him on the Dyle and had defeated his attempts to break their line. They were confident they could defend their position indefinitely. And now they were ordered to withdraw. Telling them that their retreat was necessitated by events miles away to the south, where the French front had broken, did not seem a sufficient explanation.

Even the highest officers in the army thought withdrawal was a bad idea. "It took us three and a half days to get to the Dyle (after very careful planning) with three divisions," Pownall complained. "I don't see how we can get back again in two days, in a hurry, especially as the roads are badly blocked with thousands of refugees and we may be sure that we shall get properly bombed, which we didn't on our way up."

To soften the blow, the order to withdraw was transmitted to the lower-echelon soldiers in several ways. Some were told that the withdrawal was ordered to lengthen the enemy's lines of communication, or was designed to entice the Germans forward so that they could be attacked on their flanks. But Col. Graham Brooks obviously did not buy this rationale. "To leave this magnificent position on the Dyle, when the BEF had its tail right up—it couldn't be true. . . . Still, we thought, we'll be back here again very soon."

The retreat was particularly hard on the Belgian soldiers, for they realized that they were abandoning their capital to the Germans for the second time in a generation. By nightfall on May 17, German troops were again marching into Brussels. Falling back with his unit on Maubeuge that day, a baffled René Balbaud wrote: "We don't understand. A liaison officer's driver brings strange news. The Germans, he says, have entered France at Sedan . . . . Somehow the old jokes about our coming occupation of Germany have become scarce."

In fact, the Germans were advancing so rapidly on the flanks of the northern Allied armies that no matter which way the Allies turned, they risked running into trouble. The predicament was particularly troubling to General Billotte. With only 14 Belgian, nine British, and 18 French divisions, including three mechanized divisions and parts of the 2nd and 1st Armored Divisions, Billotte faced 10 German panzer divisions and over 30 other types of divisions, all of which were backed up by 25 reserve divisions. During the afternoon of May 17, Billotte's staff intercepted a German radio transmission: "From now on, the pressure is off Paris and on the sea." The Germans were so sure of victory, his staff observed, that they no longer bothered to transmit their orders in code.

The Race to the Channel Begins, May 16

On May 16 the great panzer dash to the English Channel got under way. The previous day, one of Guderian's units had captured a French order, originating from General Gamelin himself, which contained these words: "The torrent of German tanks must finally be stopped!" This order strengthened Guderian's conviction that, as he put it, "the attack must be pressed forward with all possible strength, since the defensive capabilities of the French were obviously causing their high command serious anxiety. This was no time for hesitancy, still less for calling a halt." Accordingly, he gathered his troops company by company and read to them the captured French order, making plain to them its significance and the necessity of continuing the attack at once. After thanking them for their achievements to date, he told them that they must now strike with all their power to complete the victory. He then ordered them to return to their vehicles and to continue the advance.

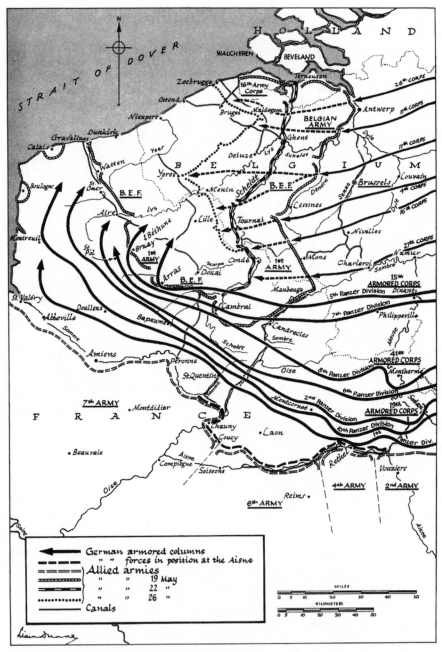

Encirclement of the Allied Northern Armies, May 17–26. (Shirer, *Collapse of the Third Republic,* Simon and Schuster)

Guderian's panzers were now moving in open country, and they advanced rapidly, meeting virtually no French resistance. Driving toward Montcornet, Guderian passed an advancing column of the 1st Panzer Division. He found its men "wide awake and aware that we had achieved a complete victory, a breakthrough." The soldiers, he recalled, cheered and shouted remarks that often could only be heard by the staff officers in the car behind Guderian's: "Well done, old boy," and "There's our old man," and "Did you see him? That was hurrying Heinz." All this was indicative to Guderian that his panzers could not be stopped.

Arriving in Montcornet's marketplace, Guderian found General Kempff, the commander of the 6th Panzer Division, which was attached to General Reinhardt's panzer corps. Kempff's troops entered the town from the west after having crossed the Meuse just as Guderian was arriving from the south. Since Kleist's panzer group headquarters had laid down no boundary between their divisions, Guderian and Kempff quickly drew up one themselves and then, as Guderian recalled, "ordered the advance to go on until the last drop of petrol was used up." By the end of the day, Guderian's lead units reached Marle and Dercy, over 40 miles from that morning's starting point and 55 miles from Sedan.

Behind Guderian's and Reinhardt's leading panzer divisions, as many as 25 to 30 miles, except for a few supply units, there was hardly a single German soldier to be found. The lead German infantry divisions did not reach Sedan until the evening of May 16. Munitions and fuel were being brought up to the advancing panzer divisions over a single, very thin, almost unprotected supply road. But the panzers' advance was so swift, they were able to refuel at French gasoline stations before the French could destroy them.

While Guderian and Kempff were planning their next moves, Guderian's men were searching houses near Moncornet's market place. Within a few minutes they had collected several hundred prisoners, Frenchmen from various units whose amazement at the German arrival was written all over their faces. A French tank company, which had tried to enter the town from the southwest, was taken prisoner. It belonged to General Charles de Gaulle's 4th Armored Division, which had been organized only the previous day, and whose presence, Guderian learned, was in the area north of

Laon. Guderian was not bothered. He knew that the Stukas controlled the skies and that consequently the threat posed by de Gaulle was not serious enough to delay his advance to the sea. He realized from the scenes he had witnessed as he advanced across France that the entire French command structure, all the way down to the tactical level, was totally disrupted. Every mile farther that he could thrust his panzer sword into the body of France would only accelerate this process.

THE PANZERS ARE HALTED, MAY 16–17

Army Chief of Staff General Franz Halder also was pleased with the progress of the panzers' advance. On May 16 he wrote in his diary that the breakthrough was "developing on almost classical lines." The French had not yet thrown in their "principal reserves," which he estimated at 30 divisions, nor did they show any signs of preparing to do so. Nevertheless, he issued orders to keep a watch on them. But on the whole, he was not worried. He did not believe the French high command would get around to mounting a counterattack against the rapidly lengthening flanks of the advancing panzers before he could reinforce them sufficiently with the infantry divisions that were coming up from behind.

However, Army Group A's commander, Gerd von Rundstedt, was nervous about the panzers' flanks. His chief of operations and biographer, General Guenther von Blumentritt, recounted how Rundstedt was amazed—and frightened—by the success of the Meuse crossings. He called them a "miracle he could not understand." In fact, at various crucial moments during the campaign Rundstedt would show himself to have been almost as strongly conditioned by his personal experiences in World War I as any of the French generals. During that conflict, Rundstedt's own unit came within sight of Paris shortly before his commander, General Alexander von Kluck, turned his army eastward. In doing so, Kluck exposed the flank of the German army to the devastating counterattack that came out of the French capital. It struck the Germans as they were advancing to the Marne River and robbed them of a quick victory, prolonging the war and contributing directly to Germany's ultimate defeat. Scarred by the memory of this disaster, Rundstedt was determined that it would not be repeated.

By May 16, Rundstedt's fears finally overflowed. That day, the French repeatedly attacked the turning hinge of Kleist's panzer group at Stonne, causing substantial losses to the German infantry that were arriving there to relieve Guderian's 10th Panzer Division. By then, Guderian's lead tanks, in the 1st and 2nd Panzer Divisions, were preparing to cross the Oise River. That evening, Rundstedt ordered all panzers to halt their westward movement until infantry could be brought up to protect the panzer corridor's flanks.

The German supreme commander, Adolf Hitler, also was worried that powerful French armored units might attack the panzers' flanks and steal a great triumph from him. Like Rundstedt, the Führer's mind was very much on the last great war. On May 18 he wrote to Italian dictator Benito Mussolini that "the miracle of the Marne of 1914 will not be repeated!"

To ensure this, during the morning of May 17, Hitler decided, for the first time in the campaign, to see his field commanders. At 1:00 P.M., he was driven from the Eagle's Nest to a nearby airfield, where a plane was waiting to fly him to Rundstedt's headquarters near Bastogne, the town whose name would enter American history four and a half years later. There he was relieved to learn that Rundstedt had already issued the order halting the panzer advance. Rundstedt said he expected "a great surprise counteroffensive by strong French forces from the Verdun and Châlons-sur-Marne area northward . . . against the ever-lengthening left flank of the armies pressing forward."

Hitler emphasized that there must not be an Allied counterattack. The importance of this, he said, went beyond purely military effects; it was also "political and psychological." In the absence of a successful French counterattack, Hitler insisted, the English would realize that they must leave the Continent. Then he would make peace with them. At the moment, he told Rundstedt, the final decision "depends not so much on a rapid thrust to the Channel, as on the ability to secure as quickly as possible an absolutely sound defense on the Aisne in the Laon area and, later, on the Somme." He spoke briefly, cut the conversation off, and returned to the Eagle's Nest before supper.

General Halder, who was not present at this meeting but heard about it later, kept peppering his diary with notations all that day refuting the idea that the French could seriously counterattack the exposed southern flank of the advancing panzers. "The enemy has only six divisions there, which is not enough to attack with. Therefore, no danger." He closed his diary by noting Hitler's nervousness: "He is worried over his own success, will risk nothing, and so puts the reins on us. And all because of his concern with the left flank!" His calls and talks to the army groups, Halder concluded, "have caused only bewilderment and doubts."

The next day, Hitler told both Brauchitsch and Halder that he had ordered a slowdown in the advance in order to avoid falling into a French trap. Although the generals knew there would be no trap, because the Allied armies were already in disarray and in retreat almost everywhere, they obeyed his order. Ominously, it was the first time that Hitler directly involved himself in a battlefield decision. His growing conviction that he knew more about strategy than Brauchitsch and Halder convinced him that he must intervene to save the victory.

Ironically, however, it was the Führer, not the army high command, who was being excessively cautious. Far in the rear, he could not comprehend either the quickness or the totality of the French collapse on the Meuse. The absence of a strong French counterattack naturally seemed too good to be true. After all, every army maintains reserves for just such an eventuality as the French now faced. But there were no French reserves in the area. After crossing the Meuse and turning westward, Kleist's panzers met little resistance as they drove to the sea.

Early in the morning of May 17, Guderian received a message from the headquarters of Panzer Group Kleist: the advance was to be halted at once and he was personally to report to General Kleist, who would come to see him at Guderian's airstrip at seven o'clock. Kleist arrived punctually and, as Guderian recalled, "without even wishing me a good morning, began in very violent terms to berate me for having disobeyed orders." The previous evening, Guderian had conveniently overlooked Rundstedt's halt order, which had been relayed to him by Kleist, and blandly sent out radio orders to his divisions to continue the advance the next day. Unfortunately, Guderian's radio-delivered orders were monitored by Kleist's headquarters. When Kleist "stopped to draw breath," Guderian immediately asked to be relieved of his command. Kleist was momentarily taken aback by the request, but then nodded and ordered Guderian to hand over his command to the most senior general in his corps.

Guderian returned to his headquarters and asked General Rudolf Veiel, commander of the 2nd Panzer Division, to come to see him. He then sent a message to Rundstedt's headquarters by radio, informing him that he had handed over his command to Veiel and would be flying there at noon to make a report on what had happened. Guderian received an almost immediate reply: he was to remain at his headquarters and await the arrival of Colonel-General Sigmund Wilhelm von List, who was in command of the 12th Army, which was following behind him and who had been instructed by Rundstedt to clear up this matter. The last thing Rundstedt wanted was one of Hitler's favorites out of action. However, until List arrived, all units were to remain where they were.

Guderian took advantage of the interval to write a letter to his wife, Gretel. While the letter no longer exists, its purport is evident in her reply, which was written on May 27. "Darling," she wrote, "I beg of you, from the bottom of my heart, not to do this [resign]. If you have to act, I think you should send a direct report to the Fuehrer: anything else would be, as always, to your disadvantage."

Well before that letter proved necessary, however, List arrived early in the afternoon of May 17 and informed him that he would not be permitted to resign his command. The order to halt the advance came from the Führer himself, List explained, and therefore had to be obeyed.

Guderian was surprised. "After our splendid success on the 16th of May," he recalled, "it certainly never occurred to me that Hitler, himself, who had approved the boldest aspects of the Manstein plan and had not uttered a word against my proposals concerning exploitation of the breakthrough, would now be the one to be frightened by his own temerity and would order our advance to be stopped at once."

List sympathized with Guderian's reasons for wanting to continue the advance. With the army group's approval, he permitted Guderian to carry out a "reconnaissance in force," provided that his headquarters "must in all circumstances remain where it is, so that it may be easily reached."

Guderian expressed his gratitude to List and asked him to clear up the misunderstanding between Kleist and himself. Then he put the "reconnaissance in force" in motion. And while he kept his corps headquarters in its old location in Soize, he had a wire laid from it to his advanced headquarters. In this way, he would not have to communicate with his staff by radio, and his orders could not be monitored by the radio intercept units of Kleist's headquarters! By the evening of that day, Guderian's advanced units had established a bridgehead across the Oise River, near Moy, 15 miles from Dercy and 70 miles from Sedan. The English Channel was only 70 miles away.

Among the panzer troops, however, there was no doubt that the halt order of May 16 was an unmitigated blessing. It was, Major Kielmansegg pointed out, "the first real day of rest since the beginning of the campaign." Besides enabling the outdistanced infantry and supplies to catch up, here at last was an opportunity to get some badly needed sleep, to grease up the tanks, and to replace their numerous worn-out parts.

It also was an opportunity for the French high command to collect itself. Unfortunately for France, that opportunity was not seized.

DE GAULLE'S COUNTERATTACK, MAY 17

On May 16, General Georges ordered General Henri Giraud and General Robert-Auguste Touchon, respectively the recently appointed commanders of the 9th Army and the newly created 6th Reserve Army, to counterattack the vulnerable flanks of the German panzer corridor and "clear" the "gap" between the Oise and the Aisne rivers. The operation, which was set to begin on the morning of May 17, was to be carried out by three armored divisions: the 1st, 2nd, and 4th.

But all this was wishful thinking, for on the morning of May 17, unknown to Georges, there was only one, not three, armored divisions available to clear the vast area between the two rivers. The 1st Armored Division was all but annihilated after it had arrived with empty fuel tanks near the Meuse on May 14. The 2nd Armored Division, whose tanks were severed from its wheeled vehicles, had been completely dispersed by the German panzer thrust. The only armored division available for the counterattack was Charles de Gaulle's 4th Armored Division.

On May 15 de Gaulle had been summoned to Georges's headquarters and informed that General Touchon would try to establish a defensive front that would block the way to Paris. Operating from the Laon area, de Gaulle was directed to "gain time" for Touchon. "Calm, cordial, but visibly overwhelmed," de Gaulle recalled, General Georges sent him on his way with the words: "There, de Gaulle! For you, who have so long held the ideas which the enemy is putting into practice, here is the chance to act."

But act with what? De Gaulle was supposed to have under his command two battalions of 60 31-ton "B" tanks and two battalions of 80 12.5-ton Renault tanks, one rifle battalion, and two groups of artillery with 75mm guns. Yet on the evening of May 15, when he arrived in Laon, about 20 miles southwest of Montcornet, where these forces were to assemble, all he found was a number of French troops from several different units, completely unrelated to his own. He had no idea when his own units would arrive.

Nevertheless, the next morning de Gaulle set out to inspect the terrain east of the Sissonne Canal, on which his offensive would take place, provided his forces arrived to carry it out. He was appalled by what he saw. All the roads from the north were packed with pitiful convoys of refugees and unarmed soldiers who, overtaken in their flight by the panzers, had been ordered by the Germans to throw down their rifles and head south, so as not to clutter the roads. "On hearing of that contemptuous piece of insolence on the part of the enemy," de Gaulle remembered, "I was filled with indescribable fury. . . . If I lived, I would fight, wherever I had to, so long as I had to, till the enemy was defeated and the national taint expunged. What I was able to do later, I resolved upon that day."

All throughout May 16, de Gaulle's units straggled into Laon, many of their men completely exhausted. But only one of his division's two heavy tank battalions arrived, and only after a series of misadventures during the previous night. The two light tank battalions also drove in, but the artillery groups and rifle battalion did not arrive with them. To fill that void, de Gaulle commandeered some unattached artillery units. Nevertheless, the 4th Armored Division was in no condition to go into battle. However, de Gaulle's commanding officer, General Giraud, could not wait until it was.

That evening, de Gaulle learned that a German column (the 1st Panzer Division) was moving west of Montcornet, along the Serre River, 10 to 12 miles north of where his forces were deployed. De Gaulle decided to attack northward the next morning. He would attempt to cross the Serre in order to block the junction of roads that led west and south to St. Quentin, Laon, and Reims. His immediate objective was the seizure of three bridges crossing the canal at Montcornet, Agincourt, and St. Pierremont.

By dawn on May 17, an additional battalion of tanks had arrived, giving de Gaulle a total of three: one composed of heavy "B" tanks, equipped with 75mm guns, the other two of light Renault 33s mounting obsolete short-range 37mm guns. De Gaulle's division had no proper antiaircraft weaponry, nor could it call upon any air support worth the name. Nevertheless, at daybreak, clad in his leather jacket and puffing incessantly on a cigarette, de Gaulle set out on his mission. That day, he would finally engage units belonging to that other great protagonist of armored warfare, Heinz Guderian.

The day began well for de Gaulle, with his tanks charging up the road from Laon to Montcornet. Crossing the Sissonne Canal at Chivres, they captured the village against some resistance and overran a German reconnaissance column. One of de Gaulle's tank commanders, Captain Idée, described the carnage the French attack produced: The German "motorcycles, their passengers inert, crumpled up in the side-cars or slumped over the handle-bars; a truck in flames; an armored car knocked out by our 47-mms; infantrymen mown down while they were withdrawing behind a farm; yet another armored car, shot up on the road to Machecourt."

By 3:00 P.M., de Gaulle's tanks had fought their way into Montcornet, "destroying everything which had no time to flee."

Major Kielmansegg, the 1st Panzer Division's chief of staff, was driving to the division's advanced headquarters, some eight miles to the west of Montcornet, when de Gaulle's division attacked. "As I came out of Montcornet and continued along the main road," Kielmansegg recalled, "I saw several German soldiers running back towards me. They were engineers, who insisted that French tanks were coming behind them. . . . There was no longer any time to consider where the tanks were coming from. I ordered the engineers, who had already laid some mines, to set up a barricade at the entry to Montcornet."

After establishing a hasty defensive line in front of the town, Kielmansegg rushed back to his division's headquarters at Lislet, which was totally undefended. Here he found, "lying blissfully and peacefully ignorant in the warm sunshine, a field service ammunition column halted on two of the roads leading to the village and waiting to push on ahead." Kielmansegg ordered them to turn around. As they were doing so, a lookout ran up, shouting, "They're coming, Herr Hauptmann, they're coming!" As the first French tanks swung into the streets of Lislet, Kielmansegg ordered his men to retreat. "Under these circumstances," he observed later, "prudence was the better part of valor, for even with the best will in the world, one cannot hold up a dozen enemy tanks with a pistol."

Kielmansegg then drove back to Guderian's headquarters at Soize to alert it. On his way, he encountered a small number of advancing panzers that had just been repaired. He immediately ordered them off in the direction of the oncoming French tanks. On returning to Lislet, Kielmansegg was informed that the panzers, supported by a few flak guns firing from the heights behind the town, were able to knock out several of de Gaulle's tanks and to beat back the rest. The town, he remembered, was "burning from one end to another," with two shot-up French tanks in the village itself and several others on the road to Montcornet.

A second French attack, led by four heavy "B" tanks, later that afternoon was also beaten back. Although Kielmansegg's light flak guns could not penetrate the French tanks' armor, by firing at their tracks, the German guns forced them to withdraw. Kielmansegg bragged that "the lack of fighting spirit of the enemy became abundantly clear to us—German tanks against so weak a defense would certainly not have turned round." But Captain Idée explained that the "B" tanks were compelled to withdraw from Lislet because they lacked infantry support.

❁

To the east, the advance of another of de Gaulle's tank columns was checked by German self-propelled guns, firing across the Serre River. Lacking artillery with which to engage the German guns, the French tanks were forced to withdraw. "We were lost children twenty miles in advance of the Aisne," de Gaulle exclaimed, "we had got to put an end to a situation that was, to say the least, risky."

On their way back to their morning starting point, they were attacked remorselessly by wave after wave of Stukas. Captain Idée recalled the incendiary bullets ricocheting by the thousands off his armor as he thought grimly: "We shall not get out of this. I am blinded by sweat. I wipe myself with my sleeves—and the medallion of Saint Thérèse, which I carry on my wrist, smiles at me. I kiss it." Idée survived, though his battalion lost one more tank from the air attacks.

With the German panzers beginning to infiltrate his lines and nightfall approaching, de Gaulle decided to withdraw his division, along with 150 prisoners. He had lost 200 men, 10 of his heavy tanks, and 40 of his light ones. Despite this, his counterattack had only minimal impact on the course of the conflict. While it did create some momentary alarm within the 1st Panzer Division, "it did not," General Kleist recalled, "put us in any such danger as later accounts have suggested. Guderian dealt with it himself without troubling me, and I only heard of it the day after." No doubt Guderian had his own reasons for not informing Kleist, but the fact remains that the German high command knew nothing of de Gaulle's counterthrust until the order to resume the advance had already been made. Considering OKW's state of extreme nervousness, had de Gaulle's counterattack been strong enough to make itself heard at Rundstedt's headquarters, the halt order would most certainly have been extended.

HITLER LIFTS THE PANZER HALT ORDER, MAY 18

The next day, May 18, Hitler's nerves were even worse than the day before. "The Fuehrer," Halder scribbled in his diary, "has an unaccountable worry over the south flank; he rages and screams that we are on the way to ruining the whole operation and risking the danger of defeat. He will absolutely not go along with continuing the operation westward." This, he added, was the subject of "a most unpleasant discussion at his headquarters" at nine o'clock that morning between Hitler, Brauchitsch, and Halder. Hitler, according to General Jodl, berated Brauchitsch for not building up the southern flank quickly enough.

Then, around midday, army headquarters received news that Antwerp, Cambrai, and St. Quentin had been captured. Neither Halder nor Brauchitsch intended to let victory fall from their grasp because of what they considered the groundless fears of a World War I corporal. Without attempting to get Hitler's approval, Halder immediately issued orders for the panzers to push on westward with reconnaissance forces. Then, at 5:00 P.M., he again met with Hitler and, after explaining the new situation, "demanded freedom of movement." This time, the Führer reluctantly agreed and lifted the halt order. That evening Halder smugly noted in his diary that "the correct thing finally came to pass; but with ill temper all round and in a form that, seen from the outside, gave the appearance of being a measure concluded by the OKW"—that is, by Hitler.

Pétain and Weygand Are Recalled to Paris, May 17

As Hitler's panzers drove deep into the heart of France, Paul Reynaud looked for a savior. On the morning of May 17, the French premier summoned to Paris from his post as ambassador in Madrid the 84-year-old World War I hero Marshal Henri Phillipe Pétain. The next day, he made Pétain his deputy premier. That evening, Reynaud made a radio address to the nation. "The victor of Verdun, Marshal Pétain," he declared, "will now be at my side . . . putting all his wisdom and all his force in the service of the country. He will remain there until victory is won." The press was ecstatic. The "Victor of Verdun" would once again make the French army invincible. Pétain, however, had no such illusions. On leaving Madrid, he told Francisco Franco, the Spanish dictator: "My country has been beaten and they are calling me back to make peace and to sign an armistice. . . . This is the work of thirty years of Marxism."

In the face of the "immensity" of the developing disaster, as Reynaud put it, he also reshuffled his cabinet during the evening of May 18. He took over the Ministry of Defense and sent Daladier, who had tenaciously clung to that post for four uninterrupted years, to the Foreign Ministry. Daladier, who had refused to accept this arrangement in March, now gave in. Like the top generals who had helped him fashion the French army, Daladier was stupefied to see it fall apart in only nine days.

At about eight o'clock in the morning of Friday, May 17, some 2,000 miles from Paris, a telegram from the Ministry of Foreign Affairs arrived at the high commission in Beirut, Lebanon. It was addressed to General Maxime Weygand, the commander-in-chief of French military operations in the eastern Mediterranean. Weygand, who was busy getting dressed, asked his secretary, Capt. Roger Gasser, to decipher the coded message. Bearing Paul Reynaud's signature, it read as follows: "The grave situation on the western front is worsening. I ask you to return to Paris without delay."

Even before he had finished, Gasser had a premonition it did not contain good news. "It's just as I thought," he said when he passed the decoded text to Weygand. Reading the text, Weygand sighed, "And yet I had prayed to God to spare me this cross." Then, recovering immediately, he looked back at Gasser: "When do we go?"

"Give me time to pack the bags, General!" Gasser replied.

At 3:30 in the morning of the next day, Weygand, accompanied only by Gasser, set off for the nearby airport, where a Glenn-Martin plane awaited to fly them to Paris. As he was leaving his command in Lebanon, Weygand said that "the military situation in France was already so irremediably compromised that it would be necessary to accept a reasonable armistice."

Had Reynaud himself become a defeatist? In a frank letter to William Shirer on August 29, 1965, Reynaud wrote: "I called in Pétain and Weygand in order to save the honor of the army, hoping they could improve matters after the collapse of Corap's army. This result, the only one I could hope for, was obtained. . . . My objective: defeat with honor."

Reynaud clearly believed by this early date—but would not publicly admit—that the war was lost, for England as well as for France. Late that evening, he told U.S. Ambassador Bullitt: "If the Germans should reach the Channel, although France would continue to fight to the bitter end, the German machine would swing down and finally take Paris. . . . The war might end in an absolute defeat of France and England in less than two months."

The Anglophobe Bullitt blamed the British for not throwing in the entire RAF into the defense of France. He suspected that they were holding back their air force in order to be able to make a separate peace with Hitler after France fell. In a cable to President Roosevelt that day, Bullitt warned that "in order to escape from the ultimate consequences of absolute defeat, the British may install a government of Oswald Mosley . . . which would cooperate fully with Hitler." However, hardly anyone, including

Hitler, took seriously the possibility of a British government headed by Mosley, the leader of a small and inconsequential British fascist party.

In London, Winston Churchill also began to have doubts about France's ability to stick it out. On May 18, the day Reynaud appointed Pétain to his cabinet, the British prime minister reminded Lord Ismay that in considering more troops for France, "one must always be prepared for the fact that the French may be offered very advantageous terms of peace, and the whole weight be thrown on us."

In fact, two days later, on May 20, Reynaud did receive a peace offer from Hermann Göring. It was delivered to him by Raoul Nordling, the Swedish consul-general in Paris. Nordling was instructed by Göring to "tell Reynaud he should immediately make us propositions for an armistice. We are ready to accord France reasonable conditions. . . . The more France delays in recognizing the facts, the severer will be our conditions."

When Nordling gave Reynaud Göring's message, the French premier was outraged. "If I did not know you," Reynaud told him, "I would have you arrested on the spot for sowing defeatism."

Gamelin "Acts!" May 17

Early on May 17, General Gamelin was informed by Daladier that Reynaud had recalled Pétain and Weygand to Paris. The implication did not escape the generalissimo: his head was on the block. That day, at Reynaud's urging, he reluctantly issued a new and ringing Order of the Day: "The fate of the country, that of our Allies, the destiny of the world, hangs on the battle now in course. . . . All troops which cannot advance must let themselves be killed rather than to abandon a parcel of our soil. . . . Conquer or die! We must conquer." Gamelin's words had a hollow sound to the weary, retreating soldiers of France.

The next day, Gamelin drove to General Georges's headquarters at La Ferté to see what the Northern Front commander was planning to do about the panzers driving to the English Channel. Gamelin was shocked by the appearance of Georges's office. It was, he recalled, in "complete disorder. . . . Liaison officers came and went. Letters and telegrams were brought in directly. Everyone talked at once. A waiting room, not a working room." Georges himself, Gamelin added, gave "incontestable signs of weariness. . . . he was not tranquil. . . . How could one dominate events in such an atmosphere and without withdrawing to think things over?"

Gamelin spoke privately about Georges's condition to General André Doumenc, the chief of the French general headquarters, whom he had brought along on the visit.

"General Georges," Doumenc said, "has always shown me sympathy and confidence, and I'm grateful to him. But it is going to be necessary for you to take over effective command yourself. It must be done, however, without hurting him."

"Certainly," Gamelin replied. "Tell me the moment and the occasion."

Surely, with Georges "weary" and his command post in "complete disorder," "the moment and the occasion" for Gamelin to act had indeed arrived. Moreover, that afternoon, French aerial reconnaissance planes reported a "complete vacuum" in the Laon-Montcornet area, immediately behind the cutting tip of the panzer divisions. But the sixty-eight-year-old generalissimo had no will to act, and the opportunity to do so passed quickly. The vacuum behind the rapidly advancing panzers was fast being filled by German infantry.

That same afternoon, after Gamelin had returned to his headquarters in Vincennes, he received a call from Georges, who said that Reynaud and Pétain were en route to La Ferté to assess the situation for themselves. They would then visit Gamelin at his headquarters. The generalissimo spent the rest of the afternoon awaiting their arrival, in what he said was an "affectionate and confiding conversation" with Daladier, the deposed defense minister. "It is the first time in ten days," Gamelin commented, "that I am left without something precise to do."

Reynaud and Pétain finally arrived at Vincennes at 6:20 P.M. To Reynaud, Gamelin seemed to be "concerned, but elegant and fluent as usual," as he stood before a map and briefed them. But, Reynaud recounted, the generalissimo's presentation dealt primarily with "what appeared to me to be the causes of our defeat."

After Reynaud and Daladier had departed, Gamelin escorted Pétain to his car. Shaking hands "affectionately" with Gamelin, the old soldier said, "My heart goes out to you," to which the generalissimo replied: "I think only of the country." The marshal waved warmly to him. "It was the last time," Gamelin recalled, "that I was to see him."

May 19 also proved to be Gamelin's last day in command of the French army. Around five o'clock that morning, General Doumenc called him: "The moment," Doumenc said, "has come for you to intervene." Gamelin asked Doumenc and Air Force Chief General Joseph Vuillemin to meet him at La Ferté at 8:00 A.M.

On his way there, Gamelin was filled with thoughts about Georges's failures. "I considered it particularly regrettable," he recounted, "that the commander of the Northeast Front had not taken effective direction of the battle at two crucial moments, on May 10 and on May 15."

General Doumenc greeted Gamelin as he arrived at La Ferté and again urged him to immediately take over command of all military operations. Gamelin found Georges, recalled Colonel Jacques Minart, a staff officer in Gamelin's headquarters, "in a state of profound physical and moral depression." Gamelin asked for a pencil and paper and retired to a small room on the second floor. "I wish to work in complete tranquillity," he said.

The plan Gamelin drafted was prefaced with the sentence, "Without wishing to interfere in the conduct of the battle." It then outlined his intention to launch a pincer attack against the panzers' southern flank with General Robert Touchon's 6th Army and against their northern flank with General Billotte's army group. Gamelin's last line read: "All is a matter of hours." At 9:45 A.M., he put his signature to what General Roton labeled his "military testament."

Later, Georges recalled that Gamelin returned with his "paper," placed it on his desk, and said: "You will read it after my departure," whereupon he took his leave. In those circumstances, Georges insisted, he did not think "the paper was urgent. I did not open it until some moments later, when I perceived it was a personal and secret instruction written in pencil. It had been a long time since I had received one! . . . I was stupefied!"

Perhaps Georges already knew that Weygand was on his way to replace Gamelin, for he made no effort to implement the directive, which he later insisted was only a set of "suggestions." Georges had already ordered the extension of the 7th Army's front to cover Paris, as well as the massing of the Cavalry Corps on Billotte's right. That evening, Georges also gave to General Antoine Besson, the commander of the 3rd Army Group, the responsibility for overseeing the 6th and 7th Armies on the Somme front. And this was as far as he acted.

Before departing La Ferté, Gamelin had a "quick lunch" with Georges. The chef, "dispirited, like all of us by the defeat," one staff officer recalled, "had put all his frustrated patriotism into the confection of a true wedding banquet." But the lunch assumed more "the atmosphere of a funeral repast. . . . Then came the dessert; a huge raised pudding covered with *cheveux d'ange*. It was grotesque and pathetic." Only Gamelin seemed to have had a good appetite.

GORT DECIDES TO WITHDRAW
TO THE COAST, MAY 19

For the first time, shortly after midnight on the morning of Sunday, May 19, General Billotte visited Gort's BEF headquarters at Wahagnies. Billotte was at the end of his tether. "I am completely done in, and I can't do a thing against these panzers," he said to his British liaison officer, Major O. J. Archdale, as they drove to Gort's headquarters.

Archdale, for his part, was determined that Gort should not remain ignorant of the "malignant inaction" at 1st Army Group headquarters. He had seen that all Billotte could do was to stand in front of a map that showed the positions of the 10 German panzer divisions, count them up one by one, and say, "Against them, I can do nothing." Archdale had decided to arrange Billotte's visit to Gort's headquarters so that the British commander-in-chief could have an "eye opener."

Billotte, whom Pownall described as "quite calm but very tired," began the meeting by discussing the measures that had been taken to prop up the French 9th Army. But Billotte, Pownall remembered, "clearly had mighty little hope that they would be effective." Producing a situation map on which the spearheads of 10 panzer divisions were shown to be little more than 30 miles from the Channel coast, and with no French troops between them and their objective, he asked the British for help in launching a counterattack against the panzers' northern flank, breaking through it, and forcing their way south to the Somme River. Until this point, the French had regarded Britain's small contribution to the land war with a certain amount of contempt. Now, in this moment of crisis, they were calling upon the small but relatively intact BEF to play a key role in saving France.

It was obvious to Gort from Billotte's despairing remarks that there was no possibility that the BEF could break through the German front and reach the Somme. Gort's army was already holding down about a third of the Escaut line. How, he asked, did Billotte expect him to hold a southern line almost twice as long, not to mention launch a counterattack to break through the panzer corridor? And in doing so, Gort was supposed to rely on the assistance of the French 1st Army, which had suffered heavily, and the Belgian army, which was losing heart. Gort argued later that even if the maneuver to the Somme had been possible, "it would have obviously been unwelcome to the Belgians, who would have been faced with the alternatives of withdrawing with us, and abandoning Belgian soil, or fighting on a perimeter on their own, or seeking an armistice."

Clearly, Gort also did not have much faith in the French high command's ability to orchestrate such a withdrawal. From at least May 15, he had received reports from his liaison officers describing the French army's administrative chaos, as well as the demoralization and "malignant inaction" that were permeating both Billotte's and Blanchard's headquarters. According to Gort's liaison officer at Blanchard's 1st Army headquarters, "Blanchard was every day losing the respect of his officers," who, "with one or two exceptions," also did not deserve his. (The French liaison mission at Gort's headquarters, for its part, began to detect and to report the British command's growing lack of confidence in the French military, all of which was accentuated by the discovery that Gort had shipped his personal luggage back to England on May 18.)

Even worse, from Gort's perspective, he realized that with the panzers advancing to the Channel, the BEF's position in Belgium was quickly becoming untenable. Its supplies, which were brought from England through Cherbourg and Brest, two ports over 200 miles away, were about to be cut off. Moreover, the panzers already had cut straight through his lines of communication and forced him to improvise new lines to Boulogne, Calais, and Dunkirk. Yet each of these ports could be threatened by the Germans in a matter of a few days.

For Gort, there was no alternative but to withdraw to the coast. This move would allow the BEF to fall back on its lines of communication and keep in touch with the Belgian army. But more importantly, withdrawal to the coast would enable the BEF to evacuate to England, if that proved necessary—and to Gort, that possibility now seemed inevitable. Yet he was reluctant to consider this option, for it would have amounted to abandoning the French at a time when they were in need of all possible support. Nevertheless, Gort also realized that his primary duty was the preservation of the BEF, not the maintenance of good relations with the French.

At 11:30 A.M. on May 19, Gort instructed General Pownall to telephone the War Office in London and inform the director of military operations that, ultimately, the only course open to the BEF might well be evacuation to England. He then ordered his staff to draw up a preliminary plan for withdrawal to the coast. "Every useless mouth," including all headquarters troops not required for fighting, would be moved first, to Dunkirk and then to England. Gort also directed all RAF units in the path of the German panzers to leave France immediately; three fighter squadrons left that day.

Gort also took action to protect his southern flank. He ordered his reconnaissance regiment to move to Arras and deployed the 50th Infantry Division just north of that city, with the British 5th Division nearby in reserve. However, Gort had only two partially filled-out divisions, the 12th and 23rd British Territorial Infantry Divisions, between the Germans and the sea. The 23rd Division was assigned 16 miles of front along the Canal du Nord, while the 12th Division was ordered to man strong points in Albert, Doullens, Amiens, and Abbeville.

The War Cabinet, May 19

That Sunday morning, May 19, Winston Churchill thought he could spend some time at his home, Chartwell, some miles outside London. It would be his first visit since he had become prime minister nine days earlier. Once there, he discovered that some of his swans had been eaten by foxes. However, his favorite black swan had survived and was floating serenely on the water, craning and pecking at whatever he threw to it.

Not long after arriving, however, the prime minister's meditation was abruptly interrupted by a telephone message. The French 1st Army had collapsed, it stated, leaving a vast gap on the right flank of the BEF. Churchill quickly drove off for London, his driver disregarding all traffic lights, the bell of the accompanying police car ringing incessantly. Arriving at Downing Street, the prime minister was relieved to learn that the report of the French 1st Army's demise was greatly exaggerated.

Churchill also was informed that General Pownall had telephoned to say that Gort was contemplating a retreat to the sea. Although Churchill, two days earlier, had directed the preparation of plans for such an eventuality—an order that marked the genesis of "Operation Dynamo," the evacuation of the BEF from Dunkirk—he had considered his order merely a precautionary move for a remote possibility. He was shocked that Gort was considering its implementation so soon.

Gort's suggestion that the BEF might abandon the fight in France relatively soon touched off a furor in the British War Cabinet. General Sir Edmund Ironside, the chief of the Imperial General Staff, was appalled by that prospect. He told the War Cabinet that it might be possible to keep the army supplied for a limited time on a bridgehead resting on the Channel ports, but "we could certainly never evacuate the force completely." Instead, he preferred "that the BEF should advance southwest, with its left somewhat reduced, in order to get back on to its lines of communication."

Arthur Greenwood, a Labour member of the War Cabinet, angrily reacted, calling the French "bloody Allies." But Ironside rejoined "that it was not right to say 'these bloody Allies.' It was for them to say that of us." He explained: "We have lived in a fool's paradise. Largely depending upon the strength of the French army. And this army has crashed or very nearly crashed. . . . At the moment, it looks like the greatest military disaster in all history."

Churchill agreed fully with Ironside. If the BEF withdrew to Dunkirk, he said, it "would be closely invested in a bomb-trap," and its total loss would be only a matter of time. "Our forces," Churchill continued, "must therefore, at all costs, move back towards Amiens." This, he admitted, however, would entail giving up the Channel ports; it also would mean that the Belgian army "might be lost altogether." No one disagreed with his assessment. The meeting concluded after it was decided that Ironside personally should go at once to deliver the War Cabinet's instructions to Gort.

Nevertheless, as a precautionary measure, Churchill also thought that the Admiralty should begin to assemble a large number of small vessels and prepare them to proceed to the ports and inlets of northern France. In fact, as early as the evening of May 17, General Ironside had asked the Admiralty to begin that very task. As a result, by May 20, 30 passenger ferries, 12 naval drifters, and six small coasters were assembled as a first installment. The overall responsibility for drawing up the contingency plan for the evacuation was assigned the previous day to Vice Admiral Sir Bertram Ramsay, commanding at Dover. He immediately put the assembled ships to work gathering Gort's "useless mouths."

At nine o'clock that evening, Churchill delivered a radio speech to the nation for the first time as prime minister. Although it would be foolish to "disguise the gravity of the hour," he said, "it would be still more foolish to lose heart." He expressed his confidence that the front in France would be stabilized soon, but he also warned that once this was achieved, German aggression would be turned "in a few days" upon Britain. "In that supreme emergency," his voice rose, "we shall not hesitate to take every step, even the most drastic, to call forth from our people the last ounce and the last inch of effort of which they are capable." Churchill then referred to Premier Reynaud's pledge "that whatever happens," France would fight on to the end. "We have differed and quarreled in the past," Churchill said, "but now one bond unites us all: to wage war until victory is won, and never to surrender ourselves to servitude and shame, whatever the cost and the agony must be."

Churchill's first broadcast as prime minister caught the imagination of millions of Britons. That evening, Anthony Eden wrote to him: "My dear Winston, You have never done anything as good or as great. Thank you, and thank God for you." Churchill's private secretary, John Colville, who had been critical of the new prime minister's character and judgment just a few days earlier, now said, "His spirit is indomitable."

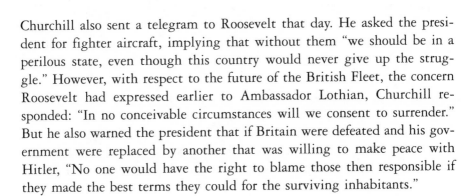

Churchill also sent a telegram to Roosevelt that day. He asked the president for fighter aircraft, implying that without them "we should be in a perilous state, even though this country would never give up the struggle." However, with respect to the future of the British Fleet, the concern Roosevelt had expressed earlier to Ambassador Lothian, Churchill responded: "In no conceivable circumstances will we consent to surrender." But he also warned the president that if Britain were defeated and his government were replaced by another that was willing to make peace with Hitler, "No one would have the right to blame those then responsible if they made the best terms they could for the surviving inhabitants."

WEYGAND TAKES OVER, MAY 19–20

For General Weygand, who had turned seventy-three the previous January, the flight to Paris proved to be eventful and uncomfortable. Seated on a shaky garden chair in the tail section of the heavily loaded Glenn-Martin, he could only catch a glimpse of the sky by looking between the long legs of his aide, Captain Roger Gasser, who was perched on the gunner's seat in front of the general.

The plane's pilot, Commander Pepin, had counted on reaching Tunis in one hop, where he had planned to refuel and then arrive in Paris the same night. But violent head winds around Benghazi, Libya (then a colony of the dubious neutral, Italy), forced Pepin to return to the British base at Mersa Matruh in Egypt, causing the flight to be delayed three hours and compelling his passengers to spend the night in Tunis.

The plane left Tunis early the next morning, Sunday, May 19, and, four hours later, landed at Étampes military base near Paris. But upon landing, due to the weight of the plane's cargo, its undercarriage collapsed, blocking the exit door. Weygand had to squeeze out of the plane through its gun turret dome. As he got out of the plane, air raid sirens were blaring. "Hurry, General!" Pepin yelled. "We could be attacked any minute!"

As Weygand made his way to Reynaud's office in the War Department, the members of the French government, led by President Lebrun, Reynaud, and the venerable Marshal Pétain, were praying at Notre Dame, the great Gothic cathedral in the heart of Paris, for a repeat of the "Miracle of the Marne." The names of the great saints of France, St. Geneviève and St. Louis, were invoked as their relics were paraded before the congregation. U.S. Ambassador Bullitt sat in the front pew, unable to hide his tears.

After the services, Reynaud drove back to his office with his aide, Paul Baudouin, who urged him to lose no time in replacing Gamelin with General Weygand. But now that Weygand was in Paris, Reynaud became reluctant to change commanders-in-chief in the midst of the battle. He said it might be better to keep Weygand at his side as chief of the General Staff. "You can't offer Weygand half a loaf," Baudouin replied. "A situation as grave as this demands a sole chief." Nevertheless, when Weygand arrived at the War Department at 2:30 P.M., looking as dapper as a horse jockey, Reynaud merely told him to see Georges and Gamelin and then return that evening with his impressions of the military situation.

After arriving at Vincennes, Weygand did not inform Gamelin why he had been recalled to France. And the generalissimo thought it beneath his "dignity to ask him." Weygand merely said that Reynaud had asked him "to have a look at things."

Gamelin proceeded to brief him on the military situation and to explain the order for a counteroffensive that he had just given Georges.

As Weygand was leaving, he said to Gamelin: "You know that Paul Reynaud does not like you?"

"I know it," the generalissimo replied.

Weygand had made little effort to question Gamelin about the military situation. He preferred to get that information from General Georges, who, he felt, was better qualified to give it.

When Weygand arrived at Georges's headquarters, one of its staff members, General André Beaufre, was struck by his "swagger, passion and fierce will, which contrasted sharply with the pale and curdled calm of his predecessor." But Weygand, for his part, was shocked by Georges's demeanor. He was, Weygand recalled, "like a man who had received a violent blow in the stomach and finds it difficult to pull himself together again." However, Weygand soon became depressed himself after Georges explained the military situation. In just 10 days, Georges said, the French army had lost 15 divisions. In the north, another 45 divisions were in danger of being thrown into the sea. The gap in the French front was nearly 100 miles wide, and there were no reserves to check the German avalanche.

The proper moment for a coordinated counteroffensive, Weygand responded, should have been on May 15 or 16. Now, he said, it might be too late.

After seeing Gamelin and Georges, Weygand returned to Reynaud's office, where the premier asked him to replace Gamelin. Weygand accepted the "heavy responsibility" cast upon him. But, he added pessimistically, "You will not be surprised if I cannot answer for victory, nor even give you the hope of victory."

As he left, Paul Baudouin inquired about Weyand's immediate plans. "I am dead tired," the new generalissimo replied, "for I had only three hours of sleep at Tunis. I shall begin by getting some sleep." He would decide what to do the next day. For France, this meant that another 24 hours would pass without a meaningful response to the onrushing German panzers.

At 8:15 that same evening, "without any previous notice of any kind," Gamelin recalled, an officer arrived with an envelope from Reynaud. It contained two decrees signed by the president of the Republic, naming Weygand the new chief of the General Staff as well as commander-in-chief of the army. An attached note by Reynaud thanked Gamelin for his years of service to the country.

The French press praised Weygand's new appointment as lavishly as it acclaimed the naming of Pétain as deputy premier. Wrote Emile Buré, the editor of *L'Ordre,* Weygand had been "the brains of the General Staff in the last war. . . . His is not a name of defeat or of capitulation." One columnist, Madame Tabouis, went so far as to announce that Weygand was the man Hitler feared most.

Charles de Gaulle, however, was not impressed. "Weygand," he wrote, "was neither made, nor prepared, to take action, to confront destiny as a great commander. In the course of his whole career he had never exercised command in battle. . . . To choose him to take command at the gravest hour in our military history—not because he was judged capable but under the pretext that 'he was a banner'—that was the great mistake."

Nor was General Spears impressed with Weygand. On arriving from Lebanon, Weygand looked at a map of the German advance and reportedly said: "If I had known the situation was so bad, I would not have come." To Spears, Weygand's comment "meant he was thinking of his reputation"— not the salvation of France.

❈

The next morning, May 20, Weygand arrived at Vincennes to assume command. His last meeting with Gamelin was cool and brief. To Weygand, Gamelin appeared "relieved to be rid of his heavy load." Gamelin, for his part, thought his successor was too abrupt. "Not one single word from the heart," he later complained. "Has this man a heart, like Joffre and Foch?"

Gamelin also observed that Weygand seemed "awfully sure of himself." When Gamelin said he thought that only the execution of his last order to Georges "could save the situation," Weygand slapped his hand on his notebook and replied: "But I have the secrets of Marshal Foch!" Gamelin recounted that he could have replied that he himself had possessed the secrets of Marshal Joffre, "but that they had not sufficed." However, Gamelin said nothing.

What really shocked Gamelin was Weygand's statement that "We must change this whole business of politics. We must finish with all these politicians. They're all the same, one as bad as another." But, again, Gamelin did not reply.

The meeting ended with both men shaking hands "coolly," as Gamelin recalled. The ex-generalissimo then drove off to his comfortable but modest apartment on the Avenue Foch. He would not see Weygand again until the end of 1943, when both generals found themselves imprisoned by the Germans in a Tyrolian castle.

IRONSIDE'S VISIT TO GORT, MAY 20

Meanwhile, General Ironside made his way to Gort's command post at Wahagnies, arriving there at 6:00 A.M. on May 20. He brought with him the War Cabinet's instruction ordering Gort to move the BEF south toward Amiens.

Gort told Ironside that he could not accept the order. He calmly pointed out that by disengaging the seven British divisions facing the Germans on the Escaut, he would precipitate the collapse of the tottering Belgian army on his left flank and thus guarantee disaster. Furthermore, he pointed out, the area to be attacked was occupied by several German panzer divisions; the BEF's communication lines and connection with its supply bases were on the point of being disrupted, and its supply of ammunition was precarious. With Amiens about to be in German hands, Gort wrote later, "the picture was no longer that of a line bent or temporarily broken, but of a besieged fortress. To raise such a siege, a relieving force must be sent from the south and, to meet this force, a sortie on the part of the defenders was indicated."

Gort attempted to overcome Ironside's objections by telling him that he already had planned to launch a limited attack southward from Arras the next day. It would be conducted by his two reserve divisions, the 5th and the 50th Infantry Divisions. They would be supported by two divisions from General René Altmayer's French 5th Corps. This was the most he could do, especially since he also had to take steps to defend his own rear, which extended along the canal lines running from La Bassée through St. Omer and then to the sea at Gravelines. However, Gort also cautioned Ironside that the attack would have to be approved and coordinated by General Billotte, who, Gort said, had given the BEF no orders for eight days. Billotte, Gort complained, was "just jelly—he has nothing and does nothing."

Pausing only to get Pownall, Ironside angrily set off for Billotte's headquarters near Lens. After a tiresome journey on roads blocked by refugees, Ironside found Billotte with General Blanchard, commander of the French 1st Army. The two French generals, according to Ironside, were "in a state of complete depression. No plan, no thought of a plan. Ready to be slaughtered. Defeated at the head without casualties. Worn out and nothing doing." When the trembling Billotte voiced his despair about halting the panzers, Ironside, whose six-foot-four-inch stature earned him the inevitable nickname "Tiny," lost his temper and, seizing the French general by his tunic buttons, administered a vigorous shaking. The startled Billotte immediately accepted the British proposal to attack the next day and promised French support.

Ironside then rushed back to Gort's headquarters with the good news, but Gort told him that the French would not carry through with their promise. Gort's negative reaction prompted Ironside to telephone General Weygand to complain that there was no coordination in the north and that Billotte should be relieved of his command, advice the new French generalissimo did not at all appreciate from a British general. Ironside also sent a threatening telegram to General Georges, warning him that unless he launched a counterattack northward against the panzer corridor, Billotte's army group would be completely and finally cut off. In Pownall's mind, the attack the British were planning would be "do or die." Ironside then abruptly departed for London. That evening, his diary closed with the lament, "God help the BEF. Brought to this state by French incompetence."

GUDERIAN REACHES THE CHANNEL, MAY 20

While the Allies were planning to break out of the bag the Germans had thrown around their northern armies, Heinz Guderian's panzers were closing the bag's still-open southern side.

Shortly after midnight on May 20, Guderian ordered his 19th Panzer Corps to strike out for Amiens and Abbeville, a move that would bring its panzer divisions to the English Channel and thereby complete the encirclement of the Allied armies in the north. Guderian prefaced his orders with the words, "The enemy opposite the corps's front has been defeated." The latest aerial reconnaissance patrols certainly confirmed this view; they could find virtually no Allied formations ahead of the panzers. French air patrols concurred. One reported a "whirlpool of armor" about to burst westward. With the Canal du Nord behind the panzers, there was now no natural barrier between them and the coast, just mile upon mile of the flat, featureless Picardy plain.

Guderian, not wanting to miss the historic moment when Amiens was captured, was on the road with the 1st Panzer Division at 4:00 A.M. Later that morning, the division's 1st Panzer Brigade, now under the command of Lieutenant Colonel Hermann Balck, ran into British soldiers for the first time near the town of Albert. The 1st Panzer Division's official historian describes the British soldiers as having "fought toughly and bravely without, however, being able to prevent the fall of Albert." By midmorning, Balck's tanks were at the gates of Amiens, having advanced nearly 35 miles since dawn.

Never had the 1st Division's panzers moved faster. Recalled Major Kielmansegg, "We had the feeling, such as a fine racehorse may have, of having been held back by its rider, coldly and deliberately, then getting its head free to reach out into a swinging gallop, and then speed to the finishing post as the winner."

William Shirer, who that day had finally been allowed to follow in the wake of the advancing panzers, was overwhelmed by the efficiency of the German army: "It is a gigantic, impersonal war machine, run as coolly and efficiently . . . as our automobile industry in Detroit. . . . thousands of motorized vehicles thundering by on the dusty roads, officers and men alike remain cool and business-like. Absolutely no excitement, no tension." Shirer added that it was "curious, not a single Allied plane yet . . . and these endless columns of troops, guns, supplies, stretching all the way from the German border . . . what a target!"

Guderian's panzers were advancing so fast, in fact, that they nearly captured an RAF unit on an airfield outside Amiens; the British fighters took off literally in the faces of the lead German tank crews. Bombed relentlessly by the Luftwaffe since the previous day, Amiens was still on fire as the 1st Panzer Division approached. The only Allied force remaining in the town was a battalion of the Royal Sussex Regiment, a unit attached to the 12th Territorial Division. It was quickly overrun by Balck's panzers. By midday, the Germans had spread a huge swastika flag in front of Amiens's post office to show the Luftwaffe that the city had been captured. The panzers then established a bridgehead about four miles deep on the south bank of the Somme River, in preparation for phase two of the battle of France, which would follow the defeat of the northern Allied armies.

Guderian arrived in Amiens shortly after it fell to inspect the great city that even General Ludendorff had failed to capture in 1918. Somehow he even found time to visit the city's great cathedral, before rushing off to see how the 2nd Panzer Division was doing.

That division was in Albert, where it was nearly out of fuel. Its staff proposed to halt there until gasoline could be brought up. But, Guderian recorded, "they were soon disillusioned." He ordered them to find fuel immediately and push on at once to Abbeville. After the division commander found the requisite gasoline, Guderian explained the moral of the incident: "One must always distrust the report of troop commanders: 'We have no fuel.' Generally they have. But if they become tired, they lack fuel." The division soon was on its way to Abbeville, some 45 miles distant.

Guderian then drove off to his new headquarters at Querrieu, northeast of Amiens. Arriving there, he was attacked by German planes. "It was perhaps an unfriendly action on our part," he recalled, "but our flak opened fire and brought down one of the careless machines. The crew of two floated down by parachute and were unpleasantly surprised to find me waiting for them on the ground. When the more disagreeable part of our conversation was over, I fortified the two young men with a glass of champagne. Unfortunately, the destroyed machine was a brand-new reconnaissance plane."

By six o'clock that evening, the 2nd Panzer Division reached Abbeville, moving so quickly it took by surprise a French unit drilling on its parade ground. The panzers then broke through positions held by the British 35th Brigade. With few tanks and practically no artillery, the British were quickly overrun. Pushing on from Abbeville, down the Somme River, Lieutenant Colonel Spitta's battalion reached the English Channel at Noy-elles by dusk. With understandable joy, the panzer crews, who had crossed the Meuse only a week before, filled their lungs with the sea's air and their eyes with its sight. In 10 short days, the exhausted but elated panzer sol-diers had traveled some 200 miles and had completed the encirclement of the Allies' best armies. That night, Guderian told his corps: "Today's battles have brought us complete success. Along the whole front the enemy is in retreat in a manner that at times approaches rout."

Far to the rear, the news of Guderian's arrival on the Channel caught the German high command by surprise. As late as the morning of May 20, General Halder had expressed concern that General Bock's advance on the German northern flank might result "in driving the game away, as it were, past Kleist."

But at the *Felsennest,* Hitler was "beside himself with joy," General Jodl recorded, after he received the news of Guderian's achievement. The Führer "talks in words of highest appreciation of the German army and its leadership," Jodl added. He "is working on the peace treaty," which would be signed in the Forest of Compiègne, where the German army surren-dered in 1918.

Yet Hitler was still anxious about the panzers' exposed flanks. And so was Rundstedt. "A critical moment in the drive came just as my forces had reached the Channel," he recounted at the postwar Nuremberg trial of Nazi war criminals. "It was feared that our armored divisions would be cut off before the infantry divisions could come up to support them." It was this fear that ultimately would save the British army.

CHAPTER SEVEN

The Weygand Plan, May 20–26

FRANKFORCE, MAY 20

At nine o'clock in the morning of Monday, May 20, General Sir Harold Franklyn, the commander of the 5th Division, arrived at Gort's headquarters. The BEF's chief informed him that in addition to his own division, he would now be commanding the 50th Northumbrian Division and the British 1st Army Tank Brigade. With this force, which Gort labeled "Frankforce," Franklyn was to move to Arras and relieve French and British troops holding the line of the Scarpe River east of that town. In so doing, he also was to gain as much "elbow room" as possible in order "to block the roads south of Arras, thus cutting off the German communications from the east." Although Franklyn had never commanded troops in battle before, he was confident that he could successfully carry out Gort's orders.

First, however, Franklyn would have to assemble his forces. The 1st Tank Brigade, during its 90-mile retreat from Belgium, had been reduced by breakdowns to 58 weakly armed Mark I tanks, which carried only a medium machine gun, and only 16 of the more powerful Mark IIs, which were equipped with a 2-pounder (37mm) gun. The tank brigade still had to travel another 30 miles to get to Vimy, its assembly point. The movement of the 5th and 50th Divisions also was held up by the allotment of only one troop-carrying company to each division, presumably because of the immense strain to which the other six companies had been subjected during the BEF's withdrawal to the Escaut. This meant that the only troops available to attack south of Arras the next morning would be a brigade belonging to the 50th Division.

Later that morning, Franklyn drove to General René Prioux's command post, six miles north of Arras. The tanks of Prioux's cavalry corps, which had performed brilliantly in holding up the panzer advance through the Gembloux gap, were now patrolling the Scarpe River just east of Arras. When Franklyn arrived, he found Prioux in conference with General Blanchard, the French 1st Army commander, and General René Altmayer, who commanded its 5th Corps. They soon were joined by General Billotte, the commander of the 1st Army Group.

Franklyn described Prioux as "a pleasant, cheerful, little man and obviously efficient" who was eager to make offensive use of his cavalry corps, which now included the reduced 1st Light Mechanized Division from the 7th Army, as well as the 2nd and 3rd Light Mechanized Divisions. On the other hand, General Altmayer looked haggard and worried, and was gloomily examining a map illustrating the planned counterattack. Billotte merely shook hands with Franklyn, who neither had met the French general before nor even heard of him. But clearly Franklyn had expected the commander of the Allied army group to display a more dashing demeanor. Instead, he found Billotte to be "a small, wizened man, which shows how anxiety can reduce a man's physical stature."

The French generals told Franklyn that they were planning a counterattack, southward, toward Bapaume and Cambrai. They asked Franklyn to cooperate by attacking toward Bapaume on the following day, May 21. Franklyn replied that he could not undertake more than the limited operation that Gort had assigned him, namely an advance south of Arras to relieve Prioux's cavalry of the responsibility for defending the Scarpe River east of that town. In return, Franklyn asked Prioux to move his cavalry to the west of Arras and watch that flank. Prioux offered to do even more than that. He promised that part of a mechanized cavalry division would advance on the outer flank of the British attack the next day.

Like Franklyn, however, Prioux had trouble assembling his forces. Many of his tanks had been dispersed among infantry units whose commanders now refused to return them. Learning of this, Prioux angrily fired off this order: "Today, May 20, the greater part of the fighting vehicles have not been returned to the light mechanized divisions. . . . This order will be carried out immediately. I will not hesitate to bring any formation commander who disobeys this order before a court-martial!" But even this threat did not work. As a result, only a few weak detachments of Prioux's 3rd Light Mechanized Division were available to assist "Frankforce's" operation.

To make the prospects for success of Franklyn's offensive even worse, that evening he learned that General Altmayer's force would not be ready to attack before May 22. According to Major Vautrin, a French 1st Army liaison officer with the BEF, when Altmayer received the order for the attack, "he sat on my camp bed and wept silently. He said . . . he would not continue to sacrifice his army corps, which had already lost half its strength."

Franklyn went ahead with a plan for the next day's attack anyway. It called for a two-pronged advance by two adjacent columns, each comprised of a battalion of tanks and one of infantry, as far as five miles to the south and east of Arras. The plan was accepted with more enthusiasm at Gort's headquarters than Franklyn had anticipated. As he was leaving there, General Ironside warmly grabbed him by the arm and wished him the best of luck. Clearly, Ironside hoped that Franklyn's impending attack would satisfy Churchill's and the War Cabinet's demand for action against the German panzer corridor. But, obviously, this ambition was not conveyed to Franklyn. When he asked Gort if he had any new instructions, he received a negative answer.

However, later that afternoon Gort sent his deputy, Brigadier General Sir Oliver Leese, to Franklyn's headquarters. Leese hinted that Gort was hoping for a more ambitious attack than he had originally planned. However, he left it to Franklyn to determine how the attack was to be conducted. But Franklyn was unaffected by Leese's intimations. He would stick to the original orders Gort had given him. They called for a limited advance beyond Arras, and that is what Franklyn intended to do.

ROMMEL ADVANCES TOWARD ARRAS, MAY 20

While Franklyn was deploying his tanks and troops around Arras during the evening of May 20, General Erwin Rommel's 7th Panzer Division was advancing toward that city from the southeast. The German high command fully appreciated the strategic importance of gaining the heights around Arras. "Only when we have seized the high ground around Arras shall we have won the battle," wrote General Halder.

Rommel planned to advance around the western flank of Arras with his 7th Panzer Division and, on its left flank, with the SS Motorized Division *Totenkopf* (Death's Head), while the 5th Panzer Division would drive east of the town. Rommel's established tank strength of 218 was now down to about 180, owing to breakdowns and casualties. Nevertheless, he was convinced that his planned attack would be as successful as all his previous battles.

Tanks and infantry belonging to Rommel's 7th Panzer Division crossing a French field. (Imperial War Museum RML132)

Rommel had intended to accompany his lead panzers himself, as was his custom, but his infantry were traveling so slowly that he felt compelled to drive back to them to hasten their advance. A mile or two north of Ficheux, he encountered part of the 6th Rifle Regiment, which was moving on the right flank of the 7th Regiment. He ordered it to speed up.

Half a mile east of Wailly, however, Rommel's infantry came under heavy fire. "One of our howitzer batteries," he recalled, "was already in position at the northern exit from the village, firing rapidly at enemy tanks attacking southward from Arras." Rommel immediately took charge. He and his aide-de-camp, Lieutenant Most, rounded up some light flak troops and some anti-tank guns, and personally gave each gun its target. "With the enemy so perilously close," Rommel recounted, "only rapid fire from every gun could save the situation. We ran from gun to gun. . . . Soon we succeeded in putting the leading enemy tanks out of action." Rommel then directed his guns to another group of British tanks, knocking out several and forcing the remainder to retreat.

Just as the Allied attack seemed to be over, Lieutenant Most sank to the ground, blood gushing from his mouth. It was a mortal wound. Most was the second ADC to fall at Rommel's side during the campaign. "The death of this brave man, a magnificent soldier," Rommel commented, "touched me deeply." Most's and Rommel's intervention, he did not mention, saved the German position below Arras.

MARTEL'S ATTACK, MAY 21

The tanks that Rommel's division encountered southwest of Arras belonged to the British 1st Tank Brigade, commanded by Major General Sir Giffard Martel, and were supported by the remnants of Prioux's cavalry corps. The Allied tanks were the armored spearhead of General Franklyn's Frankforce attack.

Martel had planned to begin his attack at 2:00 P.M. on May 21, but only one infantry brigade had arrived by that time. Hoping for additional infantry to arrive, Martel decided to delay the attack another half-hour. When none arrived, he launched the attack without them. From an open car, as was Rommel's custom, Martel led his force southward around the western side of Arras. However, without adequate infantry support and no aerial assistance, Martel's attack obviously was not going to resemble the German blitzkrieg. Nevertheless, he expected his tank brigade to reach Cambrai, less than twenty miles from the Somme River at Péronne, in two days.

To Martel's astonishment, however, fighting broke out almost immediately. His right column, led by the 4th Tank Regiment, encountered an enemy force at Duisans. The village was cleared after a brief but intense fight. A number of German prisoners were taken, but two precious infantry companies and some anti-tank guns had to be left behind to hold it. The bulk of the British column then pushed on toward Warlus, which it managed to capture, but only after overcoming substantial German resistance. The British tank column moved on to Berneville and then threw an advance guard across the Doullens-Arras road. But here the British infantry were pinned down by heavy German machine-gun and mortar fire, as well as by a 20-minute Luftwaffe bombardment. Nevertheless, Martel's tanks continued their sweep around the left flank of the German position and pushed on to Wailly.

Near Wailly, Martel's tanks ran into truckloads of German infantry belonging to the SS *Totenkopf* Division, which were trying to catch up with Rommel's advancing panzers, a few miles ahead. The men of the German anti-tank gun unit that accompanied them were startled to discover that their anti-tank shells bounced off the British armor. Unable to stop the advancing British tanks, the terrified SS troops broke and ran. Despite their fierce name, the men of the *Totenkopf* Division were Nazified recruits, not professional soldiers. "They were very young and large numbers were observed lying on the ground face downwards feigning death," the battle diary of the 1st Army Tank Brigade recorded. "Others ran up to the tanks surrendering." The brigade diary also recorded that "a large number of prisoners were taken—these were handed over to the infantry," that is, to the Durham Light Infantry Regiment.

This unit's war diary also states that "large numbers of prisoners were taken." However, on the only surviving copy of this document, which is in the custody of the British Public Records Office, the total number of prisoners taken was partially cut out; this apparently occurred during the process of clipping the paper to a file. As a result, the digit preceding the two zeros in the number is missing. Other sources, however, put the number of German prisoners at 400.

What happened to the German prisoners is still a mystery. An officer of the 7th Royal Tank Regiment, on a scouting mission, reported that he captured a German noncommissioned officer and attempted to hand him over to a captain of the Durhams. The tank commander recalled that the British soldiers in that unit "displayed great animosity towards the prisoner, and I was compelled to draw my revolver and order them off before I could reach their officer." If other captured Germans had to rely on the Durhams' officers to protect them, they clearly were in trouble—by the evening of May 21, most of that unit's officers were dead. It seems quite possible, even probable, on the basis of this limited evidence, that as many as 400 SS soldiers were murdered by members of Durham Light Infantry. At least, that is what the Germans believed happened to them. And, prompted by this belief, they would soon retaliate in kind.

While General Martel's right column was stopped near Wailly, his left column, led by the 7th Tank Regiment, managed to penetrate more deeply into the German flank, capturing four villages in the process. The British tanks annihilated a German motor transport column in Dainville at about 3:00 P.M. They then advanced another two miles and, in the process, overran a German anti-tank battery whose 37mm armor-piercing shells simply bounced off the oncoming Matildas. The British main force continued pushing south to Mercatel, which it reached about 4:20 P.M.

A smaller British force advanced as far as Wancourt, on the Cojeul River. But there it was stopped by a line of German anti-tank guns, the same guns that Rommel had hastily deployed in an arc extending from Neuville to Wailly. The German guns included 88mm antiaircraft guns, which proved to be highly effective at penetrating Allied armor. Even the 70mm-thick armor of the Matildas could not withstand the very accurate, high-velocity fire of the 88s. One 88mm battery alone claimed nine British tanks.

ROMMEL'S COUNTERATTACK, EVENING, MAY 21

Having finally stopped the British counterattack, Rommel launched one of his own. At about 6:00 P.M., he ordered the 25th Panzer Regiment to retrace its steps and attack southeastward to take the British tanks in their flank and rear. The panzers struck at Warlus and Duisans, which were also bombed heavily by the Luftwaffe. After one 40-minute attack, a subaltern in the Durhams said, "Our chaps were absolutely shattered."

General Franklyn had tried to get help from the RAF, but its Hurricanes had already shifted their bases back across the Channel. Franklyn's summons had to pass through BEF headquarters, then across to London by cable, and then down to the airfield in Kent, where the Hurricanes were now based. For some reason, his request never got there. As a result, the Luftwaffe, as had been the situation all along, had complete control of the skies over the battlefield.

One British soldier, Lance Bombardier Eric Manley of the 92nd Field Regiment, Royal Artillery, voiced the outrage felt by many of his comrades at the one-sidedness of the air war: "Where is the RAF? We are obviously at the Germans' mercy. No wonder they conquer countries overnight."

About 6:00 P.M., General Martel decided to pull back his forces under the cover of approaching darkness. He simply did not have enough infantry to hold the ground his tanks had won; in fact, he barely had enough troops to extricate his trapped rear guards before night fell. Martel's entire force did not get back to the attack's starting positions north of Arras until 2:00 A.M. on May 22. Nevertheless, while the Allied tanks had been compelled to retreat, they had succeeded in penetrating the German panzer corridor to a depth of 10 miles. They also had knocked out about 20 panzers and had captured over 400 German prisoners.

The British, for their part, had lost 46 tanks (62 percent of their total) in the nine-hour battle. And they did not even reach their first day's objective, the Cojeul River. This failure, however, was not due to any lack of effort on their part. They had attacked without sufficient infantry support, no air cover, and little help from their French allies south of the Somme River, who did not attack at all. Had they done so, Rommel would have been hard pressed to defend against simultaneous attacks on two of his flanks. As it was, Martel's tank brigade—or what was left of it—engaged in two more days of fighting north of Arras before the panzer advance around its western flank compelled it to withdraw, along with the other British forces in and around that town.

While the battle of Arras was not a tactical victory for the Allies, its impact on the campaign was enormous. For one of the few times in the campaign, the Germans were stunned by the number of burnt-out panzers that littered the battlefield. Rommel thought he had been attacked by vastly superior forces, no less, he estimated, than five divisions. And this estimate, incorrect though it was, was passed up the German chain of command. Kleist reacted by withdrawing the 10th Panzer Division from Guderian's command so that it could be used, if necessary, to check any additional British counterattacks in the Arras area. In so doing, however, Kleist weakened Guderian's drive on the Channel ports, ultimately making possible the successful Allied evacuation from Dunkirk.

Kleist's concern was fully shared by his superior, Army Group A's commander, General von Rundstedt. "For a short time," Rundstedt admitted later, "it was feared that our armored divisions would be cut off before the infantry divisions could come up to support them." At that time, there were still only three motorized infantry divisions in the western part of the panzer corridor and only three regular infantry divisions behind them. It would not be until May 24, in fact, that the panzers' flanks were really secure. Needless to say, by then the news of the British counterattack at Arras would strain Hitler's nerves to the breaking point. The result would be another, far more signficant order halting the advance of the panzers.

The Ypres Conference, May 21

On the same day, May 21, that Frankforce was attacking Rommel's division southwest of Arras, General Weygand was traveling to Ypres, Belgium, for a meeting with the principal commanders of the Allied northern armies, King Léopold, General Billotte, and Lord Gort.

Weygand had a perilous journey getting to Ypres. Originally he had planned to fly there, but he was dismayed to learn, as he arrived at Le Bourget Airport just before dawn, that no preparations had been made for his trip. While his aide-de-camp, Captain Gasser, addressed the matter, the generalissimo went into a little inn next to the airport to get something to eat.

While waiting for the woman innkeeper to make him an omelet, Weygand noticed a small photograph on one of the walls. It depicted the interior of the train coach in which the armistice was signed in 1918. Sitting on one side of the table, in the photograph, were the four German delegates, and opposite them, two British admirals, Marshal Foch, and his chief of staff, then Colonel Weygand.

"Is that really you there, General?" the innkeeper asked as she brought in the steaming omelet. After Weygand nodded, she exclaimed: "What you are doing is very fine!" The general thanked her for the compliment, which, he recalled, "I was anxious to be worthy of."

Eventually a light bomber with a fighter escort was procured for the generalissimo. However, soon after taking off, the formation was attacked by German fighters and forced to land at Calais. There Weygand received another shock. The sole soldier remaining at the airfield, a French private, told him, "They've all pissed off," and then asked what he should do about 20,000 liters of aviation fuel that was left behind. After telling him to guard it, Weygand and Captain Gasser drove off in an ancient truck on roads clogged with civilians on the run. "The difficulties we had already met on our journey," Weygand recalled, "gave me some idea of the disorganization I might expect to find when I reached headquarters."

It took almost two hours for Weygand's car to drive the 40 miles to Ypres, but he was there before the other military leaders had arrived. While waiting for the others to appear, he had the opportunity to talk to King Léopold's principal ministers, Pierlot, Spaak, and Denis. "Their faces lit up with satisfaction," Weygand recalled, when he told them that in his opinion the Belgian army had stayed too long in the east and that it should hasten its retreat toward the west to join the Allied forces.

Léopold, also held up by congested roads, arrived 45 minutes later. Weygand greeted him on the front steps of the town hall, where the meeting would take place. Much to the embarrassment of the Belgian ministers, however, Léopold asked them to wait outside the meeting room, saying that the conference was strictly about military matters. As a result, the talks began with only the king, Van Overstraeten, and Weygand. Billotte and Gort still had not arrived.

Weygand began by outlining his plan for a counterattack against the German panzer corridor. It would be undertaken by General Billotte's army group and the BEF. The Belgian army would be expected to protect the Allied eastern flank. The attack called for some of the 45 divisions cut off in the north to move southward against the northern side of the panzer corridor, while French forces south of the Somme would move northward against its southern side. Repeating what he had told Pierlot, Spaak, and Denis earlier, Weygand said he thought that the Belgian army should retreat to the Yser River, in order to protect the left flank of the Allied armies as the BEF and the French 1st Army attacked southward.

"Excuse me, General," Van Overstraeten interrupted, "but I do not agree with you." After several retreats, he said, the Belgian army was only "getting its bearings again."

"I think the Anglo-Belgian positions are too extended and too far to the east," Weygand responded. "I hope to see the Belgian army back on the Yser, retreating by night in stages."

Van Overstraeten again objected. "It has been absolutely essential to stop the retreat," he said, "because the units were beginning to break down," due to previous retreats that were conducted at night. "Another retreat would have a deleterious effect on morale." Moreover, he added, "a retreat to the Yser"—where the Belgian army withdrew during World War I—"would awaken painful memories for the army." Van Overstraeten recommended that for the time being, the Belgian army should remain in its present location but eventually should withdraw to the coast, where it could hold out indefinitely, supplied from Ostend and Dunkirk.

Weygand strongly rejected Van Overstraeten's recommendations. He said a Belgian withdrawal northwest to the coast would expose the left flank of the advancing BEF and permit the Germans to divide the northern armies. He also said it would be impossible to supply the Belgian army from the Channel ports alone, with the result that it would soon be forced to surrender. He then impatiently reminded the king and Van Overstraeten that France and Britain had come to their country's aid and now it was their turn to stand by their allies. They must help the British and French armies break through the panzer corridor.

At this point, Van Overstraeten interjected again, "Do you not know then that the Germans have captured Abbeville this morning? It was announced uncoded over the radio by the occupying detachment, and the British believe the information to be true."

"I had not heard the news," the Allied generalissimo replied, trying not to look upset.

To Van Overstraeten, Weygand's admission of ignorance was incredible. "I looked the general straight in the eye," he recalled. "I could not believe he was not telling the truth. Nor could I believe that such an event could have had no effect on him."

King Léopold then said that the decision to withdraw to the Yser could not be made until they had heard Lord Gort's views, since the movement of the Belgian army would affect the BEF. They tried to reach Gort by telephone, but his staff officers replied that he was absent and would not return until six o'clock. Since General Billotte had still not appeared, the conference was suspended temporarily until the two generals arrived.

Billotte appeared a while later and the talks resumed, but again without Gort. Weygand began by saying that he was willing to modify his plan to satisfy Van Overstraeten's objections. "If the Belgian army will extend its front to relieve part of the British army, all parties should be happy. But you must choose, and quickly," Weygand insisted. "Either you must maintain, at whatever cost, the continuity of the Allied front—which is what I want you to do—or you must cover the Channel ports and sever the front, which would be dangerous."

"The king," Weygand recalled, "did not commit himself, saying he would think about it." Billotte, for his part, also refused to play the part Weygand had assigned to him. He said that the French 1st Army was "tired and severely tested," and incapable of launching an attack. He added, however, that the British army "was still intact and constituted a powerful offensive force."

But Billotte did not give Weygand the full facts concerning the BEF, particularly the news that Gort had been able to muster only one brigade group to make the Arras counterattack. If Gort had been present at the Ypres meeting with Weygand, it seems improbable that the generalissimo could have entertained any idea that the northern armies could break out of the German trap. In the end, the success or failure of the Weygand plan fell on the willingness of Gort to play the part the Allied generalissimo wanted him to play. But Gort still had not arrived, and so it was again decided to suspend the conference until he did.

Unfortunately for the Allies, Gort did not arrive until after Weygand had left Ypres. Weygand initially had been prepared to wait for the BEF commander by spending the night at Ypres, if necessary, but Admiral Jean Abrial, who was in charge of French naval forces at Dunkirk, arrived with the news that Calais, where the generalissimo's plane and escort were waiting, was being bombed. In order to get back to Paris for a war cabinet meeting the next day, Weygand decided to accept Abrial's offer of a destroyer that would take him to Le Havre during the night. Weygand reluctantly left Ypres suspecting that Gort had purposely missed the meeting because he had already decided to withdraw the BEF to the English Channel.

❈

After General Weygand's departure, King Léopold decided to use the time awaiting Gort's arrival to talk with Pierlot, Spaak, and General Denis. The ministers were still upset that the king had rejected Weygand's request to withdraw the Belgian army to the Yser River. This could only mean that the army ultimately would be entrapped by the Germans and forced to surrender. They implored Léopold to avoid this outcome by supporting the Weygand plan and speeding up the retreat of the army, to France if necessary.

Léopold nonchalantly replied: "You need only look at the map and examine the Allied deployment to see that our right flank is covered by the British army, whose duty is to give us support. I cannot conceivably decide to retreat as it would leave the British army completely in the lurch. That is why I am waiting here at Ypres for Lord Gort, to hear his thoughts."

With that, Van Overstraeten said the troops were "too tired to retreat."

"It is better to retreat than be taken!" Pierlot angrily responded.

"But we're already taken," Van Overstraeten interjected.

"No, we are not taken!" Pierlot exclaimed. "But we will be if you do not do everything to avoid it. We are not taken as long as we have arms and can move."

Van Overstraeten did not say anything further but simply walked away.

The next day, Léopold wrote Pierlot that their talks had made a most "unpleasant impression" on him. "The ministers were aggressive and unpleasant. . . . I cannot admit that the ministers have a right to judge the army or to determine when it shall retreat." He also castigated the government for the "ridiculous haste" with which it had "evacuated to France," and concluded his letter on an ominous note: "This unjustifiable defection . . . leads me to the conclusion that, since the opening of hostilities, the government has no longer had the means of governing."

Pierlot replied the next day by apologizing for the sharpness of his exchange with the king. But he also insisted that the government "alone" was constitutionally responsible for the conduct of the war "and of the acts of the Chief of State," that is, the king. Pierlot, fearing as early as May 15 that Léopold saw surrender as the only way out of the conflict, again insisted that the "King must not link his fate to that of the army, to the point of losing his liberty." As for the government's evacuation to France, he reminded Léopold that the ministers had left the capital only at the last hour, just before the Germans entered the city.

The king and his government, obviously, were now at complete odds.

Shortly after this latest confrontation between Léopold and his chief ministers, Lord Gort, accompanied by General Pownall, finally arrived. They had been busy most of the day overseeing the British counterattack at Arras and blamed their late arrival, as the others did, on the congested roads. The conference immediately resumed with General Billotte outlining Weygand's plan to the two British generals, adding that the generalissimo expected much from the Allied counteroffensive, providing it was powerful.

"What would the French participation be?" asked Gort. But before Billotte could answer, Pownall interrupted and summarized the plight of the BEF: "Our communication lines have been cut. We have been reduced to diverting our supplies by sea to the Channel ports, which have been heavily bombarded. . . . We only have supplies for two more days, and our artillery reserves are restless and unmanageable. So we have no wish to engage in a large battle." To this, Gort added, "As far as we know, out of the entire French [1st] Army, only one division has remained vaguely intact."

Never during the course of the conversation did Gort mention that he was already preparing to withdraw toward the Channel ports, and his silence prompted a reproach from Lieutenant General Maurice Fagalde, who commanded the French ground forces around Dunkirk: "You must do what has been agreed!"

Gort responded by saying that the progress of his Arras operation was not very encouraging and added that all his available reserves were already committed. He also pointed out that if he were expected to attack southward, the Belgians would have to withdraw to the Yser to protect the BEF's left flank. Gort said the Escaut River was so low that it was useless as an obstacle to the German advance.

Reluctantly, Léopold finally agreed to pull back his army, but only to the Lys River, 10 miles farther west and some 30 miles from the Yser. Everyone present realized that the Lys line was no better than the Escaut, and probably much worse, since deployment along the Lys would leave the Belgian army with a dangerously open left flank.

Finally, Billotte asked Léopold whether he would fall back to the Yser if that proved necessary. "Evidently with some regret," Gort recalled, Léopold agreed to do so. However, the next day the king informed Weygand that the Belgian army would withdraw to the Yser only after first stopping at the Lys.

The conference ended, pessimistically, at 9:30 P.M., with every one of the participants believing that Weygand's plan was beyond their capabilities to fulfill.

As the participants were about to leave, they learned that the Luftwaffe had bombed Béthune. General Billotte was about to drive to that town, but he was apprehensive about having to travel at such a late hour along a road that would be crammed with refugees.

After the meeting, Admiral Keyes, Britain's envoy to King Léopold, told Gort privately that the decision to evacuate the BEF to England via Dunkirk was tantamount to running out on the Belgian army, but he admitted that he had not had the nerve to inform the king about it. Keyes added that the Belgian troops were already bitter about their treatment by the Allies. Gort replied, with a gesture of despondency, "Do the Belgians really regard us as awful dirty dogs?"

But Léopold was also planning to pull back to the coast. When he returned to his headquarters later that evening, he told Keyes that the planned Allied counteroffensive "had been delayed too long and that the only real hope now, at this late hour," was to withdraw to Dunkirk and the Belgian ports. He asked Keyes to inform Churchill that he did not believe the prime minister appreciated the difficulties involved in attacking toward the Somme. For one, his exhausted army would be expected to hold a front being attacked by at least eight German divisions with strong air support. He feared it would be overwhelmed.

Léopold also asked Keyes to inform Churchill that "his government are urging him to fly with them to Le Havre before the army finds it necessary to capitulate." The king added that "he has no intention of deserting his army." He realized the hostile reaction his ministers would have to this decision, but he said that "if the British Government understands his motives, he does not care what others may think."

At 5:00 A.M. on May 22, General Weygand disembarked at Cherbourg from the French destroyer that had carried him from Dunkirk and immediately set off for Paris by car. He had absented himself from his command post for a whole precious day in an attempt to work out a plan to save the northern armies. If anything, in the aftermath of that trip he was more doubtful than ever that the plan could be successfully implemented. He saw the Belgians faltering, their king at odds with their government, in no mind to accept the Allied high command's directives, and losing all hope. He found General Billotte, once noted for his energy and drive, physically and mentally worn out and with no confidence in the offensive capability of the French 1st Army, which only 10 days before had been France's best. Now, its general staff exhausted and its original 11 divisions reduced to less than three, the 1st Army was at the bottom of the French order of battle. The only counteroffensive the Allies would conduct during the entire campaign, the one carried out by Frankforce and the remnants of Prioux's cavalry corps, was now over, and apparently inconclusive. The German panzer corridor was still intact, and the panzers were still advancing on the Channel ports. Moreover, the British were giving every indication that they were trying to reach those ports before the Germans could get to them. To make matters even worse, if that were possible, Weygand would soon learn that General Billotte had been seriously injured in a car accident while driving back to his headquarters from Ypres. Billotte would die two days later. As a consequence of this tragedy, no French general in the north would understand what was on Weygand's mind regarding the Allied counterattack. Billotte's place as 1st Army Group commander would be taken, another precious four days later, by General Blanchard, the commander of the disintegrating French 1st Army.

Gort was particularly hard hit by Billotte's death. With the indecisive Blanchard in charge of the northern armies, he doubted that the French would be able to do anything right.

CHURCHILL VISITS PARIS, MAY 22

While Weygand was making his way to Ypres during the morning of May 22, Winston Churchill was becoming more and more depressed. He was losing any confidence he had left in the ability of the French to launch a counterattack against the German panzer corridor. He also was upset by his inability to contact Paris by phone. Holding the telephone receiver in his hand, he turned to his private secretary, John Colville, and said, "In all the history of war, I have never seen such mismanagement." Then Churchill's spirits began to revive. Sweeping aside the advice of his aides, he decided to go to Paris the next morning to meet with General Weygand.

As he was getting ready for bed that evening—actually at 1:30 in the morning of the next day—a dispatch arrived stating that General Billotte, whom Churchill knew well, had been severely injured in a car accident. When Colville, carrying the dispatch, knocked on the prime minister's bedroom door, he found Churchill "a comic sight clad in nothing but a vest. All he said was 'poor man, poor man'—but without much sign of grief in his tones." Churchill thought Billotte's weakness and vacillation were largely responsible for the BEF's plight.

At noon on May 22, another impeccably beautiful spring day, Churchill, along with his chief military advisers, arrived in Paris and immediately drove to Weygand's headquarters at Vincennes. General Ismay noted that despite the disaster engulfing the French army, "the *Beau Geste* flavor of the old fort was just the same—spahis with white cloaks and long curved swords, on guard duty, and the floors and chairs covered with oriental rugs." There Churchill and his party were joined by Premier Reynaud and General Weygand.

Ismay was impressed by the new Allied commander-in-chief: "He gave the appearance of being a fighter—resolute, decisive and amazingly active, in spite of his wizened face and advanced years. . . . One dared to hope that the Allied armies would now have the leadership that had hitherto seemed lacking." Churchill agreed with this assessment fully: "In spite of his physical exertions and a night of travel, Weygand was brisk, buoyant, and incisive. He made an excellent impression upon all." However, as historian Alistair Horne has pointed out, Churchill, throughout his entire career, was "susceptible to a general who gave the appearance of being a fighter, and Weygand—in sharp antithesis to the pallid intellectualism of Gamelin—clearly struck him as such."

Weygand warmly welcomed the two prime ministers and then conducted them to the Map Room, where he delivered a forceful presentation of his plan for a great Allied counteroffensive against the German panzer corridor. The plan called for all available French and British forces to "take offensive action," covered on the east and north by the Belgian army. The attack southward would be simultaneously supplemented by a northward push across the Somme River by the newly reconstituted French 7th Army, consisting of "eighteen to twenty divisions" under the command of General Aubert Frère. The counterattack would be centered against the German forces in Amiens, Abbeville, and Arras. In this way, Weygand expected, the counterattack would stop the German panzer thrust and allow the Allies to take the initiative.

Churchill gave numerous signs of approval as Weygand explained his plan. He repeatedly interrupted by saying that restoring communication and supply lines between the armies in the north and the main forces in the south was essential. To this end, he told Weygand, Gort had already begun to move certain forces toward his right flank "with the object of proceeding gradually towards Arras and Bapaume." The outcome of this battle, he said, "was vital to the further conduct of the war, for the maintenance of the British forces through the Channel ports was becoming exceedingly hazardous." Like Gort, however, Churchill made no mention of the "precautionary measure" he had ordered Vice Admiral Bertram Ramsey to prepare two days earlier: the evacuation from the Continent of the BEF.

Weygand now asked, "in firm and exact, although courteous, terms," the minutes of the meeting recorded, for British fighter and bomber forces to be engaged "up to the hilt" in the present theater of war. After what was politely called "an exchange of views," it was agreed that Weygand's wishes should be met.

As the Vincennes meeting was drawing to a close, Churchill was full of optimism. What mattered most, he emphasized, "was now to hold on everywhere at every single point where an Allied force was in possession."

But, Weygand added, it was also "necessary to act." Every time an attack was launched by the Allies, he said, "some part of the enemy force would find itself faced with difficulties."

The Vincennes meeting concluded with a written agreement to implement the Weygand plan. Both the BEF and the French 1st Army would attack southward, toward Bapaume and Cambrai, "at the earliest moment—certainly tomorrow," with a view to freeing Amiens and "joining hands" with the new French army group that would be advancing upon that town from the south.

As Churchill was leaving Vincennes, he remarked flatteringly to Weygand: "There is only one fault in you; you are too young!" He then telegraphed the text of the agreement to Lord Gort. The message concluded: "You have our best wishes in the vital battle now opening towards Bapaume and Cambrai."

Back at 10 Downing Street, six hours later, Churchill gave the War Cabinet an exhilarating account of the Vincennes meeting. "He was almost in buoyant spirits," Ironside commented, "having been impressed by Weygand," who, Churchill told his colleagues, "looked like a man of fifty."

"Provided the French fought well," he added, "there seemed a good prospect of success."

Weygand clearly had rekindled Churchill's faith in the French army. In the words of General Edward Spears, the Weygand plan had "hung like a limp sail from the mast," but Churchill "filled it momentarily with the power of his lungs." However, Spears added, "the ship did not move. . . . the vessel was grounded." It did not because the Weygand plan was simply impracticable. No army, certainly not one as large as Gort's—nine divisions, 100,000 men—could march off the field at a few hours' notice and deliver a decisive blow, in a different direction, many miles away.

Moreover, as Gort's aide-de-camp, Lord Munster, pointed out in a telephone message to Anthony Eden, the situation confronting the BEF "was very grave." There was, Munster said, a "severe shortage of the essential commodities for war, both in respect of food and munitions." All its lines of communication, including telephones, were cut. Eden said that Munster had telephoned from "some point" on the Belgian coast, after driving for two hours from Gort's headquarters.

Above all, Munster reported, "there was no coordination between ourselves and the French on our right. The Coordinator [Billotte] has had an accident and coordinates no longer." Munster added that the French forces "were not prepared to fight, nor did they show any sign of doing so." Munster's message had a chilling effect on the War Cabinet and did much to take the wind out of the briefly fluttering sail of the Weygand plan. In fact, as events would soon prove, the plan was dead before it was even born.

After General Sir Henry Pownall read Churchill's telegram at Gort's headquarters, he vented his exasperation with the prime minister's "cigar-butt strategy." In his diary, Pownall wrote: "Here are Winston's plans again. Can nobody prevent him from trying to conduct operations himself, as a super commander-in-chief? How is an attack like this to be staged involving three nationalities at an hour's notice? The man's mad."

In fact, by the time Pownall had received Churchill's telegram, Gort already had told one of his liaison officers, Major O. J. Archdale, that "he believed the time was approaching when his responsibility for the safety of the BEF was going to outweigh his obligations to the French high command."

In Churchill's defense, however, Weygand, whether intentionally or not, had clearly misled him as to what was possible. The "eighteen or twenty" divisions the prime minister was told comprised Frère's 7th Army in reality consisted of only six divisions, three of them incompletely organized, and strung out on a front 65 miles long. Weygand admitted later that he had expected too much of Frère's army. "But I calculated," he was recorded as saying, "that however feeble it might be, it would at least create an additional threat to the German flank and thus increase the chances of success for the northern offensive." By the time Frère's army finally did attack, however, the Germans were firmly established on the northern bank of the Somme. As a result, Frère's army hardly advanced beyond its prepared positions.

Nor was there much further offensive movement on the northern side of the panzer corridor. When, on May 22, General Blanchard finally launched a counterattack, after having been unable to assist Frankforce's Arras operation the previous day, the result was the same. Instead of being supported by two light armored divisions, as originally planned, General Altmayer's 5th Infantry Corps attacked with only one infantry regiment supported by two small armored assault groups. Attacking the north side of the panzer corridor just east of Cambrai, these French units, like Frankforce the day before, had some initial success. They were able to advance to the outskirts of Cambrai. But that evening they were ordered to withdraw from the territory they had occupied in order to avoid encirclement by superior German forces. Obviously, the results of this minor offensive did not augur well for the prospects of the major counteroffensive Weygand had in mind.

LÉOPOLD DECIDES TO STOP
ON THE LYS, MAY 22

The Belgians were also doing their part to undermine the Weygand Plan. At 10:00 P.M. that day, May 22, King Léopold informed General Denis that he had changed his mind and would not withdraw to the Yser River after all. Instead, the Belgian army would withdraw only to the Lys River, as he had originally intended. "What do you think?" Léopold asked Denis. "From a military point of view," Denis replied, "that is the only possible solution."

That afternoon, Léopold heard about General Billotte's accident. He also read reports from his liaison officers with Billotte's 1st Army Group headquarters describing its almost complete breakdown. The news convinced the king that the counteroffensive agreed to the previous day at Ypres was doomed to failure and that he should stand by his decision to withdraw to the Lys River without delay. He ordered the Belgian army to begin withdrawing to the new line that night.

GUDERIAN RESUMES HIS ADVANCE, MAY 21

As the battle of Arras was being fought, Guderian's panzer divisions spent the day waiting for orders. Amazingly, considering the thoroughness of German military planning, no one had yet decided what to do with the panzers once the Channel was reached. General Halder believed that the suddenness of the French collapse made it possible to capture Paris quickly, before the French could recover, rather than wait until the northern Allied armies were defeated first.

While the German high command deliberated, Guderian's soldiers, of course, did not mind having the day "off"; they were exhausted, and many of their panzers needed repair. Late in the day, however, Guderian's orders arrived. He was to swing northward, seize the Channel ports, and trap the British Expeditionary Force before it could get to the sea. He immediately decided to allot to each of his three panzer divisions one port each: Calais was assigned to the 1st Panzer Division, Boulogne to the 2nd, and Dunkirk to the 10th.

But soon afterward, he received word of Kleist's decision to remove the 10th Panzer Division from his command and place it in reserve in case the British launched another counterattack. Guderian again argued with Kleist, but this time unsuccessfully. Dunkirk would have to wait a little longer. He would begin his advance on Boulogne and Calais with his two remaining panzer divisions early the next morning.

However, during the afternoon of the next day, May 22, Guderian was informed that the 10th Panzer Division was being returned to his command after, as he put it, being "wasted" for 36 hours in reserve. The indecisiveness of the high command must have irritated the panzer leader, but there was still plenty of time to capture all the Channel ports. He decided to push the 1st Panzer on to Dunkirk and leave Calais to the 10th Panzer and Boulogne to the 2nd Panzer.

As Guderian's panzers advanced northward toward the Channel ports, they experienced, for the first time in the campaign, unopposed attacks from the RAF and from the French naval air arm. Guderian's rapid advance had taken his panzers out of range of the Luftwaffe's air cover. Nevertheless, the panzers pushed on. The 2nd Panzer launched a full-scale attack on Boulogne during the afternoon of May 22. The 10th Panzer reached Calais by the evening of the same day, after a staggering advance of over 60 miles. By the evening of the 23rd, the 1st Panzer secured bridgeheads across the

Aa canal, between Holque and the coast. Dunkirk was only a dozen miles away. In fact, by this time, the Germans were considerably closer to that port than was the bulk of the BEF. It appeared that the Germans were about to close the trap on the Allies' northern armies.

THE HALT ORDER, MAY 24

On May 24, Guderian received an order that left him, and all the other panzer commanders, flabbergasted. It stated that the panzer divisions would halt immediately on the Canal Line, the name given to the network of waterways and canals extending from Lens to the English Channel at Gravelines. The purpose of the order was "to allow the situation to clarify itself and to keep our forces concentrated."

"We were utterly speechless," Guderian recalled. The results "were to have a most disastrous influence on the whole future course of the war." He believed the order prevented General Ferdinand Schaal's 10th Panzer Division and General Kirchner's 1st Panzer Division from seizing Dunkirk and completing the entrapment of the Allies' northern armies.

While Guderian received the halt order from General Kleist, his immediate superior, its origin can be traced to the highest level of the German command. Kleist had gotten the order from the 4th Army commander, General Kluge, who was now commanding both Kleist's and Hoth's panzer groups. Kluge, in turn, received the order from its originator, General Rundstedt, commander of Army Group A, who sent out the order at 11:00 P.M. on May 23.

"Gerd von Rundstedt was a gentleman to the core," the historian Basil Liddell Hart remembered. "His natural dignity and good manners inspired the respect even of those who differed widely from him in views." Almost seventy, he was still lean, ascetic, and sharp, the very personification of the professional soldier. While Rundstedt disdained Nazism, his devotion to the army and to Germany—not to mention his innate desire to excel—prompted him to come out of retirement in 1939 and accept the command of an army group. Its brilliant performance during the Polish conflict led to his appointment as commander of Army Group A during the western campaign.

Rundstedt was a cautious commander, however, and was not at all comfortable with Guderian's blitzkrieg methods. Especially bothersome to

him was Guderian's apparent disregard for his flanks, which had become
acutely worrisome to Rundstedt after the Allied counterattacks near Arras.
But apparently it was Kluge, whose timidity would cost the Germans
dearly in the future Russian campaign as well as in this one, who raised
Rundstedt's concern to the level of action. On May 23 Kluge suggested to
Rundstedt that the panzers should "halt and close up," a move that also
would allow the Luftwaffe time to move its bases closer to the panzers'
area of operation.

Kluge's argument made sense to Rundstedt. The army group commander was concerned about the heavy losses the panzers had incurred in
their advance across France. That day, Kleist reported that 50 percent of
his panzers were unfit for action (although he did not mention that many
of these vehicles could be repaired in a day or two). If the other panzer
divisions had suffered comparable losses, Rundstedt feared, they would not
be strong enough to carry out Operation Red, the second phase in the conquest of France.

Another factor that prompted Rundstedt to halt the panzers was a
message that morning from General Brauchitsch stating that the task of
completing the encirclement of the enemy forces retreating toward Dunkirk would be handed over to Bock's Army Group B so that Rundstedt
could concentrate on preparations for the drive toward Paris. As far as
Rundstedt was now concerned, his army group had completed the work it
had been assigned in *Fall Gelb*: breaking through the French front and
advancing to the English Channel. For Rundstedt, Liddell Hart remarked,
Dunkirk "was now barely in the corner of his eye."

Yet Dunkirk was very much in the eyes of the Luftwaffe's commander-in-
chief, Field Marshal Hermann Göring. Late in the evening of May 23,
while studying the latest situation reports from the front aboard his personal train, which was stationed in the Eiffel Mountains, Göring suddenly
realized that the Allied armies in the north were almost surrounded and
that their capitulation would soon be at hand. He was determined that his
Luftwaffe should conduct the final kill.

"This is a special job for the Luftwaffe!" he bellowed, smashing his fist
on the table. "I must talk to the Führer immediately! Get through on the
phone!" he yelled to his chief of staff, General Schmidt. Within minutes,
Göring was talking with Hitler, explaining the reasons why he believed
the Luftwaffe must be given primary responsibility for eliminating the
encircled Allied armies.

While Hitler apparently did not immediately agree, he obviously was receptive to Göring's reasoning. Unlike the army and the navy, the Luftwaffe was the creation of the Nazi movement: it was established as a separate branch of the armed forces soon after Hitler came to power in 1933. Allowing the Luftwaffe to finish off the Allied northern armies would raise its prestige to a level at least equal to that of the other armed services.

Early the next morning, Hitler left his Eagle's Nest headquarters, on the edge of Germany, and flew to Rundstedt's command post at Charleville, on the western bank of the Meuse. The early morning trip was unusual for the Führer, whose custom it was to retire late and rise late. Obviously, he wanted to discuss something of great importance with the army group commander. Above all, he was still worried about the southern flank, overestimating the effect of the Allied counterattack at Arras, and not fully realizing the acute precariousness of the Allies' position. Not wanting victory ripped from his grasp by an Allied counterattack from across the Somme River—as victory was snatched from the German army in the Battle of the Marne—Hitler wanted to concentrate all the motorized formations in the Arras area and wait for the infantry to reinforce the southern flank.

Much to the Führer's pleasant surprise, Rundstedt told him that he had already ordered a halt in the panzer advance the previous evening, and for much the same reasons as Hitler's. According to Army Group A's war diary, Rundstedt told Hitler that "the possibility of concerted action by Allied forces in the north and French forces south of the Somme had to be reckoned with." Rundstedt also stressed the extreme nervousness that had gripped the headquarters of Kleist's panzer group during the Allied counterattack at Arras. In addition, he felt that the canals and marshy terrain surrounding Dunkirk were not suitable for panzer operations.

Hitler nodded his agreement. As a corporal in World War I, he had seen British tanks bogged down by the very same terrain during the Poelkapelle offensive in October 1917. He also agreed with Rundstedt that it was vitally necessary to save the panzers for the ensuing phase of the campaign. Not surprisingly, then, he fully approved of Rundstedt's order halting the panzers on the Canal Line.

But the new order, issued by Rundstedt in Hitler's name at 11:48 A.M., no longer called for a temporary halt to "clarify the situation"; rather, it changed the army's war plan fundamentally. "Dunkirk," the new order stated, "is to be left to the Luftwaffe. Should the capture of Calais prove difficult, this port too is to be left to the Luftwaffe." In addition, to avoid restricting the Luftwaffe's field of action, Hitler emphasized that it was essential to avoid pressing the surrounded Allies too hard on the ground.

General Halder was livid about Hitler's halt order. "The left wing," he wrote in his diary, "consisting of armored and motorized forces, which has no enemy before it, will thus be stopped in its tracks upon direct orders of the Fuehrer. Finishing off the encircled enemy army is to be left to the Luftwaffe!" To Halder, the new order made no sense. "I wanted to make Rundstedt's group the hammer," he wrote in his diary, "and von Bock's the anvil." Now, as a result of Hitler's order, Army Group A, which was only 12 miles from Dunkirk and had next to nothing in front of it, and which possessed nearly all the panzers (8 panzer divisions out of 10), was restricted to the passive role of the anvil. The new hammer, Army Group B, was still 34 miles to the east and faced an unbroken Allied front with only infantry units.

Brauchitsch told Halder that he had argued strenuously with Hitler, trying to get him to change his mind, but the Führer was deaf to his protestations. Göring, Hitler said, would foil any attempt by the Allies to embark from Dunkirk; the Luftwaffe would sink any boat that by some strange chance managed to reach the open sea. As exasperated as Halder was at the self-imposed delay, Brauchitsch ordered a resumption of the panzer advance the next day. But this only brought him another humiliation, for Rundstedt ignored the order and Hitler decreed that the decision to resume the panzer advance must be left to Rundstedt.

Colonel Bernhard von Lossberg, who was on the staff of OKW, also thought the order was insane. "The panzers were thrusting towards Dunkirk to cut off the British retreat," he recounted, "and there were good grounds for hoping that not a single Briton would escape from the continent."

Lossberg protested the decision to General Jodl: "I pointed out that by doing this, we were unconcernedly throwing away the chance of capturing the entire BEF. But Jodl simply answered that the war was already won, that it was merely a question of bringing it to a close, and that it was useless to sacrifice a single tank in achieving what the Luftwaffe could do much more economically."

"Very agitated," Lossberg stormed out of OKW headquarters, where he found General Keitel "contentedly smoking a cigar in the sun." After making the same arguments to him that he had just addressed to Jodl, Lossberg asked Keitel to try to change the Führer's mind. But Keitel answered that he also thought the ground in Flanders was too marshy for the panzers, and that he too was confident that Göring would be able to finish the job.

Göring's generals, however, were not at all confident that they could complete the job. "The job is completely beyond the strength of my depleted forces," General Albert Kesselring, the commander of Air Fleet 2, exclaimed. Kesselring argued that his pilots were too exhausted to bear the main responsibility for bringing the northern battle to an end. He pointed out to Göring that the blitzkrieg had succeeded so far because the army and the Luftwaffe had cooperated closely. Without panzer support, Kesselring did not think his exhausted airmen could wipe out the trapped Allied armies. But Göring simply replied, "My Luftwaffe will do it alone!"

General Ritter von Thoma recalled that when he received the halt order, he was riding with the leading panzers near Bergues, from which he could almost look into the town of Dunkirk, only five miles to the north. Thoma sent back radio messages to OKH, begging for permission to let the panzers push on. But his appeal had no effect. Referring to Hitler, Thoma bitingly remarked: "You can never talk to a fool. Hitler spoilt the chance of victory."

The next morning, Guderian drove out to Watten, a small town on the Aa canal about 15 miles southeast of Calais, to make sure that the SS *Leibstandarte* Division was obeying the halt order. When he arrived, he found that unit crossing the canal. When Guderian asked its commander, SS General Sepp Dietrich, why he was disobeying orders, Dietrich replied that the enemy on Mont Watten—a height of only some 235 feet, which nevertheless dominated the whole relatively flat countryside—could "look right down the throat" of anybody on the far bank of the canal. Dietrich therefore had decided to take the height on his own initiative. In view of the success that Dietrich's soldiers were having, Guderian approved his decision to cross the canal and even ordered the 2nd Panzer Division to move up in his support.

General Kleist also decided to ignore the halt order and pushed on across the canal. "My armored cars actually entered Hazebrouck," Kleist recalled, "and cut across the British lines of retreat. I heard later that the British commander-in-chief, Lord Gort, had been in Hazebrouck at the time. But then came a more emphatic order that I was to withdraw behind the canal. My tanks were kept halted there for three days. It was left to the infantry forces which had come down from Belgium to complete the occupation of Dunkirk—after the British had gone!"

A few days later, Kleist had the opportunity to talk to Hitler on the airfield at Cambrai. He ventured to remark that a great opportunity had been lost for reaching Dunkirk before the British escaped. "That may be so," Hitler replied. "But I did not want to send the tanks into the Flanders marshes—and the British won't come back in this war."

It is hardly surprising, considering the military's hostile reaction to Hitler's halt order, that the generals concluded that it was prompted by some secret political design. This impression was reinforced by Hitler's private remarks to Rundstedt and to two key members of his staff—Generals Georg von Sodenstern and Blumentritt—shortly after their military conference during the morning of May 24.

"Hitler was in very good humor," Blumentritt recalled; "he admitted that the course of the campaign had been 'a decided miracle,' and gave us his opinion that the war would be finished in six weeks. After that, he wished to conclude a reasonable peace with France, and then the way would be free for an agreement with Britain."

To the astonishment of his small audience, Blumentritt continued, "Hitler then spoke with admiration of the British Empire, of the necessity for its existence, and of the civilization that Britain had brought into the world. He even compared it with the Catholic Church, saying that both were essential elements of world stability. He remarked, with a shrug of the shoulders, that the creation of its empire had been achieved by means that were often harsh, but 'where there is planing, there are shavings flying.'" The Führer concluded his impromptu address by saying that his aim was to make peace with Britain on a basis the British would consider honorable.

Rundstedt, who had always favored an agreement with France and Britain, expressed his satisfaction with Hitler's words. Later, after the Führer had departed, Rundstedt remarked with a sigh of relief, "Well, if he wants nothing else, then we shall have peace at last." After the war, Rundstedt expressed his opinion to Liddell Hart that "the Fuehrer had counted on a speedy end to western operations. . . . He deliberately let the bulk of the BEF escape, so as to make peace negotiations easier."

Blumentritt also believed that Hitler's desire for an honorable peace with Britain was the main reason behind his decision to halt the panzers and, in effect, allow the British to escape. If the British army had been captured at Dunkirk, Blumentritt argued, the British people might have felt that their honor had suffered a stain that they must wipe out. By letting the BEF escape, Hitler hoped to conciliate them. According to Blumentritt, the Führer was convinced that once France was eliminated and Britain was deprived of its "continental soldier," the British would come to terms. The fact that the halt order was transmitted to the field commanders in the clear and was instantly read in London was, for Blumentritt, proof positive that Hitler was telling the British he would permit the BEF to escape destruction.

To Guderian, on the other hand, the idea that Hitler purposely allowed the British to escape from Dunkirk was "an absurd theory. . . . It was by capturing the whole of Lord Gort's forces," he argued, "that we might have brought the British to terms. To leave them with the units that would enable them to raise and provide the backbone of further armies was, on the contrary, tantamount to urging them to go on with the war and to strengthening their resolve."

SPEARS IN PARIS, MAY 25

Toward noon on May 25, General Sir Edward L. Spears arrived in Paris to serve as Churchill's personal military liaison officer with Reynaud. Half-French by birth and bilingual, Spears had served as liaison officer between the French and British armies during World War I. He knew the country and the people, and he liked them. Not all Frenchmen, however, liked Spears. One French politician, Pierre Varillon, called him a "disquieting person who, ever since 1914, could be seen to surface each time the shadow of misfortune fell across France." Nevertheless, Churchill trusted Spears more than anyone else to serve as his personal link to Reynaud. Moreover, Spears's knack for irritating people would enable Churchill to play the role of the compassionate statesman.

Spears drove immediately to the War Ministry to pay his respects to Reynaud. After exchanging greetings, the general recalled, the French premier "then began to tell me how British generals always made for the harbors." Spears replied that if Gort had fallen back, it was because he had been compelled to do so. He then begged Reynaud "to set his face against recriminations, not to tolerate them. . . . the only sensible thing we can do at the moment is to consider our common danger as calmly as we can, in complete harmony, and act together as brothers."

Reynaud, Spears recounted, "nodded his head in approval." Then, Spears continued, "he got up once or twice, his small figure very erect, the shoulders of his black jacket thrown back, and walked up and down, his hands behind his back. . . . His Chinese eyes, always so ready to emphasize his wit with a twinkle, did not smile, but his eyebrows, which were drawn high and shaped like open umbrellas, giving him an expression of unabating wakefulness and amused curiosity, shot several times half-way up his forehead, as if they had been half-closed, and lifted to avoid colliding with each other. His attitude was one of undemonstrative cordiality and underlying understanding."

Reynaud then invited Spears to attend a meeting of the War Committee, whose members were waiting in his study. Spears agreed. Present were Marshal Pétain, General Weygand, Admiral François Darlan, and Reynaud's aide, Paul Baudouin.

Looking over the assembled collection of France's primary leaders, Spears painted a literary description of each of them. The great Marshal Pétain, walking toward him, was "still erect but so much older, . . . he seemed dead, in the sense that a figure that gives no impression of being alive can be said to be dead. . . . his words of greeting were kind. . . . Then he seemed to disappear from the scene, almost from sight, for not another word did he utter, and when I occasionally looked towards him he seemed not to have heard what was being said. After all, he was in his eighty-fifth year."

Weygand greeted Spears next. "He was," Spears recorded, "in khaki uniform and riding breeches, complete even to brass spurs, wizened and yellow-skinned. Like Reynaud, he looked Oriental. His sparse moustache and parchment skin, his high cheek bones protruding from a flat face shaped like the ace of spades reversed, enhanced an impression already emphasized by his very pointed chin." Unlike Pétain, Weygand "was darting about like a minnow, as fresh as a daisy, showing no sign of fatigue."

To Spears, the navy's chief, Admiral Darlan, "looked . . . like a clean shaven Bacchus on the morning after the Bacchanalia. . . . He conveyed an uneasy sense of unreality, of something rather bogus" and then, "like Pétain, evaporated from the proceedings as soon as he had sat down."

Spears next was introduced to Baudouin, the undersecretary of state and, in effect, Reynaud's chief secretary. Spears initially received the impression that Baudouin, whom he described as "tall, clean-shaven, blue-eyed, and good looking," was a friend of Great Britain. But he came to realize "only gradually" that "we stood for things as different as night and day."

The French War Committee was meeting to hear a report from one of General Blanchard's staff officers, Major Joseph Fauvelle, on the military situation facing the northern armies. There was no hope, Fauvelle said, of the French 1st Army carrying out Weygand's plan. General Blanchard, its commander, was exhausted, and so were his troops. "The Army has only three divisions left capable of fighting," Fauvelle went on. "There is only one day's reserve of ammunition." Fauvelle added that the British army "appeared to be preparing to reembark and the Belgian army to give up." When Reynaud asked him what should be done, Fauvelle responded—as Spears described it, "in the voice of a seasick passenger asking a passing steward for a basin"—"I believe in a very early capitulation."

Fauvelle's report appeared to surprise Reynaud and Weygand, but it shocked Spears. "I have," the British general recalled, "seen broken men, but never one deliquescent, that is, in a state where he was fit only to be scraped up with a spoon." Fauvelle "was the very embodiment of catastrophe. . . . nothing short of throwing him out of the window would have been adequate."

What shocked Spears even more was the lackadaisical reaction of the French War Committee. "Pétain," Spears recorded, "said nothing, and continued staring at the carpet. Admiral Darlan was equally silent, apparently thinking that since this was not a nautical matter, it did not concern him."

However, "Weygand, with a look of absolute exasperation," Spears continued, "lifted his hands, turned his head towards Reynaud, and said with a voice like a saw on steel: 'This war is sheer madness, we have gone to war with a 1918 army against a German Army of 1939. It is sheer madness. What sort of air force have we got? Four hundred fighters and some 30 bombers capable of flying by day, and that for the whole of our front; our tanks are inadequate and insufficient, ridiculously few in numbers.'" The generalissimo finally declared that not only were the practical means of waging war totally lacking, but the whole strategic theory on which Allied plans had been made was mistaken.

Yet Fauvelle did make two constructive suggestions: that the armies in the north be permitted to move toward the sea and that General Blanchard be officially named head of the 1st Army Group. Weygand apparently agreed with the first suggestion, and definitely with the second. Later that afternoon, three days after Billotte's ultimately fatal accident left the 1st Army Group without a commander, he got off a telegram to Blanchard appointing him to that post and naming General Prioux of the cavalry corps the new commander of the 1st Army. The generalissimo added a personal message to Blanchard: "You remain sole judge of decisions to take to save what can be saved, and above all the honor of the colors of which you are the guardian."

To Spears, the idea of honor seemed to be becoming an obsession with Weygand as well as with Pétain. After the "honor of the Army" had been saved, Spears concluded, the obvious corollary was that France must ask for an armistice. Spears was shocked. "I realized that his catastrophic defeatism seemed to some extent at least to be accepted as the reflection of the real position, I felt cold fingers turning my heart to stone."

What Spears did not know was that Pétain had accepted defeat as early as May 17, when, upon leaving his ambassadorial post in Madrid, he had told Franco that France had been beaten. The very next day, he startled Reynaud's cabinet, who were discussing the possibility of evacuating the government to Tours, saying that he would refuse to quit the capital even if it fell to the Germans. The marshal added "that to find himself face to face with Hitler and to talk to him did not frighten him; that, on the contrary, between soldiers, better conditions could be obtained than civilians could get."

Later that day, Georges Mandel, the French minister of colonies, said to Spears, "I suppose you realize that Weygand is already thinking in terms of a surrender? He is obsessed with fear of revolution, of a break-up of the army. . . . He is . . . talking of the government awaiting the Germans in Paris as the Roman Senate awaited the entry of the barbarians sitting on their *chaises curules.*"

Spears asked Mandel what had happened to France. "This is much more than a military defeat," Spears added. "In the last war, defeat compressed the spring of the nation's will. Each setback produced resurgence. The people literally hurled themselves at the Germans. I feel in my bones that is not so today. Why?"

"It is certainly the fact," Mandel answered, "that the shock of what has happened has had a stupefying rather than a galvanic effect." He then told Spears, in the voice of a lecturer objectively delivering a thesis, "There is no will to fight." France, he explained, was a group of factions, rather than one nation. There was no unity.

Moreover, Mandel continued, "France could only fight with strong allies. You, the English, certainly could not answer that description, and the United States do not exist as far as Europe is concerned. As no one wanted to fight, why should France?" The result, he said, was the "moral surrender of the civil authorities . . . and the complete apathy of the population in the face of invasion."

THE FRENCH WAR COMMITTEE, EVENING, MAY 25

There was a second meeting of the French War Committee that day, one that General Spears did not attend. It began at 7:00 P.M. in the Elysée Palace and was chaired by French President Albert Lebrun. It was at this meeting that the question of an armistice was, for the first time, formally discussed within the French government. In addition to Lebrun, Reynaud, Pétain, Weygand, two other ministers and two other generals were present.

Weygand began the meeting with a long presentation, the gist of which was that the military situation was hopeless. The French armies, minus those in the north, he said, would have to hold the line of the Somme and the Aisne against German forces three times their own number and with only a fifth of their original armored forces remaining. "We will be smashed," Weygand predicted. The only thing that could be done was that "each portion of the Army must fight until exhausted, to save the honor of the country." He then stated that "France had committed the immense mistake of entering into the war without the material or the military doctrine that were needed. It is probable that [France] will have to pay dearly for this criminal thoughtlessness."

To President Lebrun's obvious horror, Weygand also recommended that the government remain in Paris, though by remaining there it would risk imprisonment. "What Weygand was asking for," Reynaud wrote in his memoirs, "was an armistice, and, as a corollary, the capture of the government." However, Lebrun and Reynaud were not yet as interested in the idea of soliciting an armistice as they were in how the government should respond in the event the Germans offered one. Reynaud had already discussed this contingency with Jules Jeanneney, president of the Senate, earlier that day. Jeanneney said he hoped any German armistice offer would prove unacceptable. It would only mask Germany's design of crushing France in two steps—much as Czechoslovakia had been betrayed diplomatically at the Munich conference in September 1938 and then occupied by German troops the following March.

César Campinchi, the minister of the navy, declared that "the loyalty of France must not be risked; a peace treaty must never be signed by France without a previous agreement with England." But, he added, "if the present government had given its word to England, perhaps another government might feel less bound to the signing of a peace treaty without the former agreement with England."

Pétain, for his part, was indifferent about the prospect of offending the British by concluding a separate peace. "I question whether there is a complete reciprocity with the British," he said. "Actually, they have given only two [actually 10] divisions, while eighty French divisions are still fighting." It was obvious to him that France owed Britain nothing.

Lebrun then asked Reynaud how soon France could expect to receive effective aid from America. The premier replied that more than a week before he had asked U.S. Ambassador Bullitt to place the same question before President Roosevelt. As of yet, he had not received an answer.

Reynaud then said that he would go to London the next day. "If offers of peace are presented," he said, "France must say to England: 'Here are the offers we've received. What do you think of them? We realize we are bound by a formal engagement to you.'"

Weygand reacted by saying that it did not make sense to sacrifice the French army to honor the alliance with Britain. What was more important, he believed, was preserving the army in order to maintain order within the country after an armistice was signed. "What troubles would result," he asked, "if the last organized force, that is, the Army, is destroyed?" Significantly, no mention was made of another option: continuing the war from North Africa if metropolitan France fell to the Germans.

LÉOPOLD MOVES TOWARD
CAPITULATION, MAY 25

Weygand was not the only Allied leader who was thinking about surrendering. At 5:00 A.M. on May 25, at the Château Wynendaele, near Bruges, King Léopold confronted a deputation of ministers—Prime Minister Pierlot, Foreign Minister Spaak, and War Minister General Denis. They had come to the king's military headquarters to beg him to accompany them out of the country and become, in effect, the head of a Belgian government in exile, one that would keep the country in the war even though its national territory was overrun by the Germans.

The king, who had returned from his military headquarters very late, had been roused from his bed by his aide, Major Van den Heuvel, to receive the ministers. The meeting took place in the large drawing room on the first floor of the château. The atmosphere was painful, tense, and dramatic, evidenced by the fact that the king and the ministers remained standing during their conversation.

Pierlot spoke first. "The Belgian Army," he began, "must beat a retreat, withdraw from Belgium, and take refuge, if necessary, as far as the Somme." Then, looking squarely at Léopold, Pierlot said: "The King cannot surrender with his army. If the King returns to Belgium to rule under German authority, he will be under their thumb like President Hácha of Czechoslovakia. The Belgian people will turn their backs on him—at least the French-speaking Belgians will—and it will divide our country." However, if the king withdrew to France, Pierlot added, "his voice, and that of his government, will be heard. He will live in freedom and the Belgian institutions will continue to function outside the country."

After a few moments of silence, Léopold responded: "I have decided to stay. I must share the fate of my people, whatever it may be. It is by remaining with them that I shall best be able to protect them."

The silence in the room was deafening. So fixed was Léopold's determination not to be swayed by his chief ministers' advice that he continued to stand rather than invite them to sit down. Finally Spaak, pleading exhaustion, asked permission to sit. The king reluctantly sat down and signaled his ministers to their chairs.

Pierlot then asked whether the king had considered all of the consequences of his decision. "Contrary to what Your Majesty said," Pierlot said, "he will not share the fate of his troops. He will not be incarcerated in a German fortress, but in his own palace. Anything he tries to do will compromise him and will compromise our independence, since Your Majesty will be acting under enemy orders. Everyone's conscience will be deeply troubled."

Léopold replied that he would never consent to anything against the interests of the Allies. "If I were ever forced into that position, I would withdraw," that is, abdicate. "The decision I am making," he added, "is a terribly painful one. Of course, life would be easier for me in France, if I went there to live with my children until this torment is over, but I believe that when one has two roads to choose from, the path of duty is always the hardest. That is the one I have chosen."

"Will Your Majesty form a new government?" Pierlot asked.

Léopold looked surprised for a moment, then replied: "Naturally! I am not a dictator!"

Finally, the ministers asked him how much longer the Belgian army could hold out. "Twenty-four hours at most," he answered.

The audience was over. The ministers took their leave of the king and left the country for France. They would not see him again until after the war.

As the ministers drove off down the road to Dunkirk and long exile, Pierlot looked out the car window at the waiting crowd. "I could not restrain my sense of unease, almost a kind of shame, passing before so many of my fellow-countrymen in whose eyes I thought I could be reproached at what seemed like our desertion."

GORT DECIDES TO WITHDRAW
TO THE COAST, MAY 25

When Winston Churchill arrived back in London after his trip to Paris during the late afternoon of May 22, he remained as determined as ever that Lord Gort should launch the southward attack as soon as possible. After learning that neither Gort's nor the southern offensive had started, he fired off to Reynaud a brusque "demand" for the "most stringent order" to execute the Weygand plan. "Time is vital," he added, "as supplies are short."

However, when Gort received a copy of this telegram, he realized that Churchill was working at cross-purposes with him. The prime minister, in Gort's mind, simply could not appreciate the fix the three northern Allied armies were in. They were caught in an elongated and highly vulnerable pocket 70 miles deep and only 20 miles wide at its narrowest point, with its mouth on a narrow stretch of the Channel coast, and the enemy pressing in from all sides. Moreover, with the French airfields in the north either captured or abandoned, and with the RAF operating from British airfields, there was virtually no air support for the three northern armies. To make matters even more precarious, Gort's army was now completely cut off from its supply bases, all west of the Somme River.

That evening, Gort drafted a message to Churchill. It stressed the gravity of the situation, the serious shortage of all essential commodities, and, above all, the lack of coordination, made worse by the fact that, as he put it, "the coordinator [Billotte] has had an accident and coordinates no longer." The French, he added, "were not prepared to fight, nor did they show any sign of doing so." He asked Churchill to send Sir John Dill, vice chief of the Imperial General Staff, to fly over to assess the situation himself.

Even before Gort's message arrived in London, Churchill's eyes had been partly opened by Admiral Keyes, who had managed to get through to him by calling from the coastal town of De Panne. Keyes related to him in graphic terms the precarious condition of the Allied armies. In response, Churchill telephoned Reynaud and asked if, in view of Gort's lack of orders from Blanchard, now Billotte's successor, combined with the continuing advance of the panzers, "whether it would not be better if the British army fought in retreat towards the coast?"

Reynaud vigorously rejected this suggestion. "We ought not to change anything," he exclaimed. "We must follow the path which we have traced out." Weygand himself was brought to the telephone to assure Churchill that the reformed French 7th Army had already begun its northward assault, and that it had already recaptured Amiens, Albert, and Péronne— all towns on the Somme River. To continue this maneuver was "the only solution," Weygand insisted. The rest "was disaster."

Churchill was overjoyed with the news that the southern offensive finally had begun. "The Prime Minister's cigar was waving cheerfully now," observed General Spears, who was present when Churchill talked to Reynaud and Weygand. "Wonderful," Spears reacted. "This really looked like business." Churchill's secretary, John Colville, recorded that "there was no reason to doubt Weygand's report, and gloom gave way to elation. The Germans must have shot their bolt; perhaps the Miracle of the Marne, that historical parallel of which everybody had been daydreaming, was going to be repeated."

But it was not to be. There was no counterattack across the Somme. Weygand had been misinformed—or was lying. Colville put the most sinister interpretation on the generalissimo's message. "Weygand was determined," he wrote in his diary, that "if the BEF could not go southward, that we should go under if they did."

Fortunately for the British, they had other, more reliable sources of information than that possessed by the Allied generalissimo. After the fall of Poland, they had obtained from Polish intelligence a machine called "Ultra" that was capable of decoding the German army's messages. That evening, Churchill read a decoded message that General Brauchitsch had radioed to his field commanders that morning, urging them to speed up their effort to enclose the Allied pocket. Bock's and Rundstedt's army groups were ordered to "continue their encircling maneuver in force" in

order to annihilate the French 1st Army Group, the British Expeditionary
Force, and King Léopold's army. To put this order into effect, Rundstedt's
divisions would have to drive to Ostend as quickly as possible, while Bock
would advance on the northern side of the pocket. "This was the signal,"
recalled one decoder, F. W. Winterbotham, "that decided both Gort and
Churchill that the time had come to get out of France."

However, historian Ronald Lewin points out that Gort also received
the text of Hitler's order halting the panzers on May 24, a message that in
effect canceled Brauchitsch's encirclement order. The new message permitted Gort to continue his preparations for a southward counterattack. It was
not until the evening of May 25, therefore, that Gort realized that the
counterattack was not possible and decided on his own to begin the BEF's
withdrawal to the Channel.

This Ultra message may have been on Churchill's mind when, at 10:30
that evening, he was summoned to Buckingham Palace by a deeply worried King George. "He told me," the king recorded in his diary, "that if
the French plan made out by Weygand did not come off, he would have to
order the BEF back to England. This operation would mean the loss of all
guns, tanks, ammunition, and all stores in France. . . . The very thought
of having to permit this movement is appalling, as the loss of life will
probably be immense."

At about 5:30 in the afternoon of May 25, Major Archdale, Gort's liaison
officer with the French 1st Army, found his commander-in-chief at his
headquarters "sitting at his table, very silent, and looking rather bewildered and bitter." Gort told Archdale that he had gotten "a raw deal" from
the French. "Not only had their army continually pleaded that it was too
tired to fight, and their staff work broken down, but from start to finish
there had been no direction or information from the high command."

To make matters worse, the military situation was becoming increasingly perilous. All that day, his two infantry divisions on both sides of
Arras, the 5th and 50th Divisions, had been pushed back by the 5th and
7th Panzer Divisions. And while a small British garrison still held on to
Arras, it was in danger of being surrounded. At the same time, the French
1st Army continued to disintegrate and was retreating northward to the
Escaut River, rather than withdrawing southward to link up with his own
lines, thereby creating another gap between the Allied armies. In addition,
Gort's own tank force had been drastically reduced: only two of the original 16 Mark II tanks, and 15 of the initial 60 more lightly armed Mark I

tanks, were still operable. Yet he was expected to support a counterattack against the panzer corridor by Altmayer's 5th Corps the next day.

Gort was torn between his intense desire, on the one hand, to fight the Germans and to be a loyal ally to the French and Belgians and, on the other, his even more binding duty to keep the BEF intact. But a number of developments that evening made Gort's choice easier. One was a telephone call shortly after Archdale left, informing the BEF commander that General Altmayer could provide only one division for the planned counterattack, instead of the three divisions and 200 tanks Blanchard had promised the previous day. It was now obvious that if Gort attacked southward, he would—as at Arras—have to go without the French. And with Martel's tank force dwindled away to only 17 tanks, he would be sending infantry divisions with virtually no armored support to do battle with panzers.

There was also his growing doubt about Blanchard's ability to coordinate the Allied counterattack. Gort received an unusual request that day that was contained in a message from Captain Guy Westmacott, who was the British liaison officer attached to the best unit in the French 1st Army, General Fournelle de la Laurencie's 3rd Corps. De la Laurencie told Westmacott he had received no orders for several days from Blanchard, whom he believed was incapable of formulating a plan. De la Laurencie wished "to have the honor" of placing his corps directly under Gort's command because, he said, the BEF commander was a fighter.

Perhaps the most important development that influenced Gort's decision to call off the counterattack and retreat to the Channel was the impending disintegration of the Belgian army. Early that morning, he had learned that the previous evening the German 6th Army had broken through the Belgian lines on both sides of Courtrai, on the Lys River, and penetrated to a depth of one and a half miles on a 13-mile front. This at once endangered the BEF's left flank by opening a gap between it and the Belgian army through which the Germans could charge, probably all the way to Dunkirk. Gort waited anxiously throughout the day for news of promised Belgian counterattacks to plug the hole in the Allied front. But when, toward evening, it became clear to Gort that the Belgians, despite a valiant effort, were unable to eliminate the German bridgehead and that the gap between his army and the Belgians was actually widening and deepening, Gort accepted that, as he put it, his "last hope of reaching the coast would be gone" if he did not withdraw immediately.

At 6:00 P.M. on May 25, Gort made his most fateful decision of the campaign. He came out of his office and walked next door to General Pownall's and said: "Henry, I've had a hunch. I've got to call off the 5th and 50th Divisions from the attack to the south and send them to Brookie [General Alan Brooke, 2nd Corps commander] on the left."

"Well, you do realize, sir," Pownall replied, "that that's against all the orders we've had, and that if we take those divisions away, the French 1st Army is very unlikely to attack without British support?"

"Yes, I know that quite well. All the same, it's got to be done."

Without asking for authority from the French command or from his own government, Gort ordered the two divisions assigned for the push south, the 5th and the 50th, to head northward toward the Channel and seal the gap around Ypres, thereby blocking the road to Dunkirk for the Germans.

"I knew for certain," Gort later recounted, "that a German thrust through Ypres, unless stopped, must inevitably cut off the BEF from the sea." He appreciated that if the British army were destroyed or captured, Britain would not have the means to successfully resist a Nazi invasion of the home islands. "A soldier at heart," F. W. Winterbotham wrote, "Gort was determined to save his men and through them his country from the danger that threatened the entire Western world."

As it was, Gort closed the gap between the BEF and the Belgian army only in the nick of time. Had the two British divisions he sent there arrived but a few hours later, they would have been too late. Bock would have secured his breakthrough and trapped the British army before it could have retreated to the coast.

Gort cabled Secretary of War Anthony Eden that evening to inform him that he was withdrawing to the coast, but he did not mention that it was also his intention to evacuate the BEF to England. He also ordered the withdrawal of the Arras garrison, since it was now evident that its men must retire or be surrounded. During that night, they managed to escape through the narrow corridor still open to them. Eden's reply the next morning recognized that "the only course open to you may be to fight your way back to the west, where all beaches and ports east of Gravelines will be used for embarkation." He added that Churchill would meet with Reynaud the following day to clarify the French attitude to evacuation of the BEF. "In the meantime," Eden's cable closed, "it is obvious that you should not discuss the possibility of the move [evacuation] with the French or the Belgians."

Gort complied with the war minister's order. He simply informed General Altmayer that BEF participation in the counterattack was off, but he made no mention of withdrawing to the coast, let alone evacuating the BEF to England.

The British Defense Committee,
Evening, May 25

At ten o'clock in the evening of May 25, shortly after the French War Committee ended its meeting in Paris, the British Defense Committee met at Admiralty House. Although Churchill was ignorant of Gort's decision to abandon the Weygand plan, he told his colleagues that "it was clear that there was no chance of General Weygand striking north in sufficient strength to disengage the Blanchard group in the north." Even Weygand, Churchill added, no longer supported the counterattack. According to a message from General Spears, Weygand had concluded "that attacks to the south by the group of armies in the north, including the British army, could serve no other purpose than to gain breathing space before falling back to a line covering the harbors."

Sir John Dill, who had just returned from his brief fact-finding mission to France, supported this conclusion. Dill, like Churchill, not yet knowing that Gort had abandoned the southward attack, warned the committee that if a British drive to the south was tried and it failed, Gort would not have sufficient strength to try the other course open to him, "namely to cut his way north to the coast."

Without hesitation, Churchill expressed his opinion "in favor of an advance north to the ports and the beaches," which the Defense Committee concluded "was the right course." Said Churchill, Gort must march "north to the coast, in battle order, under strong rearguards, striking at all forces between himself and the sea"; the navy must prepare "all possible means for reembarkation, not only at the ports but on the beaches"; the air force must "dominate the air" above the area involved; Gort would be ordered to plan the march to the sea beginning on the night of May 26.

Toward the end of the meeting, Lieutenant General Sir Henry Karslake, who also had just returned from France, reported that the French were very downhearted and were preparing to get out of the war. In this connection, Churchill told the War Cabinet that Reynaud had asked to meet with him privately the next day, and not with the War Cabinet as a whole. He said he would not be at all surprised if a peace offer had been made to Reynaud. But he insisted that if the French wanted out of the war, they must first agree to permit the BEF to leave the Continent intact, not allow the soil of France to be used as a base for attacking Britain, and not surrender the French Fleet. If an offer were made on these terms, Churchill said, he would accept it. "We could hold out in this country," he added "once we had our Army back from France."

THE BATTLE OF CALAIS, MAY 24–27

In addition to approving these steps, the Defense Committee agreed with Churchill that at all costs, it was essential to hold on to Calais for as long as possible, especially after Boulogne had fallen to the Germans the previous day. "If we attempted to withdraw our garrison from Calais," Churchill said, "the German troops in Calais would immediately march on Dunkirk."

Moreover, Churchill was stung by Reynaud's vigorous complaints about his decision to withdraw British troops from Boulogne before it surrendered and without first informing the French high command or the French defenders in that port. The French argued that Boulogne could have been defended had not the British troops departed. Accordingly, Churchill countermanded a War Department order directing the evacuation of British forces in Calais.

Calais, which was invested by the 10th Panzer Division during the evening of May 23, was defended by units of the French 21st Infantry Division and the British 30th Infantry Brigade, together with the 3rd Royal Tank Regiment. The British forces were under the command of Brigadier General Claude Nicholson, an experienced cavalry officer who, at the age of forty-two, was rather younger than most officers of similar rank.

Against the overwhelming firepower of the 10th Panzer Division, the much smaller Allied force had no chance of holding the city. Realizing this, Nicholson was obviously relieved by a message he received at 3:00 P.M. on May 24 from the War Office ordering him to prepare his troops for evacuation, beginning at seven o'clock the next morning. Nicholson responded by directing his brigade to retreat to Calais's inner perimeter, which enclosed the dock area, the old town, and the Petit Courgain.

During the early hours of May 25, however, Nicholson learned that Churchill had canceled the evacuation order. Admiral Sir James Somerville, commanding the small force of warships that had been standing offshore and bombarding German positions around Calais, sent him a War Office message that read, in part: "British forces in your area [are] now under [French General] Fagalde, who has ordered no—repeat—no evacuation . . . you must comply for sake of Allied Solidarity. Your role is therefore to hold on, [even though] harbor is at present of no importance to B.E.F."

When Churchill read this message after it had been sent to Nicholson, he was furious. He minuted to Eden and Ironside: "This is not the way to encourage men to fight to the end," and he went on to ask: "Are you sure there is no streak of defeatist opinion in the [Imperial] General Staff?" He then drafted his own message to Nicholson. He explained that the defense of the city "is of the highest importance to our country and our army" since it would tie down a large part of the German armored forces that might otherwise attack Gort's forces and prevent him from preserving a "sally port" from which portions of the British army "may make their way home." "Every hour you continue to exist is of the greatest help to the BEF." Churchill's message ended: "The eyes of the Empire are upon the defense of Calais, and His Majesty's Government are confident you and your gallant Regiment will perform an exploit worthy of the British name."

As the sun rose on the morning of May 25, Calais was the scene of desperate fighting. Following a fierce artillery barrage, the Germans launched a strong attack against the British Rifle Brigade's positions on the south of the perimeter. The brigade resisted with only a handful of scout cars, light tanks, and Bren carriers, since most of the supporting 3rd Royal Tank Regiment's tanks had already been destroyed—many of them, much to Nicholson's regret, deliberately—when the earlier order to evacuate was received.

The Germans, hoping to make a quick finish of Calais in order to be able to move on to Dunkirk, pressed their attack throughout the day with growing intensity, using the full strength of two panzer divisions, the 2nd as well as the 10th. At 3:00 P.M., they launched a concentrated ground and aerial bombardment that lasted three hours. When it was over, German infantry stormed over the canals, covered by the dust and smoke produced by the bombardment, and pierced the British line at several points, forcing Nicholson to withdraw his troops to the Citadel—the principal remnant of a 16th-century fortification—which was being held by about 800 French troops.

At 4:30 P.M., Nicholson sent out his last direct message. He reported heavy German shelling and asked for guns and air support. At about that time, a flag of truce appeared, carried by a German officer who demanded the surrender of the Citadel as the only alternative to its pulverization. As recorded in the attacker's war diary, in English, Nicholson's reply was: "The answer is no, as it is the British Army's duty to fight as well as it is the German's."

Thereafter, the attack was renewed with a terrific artillery barrage lasting half an hour, after which German infantry, led by panzers, attempted to storm the three bridges connecting the Citadel with the old town.

On the first two bridges the German infantry were forced to retreat when their supporting panzers were knocked out, but they managed to get across the third bridge and overran some of the British forward positions. However, the British counterattacked and dislodged the Germans after vicious close-in fighting. The German onslaught was broken off, according to the war diary of the 10th Panzer Division, only because "the infantry brigade commander considers further attack pointless, as the enemy resistance is not yet crushed and as there is not enough time before the fall of darkness."

While German ground forces were attacking the Citadel, Stuka dive-bombers were attempting to sink the ships of Admiral Somerville's flotilla, consisting of the British cruisers *Arethusa* and *Galatea,* the destroyers *Wessex, Vimiera, Wolfhound, Verity, Grafton,* and *Greyhound,* and the Polish destroyer *Burza.* The Stukas, about 40 in number, were commanded by Maj. Oskar Dinort, who had achieved fame as a competition pilot in prewar Germany and then participated in the blitzkrieg on Poland. Since the Luftwaffe had not developed a technique for dive-bombing warships, Dinort realized that his attack would be a learning experience. What he did not realize was that it would also serve as a dress rehearsal for a far more important mission: the destruction of the Allied evacuation force at Dunkirk.

As Dinort's planes approached the coast, the reflection of the early morning sun on the English Channel, combined with the smoky haze rising from Calais, made it difficult for his pilots to find their targets. Suddenly, however, a group of ships came into view. Over the radio, Dinort ordered his two group commanders, Hauptmann Hirtschold and Hauptmann Bruckers, to select their own targets while he led his own section of three Stukas in a dive on a destroyer. Diving from 12,000 feet, Dinort placed the British ship squarely in his sight, only to see it drift out again as it took evasive action. Easing out of the dive slightly, Dinort captured the warship once more, then lost it again as it turned the other way. The sea was fast racing up to meet him by now, and in desperation he kicked the rudder bar, releasing his bomb as the gray hull of the destroyer swung through his sight for the last time. As he pulled out of his dive and raced away through a maze of antiaircraft bursts, he looked back to see his bomb explode in a geyser of spray 100 yards from its target.

Everywhere, Dinort's other Stukas experienced the same results. Obviously, air attacks on warships maneuvering at high speed were going to call for a higher degree of expertise than other targets had required before. Nevertheless, some of the Stukas did find the target. They sank the destroyer *Wessex* and damaged both the *Vimiera* and the *Burza.*

As Dinort and his pilots were flying home, half a dozen sleek aircraft, firing their machine guns, swept through the German formation. The attackers did not display the familiar humpbacked silhouettes of British Hurricanes, which until now had been the Luftwaffe's main RAF adversary in the skies over the coast. From now on, the Luftwaffe would also have to contend with Spitfires.

"English fighters behind us!" Dinort's radio crackled.

Dinort immediately throttled back and stall-turned his Stuka to starboard, a maneuver that enabled his much slower plane to avoid the hail of bullets fired from a Spitfire on his tail.

Fortunately for Dinort, the British fighters were immediately engaged by German Me-109 fighters, allowing his Stukas to escape. However, during the previous 24 hours, eight Stukas from other units fell victim to Spitfires in aerial engagements along the coast.

Early in the morning of May 26, the German bombardment of Calais resumed with greater violence than ever, additional artillery having been brought up from Boulogne. Although the German panzers and infantry were again repeatedly repulsed, the defenders were gradually forced back into the northern half of the old town. At about 3:30 P.M., the Germans finally broke into the Citadel and captured Nicholson and his staff. As evening arrived, the remaining British forces in the city also surrendered. They were marched off to prisoner-of-war camps, where most of them would spend the rest of the war. Nicholson, however, did not survive internment. He died in captivity writing his own version of the battle.

The remaining French forces, holding out in the city's old fortress, did not surrender until the following day. The survivors were marched out of the fort, stripped of their watches, rings, and other valuables, and then reassembled and photographed by Nazi propagandists. They then were marched out of the city on their way to prisoner-of-war camps in Germany. All totaled, from Calais, the Germans took 20,000 prisoners, 3,500 of them British.

While the British and their French allies were finally overwhelmed at Calais, they had engaged two of Guderian's three panzer divisions and held them off for three critical days. In so doing, they bought time for Gort's 3rd Corps to establish a defensive line west of Dunkirk, thereby preventing Guderian from breaking into the rear of the BEF as it retreated to that port. Of their sacrifice, Churchill later wrote: "Calais was the crux. Many other causes might have prevented the deliverance of Dunkirk, but it is certain that the three days gained by the defence of Calais enabled the Gravelines waterline to be held, and that without this, even in spite of Hitler's vacillations and Rundstedt's orders, all would have been cut off and lost."

The Demise of the Weygand Plan, May 26

News of Gort's decision to withdraw from the Weygand plan had reached General Blanchard three hours after it was made. He reacted by canceling the planned counterattack and by ordering the three Allied armies in the north to "regroup progressively behind the waterline demarcated by the Aa Canal, the Lys, and the Canal de Derivation, so as to form a bridgehead covering Dunkirk in depth." Blanchard then sent a telegram to Weygand blasting Gort's decision.

Weygand did not need any prompting from Blanchard. Gort's retreat from Arras had already convinced the generalissimo that the BEF was heading for the coast. In fact, Weygand believed that this was the real reason why Gort had failed to meet with him at the Ypres conference five days earlier: The BEF commander did not want to risk displaying his duplicity in a face-to-face encounter.

Weygand immediately informed Reynaud, who at once indignantly telegraphed Churchill: "The British withdrawal had obliged General Weygand to modify his whole plan. He was now compelled to give up his attempt to close the breach and establish a continuous front." The stillborn Weygand plan was officially dead, and in the minds of the French leadership, Gort was the man responsible for its demise.

But Weygand knew better. He admitted after the war that he had no expectation that a counterattack of any significant strength could have been launched from the southern side of the Somme. He had hoped "that however feeble it might have been, it would have at least created an additional threat to the German flank and thus increased the chances of success for the northern offensive." Without pressure from the south, however, there was no chance of cutting the Germans off from the northern side of the panzer corridor.

Churchill replied at once to Reynaud's cable, seeking to justify Gort's action. He pointed out that the British commander-in-chief had been forced by the pressure on his western flank and by the need to keep Dunkirk open for essential supplies "to place parts of two divisions between himself and the increasing pressure of the German armored forces." How, he went on to ask, could Gort move southward, according to the Weygand plan, and disengage his northern front, "unless he throws out this shield on his right hand?"

Yet Churchill, obviously, was being as duplicitous as Weygand, for he again made no mention of the preparations he had initiated to evacuate the BEF to England or that evacuation was the primary reason behind Gort's decision to retreat to the coast.

The French, nevertheless, saw through the British subterfuge: Their ally was running out on them. That evening, for the first time, Reynaud voiced his doubt about France's ability to continue in the war. In a conversation with Paul Baudouin, he asked, "If Germany were to make reasonable peace proposals, would public opinion allow us to reject them?" But he quickly answered his own question: "Since I have always advocated total war, I should resign if that were to happen."

CHAPTER EIGHT

The Retreat to Dunkirk, May 26–28

LONDON, MAY 26

In more ways than one, Sunday, May 26, began as a gloomy day for Winston Churchill. As he awakened, it was raining for the first time in many days. But much more importantly, the news from France was bad, very bad. The road to Dunkirk was open and the race to the sea was about to begin. If the BEF lost that race to Hitler's panzers, it could mean the end of the British Empire, certainly, at least, the end of the BEF. Without her army, Britain would not have the required ground forces to repel a German invasion. She would have to rely on her navy and air force, and they might not be enough.

Churchill tried to be optimistic. There was a "good chance," he told the War Cabinet at nine o'clock that morning, "of getting off a considerable proportion of the British Expeditionary Force." But he could not be sure. The Germans might beat the BEF to Dunkirk and close the trap door before it could escape.

At the same time, Churchill's continued hold on the premiership also was by no means guaranteed. He had become prime minister by default, that is, only because the Labour Party refused to serve under Neville Chamberlain and Lord Halifax, his foreign minister, had declined the office—at least for the time being. Churchill realized that he would hold power only as long as Chamberlain and Halifax, the two leaders of the majority Conservative Party, did not turn on him. If he faltered, Halifax would be ready to step in.

Needless to say, Churchill went out of his way to treat both men with deference. Shortly after becoming prime minister on May 10, he wrote to

Chamberlain: "My first act . . . is to write and tell you how grateful I am to you for promising to stand by me. . . . With your help and counsel, and with the support of the great party of which you are the leader, I trust that I shall succeed."

On the other hand, Churchill treated Halifax as carefully as one would approach a coiled rattlesnake. The English nobleman was the chief architect of the appeasement policy, which Churchill had gone into the political wilderness denouncing. Yet Halifax, to his credit, had been the first and most important member of Chamberlain's government to advise him that it was time, following Hitler's annexation of Czechoslovakia in March 1939, to abandon appeasement and, if necessary, resist any further Nazi aggression with force.

However, unlike Churchill, Halifax never had thought much of the French army's ability to thwart Hitler. As early as the previous December, he had told the Cabinet that if France dropped out of the conflict, "we should not be able to carry on the war by ourselves." Now that this appeared to be happening, Halifax believed that it was time to explore the possibility of a deal with Hitler, one that would bring the war to an end, before Britain's cities were devastated, and on terms not too inimical to British interests.

Halifax had reason to believe that Italian dictator Benito Mussolini might be willing to serve as a bridge between the two sides, a role he had played at Munich. On May 25 Halifax sounded out the Italian ambassador, Giuseppe Bastianini, to see if Mussolini would be willing to play that role again. Bastianini told him that "Mussolini's principal wish was to secure peace in Europe." Halifax replied that the Allies would "be prepared to consider any proposals which might lead to this," provided their liberty and independence were preserved.

What Halifax did not know was that the Italian dictator had already made up his mind to enter the war on Hitler's side. That very day, in Rome, Mussolini informed his chief military leaders, Marshal Badoglio and Marshal Balbo, that he was prepared to take Italy into the war on Germany's side. "I have sent Hitler a written statement," he told the two marshals, "making it clear to him that I do not intend to stand idly by, and that, as from June 5th, I shall be in a position to declare war on France and England."

Halifax had launched his peace feeler to Italy without the knowledge or support of Churchill, whose style of leadership the foreign minister deplored. Churchill's single-minded combativeness, Halifax feared, would only produce a disastrous prolongation of the war, the outcome of which would only be the destruction of Britain and her empire.

Not believing that he alone could sway Churchill to seek a negotiated end to the war, however, Halifax planned to go over the new prime minister's head and place his case before the entire War Cabinet. Accordingly, on the morning of May 26, he informed its members that Bastianini had asked for an interview in order to put forward "fresh proposals" for a peace conference.

Churchill, predictably, was not interested in any proposal for Italian mediation. A negotiated peace at this point, he told the War Cabinet, could only be achieved "under a German domination of Europe." Such an outcome, he emphasized, "we could never accept." In fact, he added, if the British people even found out that their government was seeking another deal with Hitler, the effect on their morale and the war effort would be devastating. Hitler had demonstrated repeatedly that he could not be trusted to keep his promises.

But if France fell, Halifax responded, could Britain carry on the war alone? It "would depend," the foreign secretary answered his own question, "in the main on our being able to establish and maintain air superiority over the Germans." And, he added, once France collapsed, the Germans would "no longer need large land forces. They would be free to switch the bulk of their effort to air production."

Without coming to a decision on Halifax's proposal, the War Cabinet agreed to meet again that afternoon, after the foreign secretary had a chance to talk with the Italian ambassador, and after Churchill had met with Premier Reynaud, who was flying in from Paris, coincidentally, to discuss the possibility of a negotiated settlement of the conflict.

Before meeting with Reynaud, however, Churchill had to rush over to Westminster Abbey to attend a service launching a day of national prayer, which had been called for by King George. The king, with Queen Elizabeth, had arrived at the Abbey carrying gas masks. They were accompanied by Wilhelmina, the exiled queen of the Netherlands. Someone shouted: "Long live the Netherlands!" Wilhelmina replied with a curtsy.

Inside the Abbey, Churchill recalled, "I could feel the pent-up, passionate emotion, and also the fear of the congregation, not of death or wounds or material loss, but of defeat and the final ruin of Britain." However, having made it clear to his staff that he and the other members of the War Cabinet could stay no longer than 30 minutes, they left in the middle of the service.

Premier Reynaud arrived with his aides at Admiralty House shortly after Churchill and his War Cabinet colleagues had returned from the prayer service. The French premier informed the British leaders that France had deployed 50 divisions between the Maginot Line and the sea. But against these divisions, he added, the Germans could put three times that number. From this it was clear, he said, "that the war could not be won on land." He wanted more of the RAF's as yet uninvolved fighters.

Not prepared to send the planes Reynaud requested, Churchill instead tried to assure the French premier that they would not be needed. As soon as the situation in northeastern France had been "cleared up," he said, the Germans would make no further attacks on the French positions south of the Somme River. Rather, he believed, they would "immediately start attacking Britain itself." Britain would need all her fighters to fend them off.

Reynaud disagreed. The "dream of all Germans," he said, "was to conquer Paris." After capturing the Channel ports, the Germans would turn southward and march on the French capital. Trying to pressure Churchill into giving France more assistance, Reynaud added that if the Germans took Paris, they would gain control of the French aircraft industry. He did not have to tell Churchill that the planes produced by the French factories would be used against Britain.

Whatever happened, Churchill replied, with words that undoubtedly made Halifax cringe, "we were not prepared to give in. We would rather go down fighting than be enslaved to Germany." Churchill then tried to lift Reynaud's spirits by telling him that "if only" the Allies could "stick things out for another three months," the situation would be "entirely different."

But Reynaud did not believe the French army could last three months. And he warned Churchill that while he and General Weygand were prepared to fight on, others in the French government were ready to seek a negotiated end to the war. If Germany were to occupy a large part of France, he said, "Pétain would be likely to come out in favor of an armistice."

Yet Reynaud could not bring himself to ask Churchill the question the French War Committee had directed him to raise in London: Would the British relieve France of her promise not to conclude a separate peace? Apparently the French premier was overwhelmed by Churchill's aggressive optimism. He told the prime minister that the primary purpose for his London visit was to obtain the support of the British government "for concessions to Mussolini, in the hope of keeping Italy out of the war, and to explore the larger possibility of securing mediation, in some form, by the Italian Government."

If an approach were made to Italy, Churchill responded, what sort of terms would Italy ask? Reynaud replied that the Italians would ask for the neutralization of Gibraltar and the Suez Canal, the demilitarization of Malta, and the limitation of naval forces in the Mediterranean. Some alteration in the status of Tunis would also be asked for, and the Dodecanese Islands would have "to be put right," meaning that the islands would have to revert to Italian control. While Reynaud was under no illusion that Hitler would keep any deal, he believed that such an offer might at least keep Italy out of the war and thereby enable France to transfer many of its divisions in the Maginot Line to the Somme front.

Churchill, acutely embarrassed at again having to refuse further RAF support, did not have the heart to turn down Reynaud's request for an approach to Mussolini. He promised the French premier that the War Cabinet would consider the proposal.

While Reynaud waited at Admiralty House, Churchill again met with his colleagues in the War Cabinet at 2:00 P.M. He began by saying that it was now necessary to "persuade" Reynaud that Weygand "should be instructed to issue" an order for the British Expeditionary Force to march to the coast. Only a formal order by the Allied commander-in-chief, Churchill felt, would ensure "that the French had no complaint . . . that, by cutting our way to the coast, we were letting them down militarily." It was important, he added, that this order should be issued "as soon as possible."

Churchill then raised the matter of the Italian peace initiative. He said that while he "doubted whether anything would come of an approach to Italy," the matter was one which the War Cabinet would have to consider. He then asked Halifax to go over to Admiralty House to discuss the proposal with Reynaud.

According to the French premier, Halifax, without committing his government to a precise offer, expressed his willingness to suggest to Mussolini that if Italy "would agree to collaborate with France and Britain in establishing a peace which would safeguard the independence of these two countries . . . the Allies would be prepared to discuss with him the claims of Italy in the Mediterranean."

However, when Churchill and the other members of the War Cabinet joined Halifax and Reynaud, they expressed their opposition in principle to any concessions to the Italians. Concessions would be useless, they believed, because Mussolini would think that he could win more by entering the war on the side of a victorious Germany than he could possibly acquire by peaceful negotiations with the defeated Allies. They also believed that the Italian dictator would only understand a policy of strength; Mussolini should be made to realize that Britain was prepared to bring the war home to the Italian people, including the bombing of Italy's cities, as soon as he opened hostilities.

As a result of the War Cabinet's hostility to Mussolini, Reynaud was unable to get British support for a peace feeler to the Italian leader. Instead, he was told that he would be given an answer the next day, after the War Cabinet had a chance to discuss the matter further. But Reynaud had no doubt about what that answer would be. On his return to Paris that evening, he told Paul Baudouin: "The only one who understands is Halifax, who is clearly worried about the future, and realizes that some European solution must be reached. But Churchill is always hectoring, and Chamberlain is undecided."

Before leaving for Paris, however, Reynaud did agree to Churchill's request to direct General Weygand to order the withdrawal of the northern Allied armies to the coast. Churchill then instructed Eden to send another telegram to Lord Gort, informing him that the French had abandoned all hope of striking from the south. "In these circumstances," the text went on, there is "no course open to you but to fall back upon the coast. . . . Reynaud is communicating to General Weygand and the latter will no doubt issue orders in this sense forthwith." Churchill also authorized the Admiralty to give this order: "Operation Dynamo is to commence."

Although Reynaud agreed to direct Weygand to order the withdrawal of the Allied northern armies to the coast, he was unaware—because Churchill did not inform him—that the ultimate objective of the BEF's retreat was its evacuation to England. As far as the French leaders were concerned, the purpose of the Allied withdrawal was the creation of a bridgehead around the Channel ports that could serve as a launching pad for a future Allied counteroffensive. When they eventually did learn what was going on, the French would justifiably accuse the British of deception.

At 5:00 P.M., there was another, "informal" meeting of the War Cabinet at Admiralty House. It began with Churchill's assessment of the French situation. He said that "if France could not defend itself, it was better that she should get out of the war rather than that she should drag us into

a settlement which involved intolerable terms." There was "no limit," he said, to the terms that Germany would impose on Britain "if she had her way."

As the discussion continued, Halifax again raised the question of peace negotiations under Italian supervision. He read out an account of his lunchtime talk with Italian Ambassador Bastianini. Churchill did not like the approach Halifax suggested. It implied, he said, "that if we were prepared to give Germany back her colonies and make certain concessions in the Mediterranean, it was possible to get out of our present difficulties." Churchill's view was "that no such option was open to us." The terms Germany would demand, he felt, "would certainly prevent us from completing our rearmament."

As the meeting was drawing to a close, Churchill remarked "that Herr Hitler thought he had the whip hand. . . . We must take care not to be forced into a weak position in which we went to Signor Mussolini and invited him to go to Herr Hitler and ask him to treat us nicely." The only thing to do was to show him "that he could not conquer this country. If, as Reynaud's remarks had suggested, France could not continue with the war, we must part company."

At this point, Halifax said that he was not quite convinced that the prime minister's assessment of Hitler's aims was correct. He did not think that it was in the Führer's interest to insist on outrageous terms. "After all," Halifax observed, "he [Hitler] knew his own internal weaknesses. On this lay-out, it might be possible to save France from the wreck."

Chamberlain was now leaning toward Halifax. He said that they should not offend the French by turning down "their idea outright." Moreover, he added, "If Signor Mussolini was prepared to collaborate with us in getting tolerable terms, then we would be prepared to discuss Italian terms with him."

Churchill said that nothing should be decided until they knew how much of the British Expeditionary Force could be saved. "The operation might be a great failure," he said. "On the other hand, our troops might well fight magnificently, and we might save a considerable portion of the force."

But Halifax had the last word. "If we got to the point of discussing terms of a general settlement, and found that we could obtain terms which did not postulate the destruction of our independence, we should be foolish if we did not accept them."

The meeting, Sir Alexander Cadogan, the permanent Foreign Office undersecretary, noted in his diary, "settled nothing much." Churchill, he wrote, was "too rambling and romantic and sentimental and temperamental." Cadogan added that "Old Neville [Chamberlain] was still the best of the lot."

At eight o'clock that evening, Churchill dined with Eden, Ironside, and Ismay. The prime minister, Ismay remembered, seemed immensely sad. His spirit was not broken, but the prospect of a British *Götterdämmerung* was before his eyes. He had to abandon Calais, since all the ships were now needed for Dunkirk. He was unaware that the last British posts in Calais had fallen three hours earlier. He undoubtedly was also bothered by the revival of appeasement in Halifax's proposal to approach Mussolini, and upset that Chamberlain was also leaning in that direction. He had been unable to squelch it. For once, Churchill's appetite was gone. He ate and drank almost nothing and sat silently through the dinner conversation. After dinner, he stood up and told his colleagues that he felt "physically sick," then excused himself.

Much later, around midnight, after reading a few papers, Churchill called John Colville and said to him, "Pour me out a whisky and soda, very weak," after which he said, "There's a good boy," and then went to bed.

Withdrawal to Dunkirk Begins, May 26–27

Gort received the order to withdraw to the coast shortly before 7:00 P.M. on May 26. He immediately called a conference of his subordinate commanders to inform them that the government had authorized a full-scale evacuation of the BEF. Together they worked out the details for the move, the preliminary phase of which was to begin that night. Gort also instructed General Sir Ronald Adam, the commander of the BEF's 3rd Corps, to go to Dunkirk and make preparations for the exodus, as well as to organize a defensive perimeter around that port.

Gort, in fact, had been pulling back his army toward Dunkirk for several days before receiving the War Office's order to withdraw. In fact, had it not been for Gort's decision to disengage from Arras on May 23—which, to be sure, was assisted immeasurably by Hitler's panzer halt order the following day—any significant evacuation of Allied troops from Dunkirk would have been impossible. Even Churchill, in his memoir, grudgingly admitted that Gort had been right to act against his orders.

Getting back to the coast, however, would not be easy. There were an estimated 500,000 British and French soldiers scattered across Belgium and
northern France, and some were as far as 60 miles from Dunkirk. By the
evening of May 26, the Allied troops, along with the soldiers of the Belgian army, had been compressed into a rapidly shrinking pocket. Its bottom lay southeast of the French city of Lille, and was held by the remnants
of the French 1st Army, now commanded by General Prioux. The pocket's
mouth opened on the Channel, from Gravelines in the west to Nieuport in
the east. The disintegrating Belgian army held the extreme northern end
of the line, but only partially, for that day General Bock's army group
launched a heavy attack on the Belgian positions on the Lys River, on both
sides of Courtrai, and managed to break the Belgian army's link with the
BEF's left flank. The BEF, for its part, had to defend not only the growing
gap between its left wing and the Belgian army, but also the western side
of the Allied front, between the Channel and the French positions around
Lille. Through this narrow corridor, the Allies would have to retreat some
10 French and nine British divisions and reembark them onto ships under
attack by a numerically superior German air force.

Gort was not very optimistic. "I must not conceal from you," he replied to the withdrawal order, "that a great part of the BEF and its equipment will inevitably be lost, even in the best circumstances." In an attempt
to lift Gort's morale, Churchill sent him a personal message the following
morning: "Presume troops know they are cutting their way home to
Blighty. Never was there such a spur for fighting. We shall give you all
the Navy and Air Force can do. . . . No one can tell how it will go, but
anything is better than being cooped up and starved out."

Most of the British soldiers were surprised by the decision to evacuate to
England. Lieutenant Jimmy Langley got the news from his company commander, Major Angus McCorquodale. At the evening company conference
on Monday, May 27, McCorquodale said: "We are going home," and then
paused, "by way of Dunkirk." No one said anything. "Platoons will withdraw as quietly as possible at 22.00 hours and form up on the main road
to Lille. . . . Final destination: the harbor at Dunkirk for embarkation to
England. Any questions?"

"How far is it to Dunkirk?"

"About 60 miles."

There was a long silence as the men digested the information. Finally
they were dismissed. That night they would begin another long march,
but this time, they hoped, it would be the first step back to home.

The next morning, at dawn, there was a favorable change in the weather. The clear blue sky and blazing sun that had seemed so much a part of the BEF's retreat were replaced by banks of low gray clouds and frequent heavy showers. It was superb marching weather and unsuitable for attacks by Stuka dive-bombers or low-flying fighters. But the conditions on the roads rapidly deteriorated as more men, trucks of every description, guns, and a mass of French horse-drawn vehicles joined the retreating columns.

By afternoon, the confusion on the outskirts of Poperinge was so great that Jimmy Langley, for one, began to doubt if his company would ever make it to Dunkirk. But then, just as things were looking hopeless, a troop of Belgian Boy Scouts, immaculately dressed, carrying staves, and smiling and laughing, cheerfully led them to another way around the mess in Poperinge. Why and how a troop of scouts had come to the rescue of his outfit in the swirling mass of men, guns, and horses that choked the debris-littered street was beyond Langley's comprehension. He had always regarded the Scout movement with derision, and not infrequently cracked a joke at their expense. But not after that day.

Once around Poperinge, Langley's men were ordered to halt, in order to rest and allow stragglers to catch up. Suddenly Brigadier Beckwith "Becky" Smith, who commanded the 1st Guards Brigade, of which Langley's company was a part, drove up in his car. "Marvelous news, Jimmy," he shouted. "The best ever!" Short of the German army deciding to call it a day, which seemed improbable, Langley could think of no news deserving the qualifications of "marvelous" and "the best ever!"

"It is splendid, absolutely splendid," Smith continued. "We have been given the supreme honor of being the rearguard at Dunkirk. Tell your platoon, Jimmy—come on, tell them the good news."

After all the months Langley had commanded his platoon, the 15th Platoon, he had not the slightest doubt that they would accept the news with the usual tolerance and good humor they had previously displayed. However, he did not think they would class the news as "marvelous" and "the best ever."

"I think it would come better from you, sir," Langley responded.

"Right, right," Smith replied. After telling the men to remain seated, Smith informed them about the changed plan.

Then, to Langley's delight, Smith explained how they should deal with Stuka dive-bombers. "Stand up to them. Shoot at them with a Bren gun from the shoulder. Take them like a high pheasant. Give them plenty of lead. Remember, five pounds to any man who brings one down. I have already paid out ten pounds."

Smith's high spirits and optimism were very infectious, especially because they were genuine. "Becky," Langley observed, "genuinely regarded the task as a supreme honor, and I could see that much of his enthusiasm was shared by 15 Platoon."

THE DUNKIRK PERIMETER

Since the BEF had no choice in the matter, they were fortunate that it was Dunkirk to which they were retreating. Like other French towns on the English Channel, Dunkirk had been fortified by Marshal Vauban, Louis XIV's great engineer, and the remnants of his defenses still remained. Moreover, the port was surrounded by a network of canals as well as marshes that could be flooded. And the stretch of coast east of the port was particularly suitable for an evacuation. Extending well beyond the Belgian border, eight miles away, it constituted one of the longest unbroken beaches in northern Europe. Backed by wide expanses of desolate, rolling dunes that were studded with clumps of coarse grass, the beaches, in some places up to a mile wide, provided excellent assembly areas for large groups of soldiers.

However, the coast east of Dunkirk was not suitable for embarking soldiers on large ships. At low tide, the water was only knee-deep for several hundreds of yards into the sea. And while at high tide the sea rose several feet, the water still was not deep enough for large ships to approach closer than a half-mile from the shore. Moreover, during most of the year, even on mild, sunny days, the waters off Dunkirk are more often than not buffeted by winds that can threaten small craft manned by inexperienced sailors. Consequently, it was presumed, the evacuation would have to be conducted from Dunkirk. With seven deepwater basins, four dry docks, and five miles of quays, Dunkirk was the third largest port in France.

Adjacent to Dunkirk's docks stood a structure of immense depth and strength, known as Bastion 32. It was here that French Admiral Jean Abrial, who was both the naval and military commander of the northern coastline, had established his headquarters. Abrial's immediate task was to defend the perimeter around Dunkirk, an area up to five miles wide but stretching almost 30 miles in length, from the Mardyck fortress on the western end of the perimeter to Nieuport on its eastern side. To defend this line, Abrial counted primarily on the French 16th Corps with two divisions of the original 7th Army, under the command of Lieutenant General Maurice Fagalde. The French forces would be reinforced with BEF units retreating into the perimeter.

At 7:00 A.M. on May 27, General Fagalde met with General Adam in the bomb-damaged Hotel Sauvage in the hill town of Cassel, twenty miles inland from Dunkirk, to lay out the port's defenses. They agreed that the French would be responsible for the sector west of Dunkirk as far as Gravelines and Bergues. The British would defend the area east of Bergues as far as Nieuport, some 25 miles east of Dunkirk. The British front, most of which was behind the defendable Bergues-Furnes-Nieuport canal line, had the advantage of being behind a reclaimed sea marsh known as Les Moeres. As a precautionary measure, the sea dikes protecting the marsh had been opened on May 20, with the result that the advancing sea had turned the marsh into a shallow lake, with only the roads that traversed it standing above water. Although retreating Allied troops could safely move across the flooded marsh on these roads, the Germans would not dare attack without amphibious transport.

After these arrangements had been made, Adam and Fagalde were joined by Admiral Abrial, General Blanchard, General Prioux, and General Louis Koeltz, who was representing General Weygand. None of the French officers were aware that the British were preparing to evacuate their army from Dunkirk. And General Adam, who did know, had no authority to inform them, and he did not. Adam, considering what he knew—and his French counterparts did not know—had to have been amused when General Koeltz read a message from Weygand directing the northern commanders to expand the Dunkirk bridgehead to Calais by launching a counterattack to relieve the troops defending that port. Weygand obviously was unaware that the last French troops defending Calais were about to surrender, nor did he realize that French forces had already been driven out of Gravelines. Even the German bombardment of Cassel, which began while the Allied meeting was in progress, failed to deter Koeltz from abandoning Weygand's proposed counterattack.

General Edward Spears, in his memoir, tried to explain the divergence in the French and British strategy: For the French, "to fall back to Dunkirk represented retiring into a fortress, which might be supplied by sea, but from which there was no retreat." The French failed to understand, Spears concluded, that "behind the harbors lay God's own highway, the greatest, widest highway in the world, one that led everywhere; if the troops could get on to ships they would soon be in the line elsewhere."

Ironically, while the French generals in Dunkirk knew nothing about the British plan to evacuate, French naval officers, at a meeting in Dover that morning, agreed to participate in the evacuation. They also accepted the British proposal that Vice Admiral Sir Bertram Ramsay assume responsibility for regulating sailings of French and British vessels to Dunkirk, while Admiral Abrial, who still knew nothing about Operation Dynamo, would be the only authority in charge of all arrangements for berthing and loading ships at Dunkirk and on the coast.

OPERATION DYNAMO BEGINS, MAY 26

Shortly before seven o'clock on Sunday evening, May 26, the Admiralty sent out an order that would influence the whole course of the war: "Operation Dynamo is to commence." The order, which was drafted by First Sea Lord Sir Dudley Pound, added: "It is imperative for 'Dynamo' to be implemented with the greatest vigor, with the view of lifting up to 45,000 of the BEF within two days, at the end of which it is probable that evacuation will be terminated by enemy action." Although Dudley was a cautious man, at the time he issued his order there was not much reason to think he had underestimated the operation's goal. He could not possibly have foreseen that Dunkirk would not be occupied by the Germans until nine days later, after nearly eight times more British and French soldiers had been evacuated than he had initially estimated was possible.

Deep within the white cliffs beneath Dover Castle, in the Dynamo Room (so-called because it had housed an electrical generator during World War I), Vice Admiral Ramsay had anticipated the Admiralty's order. He had gotten the operation, named after the Dynamo Room, under way four hours earlier.

As with so much else that was connected with the "Miracle of Dunkirk," the appointment of Bertram Ramsay to direct the evacuation was providential. Slightly built and soft-spoken, the fifty-seven-year-old Ramsay was also intelligent, innovative, and determined to have his own way, qualities that often upset senior officers and almost ended what, in the end, would be a brilliant career. As chief of staff to the commander-in-chief of the Home Fleet, Sir Roger Backhouse, Ramsay believed that he had been deliberately excluded from all significant responsibilities. Not a man to sit back and accept the situation stoically, he resigned from the navy in 1938. But as war loomed, Ramsay was called out of retirement and appointed flag officer for Dover. Then, in May 1940, he was called upon to rescue the BEF. That Operation Dynamo succeeded—and indeed became a classic case of ingenious improvisation in the face of extreme adversity—was to a large extent due to Ramsay's energy and ability.

At the outset of Dynamo, however, Ramsay was under no illusion about the difficulties he would face. Working always against time, the Royal Navy would have to contend not only with the inevitable risks of wind, weather, and navigation in crowded and constricted waters, but also do so in the teeth of violent opposition from the Germans. "The situation is past belief, frightful," Ramsay wrote to his wife at the end of May 26. "I am directing one of the most difficult and hazardous operations ever conceived and, unless the good Lord is ever indulgent, there will be numerous tragedies attached to it."

Ramsay's first problem had been one of finding enough ships to evacuate so large a number of men in the short amount of time he estimated the Germans would give him. Save for destroyers and other smaller naval craft, he could not draw upon the warships of the Royal Navy. Most of the largest warships, stationed at Scapa Flow, far to the north in Britain, could not be used in the enterprise. The Admiralty could not afford to lose any of these ships, except under the most dire of circumstances, such as blocking a German cross-Channel invasion of Britain. Nor could Ramsay rely heavily upon the navy's destroyer force. Over 200 destroyers had been in service when war was declared, but many had since been lost or damaged, and many more could not be spared from duty elsewhere. At Dynamo's start, Ramsay had only 40 destroyers at his disposal.

Fortunately, the Admiralty had foreseen the need for additional water craft and had requisitioned all vessels capable of transporting men, including pleasure craft between 30 and 100 feet in length. As a result, in addition to the British destroyers and 15 French warships, the ships available to Ramsay at the outset of Dynamo consisted of 35 conventional passenger vessels (styled "personnel vessels" because of their very large carrying capacities), 22 coasters and barges, and 40 of the Dutch *schuyts,* which had managed to escape across the Channel after the fall of the Netherlands. Pronounced "skoots" by the British, these 200-ton motorized vessels had shallow drafts and large carrying capacities that made them ideal for evacuating troops from the beaches. There were also a number of cargo ships that had already been at work taking ammunition and stores to Dunkirk. By the evening of May 26, cargo ships also had already brought back to

England some 28,000 of Gort's "useless mouths," primarily noncombatant support staff of the BEF.

And yet there was still another problem that Ramsay had to solve. With the loss of Calais, the Germans had gained possession of a stretch of coast from which their artillery could shell ships transiting the last part of the short sea route from Dover. Ships sailing by this western route (called route Z) had to approach to within a few miles of Calais and then sail eastward past the shore, where enemy batteries were now deployed.

The experience of the ferry *Mona's Queen* illustrates the peril that ships using this route could expect. The ship had loaded 1,400 troops overnight in Dunkirk. At dawn she was off Calais, in full view of German gunners. Captain R. Duggan described how his ship was shelled from the shore by German batteries:

> Shells were flying all round us, the first salvo went over us, the second, astern of us. I thought the next salvo would hit us but, fortunately, it dropped short, right under our stern. The ship was riddled with shrapnel, mostly all on the boat and promenade decks. Then we were attacked from the air. A Junkers bomber made a power dive towards us and dropped five bombs, but he was off the mark too, I should say about 150 feet from us. All this while we were still being shelled, although we were getting out of range.

While the *Mona's Queen* made it back to Dover, she did so carrying 23 corpses and 60 wounded men.

It was obvious from the experience of the *Mona's Queen* that continuing to sail ships past the German guns at Calais would be mad. As a result, an alternative, more northerly route (Route Y) was opened to ships. But this diversion more than doubled the length of the passage (Route Z was 39 sea miles long, while Route Y was 87). Another route that was developed, Route X, reduced that distance to 55 sea miles. However, while the new routes diminished the exposure of ships to land-based German artillery, the longer length of time they required to make the passage increased their susceptibility to attack by both German surface vessels and aircraft. Moreover, the longer sailing times reduced by half the total lifting capacity of the available ships. As a result, the total number evacuated at the end of Dynamo's first full day, May 27, was pitifully small: only 7,669 men.

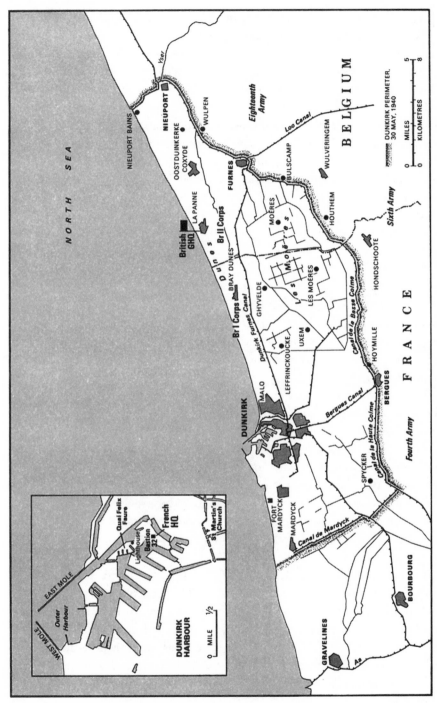

Dunkirk Perimeter and Harbor, May 30. (Nicholas Harman, *Dunkirk: The Patriotic Myth*, Simon and Schuster, 1980)

Ramsay's other main problem concerned finding suitable landing facilities for the ships the Admiralty had been able to gather. With the fall of both Boulogne and Calais, only Dunkirk remained as a usable port. But Dunkirk was only barely usable, as Captain William Tennant, chief staff officer to the First Sea Lord at the Admiralty, was about to find out.

During the afternoon of May 27, Tennant left Dover for Dunkirk, where he would assume the responsibility for organizing the shore side of the evacuation. He crossed the Channel in the destroyer *Wolfhound,* taking with him a dozen officers, communications staff, and 160 other seamen. En route, the ship was repeatedly dive-bombed and forced to take evasive action while its guns tried to blast attacking Stukas out of the sky. While the British gunners had no great success at that, they helped Tennant realize how frightening the crossing would be for the many unarmed vessels that would follow.

As Tennant's ship approached the coast of France about six o'clock that evening, a thick curtain of black smoke hung clear across the horizon. As the ship approached the outer harbor of Dunkirk, flames from burning buildings and oil tanks in and around the city illuminated the high white column of the lighthouse at the harbor's entrance, turning it orange. The inferno also silhouetted the bascule bridge that was jammed open at the entrance to the main harbor.

Tennant was appalled by the conditions he found once his ship docked. "The sight of Dunkirk gave one a rather hollow feeling in the pit of the stomach," he recalled. "The Boche had been going for it pretty hard, there was not a pane of glass left anywhere and most of it was still unswept in the center of the streets." Much of the city was still ablaze, thanks to the Luftwaffe, which had dropped incendiary as well as high-explosive bombs on it. But because the water mains had burst the previous day, the city's fire brigade could do nothing. Dead bodies and horse carcasses were everywhere. A thousand civilians died that day, and almost all of the corpses remained unburied.

Tennant quickly appreciated that the facilities of what had been one of Europe's most modern ports were unusable. The lock system for the seven main dock basins of the harbor, which were designed to keep the water at a level sufficient to float a sizable ship, was wrecked, leaving most of the five miles of the port's quays useless. The roads to the port also were blocked by rubble or licked by flames, and were crammed with leaderless men who sought refuge wherever they could to escape the almost incessant bombardment.

British warships at the mouth of Dunkirk harbor. (Imperial War Museum C1720)

Anthony Rhodes, a second lieutenant in the Royal Horse Artillery, along with other soldiers, found shelter in one of Dunkirk's many cellars. By midday, he recalled, their cellar refuge had become "rather smelly." The atmosphere was not improved by the charity of a well-intentioned soldier who had given some *foie gras* to a stray dog. The dog promptly vomited.

By four in the afternoon, the almost continuous German bomber raids had frayed the men's nerves. "The mere thought of a raid," Rhodes recalled, "was worse than its reality." One of the noncommissioned officers, wearing World War I ribbons, was crying quietly in the corner, "and several men began to make queer little animal noises, rather like homesick dogs."

One half-hour later, however, Rhodes heard a voice shouting from the street outside the cellar. A Royal Navy liaison man, a sailor from one of Captain Tennant's shore parties, was calling out for officers, some of whom had already gathered around him. Joining the group, Rhodes was told that the navy had given up any hope of evacuating troops from the harbor. Rhodes and the other army officers were advised by the sailor to gather as many soldiers as possible and, under cover of the smoke from the burning port, move the men onto the beaches to the east. There the navy would try to take off as many of them as possible using small boats.

Tennant had made the decision to shift the evacuation locus from the harbor of Dunkirk to the beaches east of the city only two hours after arriving. "During the first night," he recalled, "a party of us walked around the area of the mole and many miles of the beaches, to get a grasp of the situation. It was a sorry sight: thousands of soldiers clustering down to the foreshore with the hope of some craft coming to rescue them. They were organized to some extent, but were getting short of food and water. Their trust was pathetic, for they expected we should be able to tell them exactly when the craft were coming in to rescue them and where." That was information Tennant obviously could not give them.

The British generals with whom Tennant spoke thought that the German tanks would arrive on the beaches within thirty-six hours, so at 8:00 P.M. on May 27, he sent this message to Admiral Ramsay: "Please send every available craft to beaches east of Dunkirk immediately. Evacuation tomorrow night is problematical."

At Ramsay's Dover headquarters, Tennant's message was followed shortly afterward by a report from Lord Gort's command post, warning that the situation of the BEF was now precarious. The army was in very real danger of being cut off altogether from Dunkirk, possibly within only twenty-four hours. Ramsay immediately responded by ordering all available ships to the beaches between Dunkirk and De Panne. Soon the cruiser *Calcutta,* nine destroyers, two transports, four minesweepers, 17 drifters, and a number of skoots were in the waters between these ports, working the beaches with their lifeboats.

Captain William Bartlett was one of the many BEF soldiers who made it to the beach, late the previous evening. "I felt quite exhausted," he remembered. "I had no sleep last night and have had nothing to eat all day. And I seem to have been rushing about madly for hours. The sand-dunes looked peaceful." However, he quickly found himself in command of a bit of the beach. Although the men were strangers to him, "they were all extraordinarily patient and sensible," allowing him to arrange them into groups of about 25 before they "tucked themselves quite happily away in the sand."

Some, though, were not so easily coerced. Lieutenant Anthony Rhodes, who was now waiting in one of the long queues at the water's edge, witnessed a naval officer with a drawn pistol threaten to shoot anyone who got out of line. Nevertheless, a man suddenly rushed past him out of turn. The other men who were in front of him in the queue yelled out, "Get out! Get back, you bastard! Have him back! Have him back, the swine!" The man failed to reach the boat, which was now putting out to sea, and had to wade back to shore and get back in line, at the end of the queue. "He was," Rhodes recalled, "immediately forgotten and unobserved. . . . In our urgency, we forgot things as quickly as animals, we had the memories of monkeys."

It was soon evident, however, that there would be serious problems conducting a mass evacuation from the beaches. The big ships could not get in close enough to the shore. And in the shallows, where the tidal stream was fast, they could maneuver only at slow speed, compounding the risk of running aground with the danger of being dive-bombed. Nor were the ships' heavy, clumsy lifeboats, which were designed for deep-sea work, very efficient in ferrying out, through shallow waters, large numbers of troops to the waiting ships.

"The loading," Captain Bartlett remembered, "took a long long time. The destroyers had only two boats apiece. And these had to be rowed back and forth about half a mile with a load of a dozen men. It took six or eight hours to fill the destroyers to capacity."

Obviously, if evacuation from the beach were going to be successful, many more men would have to be taken off. Smaller, shallower-draft boats would have to be used. Fortunately, again, measures to meet this need had been taken in advance. At the Admiralty, Captain Wharton of the Small Vessels Pool had been collecting boats on his own initiative for almost a week. He already had 40 small craft moored in the Thames River near Westminster Pier. By the evening of May 28, many more were on the way from yachting centers, boatyards, and private moorings all over the southern and eastern coasts of England and from the banks of the Thames. They were the elements of a flotilla of almost 300 small craft that would lift from the beaches east of Dunkirk some 99,000 troops by the time Operation Dynamo came to an end.

However, the initially small numbers evacuated from the beaches frustrated Captain Tennant. He decided to take another look at the two long breakwalls, called moles, that stretched out on both sides of the mouth of

British troops awaiting evacuation. (AP/Wide World Photos)

Dunkirk's harbor and served to protect the harbor from wind and tide. He wondered if they could serve as piers for the larger ships. He immediately ruled out the shorter western mole. Although it was made of solid stone, its base, where troops would have to enter it, bordered the oil storage area, where tanks were blazing. On the other hand, the base of the eastern mole, which stretched almost a mile out to sea, was anchored in the relatively placid beach east of the city. The east mole's inner section was made of solid stone, but most of its length consisted of open-work concrete piles through which the sea flowed, surmounted by a wooden walkway wide enough for four men to walk abreast. However, like its western counterpart, the east mole was never intended to serve as a mooring for vessels. Tides ripping along and through its pilings could raise and lower the water level over 16 feet, making the idea of docking a ship next to it appear the height of folly.

And yet this is exactly what Tennant decided to attempt. During the evening of May 27, he directed the *Queen of the Channel* to enter the harbor and tie up at the eastern mole. The vessel gingerly eased into place alongside the breakwater and, much to Tennant's relief, was quickly and safely secured to stanchions. To Tennant, the experiment demonstrated that the east mole could serve as a major point of embarkation. There no longer was a need for the men to enter the burning harbor area. Henceforth,

Some of the small craft that participated in the Dunkirk evacuation on the Thames River. (Imperial War Museum HU3384)

troops were assembled on the beach east of the city, near the holiday resort of Malo-les-Bains, and marched out in disciplined groups straight onto the mole and then along the walkway on its top side, where ships would embark them. Almost 200,000 of the 338,000 British and French troops that ultimately escaped to England would leave France from this makeshift pier.

Having proved that the east mole would work, Tennant signaled the destroyers that had been ordered to the beaches to go there instead. At the same time, Dynamo headquarters in Dover was advised to send other ships to the mole. As darkness fell on May 27, the first ship edged up next to that breakwall, tied her bows to the pilings, and started to take on men. From this point on, the evacuation gathered momentum. The next day, May 28, 6,000 men were evacuated from the beaches and landed in England, but twice that many were taken from the east mole. Within three days, those numbers would quadruple.

HITLER UNLEASHES HIS PANZERS, MAY 26

General Franz Halder was angry when he realized the British might be able to escape before the German trap could be closed. On May 26 he confided to his diary: "Our armored and motorized forces have stopped as if paralyzed." Brauchitsch was "very nervous. I can fully sympathize with him, for these orders from the top just make no sense. In one area they call for a head-on attack against a front retiring in orderly fashion and still possessing its striking power, and elsewhere they freeze the troops to the spot when the enemy rear could be cut into any time you wanted to attack."

By then, Hitler also was upset with the slow pace of the German advance. Göring's Luftwaffe, largely grounded by poor visibility over the coast, had not been effective in smashing the Dunkirk perimeter. At 1:30 that afternoon, Halder recorded, the Führer summoned Brauchitsch to his *Eagle's Nest* headquarters and gave him permission to resume the panzer advance on Dunkirk "in order to prevent further evacuations."

Halder and Brauchitsch immediately went to work setting the panzers in motion. Kleist's panzer group was ordered to advance on Dunkirk from the west, but its main attack was directed farther south, to the Poperinge-Kemmel line, where they were expected to meet the divisions of Army Group B, which would be advancing through the eastern side of the Allied line.

Hitler's orders for the resumption of the armored attack were too late to be translated into action on May 26, but Heinz Guderian got his panzer corps moving early the next morning. The 1st Panzer Division pushed forward on its left flank, crossed the Aa Canal, and advanced along the coast. The 2nd Panzer Division advanced between the 1st Panzer Division and Arnèke. The 20th Motorized Division, supported by the SS regiment *Leibstandarte Adolf Hitler* and the infantry regiment *Grossdeutschland,* attacked between Arnèke and Cassel, with Wormhoudt as their immediate objective.

Farther south, four other panzer divisions attacked toward Armentières and Kemmel in an attempt to cut off the BEF from Dunkirk. Hoth's 6th and 8th Panzer Divisions advanced between Cassel and Hazebrouck. Farther south, Erwin Rommel's 7th Panzer Division, as well as the 5th Panzer, crossed the La Bassée Canal just east of Béthune. Their objective was Armentières, where they hoped they would meet Bock's infantry advancing from the opposite direction and, in the process, encircle the French 1st Army in its positions in and around Lille.

For his exploits during the campaign, Rommel was awarded the Iron Cross on Hitler's personal order the previous day. Yet Rommel almost did not live to receive it. During the fighting that day, German artillery shells landed only a few yards from his signals vehicle, killing one of his battalion commanders.

DEFENDING THE ALLIED POCKET

Defending the eastern side of the Allied corridor against Bock's Army Group B were General Franklyn's 5th British Division and the 143rd Brigade of the 48th Division. In order to close the gap that had opened between the British and Belgian armies, these units had traveled throughout the night from Arras to new positions along the Ypres-Comines canal line. Although the canal itself was no longer in use and contained nothing more than mud and weeds, it did form a kind of barrier in this otherwise flat and featureless stretch of Belgium.

The men of the 5th Division, who were attacked by three German divisions attached to the 6th Army—the 18th, the 31st, and the 61st— appreciated the importance of their assignment. Their inability to hold off the Germans could doom the entire BEF. Yet to them, exhaustion appeared to be the greater enemy. They had no real rest since completing their retreat from Arras, and few had slept much during the halting, bumping truck ride of the previous night. "My sergeant went about issuing the most frightful threats of what he would do to the next fellow he found asleep," one subaltern in the Inniskillings, Maj. W. M. Megaw, remembered, "but it did not do any good. The men were whacked."

The Germans did not give them much time to rest. Not long after they arrived in their new positions on the morning of May 27, the Germans attacked. By afternoon, they had managed to penetrate the 5th Division's front near Comines. Gort reacted by sending the 5th Division everything he could lay his hands on: two brigades of the 50th Division, three battalions of the 1st Division, and the 1st French Light Mechanized Division. These reinforcements enabled the British defenders to plug the gap in their line and stop the German advance.

Fortunately for the BEF, the Germans failed to exploit the six-mile gap that yawned between the British front at Ypres and the retiring Belgian flank at Zonnebeke. Had they done so, they could have moved virtually unimpeded to the sea, now only 20 miles to the north.

Meanwhile, around Lille, the French 1st Army was attacked from both sides of the narrow eastern end of the Allied pocket. The 5th Panzer Division surged forward to capture Armentières, while Rommel's 7th Panzer swung eastward to meet German infantry advancing from the opposite direction. By the end of May 27, Rommel had broken through the Allied line and threatened to cut off the whole of the French 1st Army, as well as four British divisions, which were deployed in and around Lille. That night he recorded that the rapid advance of his panzer division "was marked by the glare of burning vehicles shot up by his force." By the next morning, nearly half the French 1st Army—primarily its 4th and 5th Corps—had been surrounded. Only its 3rd Corps and Cavalry Corps were able to escape to the west and get across the Lys River.

On the western side of the Allied line, which was held by the British 48th, 44th, and 2nd Divisions, the Germans were also threatening to break through. On the morning of May 27, they attacked the railway line extending west of Wormhoudt, Cassel, and Hazebrouck—three towns roughly 10 to 15 miles south of Dunkirk—which was being defended by 44th Division. General Pownall feared that if the Germans broke through this line, they would block "the French withdrawal towards Dunkirk and drive them on to our roads." He complained that the roads were already "dreadfully congested with French transport, much of it slow-moving horse-drawn stuff, which is the devil to have mixed up with one's own motor transport. It is no good having boundaries and roads allotted as between ourselves and the French, they pay no attention and do exactly what they damn well like."

Lieutenant Eric Loveluck, on the other hand, was more concerned about the advancing Germans than he was with the movement of the French. When, on May 26, his artillery section became detached from the rest of his unit, the 115th (Leicester) Army Field Regiment, he was asked to help hold off some light panzers that had inflicted heavy losses on a pioneer battalion of the King's Own Royals, which were defending the La Bassée Canal at Merville, near Lille.

The panzers had just broken off their attack and were drawn up in the square of a nearby village, Le Saar. Their crews did not suspect that Loveluck was training two 1915-vintage, 18-pounder guns on them from a farm on the edge of Merville. Equipped only with a map, which he estimated was "250 or more miles to the square inch," Loveluck and his number two, Lieutenant John Caven, guessed the range of the panzers at about two miles. Their estimate proved so accurate that their first airburst shrapnel shell exploded directly over the heads of the dismounted crews, killing a number of them outright. Subsequent shells knocked out the rest of the panzers.

The next morning, Loveluck expected a hostile German reaction. He climbed the tower of the village church to scan the surrounding country for any enemy activity. "Suddenly," he recalled, "the air around me was alive with German fighters and light bombers. I fired my revolver at the planes in fury, they were so close. I must have been seen by a pilot whom I had missed only by inches, for he turned and climbed before diving at me with guns blazing. Clearly, discretion was the better part of valor, and I leapt inside one of the bigger bells, only to be nearly deafened by the noise of the hail of bullets striking it."

On the following day, May 28, the Germans launched another attack, this time with medium tanks. Loveluck's guns destroyed five of the panzers before running short of shells. That put his gun unit out of action, with the loss of one dead and four wounded.

Loveluck, however, was not yet finished. He next teamed up with the crew of a 2.5-pounder, which, under cover of darkness, they towed away with a tank. Loveluck was thankful that he had learned German while a student at Cambridge, for he and his comrades came upon a contingent of enemy troops who pointed an anti-tank gun at them. "I flung open the roof hatch," Loveluck recalled, "yelled some choice abuse at the unsuspecting *Feldwebel* and he leapt to attention and saluted as we swept through. It just shows what discipline can do! At the time I was wearing the service dress of a captain in the Royal Northumberland Fusiliers, yet he swallowed it hook, line and sinker."

Loveluck was attired as a Fusilier because while riding a motorcycle at dusk the previous day, he had attempted to cross a bridge. "Alas," he recalled, "the bridge was not there, so I was duly muddied and, frankly, stank. My troops scrounged up for me two old uniforms, and I had to masquerade either as a wing commander RAF or a Royal Northumberlands officer, an easy decision for me to make, with the RAF unjustly blamed by the ignorant for lack of air cover."

Loveluck was awarded the Military Cross for his leadership and bravery.

THE MASSACRE AT LE PARADIS, MAY 27

Like Eric Loveluck, the men of the 2nd British Infantry Division were also trying to stave off the Germans. This single British division was responsible for the defense of a front 20 miles in length along the La Bassée Canal, against the combined strength of three and a half recently unleashed panzer divisions and supporting SS formations. At 3:30 A.M. on May 27, the British soldiers were attacked by the 3rd, 4th, and 7th Panzer Divisions, a brigade of the 5th Panzer Division, and elements of the *Totenkopf* and *Verfugungs* SS.

The initial German artillery bombardment was an early indication of the overwhelming concentration of power that was massed against the British soldiers. The German ground assault opened an hour later and fell on both of the division's wings with equal severity. The 2nd Division's 4th Brigade, comprising the 1st Royal Scots, the 2nd Royal Norfolks, and the 8th Lancashire Fusiliers, was attacked by the 4th Panzer Division and the SS *Totenkopf* Division. The 8th Lancashire Fusiliers were the first to be overrun. At 7:50 A.M., their commanding officer reported that he was cut off from all but one of his companies. Soon after 2:30 P.M., his last received message reported that his headquarters building was on fire and surrounded by Germans. The brigade's commander, Brigadier Warren, sent his intelligence officer to deliver orders for a withdrawal after dark, but neither he nor the Lancashire Fusiliers were seen again.

The Royal Norfolks lost their right composite company first. Its men were cut off and overwhelmed by a swarm of German infantry, supported by tanks. The remainder of the Norfolks were steadily reduced in numbers and hemmed in by the advancing Germans. Yet they continued fighting. Later, from a prison camp, a rare surviving officer wrote: "I wish I could write and tell the story of the unselfish heroism of those who fought, and laughed, and died without complaint, although they knew they had no chance of getting home, and that all they could do was to fight to the end and give time to others to get home instead. Frankly, I love them and their unconscious gallantry so very much."

The remnants of the Royal Norfolk's 2nd Battalion, some 90 men, held out in a large house in the tiny village of Le Paradis, northwest of Béthune. Cut off and lacking ammunition, at about 5:15 their commanding officer, Major Ryder, decided to surrender. He and two other men emerged from the house holding a white towel. They were immediately shot down. After a brief period of great confusion, the Germans finally accepted the surrender of the other British soldiers. Pale, tattered, and in many cases wounded, they had the great misfortune of having been captured by the SS *Totenkopf* Division, the same outfit some of whose men apparently had been murdered by members of the British Durham Light Infantry.

After the prisoners were kicked, rifle-butted, and disarmed, they were marched toward a large barn, in front of which two machine guns were deployed. As the line of prisoners, with their hands tied behind their backs, straggled down the length of the barn wall, the machine guns opened fire, mowing them down from left to right. They fell into a large declivity located between the machine guns and the barn wall. Those who still showed any signs of life were shot or bayoneted.

Miraculously, two of the men, Privates Bill O'Callaghan and Albert Pooley, though shot, feigned death and survived, under the hill of bodies. After the SS soldiers left, they dragged themselves to the safety of a nearby pigsty. There they were discovered by a farmer's wife, who fed them and treated their wounds. However, when the two men discovered that she and her son were likely to be detected by the Germans, they gave themselves up to another, as it turned out, more humane unit of the regular German army, and ultimately were sent to a POW camp.

Repatriated early in the war because of his wounds, Pooley reported the massacre to his superiors, who reacted with disbelief. But Pooley did not give up. After the war, he pursued the matter, returned to Le Paradis, and gathered evidence. As a result, Fritz Knoechlein, commander of the *Totenkopf*'s 2nd Infantry Regiment, which was involved in the murders, was brought before a British court-martial in Hamburg, convicted, and hanged in January 1949.

THE MASSACRE AT WORMHOUDT, MAY 28

Unfortunately, the murders at Le Paradis were not the last committed by the SS. The next day, near Wormhoudt, a small French town some 12 miles south of Dunkirk, 99 British soldiers belonging to the 2nd Battalion Royal Warwickshires, which was attached to the 48th Infantry Division, were murdered by members of the SS *Leibstandarte Adolf Hitler* Regiment, under the command of Sepp Dietrich.

By defending Wormhoudt, the Warwickshires, like other British battalions defending the western side of the Allied pocket, were trying to delay the closing of the German pincer jaws as long as possible in order to buy time for the rest of the retreating BEF to escape to Dunkirk. They were able to perform that mission until midafternoon on May 28. However, without the assistance of mortars, aircraft, or tanks, and with very inadequate artillery support, the battalion was reduced to a few scattered infantry posts. Realizing that further resistance was impossible and taking advantage of a vicious thunderstorm, the battalion's commanding officer led about 65 of his men out of the town and onto the Dunkirk road, where they soon met other British and French troops trying to reach that port.

Everyone, however, did not escape from Wormhoudt. Over 100 prisoners were rounded up by the SS and herded into a barn. Not intimidated by the brutality of the SS guards, Capt. C. A. Lynn-Allen, commanding the Warwickshires' D Company, immediately spoke out, saying, "I wish to complain that there are wounded men inside, and there is not enough room for them to lie down."

The face of one of the SS guards reddened with anger. Reaching down for the stick grenade that protruded from his boot, he lobbed it into the barn. The explosion killed some of the prisoners instantly and wounded several others, including Bert Evans, who saw blood pouring down his right arm. Reacting quickly when the guards ran for cover, Lynn-Allen pulled Evans by his left arm and shouted, "Quick! Run for it."

The two men sprinted from the doorway and ran a couple of hundred yards, with Evans supported by Lynn-Allen. "Keep going, and stay low!" he ordered Evans. Breathless, they reached a clump of trees at the edge of a small pond of stagnant water. Without hesitation, Lynn-Allen pulled his companion into the water and said, "Get down! And keep your arm out of the water!"

Suddenly they heard the sound of boots running in their direction. They belonged to one of the SS guards, who, approaching the edge of the pond, pointed a revolver at Lynn-Allen and fired twice. The officer cried, "Oh! my God!" and then slumped face forward into the water. Before he fell, Evans saw one of the bullets pierce his forehead. He knew the captain was dead. The German then fired two shots at Evans. One ricocheted off a tree trunk in the pond and hit him in the neck. Evans fell forward into the water. The German grunted and moved off, apparently believing that he had killed both men. But Evans was only wounded. Failing to find Lynn-Allen's body, which had sunk to the bottom of the pond, Evans suppressed his desire to run from the scene and instead stayed submerged in the pond, with only his head protruding above the water.

While he hid in the pond, Evans heard, from the direction of the barn, more grenade explosions and gunshots, interspersed by the screams of men. Evans, still only a teenager, wept when he considered the plight of his comrades and his inability to help them. He scrambled out of the pond and headed for the cover of some nearby woods. Not quite there, he heard the crack of a rifle and fell to the ground. He stayed there, lying still, until he was satisfied that he was not being pursued. He then regained his feet and eventually came upon a farm where, not many yards away, a German soldier was bending over a motorcycle. Unfortunately for Evans, the German spotted him before he could hide. The soldier approached him.

"Please get it over with," Evans said, expecting the worst, "and don't mess around!" But to his surprise, the German placed him gently on the ground and then walked over to a clothesline and pulled down a bedsheet. He tore it into strips, which he used to bind Evans's wound.

Evans subsequently was taken to a German field hospital, where his arm was amputated, and ultimately to a prisoner-of-war camp. After three years of captivity, Evans was repatriated in a swap of severely wounded prisoners. The British authorities, however, showed little inclination to accept his story, so he decided to relate it to the *Daily Mirror* in October 1943. That he lived to tell his story was due to the exceptional bravery of Captain Lynn-Allen, the kindness of a German soldier, and the skill of German doctors.

The overwhelming majority of the British prisoners who were held in the barn, however, did not escape death. More SS grenades were thrown into the barn after the one that enabled Evans to escape. The explosions filled the building with smoke along with the screams and groans of the wounded and dying British soldiers. Richard Parry counted five explosions, one of which blew him partly through the side of the barn, leaving only his legs inside, one of which was wounded. However, with the top half of his body protruding through the wall of the barn, he could see through the slats between the boards much of what followed inside.

After the last grenade exploded, Parry recalled, the SS guards began yelling *"Raus!"* (out). They wanted the prisoners to come out five at a time. When they emerged, they were marched about 20 yards away to a point where an armed guard stood facing each prisoner, in firing-squad formation. When the awful intention of the Germans became clear to the helpless men, one prisoner asked if he and his comrades could have a last smoke, "Just one last cigarette." But the request was denied, and the five men were ordered to turn around and then were shot.

Then another five prisoners were brought out and shot. But when the Germans demanded the next five to come out, the prisoners refused. As the SS guards conferred among themselves, a torrential downpour began. Not wanting to become drenched as they meted out death, the guards suddenly charged into the barn and began shooting in all directions. As the dead prisoners fell, one on top of the other, some of the wounded crawled under the bodies for protection and in this way managed to survive the massacre.

During the firestorm, Richard Parry, whose trunk and shoulders were still outside the barn, was shot again, in the foot. The pain caused him to black out. Alf Tombs, who had been badly wounded in the shin, lay motionless on the ground. He heard a man cry out: "Shoot me, shoot me!" A single shot, followed by a short groan, indicated that the man's plea had been answered. One fair-haired British soldier, in a terribly mutilated condition, began to stammer the Lord's Prayer. Each syllable was slower than the last, and when he completed the petition, "Hallowed be Thy Name," he exhaled heavily and died.

George Hall finished the prayer, with several others joining in. Then he realized that the shooting had stopped and decided that whatever the outcome, he was going to attempt a breakout. He crawled to the back of the barn, where he discovered that a bottom plank looked rotten. After pulling hard on it, he managed to dislodge the board and then crawled through the opening and toward a hedge that partially concealed him.

As the Germans were leaving, one of the guards spotted Richard Parry's body protruding from the barn wall. He walked over to the wounded British soldier, who was in the process of regaining consciousness. Parry looked up at the darkened figure silhouetted against the sky. It was pointing a rifle at his head. As Parry was about to curse the German, the rifle's barrel exploded, ejecting a bullet that entered Parry's wide open mouth before it exited through the back of his jaw. It was the last bullet fired in the massacre. Believing their gruesome work was finished, the SS guards moved on.

Although 90 British soldiers were murdered in the Wormhoudt massacre, fifteen men survived, including Richard Parry, Alf Tombs, and George Hall. Unlike the La Paradis massacre, however, no Germans were punished for the massacre at Wormhoudt. Wilhelm Mohnke, who temporarily assumed command of the SS regiment the day of the massacre (because Sepp Dietrich was trapped by British gunfire in another part of the battlefield), was placed on trial after the war. But the trial ended inconclusively because the prosecution could not prove that Mohnke had been present at the barn or was even aware that a massacre had occurred. This conclusion was reached even though an SS noncommissioned officer testified that Mohnke was furious that prisoners had been taken, and then instructed they should be removed and shot.

Sepp Dietrich also escaped blame for the massacre. However, in 1946 the U.S. Army sentenced him to a 25-year prison term for his role in the murder of American prisoners at Malmédy, Belgium, on December 17, 1944. Dietrich was released after serving only 10 years of this sentence, but he was promptly imprisoned again for his involvement in the murders of Ernst Röhm and other leaders of the Nazi stormtroopers during the so-called Night of the Long Knives in 1934.

CHURCHILL VERSUS HALIFAX:
ROUND 2, MAY 27–28

When the British War Cabinet met at 11:30 A.M. on May 27, Sir Archibald Sinclair, Churchill's old friend, was present. The prime minister had asked Sinclair, who was the leader of the Liberal Party and the RAF secretary, to attend the meeting because, like Churchill, he too was a longtime opponent of appeasement; the prime minister obviously felt he needed his support against Halifax.

For additional reinforcement, Churchill read to the War Cabinet a report, entitled "British Strategy in a Certain Eventuality"—the eventuality of France dropping out of the war—which he had asked the Chiefs of Staff to prepare on May 17, the day after his first ominous visit to Paris. Churchill wanted to know if Britain could carry on the war without France. Much to his relief, the report concluded that Britain could hold out alone, without the French, provided that British air superiority could be maintained. But the Chiefs of Staff added that Britain could not survive a long war unless the United States was "willing to give full economic and financial support, without which we do not think we could continue the war with any chance of success."

Reinforced by the report's conclusion, Churchill felt more confident when the War Cabinet, later that afternoon, returned to the subject of the previous day: Lord Halifax's proposal for an Anglo-French approach to Italy.

One member of the War Cabinet, Arthur Greenwood, did not like Halifax's idea at all: "If it got out that we had sued for terms at the cost of ceding British territory," he repeated a fear expressed the previous day, "the consequences would be terrible." "Any weakness on our part," he continued, "would encourage the Germans and Italians," and would "tend to undermine morale both in this country and in the Dominions."

Churchill agreed fully with these views. He said he was "increasingly oppressed with the futility of the suggested approach to Signor Mussolini." It would "ruin the integrity of our fighting position in this country." The French must be told, he said forcefully, that Britain would fight on even without them.

Neville Chamberlain tried to work out a compromise. He said that while the proposed approach to Mussolini "would not serve any useful purpose," he thought that "we ought to go a little further with it, in order to keep the French in a good temper." He suggested that they should wait until Mussolini had answered President Roosevelt's request to stay out of the war. However, Chamberlain did not yet know that the Italian dictator had already in effect rejected Roosevelt's request.

Chamberlain's suggestion prompted the War Cabinet to digress to Roosevelt's attitude. The U.S. president, the minutes noted, seemed "to be taking the view that it would be very nice of him to pick up the bits of the British Empire, if this country was overrun." If this were true, Sinclair remarked, it was important "to get it realized in the United States that we meant to fight on."

Halifax had patiently waited for his colleagues to express their views, then calmly but sternly disagreed with them. He clearly was upset by Churchill's refusal even to explore the possibility that Britain might honorably extract itself from a war whose continuation could only bring devastation and disaster to the country. "Provided Britain's independence" were not at stake, the foreign secretary continued, he would "think it right" to "accept an offer which would save the country from avoidable disaster."

Churchill answered that the possibility of a just peace with Nazi Germany "was quite unreal and was most unlikely to arise. If Herr Hitler was prepared to make peace on the terms of the restoration of the German colonies and the overlordship of Central Europe, that was one thing. But it was quite unlikely that he would make such an offer."

But Halifax did not give up. He asked Churchill, if Hitler offered peace terms to France, and the French in response said that they would have to consult with their allies before accepting them, would the prime minister then be prepared to discuss such terms?

Churchill replied that "he would not join France in asking for terms, but if he were told what the terms offered were, he would be prepared to consider them." However, that was as far as he would go.

Chamberlain began to wobble. "He did not see," the War Cabinet minutes recorded, "what we should lose if we said openly that, while we would fight to the end to preserve our independence, we were ready to consider decent terms if such were offered to us." But, he added, "looking at the matter realistically, this may not be the time" to make the approach to Mussolini. Chamberlain was still trying to push a compromise that would mend the breach between Churchill and Halifax.

But Halifax would not buy it. He clearly was unsatisfied with—and indeed was upset by—Churchill's position. In fact, he was by now so frustrated that he was prepared to resign from the government. Recounting the War Cabinet meeting in his diary that night, he wrote: "I thought

Winston talked the most frightful rot, also Greenwood, and after bearing it for some time, I said exactly what I thought of them, adding that, if that was really their view, and if it came to the point, our ways must separate."

Later, he told Cadogan: "I can't work with Winston any longer." "Nonsense," Cadogan replied. Churchill's "rhodomontades probably bore you as much as they do me, but don't do anything silly under the stress of that." Cadogan advised him not to do anything before consulting Chamberlain.

While the War Cabinet meeting was still taking place that afternoon, Halifax, cooling down a bit, had decided to ask Churchill to take a private stroll in the garden. There he told the prime minister that he might have to resign. Churchill, Halifax later noted in his diary, was "surprised" and "full of apologies and affection." Apparently, he also was successful in persuading his foreign secretary to stay in the government, "for the sake of the country, at this grave point in its history," as Churchill put it. Nevertheless, Halifax confided to his diary, "It does drive one to despair when he [Churchill] works himself up into a passion of emotion when he ought to make his brain think and reason."

Despite the secrecy of War Cabinet meetings, the gist of Halifax's confrontation with Churchill nevertheless filtered out to London. John Colville wrote in his diary: "There are signs that Halifax is being defeatist. He says our aim can no longer be to crush Germany, but rather to preserve our own integrity and independence."

Even U.S. Ambassador Joseph Kennedy caught wind of the rift within the War Cabinet. That night he cabled Washington: "If the Germans made Britain, along with France, an offer of peace, there would be a row in the Cabinet between the 'do or die' group and the 'group that want a settlement.'" "The English people," he added, "really do not realize how bad it [the military situation] is. When they do, I don't know which group they will follow: the do or die, or the group that wants a settlement."

The possibility that Britain might succumb to Hitler's power intensified Washington's anxiety that the United States would have to face, alone, a hostile coalition of Germany, Italy, and Japan. The naval power of the Axis powers, if bolstered by the British and French fleets, would eclipse by far that of the United States. Washington was receiving reports that Hitler had threatened to kill a million Britons if Britain did not come to terms with him, terms that included giving him a portion of the British fleet.

President Roosevelt was nearly obsessed by fear that the British fleet might fall into Hitler's hands. During the evening of May 26, he delivered a "fireside" radio address to the nation, in another attempt to prepare the American people for the disagreeable steps that he believed the United States would ultimately be compelled to take. He said:

> There are many among us who in the past closed their eyes to events abroad because they believed . . . that what was taking place in Europe was none of our business; that no matter what happened over there, the United States could always pursue its peaceful and unique course in the world. . . . To those who would not admit the possibility of the approaching storm . . . the past two weeks have meant the shattering of many illusions. They have lost the illusion that we are remote and isolated and therefore secure against the dangers from which no other land is free.

The president then assured the American people that he would take whatever steps were needed to defend the nation.

Roosevelt's remarks were derided by isolationists as another of his attempts to scare the American people into supporting U.S. involvement in the European conflict. Faced with strong isolationist sentiment in the country and in the Congress, Roosevelt had to move slowly in attempting to give U.S. aid to Britain and France. Even had Congress been willing to provide that assistance—and it still was not—almost everything that the Allies needed was in short supply in the United States. However, the Army's Ordnance Division said that it could release to the Allies 500 World War I field guns, a half-million Enfield rifles, 35,000 machine guns, and 500 mortars. But Roosevelt was barred by law from sending abroad any war matériel that was not needed to defend the United States, and questions were raised about whether those weapons could really be given to the Allies in view of America's military unpreparedness. As a result, just as Britain was launching a desperate, apparently hopeless operation to rescue its trapped army, Roosevelt could offer nothing but his good wishes.

During the morning of May 28, Churchill went to Westminster Abbey to attend a short prayer service. The contrast between the bright beauty of this morning and the darkness of his own concerns was particularly poignant. "The English are loath to expose their feelings," he later recorded his thoughts, "but in my stall in the choir, I could feel the pent-up, passionate emotion, and also the fear of the congregation, not of death or wounds or material loss, but of defeat and the final ruin of Britain." He then went to the House of Commons, where he gave a summary of the "heavy tidings" from Dunkirk.

※

At 4:00 P.M., shortly after the House session was finished, the five members of the War Cabinet assembled again, this time in the prime minister's room at Westminster.

Halifax began the meeting by saying that he had now discovered what the Italian Embassy had in mind concerning a possible Allied peace feeler, namely, that Britain should give a clear indication that it desired mediation by Italy. He then read the text of the proposed approach that he had discussed with Reynaud two days earlier. Its key passage stated "that we should say that we were prepared to fight to the death for our independence, but that, provided this could be secured, there were certain concessions that we were prepared to make to Italy." Halifax added that "we must not ignore the fact that we might get better terms before France went out of the war and our aircraft factories were bombed, than we might get in three months' time."

Churchill responded by saying that "Monsieur Reynaud wants to get us to the conference table with Herr Hitler." (Churchill did not know that while this was true of some members of the French government, it did not yet apply to Reynaud himself.) Churchill again said that he was determined not to go down that "slippery slope." Moreover, he added, "nations which went down fighting rose again, but those which surrendered tamely were finished."

This remarked angered Halifax. He replied that nothing in his suggestion could even remotely be described as favoring ultimate capitulation.

Churchill responded by trying to calm his foreign secretary. He said he thought that the chances of Britain being offered decent terms by Hitler at the present time were a thousand to one against.

Halifax responded that he still did not see what harm there could be in the French suggestion of trying out the possibility of Italian mediation.

Chamberlain, now apparently siding with Halifax, added that "it was right to remember that the alternative to fighting on nevertheless involved a considerable gamble," that is, defeat and the destruction of Britain and her empire. The old appeaser in Chamberlain was reemerging: war, the ultimate evil, was to be avoided almost at any cost.

At this point, about six o'clock, the War Cabinet meeting broke up, still with no decision having been reached on Halifax's proposed approach to Mussolini. The War Cabinet agreed to take up the matter again in an hour, after Churchill had the opportunity to meet with the entire Cabinet.

Churchill looked tired as the five War Cabinet ministers filed out of the room and the other 25 members of the full Cabinet came in. He spoke to them about the critical situation confronting Britain's soldiers at Dunkirk. "How many would get away we could not tell. We should certainly be able to get 50,000 away. If we could get 100,000 away, that would be a magnificent performance."

He then said that the Italians and the Germans might offer peace terms, but he believed that they must be rejected. "It was idle to think," he explained, "that if we tried to make peace now, we should get better terms than if we fought it out. . . . We should become a slave state, though a British government which would be Hitler's puppet would be set up, under Mosley or some such person." Then he said, as he recalled in his war memoirs, quite casually, and not treating it as a point of special significance, "Of course, whatever happens at Dunkirk, we shall fight on."

These words, he recalled, brought about a sudden explosion of feeling on the part of the Cabinet ministers. "Quite a number seemed to jump up from the table and come running to my chair, shouting and patting me on the back." The ministers must have known something about his battle with Halifax, and appeared relieved that he had not lost his fighting spirit.

One MP, Hugh Dalton, told Churchill as he patted him on the shoulder, "You ought to get that cartoon of Low's showing us all rolling up our sleeves, and frame it and stick it up in front of you here." Churchill responded, with a broad grin, "Yes, that was a good one, wasn't it."

Churchill, for his part, was clearly surprised by the Cabinet's reaction. His spirits were uplifted. "I was sure," he recollected in his memoirs, "that every minister was ready to be killed quite soon, and have all his family and possessions destroyed, rather than give in. In this, they represented the House of Commons and almost all the people."

Churchill must have sensed that the Cabinet session represented a turning point in his battle with Halifax. In any event, he was heartened and reinforced by the emotional support he received, for when the members of War Cabinet returned to the room at seven o'clock, he informed them that the entire Cabinet had expressed the greatest satisfaction when he had told them that there was no chance of giving up the struggle. He said he did not remember having ever before heard a gathering of individuals who occupied high places in political life express themselves so emphatically.

The effect of the Cabinet's demonstration of support clearly influenced Chamberlain. He henceforth shared Churchill's determination, telling his four War Cabinet colleagues that Reynaud should be persuaded "that it was worth his while to go on fighting," and that there should be no negotiations with either the Germans or the Italians at this time.

Churchill also turned down Halifax's proposal for an appeal to the United States to serve as a mediator. "If we made a bold stand against Germany," he said, "that would command their [the Americans'] admiration and respect; but a groveling appeal, if made now, would have the worst possible effect."

Halifax, the last torchbearer of appeasement, was beaten. There would be no attempt to achieve a negotiated settlement of the war. Some thought he would quit the government or be fired. But Halifax would continue to serve Churchill faithfully for the rest of the war, first as foreign secretary, then as ambassador to the United States, denying to his dying day that he had ever intended to seek peace terms from Hitler.

Nevertheless, it would be difficult to overestimate the importance of the events of May 28. Churchill's victory over Halifax contributed directly to his growing power and, indeed, ultimately to the successful outcome of the war. Wrote historian Philip Bell: "There can be no doubt that if the War Cabinet had agreed to the French proposal, and approached Mussolini with a view to mediation, they could not have gone back on that decision. Once the possibility of negotiation had been opened, it could not have been closed, and the government could not have continued to lead the country in outright defiance of German power."

Churchill, once and for all, had faced down the appeasers, Halifax and Chamberlain, and won. Britain would stay in the war, with Churchill at the helm, until Hitler had been defeated.

But victory was a long way off in May 1940. Clement Attlee, the Labour Party leader who strongly supported Churchill against Halifax, warned the War Cabinet that when the British people became aware of the fate that appeared to await the BEF, they would suffer a severe shock.

Trying to stave off defeatist sentiment, Churchill that day issued a general, strictly confidential directive that stated: "In these dark days, the prime minister would be grateful if all his colleagues in the government, as well as important officials, would maintain a high morale in their circles; not minimizing the gravity of events, but showing confidence in our ability and inflexible resolve to continue the war till we have broken the will of the enemy to bring all Europe under his domination."

❊

Late that evening, Churchill phoned Reynaud to inform him that the War Cabinet had decided not to join France in seeking Mussolini's mediation. Not rejecting the idea of Italian mediation outright, Churchill simply said that it was not "the right moment." But he also added that he feared its "effect on the morale of our people, which is now firm and resolute, would be extremely dangerous." Also trying to persuade Reynaud to keep France in the war, the British prime minister said, "If we both stand out, we may yet save ourselves from the fate of Denmark or Poland. Our success must depend first on our unity, then on our courage and endurance."

LÉOPOLD SURRENDERS, MAY 27–28

While Churchill had won the support of his government for remaining in the conflict, King Léopold was moving in the opposite direction, toward surrender, against the wishes of his government.

By May 26, the Belgian army was near collapse. "Our front is fraying away," General Van Overstraeten said, "like an old rope that is about to snap." With the Lys River line having been penetrated by the Germans around Courtrai, General Blanchard urged the Belgians to fall back to the Yser River, as King Léopold had agreed to do at the Ypres conference five days earlier. But General Michíels, the chief of the Belgian General Staff, declared that another withdrawal was out of the question. The roads on which the army would have to retreat were crammed with refugees and devoid of air cover. Leaving the positions along the Lys, he said, would destroy the Belgian army faster than if it remained in its current position.

Instead of making another retreat, the Belgians wanted the British to help them to restore their front on the Lys by launching a counterattack against the southern flank of the German bridgehead. General Van Overstraeten later argued that a successful British counterattack against the German divisions, which were largely composed of infantry, not only would have encouraged the Belgians but also would have ensured the retention of two more Belgian ports, namely Ostend and Nieuport.

But Lord Gort rejected the Belgian request. He responded that under the circumstances—which he did not inform the Belgians involved the withdrawal and evacuation of the BEF to England—he could not launch a counterattack. However, after the war, Liddell Hart, the military historian, challenged Gort's reasoning. He argued that at least parts of the 5th and 50th Divisions (released from the southward move) could have counterattacked as the Belgians had wished. But by now the anti-Belgian prejudices of both Gort and Pownall had gotten the better of them, and both were unwilling to take any risks to assist the Belgian army. On May 26, Pownall wrote in his diary that the Belgians "are rotten to the core and in the end we shall have to look after ourselves."

Instead of launching a counterattack against the German bridgehead at Courtrai, Gort sent two divisions to plug the gap on the BEF's left flank and to extend its front along the Yser toward Diksmuide, only five miles from the coast. When, that evening, King Léopold was informed that Gort had rejected the request for a counterattack, he responded by warning General Blanchard that the Belgian army was in imminent danger of annihilation.

That same evening, Anthony Eden was worried about the effect that the British retreat to the coast would have on Belgian morale and staying power. He suggested to Churchill that he advise King George to personally inform the Belgians about the withdrawal, or to do so himself. Eden feared the news would crack the Belgians' resolve and prompt them to surrender. What the secretary for war did not realize, however, was that the Belgian high command had already surmised, on the basis of reports it had received of British troop movements and the destruction of stores behind the British lines, that the BEF was withdrawing to the coast and, in effect, abandoning the Belgians to their fate.

The next day, May 27, Churchill took up Eden's suggestion and ordered both Gort and Admiral Keyes to break the news to King Léopold. He also directed them to ask the Belgians to sacrifice themselves for the good of the common cause, ultimate victory, by staying in the war long enough to protect the left flank of the retreating BEF. "Our only hope," Churchill wrote Keyes, "is victory, and England will never quit the war, whatever happens, till Hitler is beat[en] or we cease to be a State." The prime minister also wanted Admiral Keyes to "make sure he [Léopold] leaves with you, by aeroplane, before it is too late." As an added plum to entice the king to leave Belgium, Churchill authorized Keyes to inform him that "we would try, if desired, to carry some Belgian divisions to France by sea."

The decision of the British to abandon Belgium was a major factor in Léopold's decision to surrender. At 2:00 P.M., General Michiels told the king that the army had already done all that it could, and that the only way to prevent a final horrific massacre was to cease fighting immediately.

The king's military headquarters already had phoned a message to Lord Gort an hour earlier that read, in part: "The King . . . wishes you to realize that he will be obliged to surrender before a debacle follows." At 3:30 P.M. the king informed Admiral Keyes and the other members of the British and French military missions that he intended to ask for an armistice at midnight. The message was received in London at 5:45 P.M. and reached Paris at 7:00 P.M.

At 3:45 P.M. Léopold sent General Derousseaux, second-in-command at the Belgian General Staff, to see General Reichenau in order to obtain the German conditions for a cease-fire. Derousseaux returned at ten o'clock and informed the king that Hitler demanded unconditional surrender. Léopold responded, "We shall lay down our arms and cease-fire at 4:00 tomorrow morning, May 28." Derousseaux returned to Reichenau's headquarters and signed the surrender instrument at 12:20 A.M. A little over three and a half hours later, the Belgian army was out of the war.

The previous evening, Léopold had had a chance to meet with Keyes before the admiral departed for England. In the course of their conversation, the king condemned his government's decision to flee to France. "They will be dragged down with the collapse of that country."

Then he asked, "What about England?"

Keyes replied, "We shall continue the struggle whatever happens."

"I am sure of that," Léopold responded. "You will get the upper hand, but not before going through a hell of a time!"

At that point, Léopold's mother, Queen Elisabeth, came into the room. She put her hands on her son's shoulders and added: "Yes, it will be hell, but England will not perish!"

Then Keyes, following Churchill's instructions, made one final attempt to persuade the king to leave Belgium with him. But Léopold walked the admiral over to the window, pointed to the crowds of refugees hurrying in all directions, and said: "It would be easy for me to leave but, even if I wanted to, I could not, after having seen such a sight." The two men exchanged farewells, and Keyes departed.

At 3:15 P.M. on May 28, General Reichenau arrived at Léopold's provincial palace at Bruges. He arrived with all the members of his general staff and a retinue of reporters from the German press. Reichenau had come, he told

the reporters, at Hitler's orders, in order to put himself at the king's disposal and to convey the Führer's greetings.

Léopold waited for Reichenau in the large drawing room on the second floor of the palace. Through one of its windows, he watched the German general's retinue enter the courtyard. He immediately called Major Van den Heuvel, the king's aide, and asked him to inform Reichenau that he refused to take part in any spectacle. Van den Heuvel realized it would be difficult to persuade the victor to comply with the wishes of the vanquished, but the German general finally agreed to Léopold's demand and dismissed his staff and the phalanx of journalists and cameramen who accompanied him. He then entered Léopold's drawing room alone.

The king was standing rigidly, in military fashion, behind his desk at the far end of the room, with a few of his aides standing next to him. After a brisk "Heil Hitler!" Reichenau strode toward the king with an outstretched hand. Then, sensing Léopold's cold impassivity, he stopped in midstride, still 30 feet away from the king.

Then Léopold spoke: "I have only one question to ask General von Reichenau. What is to become of my army?"

The German remained silent for a moment, then stammered, "I have received no instructions on the matter, Your Majesty. But you must realize that a defeated army is a prisoner."

Léopold was silent for a long time, then replied calmly, "In those circumstances, General von Reichenau should consider me his first prisoner."

Reichenau went pale, and could find nothing to say.

Then Léopold said firmly, "I consider the meeting between General von Reichenau and myself to be over. Gentlemen, please show the general out."

When Hitler was informed about the brusque reception Léopold had extended to his legate, he was furious. He ordered that Léopold be sent that day to Laeken Palace in Brussels. No sooner were its gates shut behind the king than his subjects began to pile huge bouquets of flowers against them. Like the army, the majority of Belgium's people realized that Léopold's refusal to flee to England meant that he wished to share their fate. Somehow, the news of the people's continued devotion to the king reached the members of the Belgian government who had fled to France. The president of the Senate, Gillon, told his colleagues, "In Belgium, eighty percent of the population are against us and for the king."

Churchill clearly was embarrassed by the news of Léopold's surrender. It was the first time that a European sovereign had preferred to share his people's fate rather than seek sanctuary in London. Would British prestige suffer? he wondered. Yet his initial reaction was restrained. This was due largely to the efforts of Admiral Keyes and Lieutenant Colonel George Davy, a member of the British mission attached to Léopold's military headquarters. Both men made a spirited defense of the Belgian king before the War Cabinet on May 28. Keyes said that the Belgian army had been completely demoralized by incessant bombing from large numbers of German aircraft, and that only Léopold's presence had kept it fighting during the last four days.

Colonel Davy spoke next. He said he was appalled to see a draft communiqué accusing Léopold of treachery and of surrendering without warning. Moved by Davy's reasoning, Churchill immediately drafted, in his own hand, a more moderate communiqué that included the phrase, "It is early yet to judge." He then read it aloud and said, "How about that, Colonel Davy?" "That's better, sir," Davy replied, and the whole room broke out in laughter. Churchill then said, "No doubt, history would criticize the king for having involved us and the French in Belgium's ruin. But it was not for us to pass judgment on him."

The French reaction to Belgium's surrender was much less sympathetic. When Reynaud was informed about Léopold's action, he became white with rage. "The King of the Belgians has betrayed us," he told General Spears in a voice brimming with fury. "Three weeks ago he begged us to fly to his help; today, without a word of warning, he has capitulated. There has never been such a betrayal in history," he exclaimed. "It is monstrous, absolutely monstrous." Considering Reynaud's own desperate political position, it is plausible that much of his hostility toward Léopold was motivated by a desire to make the Belgian king the scapegoat for France's collapse.

But Reynaud was also upset by Churchill's refusal to join the French vendetta against Léopold. That evening, he told General Spears that he was surprised and hurt by the British government's tepid reaction to the Belgian king's surrender. He emphasized that he needed full British support for his position against Léopold, if only to keep the defeatists in his own government in check. For this reason, Reynaud asked Spears to try his best to persuade London to change its tune. Spears apparently was successful in doing this, for in Churchill's speech to Parliament on June 4, the prime minister would be much less sympathetic to the Belgian king.

The French people shared Reynaud's anger toward Belgium. Many Belgians in France were insulted, others molested. Fearing for their safety, the Belgian government-in-exile amended a statement it had prepared that Belgian Foreign Minister Spaak later admitted originally expressed the government's continued loyalty to Léopold.

At 6:00 P.M. on May 28, Belgium's prime minister, Hubert Pierlot, read the revised version of the text to the Belgian people over Radio Paris. It stated, in part: "Ignoring the advice of the government, . . . the king has placed himself at the mercy of the enemy. From now on, he is no longer head of this country, for those duties cannot be carried out while he is under alien control. The officers and civil servants of this country are absolved from the obedience incorporated in the oath of allegiance." Pierlot concluded by saying that his government would continue fighting on the side of the Allies until Belgium was liberated.

This pledge, however, was not immediately fulfilled. After France asked for an armistice on June 17, both Pierlot and Spaak again changed their position and wrote to King Léopold asking him to intercede with the Germans so that Belgium could obtain terms similar to those ultimately granted France. But Léopold rebuffed them and instead told them to flee to England. Instead, they fled to Vichy, in unoccupied France, where they continued their efforts, unsuccessfully, to negotiate an armistice with the Germans. Only after the British threatened to set up a "free" Belgian government-in-exile on British soil did the two ministers agree to go to England. On October 18 they escaped to neutral Portugal and from there were flown to England on October 24. They would spend the remainder of the war heading the Belgian government-in-exile and renewing their pledges of loyalty to King Léopold, who continued his imprisonment in Laeken Palace.

CHAPTER NINE

Operation Dynamo, May 28–June 4

FILLING THE GAP, MAY 28

Lord Gort was not immediately informed about King Léopold's decision to surrender. He learned about it only a little before 11:00 P.M. on May 27, when General Koeltz casually asked him whether he had heard that the king of the Belgians had asked for an armistice. During the nightmarish four-and-a-half-hour journey back to his headquarters, Gort struggled with the realization that the Belgian surrender left 20 miles of his left flank wide open to the divisions of Bock's Army Group B.

Fortunately, General Alan Brooke had gotten his 2nd Corps into motion, transported in trucks northward to the Channel, even before he was informed that the Belgians had surrendered. The 50th Infantry Division led the retreat, followed by the 4th and 3rd Divisions, which had just withdrawn from the pocket around Lille. These British divisions quickly filled the gap in the northeastern side of the vital corridor that led to Dunkirk.

General Bernard Montgomery's 3rd Division moved at night, without lights, along country roads within a couple of thousand yards of the front, where a fierce battle had been raging all day. Montgomery's biographer called the successful maneuver of his division "a little masterpiece in the art of war—an operation which, for sheer nerve and skill, deserves to stand alongside any of his later achievements."

The rapid movement of Brooke's corps saved the BEF. Yet its salvation was due as much to the inability of Bock's divisions, which lacked wheeled vehicles, to move quickly into the breach in the Allied line created by the Belgian surrender. The leading elements of his 256th Infantry Division did not get under way until 11:00 A.M. on May 28. They had managed to scrape up some trucks and then rushed into the coastal area east of Nieuport, hoping to beat the British to the town. But the armored cars of the British 12th Lancers were there already and, after a brisk and bloody skirmish, stopped the Germans in their tracks. By the time the Germans launched a full-scale attack on the town later that afternoon, the Lancers had been reinforced by a brigade of the British 4th Division as well as by units of the French 60th Division, which had escaped German encirclement thanks to trucks provided by the Belgian army.

With great *élan,* the Germans rushed over the principal bridge across the Yser River, the last barrier between Bock's divisions and Dunkirk, which either the French or the Belgians had failed to destroy. But the Germans were quickly bogged down in the narrow streets and houses of Nieuport, where British and French soldiers mounted a vigorous and effective defense from cellars and barricaded streets. Even though the 256th Division was reinforced by the 208th Division, the Germans were unable to expand their narrow bridgehead as night fell. Bock, mourning his lack of armor, realized he had lost the race to Dunkirk.

The French 1st Army, May 28–29

The Belgian capitulation made it imperative for Lord Gort to meet with General Blanchard. They had to plan the redeployment of the northern Allied armies. Blanchard arrived at Gort's Houtkerque headquarters at 11:00 A.M. on May 28. The BEF commander wanted Blanchard to withdraw the French troops that had managed to retire to the Lys River, another 15 miles, and thus closer to the coast. As it was, he pointed out to Blanchard, the escape corridor to the sea was already less than 15 miles wide at its narrowest point. Even more pressing in Gort's mind was the necessity of immediately withdrawing the five divisions of the French 1st Army, which were still fighting in and around Lille. Gort, not realizing that these divisions were already encircled, stressed that they were in imminent danger of being totally cut off.

Blanchard replied that he needed another day before he could order such a withdrawal. "To wait till tomorrow night," General Pownall exclaimed, "was to give two days to the Germans to get behind us, an act of madness." While trying to convince Blanchard that the immediate retreat of the French 1st Army was necessary, it became apparent to both Gort and Pownall that the French commander was totally unaware that the ultimate object of the BEF's withdrawal to the coast was its evacuation to England. They had assumed that he had been informed by Weygand. But

Blanchard still believed that the Allied armies would withdraw no farther than the Yser River, where they would make a final stand.

Gort paused while he took out the War Office telegram that he had received on May 26. As he read the order directing him to begin the evacuation of the BEF's combat troops, Blanchard's face dropped in horror. If the order were obeyed, he exclaimed, the French 1st Army would be cut off and forced to surrender! Gort did not have to express agreement with Blanchard's prediction. Instead, he told him that this outcome could be avoided if both the French and British armies withdrew to the coast in tandem that night.

Just then a liaison officer arrived from General Prioux's 1st Army headquarters. He reported that Prioux did not consider his troops fit to make any further move and that he therefore intended to remain in the area of Lille, protected by its surrounding quadrangle of canals. Prioux's decision, exclaimed Pownall, would only result in the destruction of his army.

Gort recalled that he "begged General Blanchard, for the sake of France, the French army, and the Allied cause to order General Prioux back." "Surely," he added, Blanchard's "troops were not all so tired as to be incapable of moving. The chance of saving a part of his trained soldiers was preferable to the certainty of losing them all."

Wearily, Blanchard replied that the British Admiralty undoubtedly had already made arrangements to evacuate the BEF, but the French navy could never provide sufficient shipping for his men. Moreover, he said, evacuation from the open beaches was impossible; it was useless to even try. Even more important to Blanchard was the honor of France. It was, he said, more honorable for the 1st Army to go down fighting on French soil than to abandon any part of France by evacuating to the sea. No arguments by Gort and Pownall could persuade Blanchard to change his mind.

The French general then asked Gort a question the BEF commander was reluctant to answer: "Will the British forces pull back tonight, whatever the position of the French 1st Army along the Lys?" After a few seconds of silence, Pownall answered for his chief, "Yes." Gort then explained that he had formal orders from his government to withdraw the BEF, and that if he was to have any hope of carrying out those orders, he must continue his move that night.

That evening, Blanchard cabled General Weygand to inform him that Gort's withdrawal toward Dunkirk that night would leave the flank of the French 1st Army unprotected. After receiving the telegram the next morning, Weygand immediately telephoned Premier Reynaud and angrily demanded that he protest the "too selfish attitude of General Gort."

After the meeting with Gort ended, Blanchard rushed off to see General Prioux. Realizing that the British withdrawal would leave the 1st Army in a hopeless situation, the two French generals agreed to pull back as many of that army's units as were still mobile.

At half past three that afternoon, Major General Edmund Osborne also went to see General Prioux. Osborne's 44th Division was deployed on the right flank of Prioux's army, and he therefore wanted to know when and by what routes Prioux intended to withdraw his forces. Needless to say, he was surprised when the French general told him that only the army's 3rd Corps and what remained of the Cavalry Corps would withdraw toward the coast; the 4th Corps would remain on the Lys River, while the 5th Corps would stay in and around Lille. General Osborne tried hard to change Prioux's mind and even offered to stay and protect his flank if the whole French force would retire to the coast, but Prioux would not budge.

Osborne then drove to the headquarters of General Fournel de la Laurencie, the commander of the French 3rd Corps. De la Laurencie told him that he had been ordered to withdraw at noon on the following day but that he would not wait that long. Instead, he had decided to begin withdrawing to Dunkirk at eleven o'clock that night. De la Laurencie said that he also had been ordered to direct his regiments to burn their colors. "Why this act of despair?" he wrote in his diary. "We are not yet on our knees, and the gate at Dunkirk is still open. My men trust their officers; they have ammunition; they *can* and *will* fight. They cannot do that without colors. I shall not carry out the order, and the regiments will march past with their colors."

The ability of the French 3rd Corps to withdraw to the relative safety of the Dunkirk perimeter by that evening was a tribute to the verve and capability of General de la Laurencie. Had France only possessed more generals with his qualities of leadership, particularly his ability to make a decision and see it through to the end, she might have been able to avert the catastrophe that was about to engulf her.

Prioux, who had remained at his command post along with his staff and the commanding general of the 4th Corps, was taken prisoner by a German armored detachment at Steenwerck just north of the Lys River. The rest of the 1st Army that did not make it across that stream, at least five divisions now under the command of General Molinié, continued to put up a desperate fight in the Lille area for the next three days. In so doing, they immobilized the greater part of Reichenau's 6th Army and gained extra time for Allied units to retreat to Dunkirk. Finally, on June 1, short of food and with their ammunition exhausted, the French surrendered. The victors granted them the full honors of war before marching them off to prisoner-of-war camps in Germany.

The French units that were successful in getting across the Lys became almost hopelessly entangled with British troops retreating toward Dunkirk. Both armies had been allocated separate routes to the city, but in the confusion of the battle, units from both armies found themselves using the same roads. "The French road discipline was absolutely nil," Major John Matthew complained. "Consequently, every journey was a nightmare. They simply pushed their way through wherever they wanted to go, completely regardless of anyone else on the road."

Near Poperinge, Colonel Graham Brooks came upon what he described as the dregs of the French army: "One panic-stricken major, trying to scramble past our column, ditched his car. Rushing up to 'Boots' Brown's truck, he tried to pull the driver out of his seat, presumably in order to clamber in himself. When 'Boots' shouted at him, the major pulled his revolver; he was mad with terror. Bang went the *entente cordiale* as 'Boots' slugged him hard on the jaw."

The gunnery lieutenant and former Cambridge languages student Eric Loveluck found a more diplomatic way of dealing with demoralized French troops. "A whole battalion lay in the ditches while their officers stalked apprehensively up and down the road," Loveluck recalled. "I spotted their colonel, saluted and advised him that, although some of us had lost a battle, we hadn't lost the war and that if they sat on their *culs* [asses] much longer, they would all be in the bag, with all the deprivation that would mean. He was so delighted he invited me to address his battalion; I did so." The French soldiers were soon on their way again.

In spite of the traffic jams, by midnight on May 29 the greater part of the BEF had managed to make it back to the relative safety of the Dunkirk perimeter, where they took up positions behind the high banks of its surrounding canals. The British 46th, 42nd, 1st, 50th, 3rd, and 4th Infantry Divisions, in that order, moved into a line extending from Bergues to Nieuport. They were assisted by the French 60th Division, deployed around Nieuport; the 2nd Light Mechanized Division, near Furnes; and the remains of the 32nd and 12th Infantry Divisions as well as the Cavalry Corps, between Furnes and Bergues.

GORT'S PREDICAMENT, MAY 28

During the afternoon of May 28, Lord Gort moved his headquarters from Houtkerque to De Panne, a small town on the coast eight miles east of Dunkirk. He was very aware that he probably would not save his entire army. He asked General Sir John Dill, the new chief of the Imperial General Staff (on May 27, Dill replaced General Sir Edmund Ironside, who was transferred to the command of the British Home Defense forces), what the government wanted him to do if he could not. In response, Churchill sent Gort this order: "If you are cut from all communication from us, and all evacuation from Dunkirk and beaches had, in your judgment, been finally prevented, after every attempt to re-open it had failed, you would become sole judge of when it was impossible to inflict further damage to enemy." In other words, Gort was given the authority to surrender if that proved necessary.

While Gort was considering the possibility that he might have to capitulate, he received an urgent telegram from General Weygand appealing to him to promise that when the appropriate time arrived, the BEF would participate in an Allied counterattack and "hit hard" at the Germans. Gort could only conclude that Weygand "had no accurate information of . . . the powers of counterattack remaining to either the British or French."

OPERATION DYNAMO, MAY 28

While the BEF was withdrawing to the beaches around Dunkirk, Operation Dynamo was beginning to show results, small though they initially were. On May 28, approximately 17,000 troops had arrived in England.

The relatively slow start was due to a number of factors. "The initial problem," Vice Admiral Ramsay explained, was "in the way small boats were thrown on the beaches before adequate provision had been made for their maintenance off the coast." This included "such matters as relief of the personnel and the provision of large beach parties." Moreover, there simply were not enough small craft available at first to bring the soldiers from the beaches to the ships waiting for them in the deeper water. As a result, Dover was inundated with complaints that there were "no boats" at the beaches, complaints that led many people, including Gort, to conclude that the attempt to evacuate troops from the beaches was failing.

However, from Ramsay's perspective at Dover, where, as he pointed out, "the whole operation could be viewed, it was clear that the evacuation from the beaches . . . was, in fact, achieving considerable success." Thanks largely to the advance planning of the Admiralty, small powerboats and beach craft began appearing in ever-increasing numbers as early as the morning of May 28. By the end of that day, 17,804 troops were transported to England. Of these, 11,874 were lifted from the Dunkirk east pier, and 5,930 from the beaches.

The rescued men were treated as heroes as they disembarked at Dover, Ramsgate, Sheerness, and other ports in southeastern England. They were handed sandwiches, tea, beer, and cigarettes and then were bundled into waiting trains that transported them to collecting centers all over the country. There they would be reclothed, fed, sorted out, and then reformed into old or new units.

The increased tempo of the evacuation on May 28 was due also to the heavy pall of smoke that hung over Dunkirk and helped to reduce enemy air attacks on the harbor. In addition, the RAF intensified its efforts over Dunkirk that day. Early that morning, all involved units of the RAF were told: "Today is likely to be the most critical day ever experienced by the British army." Pilots were expected "to make their greatest effort to assist their comrades of both the army and navy." That day, the RAF flew about 320 sorties over Dunkirk, and the size of its patrols increased from an average of one squadron to an average of two squadrons. As a result, 19 German Me-109s and four bombers were shot down that day, while the RAF lost only 13 fighters. On the following day, May 29, fighter patrols were strengthened to five squadrons, all operating within a radius of 10 miles from Dunkirk.

Still, as a consequence of increased German shore fire, combined with continued Luftwaffe attacks, personnel vessels and warships plying to and from the evacuation zones became increasingly vulnerable. Admiral Ramsay was compelled to prohibit the use of personnel vessels during the daylight hours and rely only on destroyers. As it was, destroyers were already transporting the most troops. On May 28, 16 destroyers carried 11,835 of the 17,804 troops evacuated that day. Yet this was still not enough. Prompted by Captain Tennant's urgent message declaring that evacuation on the night of May 28–29 would be "problematical," the Admiralty directed every available destroyer to sail to Dunkirk.

NAVAL LOSSES, MAY 29

May 29 proved to be a particularly costly day for the Royal Navy. It opened very early in the morning with a monumental tragedy. After taking on 640 British soldiers from the beaches shortly before midnight, the destroyer *Wakeful* was racing homeward along the northerly Route Y. The troops were packed as low in the ship as possible—in the engine room, the boiler room, the storerooms, wherever empty space could be found—to give the ship maximum stability in case her skipper, Commander Ralph Lindsay Fisher, had to maneuver quickly to avoid air attack.

At about 12:45, near the Kwinte Whistle Buoy off Ostend, where British ships from Dunkirk turned west for England, Lieutenant Wilhelm Zimmermann, the skipper of the German torpedo boat *Schnellboot-30,* spotted the black silhouette of an approaching ship against the phosphorescent night sky. "There, dead ahead!" he told his helmsman, standing behind him. "It must be a destroyer." The torpedo boat turned toward the target, aiming its bow at the onrushing ship. "Fire!" Zimmermann shouted, and two torpedoes plunged into the sea.

Commander Fisher was on the bridge of the *Wakeful* when he saw two glistening parallel streaks heading toward the starboard side of his ship, one slightly ahead of the other. Torpedoes! He ordered the helmsman to turn hard to port, and the first torpedo passed harmlessly across the destroyer's bow. But the destroyer could not dodge the second torpedo, which exploded with an ear-shattering roar and a blinding flash in the vessel's forward boiler room. The *Wakeful* immediately cracked in half and sank in 15 seconds. Most of its passengers, deep within the ship's bowels, never had a chance. Only one soldier who happened to be topside sneaking a cigarette survived, along with the sailors on deck, including Commander Fisher, all of whom were thrown into the sea. The sinking of the *Wakeful* was the greatest single loss of men during the entire Dunkirk evacuation.

Within a half-hour of *Wakeful's* sinking, two small drifters, *Nautilus* and *Comfort,* approached Kwinte Buoy bound for De Panne via Route Y. Their crews spotted men bobbing in the water, crying for help. Six were picked up by *Nautilus* and another 16, including Commander Fisher, were rescued by *Comfort.* They soon were joined by the minesweepers *Gossamer and Lydd,* both carrying hundreds of troops loaded from the eastern mole, followed by the destroyer *Grafton,* with a full load of soldiers lifted off Bray-Dunes beach. The new arrivals lowered their lifeboats into the water and fired flares in the hope of finding additional survivals.

A thousand yards away, near Kwinte Buoy, the commander of the German submarine *U-62,* Lieutenant Michalowski, peered through his periscope at the flashing lights on the surface of the sea. He ordered his helmsman to move the sub toward them.

Commander Fisher quickly appreciated the vulnerability of the hud-
dled British ships. Taking command of *Comfort,* he directed the vessel
toward them. He hailed *Gossamer* and warned her captain that the attacker
was probably still nearby. *Gossamer* quickly got under way. After warning
Nautilus and *Lydd,* Fisher eased *Comfort* alongside the *Grafton* and again
called out his warning. But he was too late. Seconds afterward, a torpedo
ripped into *Grafton's* wardroom, killing some 35 army officers.

Down in the captain's cabin of the *Grafton,* Captain Basil Bartlett, who
had been evacuated from the Bray-Dunes beach, stumbled around in the
dark, trying to find the door of the unfamiliar room. "The whole ship was
trembling violently," he recalled. "There was a strong smell of petrol."
Wearing only a battle-dress top and pajama trousers, Bartlett managed to
find his way to the upper deck of the burning ship. It was, he remembered, "a mass of twisted steel and mangled bodies." He soon discovered
that he had lost three of his front teeth, apparently when his face collided
with the cabin's wall after the torpedo exploded, only 15 feet away. Still,
Bartlett realized that he was lucky to be alive. "If I'd gone on board a little earlier," he recounted, "I should have been put in the Ward Room. I
only slept in the Captain's cabin because there was no room for me anywhere else."

Unfortunately for the British, this was not the end of the night's losses.
The *Comfort,* which was lying alongside *Grafton,* was nearly swamped by
the exploding torpedo, but she soon bobbed back to the surface. However,
all of her on-deck crewmen were washed overboard, including, once again,
Commander Fisher.

Comfort, pilotless and with her engine jammed at full speed ahead,
moved off into the blackness of the night in an ever-widening circle. Nevertheless, Fisher managed to grab a rope as the ship passed him and hung on
for a brief, wild ride before he finally had to let go. He then began paddling back toward the other ships.

Meanwhile, on *Lydd,* its skipper, Lieutenant Commander Rudolph
Haig, saw a small vessel off in the distance, circling his ship at high speed.
He thought it was an enemy torpedo boat. He had been warned by a
Wakeful survivor that a German torpedo boat, rather than a submarine, had
sunk that destroyer. Gunners on both *Lydd* and on the sinking *Grafton*
opened fire on the vessel, not realizing it was the *Comfort.* The shells
knocked out the *Comfort's* engine, stopping her dead in the water.

Lydd then rammed the luckless ship at full speed, cutting her in half
just as Commander Fisher was trying to climb back aboard her. Back into

the sea went Fisher. He continued paddling around until 5:15 in the morning, when he was picked up by a Norwegian freighter, the *Hird.* In spite of the numerous dunkings he was forced to endure, Fisher was lucky. When three of the other remaining survivors from *Comfort* tried to scramble aboard *Lydd,* they were mistaken, in the darkness, for a German boarding party. One of the men was shot and killed before the error was realized.

As *Lydd* was engaging *Comfort,* the crippled *Grafton* began to list, compelling the survivors to move about its deck in an attempt to redistribute their weight as evenly as possible. After it appeared that *Grafton* would be able to look after herself, the *Lydd* set course for Ramsgate.

Shortly before dawn, the railway steamer *Malines* appeared on the horizon. Arriving alongside *Grafton,* she began taking on survivors. "The men," Captain Bartlett recalled, "showed wonderful discipline. There was no ugly rush. They allowed themselves to be divided into groups and transferred from one ship to another with the same patience that they had shown on Bray-Dunes beach." After the men had been embarked and the *Malines* moved off a considerable distance, the destroyer *Ivanhoe,* which also had arrived on the scene, put two shells into the *Grafton*'s heavily listing hull. We watched her sink," Bartlett remembered, "carrying with her a load of unknown dead."

THE ATTACK ON THE EAST MOLE, MAY 29

As bad as the destroyer losses at sea were during the dark morning hours of May 29, even more of the warships would be lost at Dunkirk's east mole during the afternoon. Until then, the smoke and low cloud cover over the port had caused the Luftwaffe to virtually ignore the harbor area. As a result, a steady stream of vessels was able to pull in and out of the east mole all morning.

In fact, the evacuation from the mole was proving to be so successful that Captain Tennant asked for permission to concentrate the entire evacuation there. But Admiral Ramsay turned down his request. There now were so many soldiers pouring into the Dunkirk perimeter that Ramsay believed that it was necessary to use both the mole and the beaches for the evacuation. Moreover, he wanted to reduce the risk of losing more ships, realizing that a large concentration of vessels in any one area would only draw the Luftwaffe's attention. Nevertheless, that day, for the first time, the east mole became the primary locus of the evacuation. During the afternoon, 11 British ships were moored at the mole and two French ships were alongside the harbor jetties.

About 3:00 P.M., weather conditions for the evacuation took a turn for the worse—from the Allied perspective. The wind shifted toward the north, clearing the smoke that had covered the port all morning. Conditions were now ideal for the Luftwaffe to deliver one of the most disastrous air onslaughts on the ships engaged in Operation Dynamo.

The German aircraft struck between 3:30 and 8:00 P.M., attacking in four separate waves. The first was made by 12 bombers, which dropped 20 or 30 bombs on the harbor. Fortunately, most fell wide of their targets. However, the trawler *Polly Johnson* was severely damaged by a near-miss. The second attack, which began at 3:50 and was conducted by dive-bombers delivering salvos of four bombs each, was more successful. A near-miss severely damaged the destroyer *Jaguar.* It ripped a hole near her waterline and knocked her engines and steering gear out of action. The destroyer, listing to port, drifted helplessly until 4:45, when she almost struck a wreck only 50 yards away. She was saved by the destroyer *Express,* which moved alongside and nudged her away from the approaching wreck. *Express* then took on some of *Jaguar*'s passengers. *Jaguar* limped back to Dover, but was too badly damaged to continue to participate in the evacuation.

The third Luftwaffe attack began at about 5:50 and was carried out by waves of bombers, which altogether dropped about 100 bombs. Allied fighters—two Hurricane squadrons and two squadrons of Spitfires—were over Dunkirk at the time, but they were kept busy by German Me-109 fighters, which were flying cover for the attacking bombers. As a result, the German bombers met little interference from the RAF.

One bomb just missed the destroyer *Grenade.* Nevertheless, the explosion blew a hole in her hull. But two other bombs that followed scored direct hits, knocking out *Grenade*'s engines and setting her on fire. As the crippled ship swung round, some of her crew were able to escape to the nearby *Polly Johnson.* The burning ship then began drifting toward five trawlers. One of them, the *John Cattling,* managed to pull *Grenade* clear of the other ships and then guided her into an empty slip just to the west of the main channel. There she burned fiercely for some hours before blowing up. A little later, the *Polly Johnson,* leaking badly and with a damaged engine, was abandoned. Her crew and troops were transferred to the *Arley* before that ship turned her guns on the *Polly Johnson* and sank her.

About six o'clock, the *Crested Eagle* managed to get away from the east mole. Shortly afterward, however, she was hit by four bombs that set her ablaze and out of control. About a half-hour later, she ran aground west of Bray Beach. When her survivors, some 200 in number, tried to swim for shore, they were strafed by German planes, which also bombed the ships that came to their rescue. Some of the survivors, several with severe burns, were finally picked up by the minesweepers *Hebe* and *Lydd*.

The fourth wave of the German air attack began about 6:30 and ended near 8:00 P.M. The bombers concentrated on ships returning to England as well as those off Bray Beach. During this phase of the German onslaught, the destroyer *Saladin* was attacked 10 times. Her engine room was so severely damaged by a German near-miss that she had to return to Dover at 15 knots and took no further part in Operation Dynamo.

All totaled, that day three destroyers—*Wakeful, Grafton,* and *Grenade*—were sunk and six more badly damaged. Indeed, it was only by good fortune that the vital channel through Dunkirk harbor was not blocked by sinking ships.

BACK TO THE BEACHES, MAY 29

As destructive as the aerial attack was, it was not the end of the bad news that Vice Admiral Ramsay received that day. About 7:00 P.M., he received a message delivered by telephone from a naval shore party officer based at De Panne, Commander J. S. Dove, who reported that Dunkirk's harbor was blocked by sunken ships. But Dove was wrong. The harbor was littered with wreckage and dotted with burning ships, but it was not blocked. Moreover, the mole was still usable.

Ramsay, however, had no immediate way of confirming or discounting Dove's report, since radio contact with Dunkirk could be made only through destroyers when they were tied up at the mole. Ramsay believed he had no option but to order all ships to avoid the harbor. They were diverted to the beaches. As a consequence, for the rest of that day and during the following night, May 29–30, only five small ships entered the harbor. It is plausible that about 10,000 troops could have been lifted from the Dunkirk harbor during the night had it remained open. To make matters worse, it would take over two days to overcome the results of the false report. Radio contact with Dunkirk was not established until 11:00 P.M. on the following day, May 31.

The Allied troops awaiting evacuation did, however, catch a major break on May 29: Hitler decided to withdraw the panzer divisions from the attack on Dunkirk.

THE PANZERS ARE WITHDRAWN, MAY 29

On the morning of May 29, General Heinz Guderian, with the leading tanks of his 1st Panzer Division only a bare eight miles from Dunkirk's harbor, inspected the intervening terrain and concluded: "A tank attack is

pointless in the marshy country which has been completely soaked by rain.
. . . Infantry forces are more suitable than tanks for fighting in this kind
of country, and the task of closing the gap on the coast can therefore be
left to them." Guderian was now more than happy to turn away from the
mud of Flanders and the British 2-pounders and concentrate on the next
stage of the offensive, the main assault on France. In fact, he was already
poring over his maps of the lower Seine Valley.

Generals Brauchitsch and Halder were more than willing to comply
with Guderian's recommendation. Since Bock had been entrusted with the
task of crushing the Dunkirk perimeter, Halder recorded in his diary,
Brauchitsch was "rather restless for want of something to do" and could
"hardly wait" until the detailed regrouping orders for the second phase of
the campaign, Plan Red, had been worked out by the General Staff. Those
plans were finally completed and accepted by Hitler after a brief skirmish
on May 28. So confident was Halder that Plan Red would take France out
of the war altogether, and thereby bring Britain to terms as well, that he
began to think about the composition of the peacetime German army.

At 10:00 A.M. on May 29, Brauchitsch, with Hitler's permission,
ordered the panzers out of the battle. General Gustav von Wietersheim's
motorized infantry was directed to take over Guderian's front. The panzers
moved south, away from the battle zone, to rest and refit for the coming
invasion of central France.

While the withdrawal of the panzers did much to ease the pressure on the
Allied soldiers defending the 35-mile-long Dunkirk perimeter, it did not
mean that they were home free. On the contrary, they were still compelled
to fend off 10 German infantry divisions. At the western end of the
perimeter, Fort Philippe fell to the Germans around noon on May 29, and
the port of Gravelines followed soon thereafter.

On the eastern side of the perimeter, the German 56th Infantry Division was attacking Furnes. About 3:30 P.M. one of its units, the 25th Bicy-
cle Squadron, collided with a French column that also was trying to cross
into the perimeter. After a brief firefight, the French soldiers surrendered.
Soon afterward, two unsuspecting French tanks, their turrets still open,
approached the German bicyclists. One of the Germans, Corporal Gruen-
vogel, jumped up on one of the tanks, pointed his pistol down the open
turret, and ordered the crew to surrender. They did. The crew of the second tank immediately followed suit.

Emboldened by the weak French resistance he encountered, the commander of the cyclist squadron, Captain Neugart, sent two of his men,

along with a captured French major, into Furnes to demand the surrender of the entire town. By this time, however, Allied troops were barricading the streets of the town and were in no mood to surrender. They scornfully rejected the German demand.

French Evacuation, May 29–30

By May 29, French troops were beginning to pour back through the perimeter line in greater numbers. French officers were under orders to gather their forces and supplies in Dunkirk and use them to break out as soon as possible toward Calais. To do that, they would need every gun and vehicle they could muster. On the other hand, British soldiers, believing they would be evacuated to England, realized they could not hope to take their guns and vehicles with them. Moreover, to ensure that no unnecessary clutter was brought into the Dunkirk perimeter, they were under orders to destroy any vehicles—other than those carrying necessary ammunition—before their occupants crossed the canals that surrounded the perimeter.

Considering their contradictory orders, clashes between the soldiers of the two Allied armies were inevitable. Occasionally British military police and provost sergeants manning the checkpoints were compelled to use pistols to persuade resisting French soldiers to destroy their trucks. A French gunner major angrily recounted to Captain Jean Beaux, attached to Admiral Abrial's headquarters, how British military police had let his guns go across the canal and then put pickaxes through the engines of the trucks carrying their ammunition. French troops, most of whom were still determined to fight, considered the forced destruction of their equipment another humiliating sign of their impotence.

Captain Barlone, a French officer who admired the British, recounted his experience upon arriving at the perimeter: "A fresh traffic block, a mile long . . . where the British have barricaded all exits. . . . The French are wild. Some gunners talk of training their guns and shooting. . . . I take command and order two officers to take a hundred men and drag away the heavy British tractors which bar the road. Then I go out and find an English major, and in five minutes everything is arranged."

The British, on the other hand, grew increasingly contemptuous of the French for resisting their orders. General Brooke wrote in his diary that the French army had become "a rabble . . . Troops dejected and surly, refusing to clear roads and panicking every time German planes come over." Due to the breakdown in communications, however, Brooke was unaware of the spirited defense the French were putting up on the right side of the perimeter defense line. They were making it possible for the entire BEF to be evacuated.

※

There also was increasing friction on the beaches as more and more French and British troops poured onto them. When the exhausted *poilus* finally made it to the coast, they were enraged to discover that the British had organized the evacuation with only their own troops in mind. A party of about 20 French soldiers, not familiar with the British method of queuing, made a rush for the shore, grabbed a rowboat, and started rowing. They did not get very far before a burst of fire from a British Bren gun flipped their boat over, leaving French bodies floating in the water.

The British also could be tough with French officers. A French colonel who angrily refused to be directed to an area of the beach reserved for French evacuation had to be ordered away at gunpoint. To the French, it seemed that not only had the British rushed to the sea to escape the Germans, they also had taken exclusive possession of the beaches as well.

But not all British sailors were rough on the French. "Let's help the Froggies, too," Bob Hilton suggested to Ted Shaw as they rowed troops from the beach to the ships lying off Malo-les-Bains. Shaw agreed, and they never considered whether any of the soldiers they transported were French or English.

※

However, it was not that simple with the higher-ups. When the evacuation began, both the British Admiralty and the army assumed that British troops would be taken off by British ships, while French troops would be transported by French ships. As a result, part of the beach at Malo was reserved solely for French use, and the British even urged the French to send more ships to take off their men.

The British Admiralty assumed that Premier Reynaud had been informed about these arrangements and had conveyed them to Admiral Abrial. However, Churchill simply could not bring himself to inform Reynaud about the British intention to evacuate when the French premier visited London on May 26. That information, he feared, would have sapped what remained of the French will to fight.

As a result, when Gort arrived at Abrial's Bastion 32 headquarters during the afternoon of May 29, he had no idea that the French admiral was still totally unaware that the BEF was evacuating. Abrial, whose "troglodyte habits" endowed him, as General Spears put it, "with the confidence and aggressiveness of a rhinoceros, and similarly limited vision," was still under the impression that the British were merely embarking rear units to clear space for the establishment of a permanent fighting bridgehead around Dunkirk. The French admiral still intended "to hold on to Dunkirk till the last man and the last round," and he expected the British to do the same.

One can only imagine Abrial's astonishment when Gort told him that the entire BEF was pulling out. Abrial insisted that they both immediately obtain clarification of their orders from their respective governments. Much to Gort's surprise, the clarification he received from London stated that henceforth French soldiers would be evacuated on an equal basis with British soldiers and that they would be embarked on British ships as well as any French vessels that were available. To Gort, the message was another example of Churchill's excessive interference in what the BEF commander regarded as purely a military matter.

Earlier that day, Gort and Sir John Dill, the new chief of the Imperial General Staff, had discussed, via the Channel telephone link, the mounting French suspicion that the British were abandoning them. To counter that impression, Gort told Dill that he was prepared to embark Allied troops with "mutual cooperation," but he said that the French would have to provide their own ships to carry them. Ignoring the fact that the main French naval strength was concentrated in the Mediterranean by previous agreement with the British government, Gort reminded Dill: "My instructions are that the safety of the BEF is the primary consideration. Every Frenchman embarked is in place of one Englishman."

The proof that Gort was sincere in this belief was demonstrated in the treatment he accorded to General Champon, head of the French mission to King Léopold. Following the Belgian capitulation, Champon and his staff, just over 100 strong, had been ordered by General Georges to make their way to Gort's headquarters in De Panne in order to make arrangements for their evacuation. Champon asked Gort to provide space for himself and his men on some British ship. To Champon's surprise, Gort responded by asking him why he and his men could not be rescued by a French destroyer. The discussion bounced back and forth between the two Allied high commands for another full day before Champon and his staff were finally evacuated at 8:00 P.M. on May 30. If it was this difficult for the British to make room for 100 French staff officers, the evacuation prospects were not bright for the thousands of ordinary *poilus* now pouring into the perimeter.

⊠

From Churchill's perspective, and contrary to what Gort thought, political considerations could never be divorced from military matters. The prime minister was shocked by the implications of a telegram from Reynaud intimating that the exclusive nature of the BEF's evacuation proved that Britain was abandoning France. If not corrected, this impression could only push the French into a separate peace with the Germans. He had to boost Reynaud's morale and, through him, sustain the will to fight of Generals Weygand and Georges.

That evening, Churchill telegraphed the French premier and asked him to convey this message to Generals Weygand and Georges: "We wish French troops to share in the evacuation to the fullest possible extent, and the Admiralty have been instructed to aid French marine as required. We do not know how many will be forced to capitulate, but we must share this loss together as best we can, and, above all, bear it without reproaches arising from inevitable confusion, stresses and strains."

In a further attempt to convince the French that they were not being abandoned, Churchill outlined to Reynaud a scheme to "build up a new BEF" south of the Somme River. Equipment sufficient for five divisions, he wrote, was being moved south of Amiens. Reinforcements also were on their way from India and Palestine, and regular British, Australian, and Canadian troops would be "arriving soon" and would be sent "for reinforcement of our troops in France." Churchill ended his message with reassuring words: "I send this in all comradeship . . . Do not hesitate to speak frankly to me."

⊠

General Spears was summoned to the British embassy at 4:00 A.M. on May 30 to receive Churchill's telegram. He was told to personally deliver it to Reynaud at once. After several hours of fruitless searching, Spears found the French premier at his private flat, dressed in a kimono and doing physical exercise.

Churchill's cable, Spears recalled, "evidently gave Reynaud neither satisfaction nor solace. . . . He said sourly, almost sarcastically, that he was very glad Churchill had emphasized that the French would be evacuated in equal numbers with the British. If this were not so, French opinion would be *déchainée*—unleashed—against Britain."

Spears could only restrain his own anger with difficulty: "I answered that . . . it was only Winston's strong hand that prevented British opinion from being *déchainée* against the French command and the French generally. We looked at each other steadily for a moment after this.

"When Reynaud broke the silence," Spears continued, "he said, in a tone I had never heard him use when talking of Churchill, a tone whose impatience was emphasized by a shrug of annoyance, that his resentment was as deep as was his incomprehension of the prime minister's attitude towards the King of the Belgians."

FRENCH PLEAS FOR ASSISTANCE, MAY 29–30

Churchill had good reason to worry about the staying power of the French. That morning, General Weygand had presented Reynaud a note advising the French government to plan the actions it would have to take if the Somme front collapsed. He warned that the loss of Paris, where 70 percent of the nation's war industries were concentrated, would render France "incapable of continuing a struggle which ensured a coordinated defense of her territory." This point, Weygand believed, would be the time to end French participation in the war. And he recommended that the British should be so informed, if only to add pressure on them to provide more assistance immediately.

Prompted by the catastrophic military situation in which France found herself, Reynaud prompted Amabassador Bullitt to send this message to President Roosevelt: "It is now or never for the United States. If you can send your Atlantic fleet to Tangier and inform Mussolini that you are doing so after the fleet has started, he will dare not strike [France]. Otherwise he will strike, and in a very few months you will face a joint attack by Germany, Italy and Japan alone."

At the same time, Arthur Purvis, the chairman of the Anglo-French Purchasing Board, was in the United States attempting to obtain the release of American war matériel for immediate despatch to Britain and France. On that very day, May 29, however, he was told by U.S. Treasury Secretary Henry Morgenthau that President Roosevelt had decided that it would be impossible at this time to gain congressional approval to modify the Neutrality Law to permit such a transfer. Morgenthau also warned Purvis that it would be both "useless and dangerous" for the Allies to take any action to "attempt the impossible."

Nor would the United States satisfy an earlier French request to station a U.S. naval fleet in the Mediterranean Sea in order to deter an Italian attack on France. U.S. Secretary of State Cordell Hull informed Ambassador Bullitt that it was "Mr. Roosevelt's decision that it was absolutely impossible to consider sending the fleet to the Mediterranean." Roosevelt considered the presence of the U.S. fleet in the Pacific "a very practical contribution to the maintenance of peace in that ocean." In short, there would be no meaningful U.S. assistance for France.

Spurned by the United States, the French increased their pressure on the British for immediate additional assistance. On May 30, Churchill informed the War Cabinet that General Weygand had "begged" Britain to send every possible soldier to the Somme front. One British division, Weygand said, would make all the difference. General Spears cabled that he had tried to convince the generalissimo that this was quite impossible, but Weygand replied that France was at the limit of what she could do to stem the anticipated final German onslaught.

Churchill told the War Cabinet that the French pleas for additional assistance made it appear that they were looking for excuses to leave the war, since they must realize that Britain could not do more than she already was doing. He then suggested to his colleagues that he should go to Paris the next day to tell the French leaders personally that Britain could do no more at the present time, but that if France could continue to hold out, additional help would be on its way eventually. The War Cabinet approved this suggestion, and the next day, Churchill, accompanied by Attlee, Dill, and Ismay, would leave for Paris.

THE EVACUATION CONTINUES, MAY 30

During the morning of May 30, the Admiralty sent over to Dunkirk Rear Admiral W. F. Wake-Walker, a 52-year-old former battleship commander who was directed to supervise "sea-going ships and vessels off the Belgian coast." Tennant now would be able to concentrate on the evacuation from the east mole.

Wake-Walker found the beaches packed with troops. While they were orderly, the sight of that many soldiers awaiting evacuation—and more arriving steadily—was almost dismaying. "At the back of our minds all the time," he recalled, "was the question of how long the defense line could hold and the weather remain fair." That day, members of Gort's staff would tell Admiral Ramsay that daylight on June 1 was the latest time the eastern perimeter could be expected to be held.

Much to Wake-Walker's surprise, when he visited the east mole he discovered that despite the previous day's bombing, it was still perfectly usable. Even better, the Germans were convinced that it was unusable. That conviction, along with the perpetual smoke from the nearby burning oil tanks, had made the mole almost completely immune from air attack throughout the day. Convinced by now that evacuation from the beaches alone would be far too slow and the exposure time to air attack of the waiting ships offshore far too long, Wake-Walker signaled Ramsay to return all available destroyers to the mole.

By this time, however, Ramsay also had become convinced that the destroyers must be sent back to the mole. The destroyer *Vanquisher,* which Ramsay had dispatched that morning to take a close look at the harbor, reported back about 4:00 A.M. that the channel was clear. While the port had sustained serious damage, it was not blocked by any sunken ships. In fact, five small ships had entered the harbor and left safely during the previous night.

Moreover, Captain Tennant had sent Ramsay a cable in which he stated his belief that Dunkirk would be "untenable" by the next morning, May 31. Embarkation, Tennant added, could continue until then, but its effectiveness would depend upon large ships and destroyers being sent to the mole that night. He reminded Ramsay that "a destroyer going full out, with her boats to the beaches, could only embark 600 men in 12 hours, whereas this could be done in 20 minutes at the mole."

Prompted by the urgent tenor of Tennant's cable, early that afternoon Ramsay phoned Admiral Pound in London and insisted that the modern destroyers must be returned to the evacuation operation if he was to get everybody off in the time he had left. After a heated exchange, Pound finally relented, and at 3:30 P.M. the destroyers were ordered back to Dunkirk.

By the end of the day, a steady stream of destroyers, along with minesweepers, Channel steamers, and trawlers, had pulled alongside the mole, loaded up, and carried off over 24,000 men. Many more would have been evacuated had the east mole remained opened the previous day. Nevertheless, May 30 witnessed the peak of the evacuation: 50 ships embarked a total of 53,823 troops, including 29,512 from the beaches. By now a total of 126,606 troops had been brought back to England, and it was beginning to look as though far fewer troops would be captured by the Germans than had seemed inevitable only the night before.

That day, staff officers from Gort's headquarters arrived in Dover to discuss with Ramsay arrangements for the final evacuation of the BEF. Gort had estimated the number of British troops remaining in the perimeter at 80,000. It was expected to be reduced to 4,000 men plus naval beach parties by 1:30 P.M. on Saturday, June 1. Ramsay was informed that the army hoped to be able to hold the eastern half of the Dunkirk perimeter until early Saturday morning. The admiral assured Gort's staff that the increasing rate of the evacuation gave every indication that the main body of the BEF could be embarked by then.

For Gort, however, defending the perimeter until the last troops could be evacuated would be no easy task. The problem, as he saw it, was how to thin out his army while keeping enough men in line to hold off the Germans. The task was complicated by the order he had received to evacuate French soldiers in a proportion equal to the number of British troops being withdrawn. The order necessitated a prolongation of the time that the existing perimeter, or a smaller one, must be held to enable all the troops to embark. Yet German pressure was increasing as the perimeter was shrinking.

After discussing the situation with his corps commanders, Gort decided that the eastern end of the perimeter could not be held much longer. The Germans were already shelling the beach at De Panne. Gort then drove over to Dunkirk to discuss with Admiral Abrial the necessary arrangements for embarking British and French troops in equal proportions and for the final defense of the perimeter. Gort intended to stay with his troops to the very end, even if that involved their surrender. However, Churchill had something else in mind for the BEF's commander-in-chief.

GORT IS ORDERED HOME, MAY 30

Early in the morning of May 30, Churchill summoned to 10 Downing Street Lord Munster, General Pownall's aide, who had arrived from Dunkirk the previous day. Churchill was taking a bath when Munster arrived, but this prime minister could conduct business anywhere. He asked Munster how the evacuation was going. While telling him, Munster informed him that Gort intended to stay until the end. Churchill was horrified. Why give Hitler a propaganda coup by allowing him to capture and display the BEF's commander-in-chief? he exclaimed.

After discussing the matter with Eden, Dill, and Pownall, Churchill wrote an order in his own hand that left Gort no choice in the matter.

Gort received it at 3:30 that afternoon. It read, in part: "If we can still communicate, we shall send you an order to return to England . . . no personal discretion is left to you in the matter. On political grounds it would be a needless triumph to the enemy to capture you when only a small force remained under your orders."

At 6:00 P.M., Gort read the order aloud to his staff at his beachfront headquarters. They then discussed plans for the final phase of the evacuation. It was decided that the 1st Corps would be the last to go, and its commander, General Michael Barker, would take over from Gort when he left. Barker was told that he must hold out as long as he could and then, when no other option remained, surrender. Barker, in effect, was expendable.

After the meeting, however, General Montgomery asked to talk to Gort, privately. Once the two generals were alone, Montgomery unburdened himself. He said that Barker, a high-strung man given to bouts of anxiety, "was in an unfit state to be left in final command." What was needed, Montgomery suggested, was a man with a calm, clear brain who might well succeed in bringing everyone away and thus avert the necessity to capitulate. Montgomery said such a man was Major General Harold Alexander, the commander of the BEF's 1st Division.

Gort listened but did not commit himself. Like many who came in contact with Montgomery, Gort found his arrogance irritating. But he ultimately would agree that Montgomery was right about Barker, and he would give command of the rear guard to Alexander. When Barker was informed about Gort's change of mind the following day, he broke down and wept from humiliation.

That evening, May 30, Rear Admiral Wake-Walker visited Gort at his De Panne headquarters to work out better coordination between the navy and the army. Gort invited him to stay for dinner. As Wake-Walker sat in the dining room, with its French windows open to the sea, and shared Gort's last bottle of champagne, he was amazed. With their country facing the greatest military disaster in its history, they were making small talk and sipping champagne as though they did not have a care in the world.

There was, however, serious business to discuss after dinner. As far as Gort and his staff were concerned, they had gotten the BEF to the coast more or less intact, and their part of the job was done. Now, it was up to the Royal Navy to get the men home. And in that regard, the generals expressed their collective opinion that the navy, so far, had not done enough.

Wake-Walker tried to explain the difficulty of getting large numbers of men off the beaches. He urged Gort to shift more of the men into Dunkirk, where they could be evacuated from the east mole. But Brigadier General Sir Oliver Leese, the deputy chief of Gort's staff, rejected that suggestion. The army, he said, had marched enough. Except for the "ineptitude of the navy," Leese charged, the men could be evacuated from the beaches.

"I could not let this pass," Wake-Walker recalled, "and told him he had no business or justification to talk like that."

Around 10:00 P.M., Wake-Walker headed back to his flagship, the destroyer *Worcester*. Arriving on the beach, he spotted a large inflated rubber boat and got eight soldiers to paddle him out. As Tennant and Leese watched them depart, the boat, overloaded with men, began to sink. Its passengers jumped out and waded back to the beach. They would make another attempt with fewer paddlers. "Another example of naval ineptitude," Wake-Walker said dryly to Leese.

THE EVACUATION, MAY 31–JUNE 1

At 4:00 A.M. on May 31, Admiral Ramsay issued his order for the day. His plan called for delivering three big batches of ships' lifeboats across the Channel to three points off De Panne. The next morning, the lifeboats would ferry the rearguard of the BEF from the beach to minesweepers waiting offshore. Escorting destroyers, which would provide covering fire if the enemy tried to interfere, were instructed to consider "All tanks hostile." The task of getting the assortment of vessels to De Panne was entrusted, for the most part, to tugs or skoots. However, a few of the larger motor cruisers and yachts also towed smaller craft. What became known as the "special tows" set off from Ramsgate at 1:00 P.M. Soon there was a continuous line of ships stretching over five miles.

Many of the little boats made it across the Channel. But the upriver boats, in particular, had trouble getting across. Towed at speeds faster than they were permitted on the Thames, the ropes that bound them to the towing tugs often ripped off their stanchions. Several times the tugs had to stop and attach new ropes to the lifeboats, only to have them pulled right out of their hulls.

The boats that made it across experienced considerable difficulty getting the soldiers off the beaches. The gentle slope of the sand into the tidal waters caused motor- and rowboats to run aground in knee-deep water. In this awkward position, it was not unusual for boats to be engulfed by as many as a dozen soldiers, whose extra weight would bury the boats' keels deeper into the sand, forcing the passengers to get out, push off, and get back in again.

A coxswain on one of the lifeboats described the difficult conditions off the beach: "There was a nasty surf. Troops were rushing out to us from all directions and were being drowned close to us . . . we could not get to them . . . it seemed to me we were doing more harm than good by drawing the men off the shore, as with their heavy clothing, the surf was knocking them over and they were unable to get up."

At 10:35 A.M., Wake-Walker informed Ramsay that as a result of the poor weather conditions off the beaches, any large-scale embarkation from them was no longer practicable. He suggested that the only hope of embarking any significant number was at Dunkirk. However, Lieutenant Harold J. Dibbens of the Military Police had a brilliant idea. Why not, he asked, push into the water the abandoned trucks that littered the dunes, and use them as makeshift piers? The idea caught on, and as many as fifteen or more trucks were moved into the water and linked together with planks, forming piers as long as 150 yards. With the makeshift piers in place, the small boats could stay in relatively deeper water while they embarked soldiers. Unfortunately, however, the makeshift piers fell apart when the tide swirled back in, causing the trucks to float and rock, and junk to spill into the surf and often into the propeller-driven boats. The makeshift piers would have to be repaired at low tide.

Britain's allies also played a larger role in the evacuation. The French contributed about 50 vessels, mostly small naval craft or fishing boats commandeered by the navy. Several small Belgian fishing craft also participated. They had been sailing along the coast at the time of the German invasion, often carrying refugees, and fled to England when their home ports were seized. Now they returned to the Continent with crews provided by the French navy. With their shallow drafts, the Belgian fishing boats proved to be ideally suited for use in the harbor, whose waters were shallow at low tide and by now filled with wrecks. During the evening of May 31, 16 of the fishing boats sailed right into the Quai Felix-Faure, in the channel linking the inner and outer harbors, and embarked 40 or 50 men each in the space of two and a half hours. They returned safely to Ramsgate at midday on June 1.

General Alan Brooke landed at Dover and, after reporting to Admiral Ramsay, drove to London. He could not get over the contrast between the beauty he saw in the viridian English countryside, unscarred by the horrors of war, and the scenes he had left behind in Belgium and France, with their burning towns, dead horses and cows, broken trees, and exploding guns and bombs. "To have moved straight from that inferno into such a paradise within the spell of a few anguished hours made the contrast all the more wonderful," Brooke recalled. After conferring with General Dill in London, he caught the train to Hartley Wintney, his hometown. Awaiting him there on the platform were his wife and children. They whisked him home and then to bed, where he slept for 36 straight hours.

At Galway in Ireland, another kind of evacuation was in preparation. The liner *President Roosevelt* was on its way to transport back to the United States Americans who were anxious to escape the war zone. When, on June 5, the vessel finally left Galway for the return trip home, it carried 725 passengers instead of the normal 460, crowding some of them into makeshift berths in the ship's post office and baggage compartments. Large American flags were painted on the sides of the ship, which was lit up like a Christmas tree, to leave no doubt about its identity. In addition, both the British and the Germans had been informed of its route. The *Manchester Guardian* reported, "Very few friends [of the passengers] had been able to get to Galway to say good-bye to the Americans returning to a land where there are still lighted streets."

Churchill in Paris, May 31

As Churchill prepared to fly to France on the morning of Friday, May 31, the news concerning the Dunkirk evacuation gave him considerable cause for relief: 133,878 British troops and 11,666 Allied troops, mostly French, had been successfully evacuated as of 7:00 A.M.

Churchill's flight to Paris, however, was somewhat disconcerting. As his plane and its fighter escort approached the airport, the presence of German fighters north of the city forced the British planes to make a wide detour around the city. The failure of Churchill's plane to arrive on time caused those who awaited it to fear the worst. One of them was General Spears. "After a painful period of waiting," he recalled, "some keen-eyed fellow cried that he saw them, then we all did, and almost at once there was a mighty roar. The plane landed, and out stepped the rather hunched but resilient figure of Winston, a stick on which he did not lean in his hand."

Churchill emerged from the plane after it had landed, looking, Spears recalled, "as fresh as a daisy, obviously in grand form. He might not have had a care in the world." Spears was especially pleased when the prime minister approached him, stopped, and then stood for a moment looking directly at him, displaying an enormous grin, and then poked him in the stomach. "This," Spears wrote, "was far more eloquent than any phrase even he might have coined." Churchill and his party then drove off to the French capital, where they were scheduled to meet with Reynaud in his War Ministry office at 2:00 P.M.

The threat of the imminent collapse of France loomed above the meeting of the Supreme Allied War Council that afternoon. Churchill; the British ambassador, Sir Ronald Campbell; and Generals Dill, Ismay, and Spears moved to one side of a large baize-covered table. On the other side, awaiting them, were Reynaud, Marshal Pétain, Admiral Darlan, and General Weygand, the latter wearing a huge pair of riding boots that made him look, Spears commented, "like Puss in Boots."

Ismay, for his part, was struck by the appearance of Pétain. "As we were standing round the table waiting for the discussion to begin," he recounted, "a dejected-looking old man, in plain clothes, shuffled towards me, stretched out his hand and said: 'Pétain.'" It was hard for Ismay to comprehend that this was the great hero of Verdun, the man who had done more than anyone to restore the morale of the French army during World War I. "He now looked senile, uninspiring, and defeatist."

When the meeting began, Churchill spoke first. He thought that the French would be very happy to hear the latest news from Dunkirk: as of noon that day, 165,000 men, including 10,000 wounded, had been evacuated.

"But how many French?" Weygand asked sarcastically. "The French are being left behind."

Churchill looked at the Allied supreme commander for a moment, Spears recalled. "The light had died out of his face, his fingers were playing a tune on the edge of the table; out came his lower lip, as if he were going to retort, and I expected one of those sentences that hit like a blow, but his expression changed again. . . . A wave of deep emotion swept from his heart to his eyes, where tears appeared not for the only time that afternoon." Then he said: "We are companions in misfortune. There is nothing to be gained from recrimination over our common miseries." Spears felt that the note Churchill had struck "was so true, went so deep, that a still- ness fell over the room."

The prime minister then did his best to explain the awkward dispar- ity in numbers. The predominance of British troops among those rescued "up to the present," he said, was primarily because the French troops had received no orders to evacuate. "One of the chief reasons he had come to Paris," Churchill told Reynaud, "was to make sure that the same orders were now given to the French troops as had been given to the British."

Weygand interrupted to say that he had already—only two days ear- lier—ordered the French evacuation to begin and that his orders "were already being acted upon."

The French premier then read a telegram that was to be sent to Admi- ral Abrial. It stated that French troops were to make their way to the points of embarkation, "the British forces embarking first."

At this moment, without waiting for a translation, Churchill inter- rupted, *"Nong! Partage bras dessus, bras dessous* (In partnership, arm in arm)!" The telegram to Abrial was amended. The evacuation of the remaining troops would proceed on equal terms between the British and the French.

To further reassure the French that they were not being abandoned, Churchill went on to promise that the British would keep three divisions on the Dunkirk perimeter in order to enable as many as possible French troops to get away. "So few French have got out so far," he declared, "I will not accept further sacrifices by the French." But the British generals thought this was a lot more than arm-in-arm and was going too far. After more discussion, the final draft of the minutes simply said that the British troops would act as rear guard "as long as possible."

After Churchill promised Reynaud that Britain "would strike hard" at Italy if she entered the war by attacking France, the official phase of the meeting ended. Churchill marked that moment by exclaiming, *"Fini l'a- genda,"* which, Spears noted, "was . . . a sign of either exhilaration or good humor." Churchill, Spears added, "beamed as he said it and this caused general relaxation, a feeling enhanced by the predisposition to pleased amusement among the French whenever he spoke their language."

Churchill, however, was not finished talking. He said, now in English, that he was absolutely convinced that they had only to carry on the fight and inevitable victory would be theirs. The French had been listening only with polite attention.

"Then suddenly," Spears recorded, "his voice changed and the atmo- sphere of the conference was transformed. It was as if the great wings of Rude's Angel leading youth to victory were beating in the room, changing the air, filling it with sound." His words now, Spears continued, "were rolling on like waves, symmetrical and formidable, crashing on to our consciousness."

"If Germany defeated either ally or both," Churchill predicted, "she would give no mercy. We should be reduced to the status of slaves for ever. The peoples of France and Britain were not born to slavery, nor can they endure it. . . . It would be far better, he said, that the civilization of Western Europe, with all its achievements, should come to a tragic but splendid end, than that the two great democracies should linger on, stripped of all that made life worth living."

"The British people will fight on," he promised, "until the New World reconquers the Old." "Even if one of the Allies should be struck down," he said, "the other must not abandon the struggle. Should one of the comrades fall in the battle, the other must not put down his arms until his wounded friend is on his feet again."

Everyone in the room, Spears recalled, "was deeply moved, carried away by the emotion that surged from Winston Churchill in great torrents." Reynaud thanked him for his "inspiring words." He added that if France could hold the Somme with the help of Britain, and if American industry came in to "make good the disparity in arms" now that a great part of France's industrial areas were occupied by Germany, "then they could be certain of victory." If one country went under, Reynaud concluded, "the other would not abandon the struggle." But none of the British knew how far, or for how long, Reynaud would be able to adhere to his promise.

That night, Churchill, Attlee, Dill, and Ismay stayed at the British Embassy in Paris. They were joined for dinner by Reynaud and a few of his aides. During the dinner, as Spears later recalled, Churchill's mind "was running on [about] the creation of bands to attack German tank columns." The French, however, were not impressed. For them, Churchill's suggestions appeared like someone "trying to stop a charging elephant with a pea-shooter."

After Churchill's French guests left and he said good night to his fellow Britons, he walked over to Spears, who was standing alone in the room, to say a few words before taking his leave. "More from his tone than from the few words Winston said," Spears recalled, the prime minister "realized in his heart that the French were beaten, that they knew it, and were resigned to defeat. He had not said so; it was as if he would not permit the thought to dwell consciously in his mind. But he knew."

Before falling asleep, Spears jotted down a final note in his diary about the day's meeting. "One sentence," he wrote, "seems to float over the conference in my memory, like a wisp of cigarette smoke circling over the table, Winston's phrase: 'The partner that survives will go on,' and an impression remains, more vivid than others, the way Reynaud clutched at those words as if to a lifeline."

GORT LEAVES, ALEXANDER TAKES OVER, MAY 31

During the morning of May 31, Lord Gort visited Admiral Abrial's Bastion 32 headquarters for the last time. In addition to Abrial, Generals Fagalde and de la Laurencie were present, and they were joined later in the meeting by General Blanchard.

Gort informed the Frenchmen about the new "equal numbers" evacuation policy and also offered the French equal access to the eastern mole. If it seemed somewhat odd that a British general should be offering French generals the use of a French facility in a French port, they did not express their incredulity. Gort also said that British troops would participate in the perimeter's rear guard and then announced that he had been ordered home. He invited Blanchard and de la Laurencie to accompany him to England, but both politely declined. Said de la Laurencie: "My flag will remain planted on the dunes, until the last of my men have embarked."

Returning to De Panne, Gort summoned General Alexander to the seaside villa that served as his general headquarters. He informed Alexander, a handsome and imperturbable officer of the Irish Guards, that he, rather than Barker, would assume command of the BEF, that is, the remnant still on the Continent: the three rather depleted divisions of the 1st Corps. As agreed to by Churchill during his Paris trip, Gort's successor would serve under Admiral Abrial and "assist our French Allies in the defense of Dunkirk."

However, Gort told Alexander that he could invoke an important escape clause in his orders, if in his judgment that proved necessary. It stated: "Should any order which he [Abrial] may issue to you be likely, in your opinion, to imperil the safety of your command, you should make an immediate appeal to His Majesty's Government." Appended to it was the War Office's authorization to surrender if that proved necessary "to avoid useless slaughter." At six o'clock that evening, Gort was ferried out to a waiting destroyer that would take him back to England.

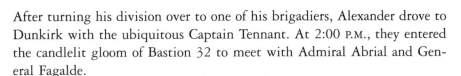

After turning his division over to one of his brigadiers, Alexander drove to Dunkirk with the ubiquitous Captain Tennant. At 2:00 P.M., they entered the candlelit gloom of Bastion 32 to meet with Admiral Abrial and General Fagalde.

Abrial informed Alexander that he intended to hold the perimeter until all troops, French as well as British, were embarked. A French corps would continue to defend the Allied right flank, which extended from Gravelines to Bergues (even though Gravelines was now under German control). Abrial wanted Alexander, with a mixed French and British corps, to defend a line running from Bergues to Les Moeres and onward to the sea. The task of Alexander's corps would be to act as a rear guard, holding the beachhead indefinitely, while the rest of the Allied troops embarked. Then, presumably, the rear guard also would be evacuated.

After Abrial finished explaining his plan, Alexander stunned the admiral by stating bluntly that he had no intention of serving as a rear guard for the French army. He said that Lord Gort, before leaving, had instructed him to withdraw as many troops as possible to the sea for embarkation, and to do so by midnight.

But just that morning, Abrial interjected, Gort had promised that Alexander would help defend the perimeter as long as necessary to permit the greatest possible number of French soldiers to be evacuated.

"General," Abrial scolded Alexander, "you must stay. It is a matter of England's honor. French soldiers have let themselves be killed to protect the embarkation of the British army. Now your last troops must take part in the defense of Dunkirk to permit the evacuation of the greater part of our troops."

To Alexander, however, it was not a matter of honor, but rather—although he would not have said so out loud—his lack of confidence in Abrial's judgment. The admiral's continuing reluctance to leave his subterranean fortress, in Alexander's view, rendered him incapable of appreciating what was possible and what was not. Alexander bluntly said that Abrial's plan would not work. Protracted resistance, he explained, was out of the question; the troops were simply too tired to continue fighting. When Abrial suggested that they shorten the defense perimeter, Alexander responded by saying that such a move would bring the harbor and the beaches within range of German artillery and imperil the evacuation. As an alternative, Alexander proposed that they wind up the evacuation as soon as possible, by the following night, June 1–2. Abrial was unimpressed. If the British insisted on leaving, he threatened, "I am afraid the port will be closed."

Alexander decided it was time to invoke the escape clause in his orders. He would have to refer the matter to London. Hurrying back to BEF headquarters at De Panne, he was relieved to see the telephone connection with London was still intact. He called Anthony Eden and told him that the delay Abrial had in mind would lead to the loss of some of Britain's finest troops. Eden, who apparently was not yet informed about Churchill's Paris offer to use British troops as the Allied rear guard, agreed. He authorized Alexander to wind up the evacuation of British troops by dawn on June 2. However, Alexander also was instructed to embark his troops "on a 50–50 basis with the French army." Alexander agreed to do just that. However, since there were still almost 200,000 French soldiers in the perimeter, and not much over 50,000 British, a withdrawal by equal numbers meant the British still would be leaving the French in the lurch.

While Alexander was calling Eden, Abrial wired General Weygand. He complained that Alexander had refused to follow his instructions to fight on and instead had announced that he planned to embark the last British troops on the night of June 1–2, "thus abandoning the defense of Dunkirk." Weygand, however, could do little more than pass Abrial's complaint to London.

In the meantime, Alexander arrived back from De Panne and informed Abrial that he would hold his sector of the perimeter until the end of the next day and then withdraw to the beaches under cover of darkness. He added that the French could share British shipping if they also withdrew. Abrial decided that he had no alternative but to accept Alexander's dictat.

By now it was after 11:00 P.M. Alexander did not want to risk trying to get to his new headquarters in the dark, so he decided to stay overnight at Abrial's bastion. He and his aide, Colonel Morgan, went to sleep on the concrete floor, which seemed to be as hard and as cold as the relationship between the two Allied military commands.

THE GERMAN ATTACK
ON THE PERIMETER, MAY 31

For the Germans on May 31, it was hard to escape the feeling that the battle for Dunkirk was all but over. Some 10 German infantry divisions were engaging a few thousand Allied soldiers. It seemed to the Germans that only one more push would finish off Dunkirk, but no one yet was assigned the task of arranging it. There were too many overlapping commands and too little coordination between the German armies attacking the perimeter.

Brauchitsh and Halder were still fuming about Hitler's decision to halt the panzer drive toward Dunkirk. "The pocket would have been closed at the coast if only our armor had not been held back," Halder complained in his diary. "As it is, the bad weather has grounded our air force and now we must stand by and watch countless thousands of the enemy getting away to England, right under our noses." However, Halder's attention also had drifted from Dunkirk. He spent most of the day far behind the lines, checking communications, the flow of supplies, and the status of Army Group C, all as a way of preparing for the next phase of the campaign against France, Plan Red.

Finally, at 2:00 A.M. on May 31, one man was put in complete charge of the 35-mile-long Dunkirk front: General Georg von Kuechler, the commander of the 18th Army. The next morning, Kuechler would launch a simultaneous attack by all his forces along the entire length of the perimeter. Surprisingly, the relatively leisurely pace of the German preparations was not accelerated even after an intercepted British radio message announced that the BEF was abandoning the eastern end of the perimeter that night. As a result, Kuechler lost a golden opportunity to attack the British forces when they were most vulnerable: on the beaches, awaiting evacuation.

Nevertheless, the preparatory artillery bombardment and the intensified Luftwaffe attacks that began during the afternoon of May 31 did increase the pressure on the ever-thinning British lines. Singled out for special attention were the dunes west of Nieuport, where British artillery was giving Kuechler's 256th Infantry Division an especially hard time. The Luftwaffe attacked it roughly every 15 minutes; the Germans even sent an observation balloon aloft to direct artillery fire on that sector.

Earlier that day, May 31, near Nieuport, German infantry broke through the Dunkirk perimeter for the first time. They crossed the canal in rubber boats and stormed the brickworks held by the 6th Battalion East Surreys. By noon, the British troops were in danger of being outflanked, but before that could happen, they were reinforced by their "sister" battalion, the 1st East Surreys. Together, the two battalions were able to stop the German advance.

Later in the afternoon, however, the Germans began massing for another assault across the canal. Fortunately for the exhausted Surreys, 18 RAF bombers, supported by six planes from the fleet air arm, swept in from the sea and bombed and scattered the German infantry. It marked the first and only time in the campaign that British ground forces received close air support.

Civilians also played a part in resisting the German advance. One was Jean Duriez, the mayor of Steene, a small town near Bergues, who also was an industrial alcohol manufacturer. Duriez opened the faucets of his factory's 10 vast stills and sent two million gallons of raw spirits gushing across the countryside. To his astonishment, the flooded fields were turned into a raging sea of flames by an exploding artillery shell. The inferno turned two panzers into white-hot hulks and brought the German advance on Steene to an immediate halt.

Just to the east of Bergues, along the canal that extended to Furnes, the 2nd Coldstream Guards defended some 2,200 yards of the Allied front. Lieutenant Jimmy Langley's platoon garrisoned a small brick cottage directly north of the canal. He described the cottage as "a fine example of a Flemish farm cottage, standing in its own land, overlooking the canal, with a superb view over the fields both towards the sea and inland."

Langley, a particularly lively and immensely resourceful Guardsman, had converted the cottage into a miniature Gibraltar. The 37 men of the company, of which Langley's platoon was a part, had scrounged up an impressive arsenal of weapons from the scores of trucks that had been abandoned along the canal bank: 12 Bren guns, three Lewis machine guns, one Boyes anti-tank rifle, 30,000 rounds of ammunition, and 22 hand grenades. In the attic of the cottage, Langley's men used some pieces of old furniture and several crates of empty beer bottles to construct two Bren gun nests. "Careful removal of the roof tiles," Langley recorded, "gave the gunners good observation, and I much doubted if the muzzles of the guns would be spotted even by the keenest Hun eye." The only drawback of Langley's "Gibraltar" was that neither its roof nor its walls appeared strong enough to protect its defenders against enemy fire. However, under attack they could jump to the relative safety of the ground floor or nearby slit trenches in a matter of seconds.

Nor was Langley's platoon hurting for food. "The living room-kitchen in the cottage," he recalled, "took on the appearance of a small country grocer's shop, with stacks of bully beef, tinned milk, vegetables, and stew, but best of all, marmalade and Wiltshire bacon." There also were plenty of chickens around the farm, as well as a cow. In addition, he recalled, "some genius found two cases of white wine, *tres ordinaire* but nonetheless very drinkable, and a couple of crates of beer." Two buckets of cold water, for the dual purpose of cooling the wine, the beer, and the Bren gun barrels, completed Langley's preparations for the expected German attack the next morning.

Langley and his men spent the rest of the afternoon watching spectacular aerial dogfights over Dunkirk. They obviously were pleased, as Langley recorded, when they "saw more than one German bomber go down in flames." The only aircraft that came anywhere near their position was a British Lysander, flying very low along the canal. Langley's men had been ordered to treat all low-flying aircraft as the enemy, regardless of their markings. "I happened to be standing by a Bren on anti-aircraft mountings and got in a good burst," he wrote, "without success, I am pleased to say, as I was later informed that it contained Lord Gort, who was having a last look at the final line of the BEF."

EVACUATION FROM DE PANNE, MAY 31

That afternoon, because of the increasing German pressure on the eastern perimeter, Admiral Ramsay was told by General Alexander's headquarters that the plan to evacuate the rear guard of the BEF had to be changed. It was no longer possible to defend the original position with only 4,000 troops, so the perimeter would have to be shortened. Under the new plan, De Panne would be abandoned. The troops on its surrounding beaches would be moved westward to Bray, Malo, and Dunkirk. The troops on the far left of the perimeter would disengage first, after last light, and fall back on De Panne beach, where they would be evacuated. Speed and guile were essential, needless to say, because once the Germans realized what was happening, they were sure to charge into the evacuated area.

For the Royal Navy, the change in the army's defensive plan required concentrating the special towboats and the minesweepers into a stretch of sea opposite the beach, from Zuydcoote to a point one mile east of De Panne. In addition, the commencement of the operation would have to be advanced by one hour. There was, however, a risk involved in changing the plan, since the tugboats pulling the tows were not in communication with Ramsey's headquarters. Consequently, it was necessary for the minesweepers to make sure that the tugs delivered their towboats to the new evacuation positions.

That night, beginning about 10:00 P.M. and continuing until about 2:30 A.M., British soldiers all along the eastern end of the perimeter fell

back on De Panne. But despite the cover of darkness, crossing through
that city to get to its beach was a perilous undertaking. Much of the once
prosperous and modern city, its main streets lined with new buildings of
concrete and glass, was in ruins. To make the withdrawal even more dangerous, German spotter planes were dropping flares to light up the city.
They were followed by "the thump of distant guns followed by the whine
of approaching shells," one soldier remembered. Officers yelled, "Off the
streets! Into the shops!" The soldiers needed no prodding. Their rifle butts
quickly shattered great plate-glass windows of shops that might provide
protection from the German bombardment. In front of one restaurant,
however, the soldiers were confronted by the owner, who, behind its glass
window, gesticulated excitedly to the troops to spare it. The soldiers
paused, butts poised, while the owner hastily unlocked his glass door,
allowing them in, plate glass still intact.

For Wake-Walker, who was on his flagship, the destroyer *Keith,* off
De Panne, everything was black that night. Ships and boats offshore
showed no lights, and although arrangements had been made for lights to
be shown toward the sea to guide boats inshore, none could be seen. During the darkness, low-flying German aircraft were patrolling continually
overhead and promptly bombing all lights they could observe, which no
doubt explains why Wake-Walker did not see the prearranged shore lights.

   Wake-Walker had received a message from the shore that thousands of
men were waiting but there were no boats to lift them off. Yet other messages from the rescue ships, inexplicably off Bray rather then De Panne,
said that their boats could find no one on the beach. At 10:23 P.M., Wake-
Walker asked Ramsay to inform Captain Tennant in Dunkirk that the
troops around De Panne had to be moved down to Bray.

Around midnight, Royal Navy Lieutenant Commander J. W. McClelland
was making his way along the beach toward Bray. McClelland, who was in
charge of naval signal arrangements at De Panne, heard rifle shots in the
distance. He soon learned that the shots were coming from groups of soldiers firing rifles into the air, trying to attract the attention of the ships at
anchor offshore.

   Realizing that there were ships off Bray, but without his signal lamp,
which had been smashed by a splinter from an exploding artillery shell,

McClelland decided to swim out to the ships. However, a wound in his ankle, from the same shell explosion that had smashed his lamp, made what otherwise would have been a good exercise an exhausting ordeal. He finally was picked up by the minesweeper *Gossamer*. Before collapsing, he was able to tell her captain about the change in the evacuation plan and that men were waiting on the shore. He asked the captain to inform both Wake-Walker and Ramsay and ask them to send more boats.

But Ramsay could offer no more help. In spite of the enormous number of boats sent over to Dunkirk that day, the flotilla—crippled by weather, accidents, mechanical breakdowns, exhaustion of crews, and enemy action—was still unable to meet the needs of the soldiers. Accordingly, the *Gossamer*'s urgent request for more boats received the curt reply: "It is now impracticable to send more boats. You must do your utmost with yours."

For the troops on the beaches, as the night slowly gave way to dawn, rescue back to England still seemed a long way off. However, despite the difficulties and delays, the anguish and the casualties, by midnight on May 31, the sixth day of Operation Dynamo, 68,014 more men had been brought back to England—more than on any day so far. Moreover, that day, for the first time, British ships evacuated a respectable number of Frenchmen: 10,842. This was not enough to satisfy Reynaud, but it was at least a beginning. Yet London's growing elation with the unexpected success of the evacuation was severely tempered by the realization that tens of thousands of men still remained on the Continent, and that the chances of saving them were growing slimmer by the hour.

That evening, Captain Tennant visited General Alexander. "I suppose," he said, "if they break through, we shall have to capitulate. How does one capitulate?"

"I don't know," Alexander replied. "I have never had to capitulate."

The Defense of the Perimeter, June 1

As first light appeared over Lieutenant Jimmy Langley's fortress cottage on the morning of Saturday, June 1, the fields were covered with a thick mist. It rapidly disappeared as the sun rose and revealed, to the utter astonishment of the lieutenant and his platoon, some hundred or so German soldiers standing in a field of dew-covered corn about 600 yards away. Langley took a quick glance through his binoculars and saw that the Germans were holding spades, rather than rifles, in an utterly lackadaisical way, presumably preparing to move off.

Suddenly Langley's section commander shouted, "Number-1 gun, 600. Number-2 gun, 800. Fire!" The burst from the Number-1 gun cut through the corn field about 50 yards short of its intended target.

"Both guns, 700!" Langley yelled above the din. The resulting massacre—it was not less—made him slightly sick. "The corn," he recalled, "was high enough to conceal a man till he started to crawl, but that did not really matter, as we simply sprayed the whole area for a couple of minutes till nothing moved."

Then Langley got another surprise. From a group of buildings about 1,000 yards away, several figures emerged, formed themselves into a rough line, and started to advance. As they approached, he saw that they were civilians, mainly women, with an odd German soldier here and there, carrying a stretcher on his shoulder. Their object was clear: collecting up anyone they could lay their hands on to carry back the wounded and to shield themselves against more British fire. The Germans were relying—correctly, as it turned out—on the assumption that the British guns would not fire on women and old men. However, British rifles did continue firing, and three more Germans went down.

Around midday, the Germans mounted an attack on the area where the bridge across the canal had been blown. Langley's platoon made good use of its Bren guns until the inevitable occurred. The Germans rushed up what looked like an anti-tank gun on wheels. Langley's men watched with interest as it was pointed their way and then was fired. At first, nothing happened. Then, as they turned a Bren gun toward the German weapon, a frightful explosion knocked them over, followed by a brightly lit object that whizzed around the attic and finally came to rest at the foot of the brick chimney stack. One glance was enough for Langley: it was an incendiary anti-tank shell. The British soldiers, Bren guns and all, jumped to the ground floor. The Germans put four more shells into the attic and then stopped firing. After a decent interval, Langley and his men climbed back into the attic but were unable to see the Germans, who by now were out of sight in the houses of the small hamlet on their side of the bridge.

Just then, Langley's company commander, Major Angus McCorquodale, arrived. McCorquodale was a throwback to an earlier, glorious age in British military history. He scorned the new battle uniform, preferring, and wearing, traditional polished brass and leather. "I don't mind dying for my country," he declared, "but I'm not going to die dressed like a third-rate chauffeur."

While waiting for the next German attack, Langley regaled McCorquodale with the gist of an interview that he and his men had heard over their portable radio. It was conducted with a soldier who alleged that he was the last man out of Dunkirk. This soldier bragged that he had managed to hold back the advancing Germans singlehandedly until he jumped into a boat and escaped across the Channel.

Shortly afterward, Langley's conversation with McCorquodale was interrupted by the arrival of the captain who commanded the company on their right flank. He said that the Germans were massing for an attack on the bridgehead; he proposed that they withdraw while the going was good. McCorquodale merely said: "I order you to stay put and fight it out!"

"You cannot do that," the captain responded. "I have over-riding orders from my colonel to withdraw when I think fit."

McCorquodale did not beat around the bush. "You see that big poplar tree on the road, with the white mile stone beside it? The moment you or any of your men go back beyond that tree, we will shoot you."

The startled captain began to expostulate, but McCorquodale cut him short. "Get back or I will shoot you now and send one of my officers to take command," and his hand moved toward his revolver. The captain departed without saying another word.

Some minutes later, the German artillery opened up on the British positions. Shells exploded all along the canal bank and uncomfortably close to Langley's cottage. The German infantry then attempted to advance, but were eventually stopped down the road from Langley's cottage. After the firing had died away, Major McCorquodale got a couple of bottles of sherry and some glasses and shared them with Langley's men. Raising his glass, McCorquodale proposed a toast: "To a very gallant and competent enemy."

Somewhat later, the Germans resumed their attack. Langley and his men climbed back into the attic with their Bren guns and managed to set three German trucks on fire, effectively blocking the road. Nevertheless, the Germans got into a cottage on the other side of the canal, opposite Langley's. They poked a machine-gun through its partially blown-away roof, but Langley's men blasted it away with a Bren gun before it could fire.

Langley then engaged in his favorite "sport": sniping with a rifle at anything that moved. "I had just fired five most satisfactory shots," he remembered, "and, convinced I had chalked up another 'kill,' was kneeling, pushing another clip into the rifle, when there was a most frightful crash and a great wave of heat; dust and debris knocked me over. A shell had burst on the roof. There was a long silence and I heard a small voice saying 'I've been hit,' which I suddenly realized was mine."

Langley was hit in the arm. Covered with blood, he was half-carried, half helped down from the cottage's attic loft and then placed into a wheelbarrow. Somewhat later, splints made out of a broken wooden box were tied around his arm. He then was put into an ambulance and rushed off. After a bumpy ride that seemed to last for hours, the door of the ambulance finally opened. As Langley's stretcher was pulled out, he could see sand dunes in the half-light of the next day's dawn. Then he heard a voice say, "This way. The beach is about two hundred yards ahead of you."

A gray lifeboat lay at the water's edge with a man in a long dark blue naval overcoat standing by it. He came over to Langley. "Can you get off your stretcher?"

"No, I do not think so," Langley replied.

"Well, I am very sorry, we cannot take you. Your stretcher would occupy the places of four men. Orders are, only those who can stand or sit up."

Langley said nothing. He was too tired to sit up, stand up, or argue.

He was carried back to the ambulance and then driven to a bombed-out building in Dunkirk. There he encountered a new face and a gruff hard voice. "Have you had your anti-tetanus injection and when?"

"Never."

"Just like you bloody officers. Avoid anything unpleasant. I hope this kills you!"

A large syringe, Langley remembered, "more suitable for a horse than a man, full of grey liquid," was pushed into his right arm. He then was left to his own devices.

The Evacuation, June 1–2

On the bridge of the destroyer *Keith,* Rear Admiral Wake-Walker had greeted the mist and low clouds of the morning with relief. But the "good" weather did not last. The cloud cover lifted, and soon thereafter, swarms of German aircraft returned to the skies over the harbor and beaches. The enemy planes were able to inflict destruction at leisure on the rescue ships in the lengthy intervals between the RAF patrols over the evacuation area. Wave after wave of German dive-bombers, medium bombers, and fighters roared out of a cloudless sky to attack rescue vessels as they arrived from across the Channel, or were taking on men, or were headed back to England. Soldiers waiting on the beaches saw ships they expected to carry them to England hit, set ablaze, and sunk.

Keith's antiaircraft guns used up all their ammunition beating off the first German attack. As a consequence, the destroyer was defenseless when the German second wave began. Bombs wrecked her engine room and blew open a hole below her waterline. Wake-Walker watched the aerial attack from the destroyer's bridge. "It was an odd sensation, waiting for the explosions, and knowing that you could do nothing." He decided to transfer to a motor torpedo boat and was rapidly followed overboard by the *Keith*'s crew and the soldiers it had just lifted from the beaches.

Another naval officer who also feared his ship was about to sink was the captain of the destroyer *Ivanhoe*. Although his ship was damaged and under attack, he shouted out to the destroyer *Havant*, which had come close to render assistance, "Get out of here or you'll end up the same as us!" He was too late. Suddenly the *Havant* was hit by bombs that quickly sent her to the bottom, near the entrance of the harbor. The *Ivanhoe*, however, was spared that fate. She was taken in tow and hauled back to England.

All totaled, three destroyers were sunk that Saturday, June 1, while four more were damaged seriously. Personnel vessels also took a battering that day.

As before, bitter complaints were voiced at the RAF for failing to provide adequate aerial protection over the evacuation ships. But RAF Fighter Command was working at a serious disadvantage: it did not have enough planes to provide continuous coverage over Dunkirk and the beaches. The Luftwaffe, on the other hand, could pick the time and place of its attacks. Only by keeping the intervals between patrols as brief as possible and through sheer luck could British fighters challenge and disrupt some of the enemy raids. Nevertheless, the RAF lost 31 aircraft that day, compared to 29 for the Germans.

At Dunkirk during the late afternoon of June 1, Captain Tennant became alarmed by the damage that the German planes were inflicting on the rescue ships. He watched six Stukas dive-bomb the old destroyer HMS *Worcester*, pounding her every five minutes without mercy. After the severely damaged destroyer limped away from the harbor, at a crippling 10 knots and with a horrifying casualty list of 350 dead and 400 wounded, Tennant radioed Admiral Ramsay: "Things are getting very hot for ships; over 100 bombs since 05:30; many casualties. Have directed that no ships sail during daylight. Evacuation by transports therefore ceases at 03:00." Tennant also informed Ramsay, with General Alexander's concurrence, that if the perimeter continued to hold, evacuation of the BEF would be completed on the following night. By that time, Tennant believed, it would be possible to lift off most of the French troops as well.

All that morning, the top commands at London, Dover, and Dunkirk also were increasingly alarmed by the pounding the rescue fleet was taking. Of the 41 destroyers that had begun the evacuation, only nine were still operational. When the last remaining daylight route, "X," came under German artillery fire that evening, Ramsay decided to suspend daylight evacuations as of 3:00 A.M., June 2.

With daylight evacuations ended, Ramsay decided to send to Dunkirk all the shipping, both British and French, that he could find for one last great liftoff during the night. All minesweepers, skoots, and small craft, except certain specially organized flotillas, were ordered to sail to the beaches east of Dunkirk. The larger personnel ships, as well as eight destroyers, were to enter Dunkirk harbor and evacuate soldiers from the east mole.

GORT IN LONDON, JUNE 1

That morning, Lord Gort arrived back in London to attend a meeting of the War Cabinet. Although its members gave him a warm reception, Gort did not, of course, return as a conquering hero. Yet he had done as much as, if not more, than anyone to save the BEF, and he did so in the face of orders that were often ill-informed, confusing, and, in reality, detrimental to the army's interests.

Obviously, the War Cabinet was anxious to hear his estimate of the prospects for getting the rest of the troops home. Gort told them that the defense line probably would hold until the following morning, but it might be a near thing. Still not impressed with Churchill's unceasing insistence that as many French troops as possible should be rescued, even if it might entail British losses, Gort said that every effort should be made to complete the evacuation that night. Apparently unaware that the successful withdrawal of the BEF owed much to the determined resistance of the French rear guard, Gort said he doubted if many French troops of fighting quality remained in the perimeter. He obviously projected onto the average *poilu* the contempt he felt for the French high command, whose incompetence he believed was responsible for his inglorious return to England.

Gort's recommendation that Dynamo should be wound up that night was echoed by the service chiefs. Admiral Sir Dudley Pound, chief of the naval staff, reported that nearly all the destroyers engaged in the operation had suffered at least some degree of damage. Moreover, the Germans had moved guns into position to shell the last Channel route through which ships had been able to reach Dunkirk with a measure of safety. In Pound's opinion, the risks of continuing the evacuation beyond sunrise the following day had become prohibitive.

The RAF was also reeling from its accumulating losses and, therefore, supported the navy's call for ending the operation that night. During the previous three weeks, Fighter Command had been operating at a rate far in excess of its ability to replace lost pilots and aircraft. Britain's fighter plane strength was said to be "already considerably below the minimum essential" for the defense of the country. Sending more Spitfires and Hurricanes to France would not only imperil the nation's defense, it would also be a futile gesture, for they could not save the French army.

However, Churchill refused to be swayed by the service chiefs. Having returned from Paris earlier that morning, where he had the previous day assured France's leaders that Britain would not abandon her, he insisted that it was essential to continue the evacuation until as many as possible of the French troops within the perimeter could be rescued. Churchill, however, was persuaded to allow General Alexander, the British commander on the spot, to decide when to wind up the evacuation. Of course, neither Churchill nor the War Cabinet yet knew that Alexander had already told Admiral Abrial that the reduced British rear guard was pulling out that night.

When, later that day, Churchill was informed that this would be the last night of the evacuation, he was compelled to cable Reynaud and Weygand to explain why—contrary to the promise he had given them in Paris—British troops would not fight until the last Frenchman was evacuated. "It is desirable that the embarkation should cease this night," he wrote. "Up to the present, 225,000 men have been shipped. Abrial would like to prolong the embarkation, but he is perhaps not the best judge, since he directs operations from a bunker. The generals on the spot should be left the responsibility of deciding when the embarkation should cease."

Not surprisingly, Churchill's message did not please Reynaud. "I note," the premier said icily to General Spears, who personally delivered Churchill's cable, "that the decision to have a united command only lasted twenty-four hours."

Reynaud's anger was aggravated by reports that French officers were being grossly abused by the British at Dunkirk. He had heard that a French general and his aide had been pulled off a rescue ship and told that if they embarked, two less British soldiers would be evacuated.

By now, however, Spears had stopped trying to smooth over the differences between Paris and London. He was now answering charge with countercharge. The French general allegedly mistreated at Dunkirk, he suggested, must have been trying to use his rank to save his own skin, not the lives of the troops under his command. Spears also firmly rejected Reynaud's criticism of Gort's performance, asserting that if the BEF commander had any failing, it was that he had not complained enough about "the abysmal collapse of the . . . French generals."

Ignoring Spears's reply, Reynaud asked, if the commanders on the spot had to make the decision to stop the evacuation, why not rely on Abrial rather than Alexander? Spears, echoing Churchill's earlier response to the same question, replied that Abrial did not often leave his bunker to see what was going on. He was not "*l'amiral* Abrial, but *l'amiral* Abri"—*abri* means a bombproof shelter. It was a "poor pun," Spears admitted, "but it helped to lower the tension."

Yet even General Alexander soon came to realize that he would not be able to complete the evacuation of the BEF by the next morning, June 2. There were still over 39,000 British troops in the perimeter, and over 100,000 French. Applying the equal numbers policy, it obviously would be impossible to lift off the required minimum of 78,000 men in the next 24 hours. Alexander now wanted more time. At 8:00 A.M., he dropped by Abrial's headquarters with a new withdrawal plan, extending the evacuation through the night of June 2–3. Abrial accepted it gladly. Captain Tennant also thought the evacuation had to be extended. There was no alternative once he had made the decision to end daylight operations.

Although the War Office in London doubted the wisdom of extending the evacuation, it also admitted that it did not know enough to make the decision. As a result, at 6:41 P.M., General Dill wired Alexander: "Impossible from here to judge local situation. In close cooperation with Admiral Abrial, you must act in this matter on your own judgment."

Alexander now had a green light. The evacuation would continue through the night of June 2–3, as he and Captain Tennant had proposed. Yet whether or not it would succeed still depended on Tennant's precondition: "if the perimeter holds." But *could* the perimeter hold another day?

Now it all depended on French soldiers. They—and not, as Churchill had promised in Paris on May 31, British soldiers—would act as the Allied rear guard. British troops were withdrawing from the front line through French formations, which were now holding, as previously arranged, a reduced inner perimeter. The French rear guard was comprised of part of the 32nd Infantry Division and the 5th Fortress Division, manning the center of the perimeter; the 60th and 12th Infantry Divisions, deployed in the old fortifications that lined the Belgian frontier; and the 68th Infantry Division, which had been defending the western flank since the beginning of Operation Dynamo.

These French forces received their first test on the afternoon of June 1, when Kuechler's divisions finally made contact with them. The Germans were stopped cold on the extreme eastern end of the perimeter by the 12th Division. It was the same story all the way to its western end. On the 12th's right, the 32nd Division launched a counterattack to retain a footing in Teteghem. On the western end, the 75mm guns of General Beaufrère's 68th Division, firing over open sights, managed to repulse an attack by the 9th Panzer Division, which was brought back into action to reinforce the attack. The French, fighting with magnificent spirit, held the Germans at bay while the remaining British units converged on Dunkirk all through the night of June 1–2.

All totaled, 64,429 men returned to England on June 1, the second-highest amount in the operation. The number lifted off the beaches fell (to 17,348) as the troops pulled back from De Panne, but a record 47,081 were rescued from Dunkirk itself. And for the first time, the number of French evacuated that day, 35,013, exceeded the number of British evacuees, at 29,416. At last, Churchill's promise of evacuation *bras dessus, bras dessous* had become an accomplished fact.

THE EVACUATION, JUNE 2–3

At 3:00 A.M. on June 2, the last ships at Dunkirk's east mole pulled up their gangplanks and set sail, to avoid further loss during the hours of daylight. However, as the ships left, the mole was still crowded with troops, standing four abreast, British on the right, French on the left. Fortunately for these soldiers, German guns fired only an occasional shell at this lucrative target and almost always missed. Realizing the night's evacuation was over, the soldiers turned about and returned to the relative safety of the dunes and Malo's cellars, there to await the return of darkness.

No one knew exactly how many troops remained. Tennant estimated that number at about 5,000 British and 30,000 French troops, but Dover believed an additional 2,000 British troops might be found in Dunkirk. As for the remaining French, Admiral Abrial estimated their number at 65,000. He hoped that 30,000 could be evacuated the next night and the remaining 35,000, who were holding the bridgeheads, on the following night.

Admiral Ramsay, however, was no longer certain that the crews manning the rescue ships could get them off. The men were exhausted. Except for brief catnaps, they had not slept for five straight days or more. It was not unusual to see ships returning to English ports with almost every crew member, including most officers, fast asleep. There were reports of men losing control or coming down with mysterious afflictions. For all, the prospect of going back to Dunkirk still another time was agonizing. Once again, they would have to dodge German shells, bombs, torpedoes, and bullets, and do so with their senses and nerves already strained to the limit.

Nevertheless, at 10:52 A.M. on June 2, Ramsay once again signaled destroyers and minesweepers to make another grand effort: "The final evacuation is staged for tonight, and the Nation looks to the Navy to see this through. I want every ship to report as soon as possible whether she is fit to meet the call which has been made on our courage and endurance."

The replies showed that despite the exhaustion that gripped the ships' crews, the men had not lost their fighting spirit. Officers responded that their crews were "fit and ready," or "ready and anxious to carry out your orders."

At 5:00 P.M. on June 2, the "final" lift of troops began. The rescue armada comprised 13 personnel vessels, 11 destroyers, 14 minesweepers, nine drifters, and a large number of tugs towing small boats. They were joined by a host of small craft and a contingent of French and Belgian boats.

Meanwhile, General Kuechler's infantry were still pinned down along the Bergues–Furnes canal line. If they could capture Bergues, the Germans would have gained access to the two good roads that ran directly to Dunkirk, just five miles to the north. But taking the town would not be easy. It was encircled by thick walls and a moat, both of which were designed by the great French military engineer Vauban. Dug in behind them was a garrison of 1,000 French troops, supported by strong artillery plus Allied naval guns off Dunkirk.

At 3:00 P.M. on June 2, the Germans began a coordinated attack on the town using Stukas and specially trained shock troops. Following a 15-minute bombardment by the Stukas, the shock troops, equipped with flamethrowers and assault ladders, stormed the wall. The French garrison, dazed by the Stuka bombardment, surrendered almost immediately.

By dusk, the Germans had advanced northward and captured Fort Vallières, only three miles from Dunkirk. There they were stopped by a costly French counterattack hastily assembled by General Fagalde.

Nevertheless, toward midnight, the weary French defenders began withdrawing from the defensive perimeter to the harbor, where they expected to be evacuated.

Kuechler did not press the attack. Why take unnecessary risks now that the campaign seemed almost over?

A couple of hours earlier, Tennant had sent Dover this message: "French still maintain front line. . . . In port, no movement. Present situation hopeful." In fact, for the first time, Tennant believed he would see England again after all. He sent for his dispatch rider, Tom Willy, and asked him to summon the remaining British officers who were still on duty along the inner perimeter to a meeting. Tennant would tell them that the final withdrawal would take place that night.

Willy was relieved when he realized that this would be his last trip to Bastion 32. "I used to dread it," he recalled. "There was a great big French *matelot* on guard there with a .45 revolver, drunk as a saint. He used to stop me every time and poke this thing into my chest, cocked, and ask for my identification. That man frightened the life out of me."

At 10:50 P.M., Tennant loaded the last of his naval party onto a waiting torpedo boat and before leaving radioed Ramsay: "Operation complete. Returning to Dover." The message was subsequently shortened for posterity to one of the most triumphant in the history of the Royal Navy: "BEF evacuated."

At about the same time, General Alexander also prepared to leave. Before doing so, however, he toured the shore of the darkened beaches in a motorboat, inquiring, with a megaphone, in English and in French, if anyone remained. There was no reply. Alexander and his party left Dunkirk on the destroyer.

Yet while the BEF was evacuated successfully, there were still tens of thousands of French soldiers in and about Dunkirk. Ironically, at 1:30 A.M. on June 3, a bewildered Wake-Walker had several vessels berthed at the mole, but no French troops could be found. He signaled Dover, "Plenty of ships. Cannot get troops."

Something had gone wrong. There certainly was a breakdown in communications between the two Allied commands. The British were unaware that the French soldiers who were supposed to have been evacuated were still busy repelling the German attack. In addition, the fierce enemy bombardment had prevented British ships from getting close to the beaches, where they would have found French troops awaiting embarkation. When no shore boats came out to them, the British vessels departed.

From Wake-Walker's perspective, it was pointless and dangerous to keep ships tied up at the mole waiting for evacuees who did not show up. At 2:30 A.M., he ordered home the destroyer *Vanquisher.* It returned with only 37 evacuees that it had picked up from a small boat outside the harbor. Another destroyer, *Malcolm,* returned to Dover with no evacuees at all. Several other ships waited an hour or more before heading back to England, also with no evacuees.

It was not until about 2:30 A.M. that the first of the French perimeter defenders, having successfully repelled the German counterattack, began filing onto the mole. By then, however, most of the rescue ships had gone back to England.

Then, at 3:10 A.M., three block ships, which were to be sunk at the harbor's entrance to prevent its use by the Germans, were towed to the mouth of the harbor. But the job was bungled. The current caught one of the sinking block ships and turned it parallel to the channel, leaving plenty of room for ships to enter and leave.

Rear Admiral Wake-Walker had expected to evacuate 37,000 men that night. Instead, he had to settle for 26,256. Between midnight and 3:00 A.M. on June 3, he estimated that a lifting capacity of about 10,000 men had not been used because the French had failed to show up. On returning to England, the crews of the relatively empty vessels complained that they had spent hours waiting in vain for French troops. This news spread like wildfire, prompting outbursts against the French for uselessly endangering British ships and their crews.

The French, however, were also angry with the British. By the time the evacuation came to an end at first light on the morning of June 3, 222,568 British troops had been removed from the Continent. However, less than 70,000 French troops had been evacuated. Moreover, there were still 30,000 or 40,000 French soldiers in Dunkirk and on the surrounding beaches. The determined resistance of many of these troops had made possible the evacuation of the BEF in its entirety. Now, to the French, it appeared that the British navy had deserted them. Moreover, the British had tried, but failed, to sink block ships that would have made it impossible for any more Frenchmen to get away.

Admiral Darlan protested strongly to the British admiralty about "the way in which it seems to have lost interest in the outcome of the Battle of Dunkirk, now that the British contingents are safe." According to General Fagalde, British planes no longer appeared over Dunkirk once the British evacuation had been completed, leaving French soldiers and ships to the mercy of the Luftwaffe. General Janssen, commander of the 12th Motorized Infantry Division, which was guarding the eastern side of the perimeter, was killed when a bomb fell on his command post.

General Weygand was furious. He fired off a telegram to the French military attaché in London urging the British to continue the evacuation for another night in order to rescue some 25,000 French troops still defending the Dunkirk perimeter. "Emphasize," Weygand wrote, "that the solidarity of the two armies demands that the French rearguard not be sacrificed."

Churchill, for his part, was upset with the French for allegedly exposing British vessels to needless danger. He telephoned General Spears in Paris to declare that he would not be sending any more ships to Dunkirk. Spears managed to calm him down. That morning, he informed Churchill, Reynaud had received news that 10,000 French soldiers had been left on the shore, almost within shouting distance of British ships that were departing empty. The French premier was furious. This apparent British betrayal was just what his critics needed to push him out of power and France out of the war. If no further attempt were made to evacuate more French troops, Spears said, even Reynaud, the most pro-British of the French leaders, would blame London.

Spears made sense to Churchill. The prime minister sent a message to Reynaud and Weygand stating: "We are coming back for your men tonight. Please ensure that all facilities are used promptly. For three hours last night, many ships waited idly at great risk and danger."

THE LAST EVACUATION, JUNE 3–4

Admiral Ramsay complied, but only reluctantly, with the order to send his ships to Dunkirk one more time. In a strongly worded telegram to the Admiralty he stated: "After nine days of operations of a nature unprecedented in naval warfare, which followed on two weeks of intense strain, commanding officers, officers, and ships' companies are at the end of their tether. . . . If, therefore, evacuation has to be continued after tonight, I would emphasize, in the strongest possible manner, that fresh forces should be used for these operations, and any consequent delay in their execution should be accepted."

Then he proceeded to try to inspire the men under his command to make one last effort. "I hoped and believed," he wrote, "that last night would see us through, but the French, who were covering the retirement of the British rearguard, had to repel a strong German attack and so were unable to send their troops to the pier in time to be embarked. We cannot leave our Allies in the lurch, and I call on all officers and men detailed for further evacuation tonight to let the world see that we never let down our Ally."

Nevertheless, Ramsay did not feel he could order ships to make even one last run. Instead, he asked for volunteers. Fortunately, an impressive number said yes. As a result, 10 transports, 13 destroyers (four of them French), eight minesweepers, nine passenger ferries (three of them French), four paddle steamers, two corvettes, 10 drifters, and, as ever, a host of small craft departed from England late that afternoon. In addition, the Dynamo Room learned that 63 French vessels were on their way to Dunkirk. Most of them were fishing boats and small naval auxiliaries capable of going into the inner quays even at low tide. Ramsay hoped that they would be able lift off the mole 14,000 troops that night.

The crew of the destroyer *Malcolm* had been planning a party to celebrate what they thought was the last night of the evacuation. Then they heard that there would be still another trip. Trying to make the best of it, the officers donned dinner jackets and bow ties for what was to be their eighth trip to Dunkirk. The destroyer *Whitshed* left Dover at 7:00 P.M. to the strains of the ship's harmonica band. It was accompanied by a torpedo boat flying the flag of Rear Admiral Wake-Walker.

Ramsay planned to concentrate this final effort at the west pier, a shorter jetty across from the east mole where hundreds of French soldiers had waited in vain the previous night. Minesweepers, skoots, and smaller paddle steamers would be sent there to take off, hopefully, another 5,000 men. Smaller boats would evacuate troops from the inner harbor, where the larger vessels could not go, to the gunboat *Locust,* anchored just outside the harbor. The remaining evacuation points—the Quai Félix Faure, deep inside the port of Dunkirk, the outer mole and the beach to its west, and the Malo beach—were assigned to the ever-growing fleet of French trawlers and fishing smacks.

When Wake-Walker arrived off the eastern mole at 10:00 P.M., he was relieved to find that unlike the previous night, there were now plenty of French troops awaiting evacuation. However, the heavy wind and the tide made it virtually impossible for the rescue ships to get alongside the mole, with the result that a huge backup of ships was created at the entrance to the harbor. Wake-Walker's ship took an additional hour to tie up at the pier and another four hours, rather than the planned three, to complete the embarkation of troops. Fortunately, there was little German shelling this night, since Kuechler's advance elements were now so close to the port that his artillery units were leery of hitting their own infantry. The Luftwaffe also was gone, having turned its attention to targets in and around Paris. As a consequence, there were relatively few Allied casualties this night.

With the British soldiers gone, the French army had been told to use the whole harbor, moles and quays alike. But when the *Lady of Mann,* the first of the personnel ships to arrive, headed for the familiar mooring at the east mole, her captain was astonished, and indignant, to find it lined with French fishing boats, which were packing in as many soldiers as they could cram aboard. Royal Navy shore patrols had regulated the movements both of troops and of vessels on previous nights, but now chaos reigned on the mole. The captains of the larger British vessels shouted to the skippers of the French trawlers to move their boats to the inner harbor, where the larger ships could not enter, but they shouted their orders in English, which most of the French men could not understand. Precious time was wasted before Wake-Walker's French liaison officers finally persuaded the French boats to leave the mole. The *Lady of Mann* had to wait two hours before it could berth at the mole.

Confusion also prevailed across the harbor, on the west mole and at the Quai Félix Faure. Royal Navy officers tried to muster French troops onto waiting vessels in the appropriate numbers, but the soldiers would obey only their own officers. Most of the French soldiers who reached the harbor had marched straight from the front line. They despised the British, who, they believed, had sneaked away while they held off the Germans. And while they accepted that they had to be evacuated to England, they wanted to arrive there organized in their respective units. The British ships took them aboard fully armed, but when they arrived on the quays of Dover or Ramsgate, they were disarmed by the British military police, marched onto trains for the more westerly ports of Southampton and Weymouth, and immediately shipped back to France. Along with their government, these French soldiers would surrender to the Germans on June 25.

Many, perhaps thousands, of the French soldiers who arrived in the harbor were not armed. They had swarmed out of the cellars of Dunkirk after realizing that the army was leaving, and then vied with the fighting troops for spaces on the rescue vessels. The troops of General Barthélemy's *Secteur Fortifié des Flandres,* who had defended the perimeter to the last moment and then were ordered to march to the harbor for evacuation, encountered the unarmed rabble near Malo. The writer Jacques Mordal, then one of Admiral Abrial's staff officers, described with disgust the encounter: "Barthélemy's column waited, while across their front passed these men from the ordnance depots, these truck drivers, these representatives of all the rear echelons." However, Mordal admitted that clearing the rabble away "could only have been done with machine guns." "What commander," he asked, "would willingly have done that?"

By the time the last British warships—the destroyers *Express* and *Shikari*—left Dunkirk soon after 3:00 A.M. on June 4, the sound of German machine guns could be heard clearly in the streets of the town. Two more block ships attempted—again not wholly successfully—to complete the job that was left unfinished the previous night. All totaled, an additional 26,209 troops (including 7 British soldiers) had been lifted off on this last night of the evacuation, bringing the grand total to 338,226 men (of these, 308,888 were British, 22,160 were French, and the remainder were Belgian, Dutch, and Norwegian).

Still, an estimated 40,000 French troops remained behind. They would surrender that day. They included a large part of the 32nd Infantry Division, whose soldiers had made a vain attempt to break out toward Gravelines after they had been denied access to the harbor. And they included almost all that remained of the 12th Division, which had continued to repulse all attacks on their positions at Bray Dunes despite the death in action of their commander, General Janssen.

These were among the best of France's fighting men. Commander H. R. Troup, who had been directing the evacuation from the center pier, marveled at their *esprit de corps.* He described how about a thousand French soldiers stood at attention, four deep, about halfway along the pier as an unidentified general and his staff boarded the last departing destroyer. Their faces, Troup recalled, "were indiscernible in the dawn light, the flames behind them showing up their steel helmets; the officers clicked their heels, saluted and then turned about and came down to the boat, and left." The time was 3:20 A.M.

There would be no further evacuations. Admiral Abrial, who, along with Generals Fagalde, de la Laurencie, and Barthélemy, crossed to England during the night, told Admiral Ramsay when he reached Dover that further evacuation was impossible, for the Germans were now closing in on Dunkirk from every side.

Admiral Wake-Walker took one last ride through the harbor on the torpedo boat that would speed him back to Dover. Its commander, Lieutenant John Cameron, observed that "the whole scene was filled with a sense of finality and death. The curtain was ringing down on a great tragedy." The fall of Dunkirk marked the end of the northern phase of the French campaign.

There were, however, a number of British troops still in Dunkirk. One was Lieutenant Jimmy Langley. He had been left behind because wounded soldiers took up too much space in the lifeboats. Langley was now spending his time lying on a stretcher located in a huge Victorian house in the Dunkirk suburb of Rosendael. The house, which served as a field hospital for 265 British troops, was capped by an odd-looking cupola with a pointed red roof that gave it its name, the *Châpeau Rouge.*

Inside the house, it was unpleasantly hot, with the air reeking of ether and the smell of unwashed bodies, and buzzing with flies. Langley asked to be moved outside. He was carried on his stretcher to the top of the granite steps that led up to a huge wood and glass double-fronted door, and was given a small tree branch to swat at flies.

Langley wondered what would happen to him when the Germans arrived. He was an officer in the Coldstream Guards, a unit with a reputation in the last war for not taking prisoners. Would the Germans remember that and pay him back in kind? The next morning, he asked a couple of orderlies to carry his stretcher to a spot near the front gate. If he was going to be killed, he wanted to get it over with quickly. On the ground, next to the spot where his stretcher was placed, Langley saw a little yellow book entitled, in huge black letters, *Fifty Filthy Facts about Hitler.* Langley grabbed it and pushed it down one of his trouser legs as far as it would go.

The Germans arrived at six o'clock that morning, June 4. Two of them, caked with dust and unshaven, sank to the ground in front of Langley's stretcher. Langley decided his best chance lay in playing to the hilt the role of a wounded prisoner.

"*Wasser?*" he asked them. One of the Germans gave him a drink from his water bottle.

"*Cigaretten?*" He was guessing about the correctness of this word. Nevertheless, he was given a lit cigarette.

Guessing that he was asking too much and giving too little, he asked "*War sie wollen?*"

"*Marmaladen,*" came the reply. Hoping there was a pot of marmalade left, Langley sent off the orderly. There was none. But a jar of jam was found and obviously pleased the hungry Germans.

"*Wo das Meer?*" one of the Germans asked.

Langley did not have the vaguest idea where the sea was, but he pointed in what he hoped was the right direction.

"*Offizier?*" the German queried.

"*Ja,*" Langley replied.

The German saluted and left. Langley was relieved. "We were not going to be massacred!"

The Surrender, June 4

The Germans who left Langley moved on into Dunkirk. Shortly after dawn, both the center of the city and the beaches east of the mole came under German small-arms fire. By now, however, French resistance had ended; white flags were everywhere. Realizing the battle was over, soldiers of the German 18th Infantry Division rode on trucks through the debris-filled streets of the city down to the waterfront. "Then our hearts leapt," the division's Daily Intelligence Summary recorded: "Here was the sea—the sea!" By 9:30 A.M., German troops had reached the foot of the eastern mole. But there were so many French troops on top of the mole that it was impossible for the Germans to round them up quickly. As late as ten o'clock, 30 French soldiers managed to escape on a lifeboat.

The Germans swiftly took control of key positions in the city, including, at about 8:00 A.M., Admiral Abrial's Bastion 32 headquarters. There they found only a handful of headquarters clerks. Shortly before ten o'clock, the 18th Division's commander, Lieutenant General Friedrich-Carl Cranz, drove up to the red-brick *Hôtel de Ville* in the center of town. He was met by General Beaufrère, the commander of the 68th Infantry and the ranking French officer remaining in the city. Beaufrère had taken off his steel helmet and now sported a gold-leaf kepi for the surrender ceremony.

"Where are the English?" Cranz asked.

"Not here," Beaufrère replied. "They are all in England."

Georg Schmidt, one of Joseph Goebbels's propaganda photographers, also was perplexed by the absence of British soldiers. Goebbels expected pictures of British POWs, but Schmidt could not find any. When he informed his section chief, he was told, "You're an official photographer. If you don't get any pictures of British POWs, then you *were* an official photographer!"

Schmidt rushed to the POW compound, where he managed to find two or three dozen Tommies among the 30,000 to 40,000 French prisoners. He quickly lined them up in front and snapped several pictures. The British prisoners saved Schmidt's job.

CHAPTER TEN

Aftermath

So long as the English tongue survives, the word Dunkerque will be spoken with reverence. For in that harbor, in such a hell as never blazed on earth before, at the end of a lost battle, the rags and blemishes that have hidden the soul of democracy fell away. . . . This shining thing in the souls of free men Hitler cannot command, or stain, or conquer. . . . It is the great tradition of democracy. It is the future. It is victory.

—*New York Times,* June 1, 1940

THE MIRACLE OF DUNKIRK

It was a nation already overflowing with gratitude and relief when Winston Churchill went to the House of Commons on the evening of June 4 to report on the evacuation from Dunkirk. The benches were filled. The Public Gallery, the Peers Gallery, and the Distinguished Strangers Gallery were all packed. The prime minister was welcomed with a rousing cheer by the assembled crowd, which then sat enthralled by that rarity—a speech devoted mainly to bad news that nevertheless lifts one's spirits to the heavens.

"When, a week ago today," Churchill began, "I asked the House to fix this afternoon as the occasion for a statement, I feared it would be my lot to announce the greatest military disaster in our long history." At that time, he had thought, perhaps 20,000 or 30,000 men might be evacuated from the continent. Instead, 98,780 men were rescued from the beaches and 239,446 from Dunkirk. They were, he said, "the whole root and core and brain of the British Army." It was around this nucleus that Britain would build the great armies that eventually would help defeat Hitler.

Churchill proceeded to explain the reasons for the "miracle of Dunkirk." He praised the Royal Navy, whose ships and sailors ran the German gauntlet to rescue men from Dunkirk and its surrounding beaches. He recognized the Allied soldiers, whose stout defense of the Dunkirk perimeter bought the time the navy needed to evacuate the maximum possible number of troops. But he placed particular emphasis on the role of the much-maligned RAF. "Many of our soldiers coming back," he said, "have not seen the Air Force at work; they saw only the bombers which escaped its protective attack. They underrate its achievements." Its fighters contested German control of the skies over Dunkirk and "showed for the first time that it was a match for the Luftwaffe."

Churchill admitted that favorable weather also played a major part. Had the winds risen and the sea become rough, the miracle of Dunkirk might never have happened. Yet what he did not emphasize was the fact that deliverance was also largely due to Hitler's first serious strategic blunder of the war: his decision to halt the panzers on May 24, when they were only a few miles away from Dunkirk. Had the panzers been permitted to advance into the virtually undefended port, most of the BEF and what remained of France's northern armies would now be on their way to German prison camps.

That this did not happen was due in large part to Lord Gort, the BEF's commander-in-chief. Gort had foreseen the possibility that the army might have to be evacuated as early as May 19, well before anyone else, and immediately began planning for it. Not favored by Churchill, however, he received no further fighting command. His career ended as high commissioner in Palestine at the end of the war. Soon thereafter, his health broke down and he died at age 60 in 1946. Yet Gort's subordinates in the BEF—Brooke, Alexander, and Montgomery—gained glory in the war. Montgomery was promoted to field marshal after winning victories in North Africa and Sicily. He also led the British and Canadian forces in the invasion of France and Germany.

Vice Admiral Bertram Ramsay also won justly earned accolades for planning and supervising the successful evacuation from Dunkirk. Rising to the rank of Admiral, Ramsay would direct the Allied naval forces in the invasion of France. Tragically, his death in an air crash near Paris on January 2, 1945, prevented him from witnessing the end of the war and the victory to which he had personally contributed so much.

Continuing his speech, Churchill cautioned his rapt listeners that "wars are not won by evacuations." The campaign had cost Britain 68,000 casualties. The loss of war matériel was catastrophic. The bulk of the BEF's heavy equipment—including virtually all its tanks, anti-tank guns, and heavy artillery, as well as 64,000 vehicles, almost all of the army's machine guns, and half a million tons of stores and ammunition—had been left behind. The navy also had paid a heavy price for its heroics. Six destroyers, five minesweepers, eight transport ships, and an additional 200 vessels had been sunk, and an equal number badly damaged. The Royal Air Force lost 177 planes over Dunkirk, against 240 for the Luftwaffe. In the period May 10–31, however, the RAF suffered a total loss of 432 Hurricanes and Spitfires.

Nor did Churchill permit the deliverance of the British army to disguise the great danger the country still faced. But he promised that Britain would continue to fight:

> We shall fight in France, we shall fight on the seas and oceans, we shall fight with growing confidence and growing strength in the air, we shall defend our island, whatever the cost may be, we shall fight on the beaches, we shall fight on the landing grounds, we shall fight in the fields and in the streets, we shall fight in the hills; we shall never surrender, and even if, which I do not for the moment believe, this island or a large part of it were subjugated and starving, then our Empire beyond the seas, armed and guarded by the British Fleet, would carry on the struggle, until, in God's good time, the new world, with all its power and might, steps forth to the rescue and the liberation of the old.

The House of Commons broke into boisterous cheers as Churchill concluded his speech. His friend Josiah Wedgwood, a Labour MP, wrote him later: "My dear Winston. That was worth 1,000 guns, and the speeches of 1,000 years." Another close friend, Vita Sackville-West, wrote her husband, Harold Nicolson, that the speech "sent shivers (not of fear) down my spine. I think that one of the reasons why one is stirred by his Elizabethan phrases is that one feels the whole massive backing of power and resolve behind them, like a great fortress: they are never words for words' sake." Replying to his wife, Nicolson wrote: "I feel so much in the spirit of Winston's great speech that I could face a world of enemies." Even his critics were inspired. That evening, Henry "Chips" Cannon, one of the staunchest critics, recorded in his diary: "I sat behind him, and he was eloquent, and oratorical, and used magnificent English; several Labour Members cried."

The significance of the miracle of Dunkirk is difficult to overstate. Had the BEF been annihilated, Britain would have found it very difficult, if not impossible, to persevere in the war. In fact, Churchill might have been ousted from power and replaced by another government, perhaps one more willing to negotiate with Hitler. Instead, thanks to the success at Dunkirk, Churchill's prestige soared and the British people became infected with his determination to resist a Nazi invasion of their island nation. Roadblocks and pillboxes sprang up everywhere, signposts were rearranged or removed, barbed wire and beach fortifications were laid. By mid-July, over a million men had enrolled in the Local Defense Volunteers.

However, few outside the British Isles expected Britain to resist for long. Having seen what the German armies had done to his own forces, General Weygand prophesied that "in three weeks' time, England's neck will be wrung like a chicken's." But largely due to the heroic efforts of the RAF in the famous Battle of Britain that summer, Hitler was unable to invade the British Isles, prompting Churchill's famous reply to Weygand's prediction: "Some chicken! Some neck!"

THE DEFEAT OF FRANCE

For the majority of the French, however, Dunkirk marked the beginning of the end. France's northern armies—24 infantry divisions, including six of France's seven motorized divisions, two light cavalry divisions, three light mechanized divisions, and one armored division—had been virtually annihilated. All totaled, France had lost some 92,000 men killed and 200,000 wounded by the time the Dunkirk operation ended. Another two million men went into captivity. This represented over a quarter of France's numerical strength and qualitatively its best soldiers. In addition, France lost 1,800 guns, 930 armored vehicles, and last but certainly not least, the economically important northern French industrial region. The end was only a matter of time.

After Dunkirk, on June 5, the German army headed south toward Paris. The French defenses along the Somme River were soon pierced, compelling the French army to stumble backward until its retreat was turned into a rout. Paris was declared an open city and on the morning of June 14 was occupied by units of General Fedor von Bock's Army Group B. Soon Bock's soldiers were marching in a victory parade past the Arc de Triomphe.

Two days later, Paul Reynaud resigned the premiership and was replaced by Marshal Pétain. The eighty-four-year-old soldier, who was described by de Gaulle as suffering from "senility, pessimism and ambition—a fatal combination," wasted no time in seeking an armistice, an action greeted with widespread relief in France. It was signed on June 22, at Hitler's insistence in the same railroad car in which the armistice of 1918 had been signed by the Germans. The agreement left two-thirds of France as German-occupied territory; the remainder of the country was left to Pétain's government, whose headquarters were moved to the city of Vichy, in south-central France.

But not all Frenchmen accepted defeat. General de Gaulle fled to England, where, from a BBC studio in London on June 18, he proclaimed the creation of a Free French Army whose goal would be the ultimate liberation of France. De Gaulle would help achieve that objective and then become active in France's political life after the war, serving first as premier in 1946, then as the architect and first president of the Fifth Republic from 1958 until 1969. He died in 1970.

Paul Reynaud, however, did not follow de Gaulle into exile. He was imprisoned by the Germans and only narrowly escaped death. After the war, he reentered politics, devoting himself to the cause of European unity, and once more became a minister. After his first wife died, he remarried in 1949 (aged 71) and begot three children, the youngest born when he was approaching eighty. Still exercising regularly in the private gymnasium he had constructed in his Paris apartment, Reynaud lived to be eighty-seven. He died in 1966.

Gamelin, along with Daladier and President Lebrun, also was imprisoned by the Germans. All three survived the war. Afterward, Gamelin threw himself tirelessly into writing his memoirs, which were published in three hefty volumes, entitled *Servir.* He died in 1958 at the age of eighty-six.

Pétain lived to an even older age, ninety-five, but he did so in disgrace, condemned by a tribunal for allowing French citizens to be marched off to Nazi slave labor camps. He died in prison in 1951.

General Maxime Weygand also survived the war. He served briefly as Pétain's minister of national defense and then was appointed governor-general of Algeria, where he acquitted himself with distinction, maintaining the spirit of his army while keeping the Germans at bay. Later, he too was imprisoned by the Germans and later still by his own country, but only for a short period. He died in 1965 at the venerable age of ninety-eight, mistrustful of the British to the very end.

The French collapse in 1940 was one of the greatest military catastrophes in world history. Why had the most powerful army in continental Europe succumbed so utterly to its hereditary enemy?

The Vichy French blamed Britain. They accused the British of secretly, then openly, violating the orders of the French high command by retreating to the English Channel. Many French could not help feeling, as General Weygand put it, that "since May 16, Churchill had played a double game, and had abandoned France to herself." And to a great extent, Weygand was right. Both Churchill and General Gort had lost confidence in the French high command, and they were not prepared to sacrifice the BEF by carrying out French orders. At the same time, Churchill was hesitant about informing the French as well as the Belgians that evacuation was being considered and preparations were under way for conducting it. He feared that the news would sap their will to continue fighting and thereby reduce the chances that evacuation could take place. The French, who had initially resisted the idea of evacuation, felt cheated out of an equal share of the participating shipping when they finally accepted it.

But General de Gaulle insisted, as the British did, that the French army and government were wholly responsible for France's defeat. France's political and military leaders, he asserted, were ill prepared for a war they knew was coming. "France has been struck down," de Gaulle charged, "not by the number of German effectives, not by their superior courage, but solely by the enemy's mechanized force, with all its offensive power and maneuverability."

Like de Gaulle, most military historians believe that France's defeat was not primarily due to the quantitative or qualitative inferiority of French manpower and weaponry but rather to the manner in which they were employed. In May 1940, the French had about 3,000 modern tanks compared to just 2,574 tanks for the Germans. Moreover, French armor and guns were on average better than those of the Germans, although German tanks were generally slightly faster and, for the most part, radio-equipped. However, France was late in forming armored divisions—possessing only three to the Germans' 10 when the western campaign began—and used tanks, almost always, as they were used in World War I, in piecemeal fashion. As a result, the French armored divisions were either swiftly chewed up or scattered by the concentrated masses of German panzers.

In addition to tanks, the French military chiefs also underrated the value of air power. As a result, the Germans were permitted to acquire a superiority in numbers of aircraft approaching 3 to 1 before the war began. At the outset of the campaign, France possessed only 1,200 first-line aircraft, of which 700 were fighters, 150 were bombers, and 350 were scout and observation aircraft. To make matters worse, many of the French planes were destroyed on the ground because the French lacked an early warning system at their airfields and had too few antiaircraft guns to defend them. German control of the air wreaked havoc with the French Army's effort to defend itself against, let alone counterattack, the advancing panzer juggernaught.

The French military leadership also failed to understand the importance of transportation and communications in modern warfare. The French high command repeatedly failed to put men and supplies in the right places, concentrate troops effectively, organize retreats, maintain communications with its fighting units, stockpile fuel, or even record the whereabouts of its soldiers.

The French high command was also deficient in intelligence-gathering and analysis. Unlike the Germans, the French had no staff structure for analyzing, filtering, or sharing intelligence data. When the Germans attacked, the French general staff did not know what was happening, even though they received plenty of evidence that hundreds of panzers were coming through the Ardennes.

Not merely did the French military leaders fail to foresee, and prepare for, the kind of blitzkrieg tactics that were used by the Germans, they also failed to react appropriately once they realized what was happening. Both the French high command and its field commanders proved chronically unable to react to unexpected changes in the flow of the battle. French generals were trained to follow orders and detailed plans rather than adapt to changed circumstances. By contrast, German field commanders were allowed to take the initiative when opportunities arose, and they did so repeatedly.

An effective French response to the German breakthrough along the Meuse River would have required the high command to maintain sufficient forces in reserve to counterattack the panzers. Instead, Gamelin sent the core of his reserve forces, Henri Giraud's 7th Army, into Holland. Nor did Gamelin tap into the more than 400,000 troops manning the Maginot Line, where, for the most part, they sat out the remainder of the war.

The absence of sufficient reserves at the critical point of the battle was a product of French strategy, which, as the Maginot Line aptly demonstrated, was geared to fight another conflict like World War I. The French high command hoped to put as much Belgian territory between France's industrial north and the German invaders as they could. This, of course, left the French army particularly vulnerable to the German attack through the Ardennes, making defeat virtually unavoidable after the battle began.

The failure of France's strategy was directly attributable to its military leaders. The French military was led by too many old men—men like Gamelin, who, more than anyone else, was responsible for the decision to send France's best armies into Belgium. Had younger, more competent generals, versed in blitzkrieg-like tactics—generals like Charles de Gaulle, for example—replaced Gamelin as commander-in-chief of the French army at the beginning of the war, and then been permitted to assemble a coterie of like-minded disciples to manage the campaign, the panzer breakthrough along the Meuse might have been prevented, or at least contained.

❋

Rather than blame themselves for the catastrophe, however, after the war, France's military leaders blamed her people and her political leaders. France lost the war, they charged, because the bulk of the French population had lost the will to resist.

Although the following words were written by a British general, Sir Henry Pownall, Lord Gort's chief of staff, they certainly mirrored the thoughts of his French counterparts:

> As nations we have got[ten] fat and lazy. We possessed great Empires, earned for us by the sweat and blood of our ancestors, that we would not take sufficient care to defend. . . . People have thought only of what they could get from the State, not of what they can give. . . . Add, too, the Pacifist movements of recent years, the influx of undesirable aliens of all kinds, the self-satisfied outlook on affairs, the failure of religion, the absence of leadership—all these things have contributed to our disaster. Of the lack of proper preparation for war, over the vacillations of the politicians, over the attitude of the Treasury . . . towards military requirements, over the treatment of the Army for the past twenty years and of the refusal of Ministers to accept the advice of their responsible Service advisers. . . . These lines of Shakespeare (*Henry VI*, Part I, Act I, Scene I) are strangely apt:
>
>> "Gloucester: 'Is Paris lost? Is Rouen yielded up?'
>> Exeter: 'How were they lost? What treachery was used?'
>> Messenger: 'No treachery, but want of men and money.'"

To be sure, the French people were traumatized by World War I, much of which was fought on French territory. As Georges Mandel, the French Minister of Colonies, admitted to General Spears, France's morale was "sapped by the feeling . . . that there would be no war because France could not stand another bleeding like that of 1914."

But there was a more fundamental division in the French polity than the one produced by the question of whether or not France should fight another war. The country was too deeply divided by internecine ideological quarrels to pay serious attention to, and prepare for, the coming conflict with Germany. The division between left and right was clearly evident in

General Weygand's concern in the waning hours of the battle about a possible Communist uprising in Paris. Generals like Weygand and Pétain resigned themselves to defeat because they regarded a leftist uprising, rather than the Germans, as the greatest threat to France.

France's collapse was also the fault of other countries. With 17 million fewer people than Germany—and consequently with fewer soldiers, workers, and industrial might—France needed allies. But France's allies did not provide the degree of help the French required to stave off defeat, as they had in World War I.

The British never sent the number of divisions to France that they had committed in World War I (25), or even the much smaller number that they had promised to send to France after war was declared in September 1939.

In his speech to Parliament on June 4, Churchill placed part of the blame for the Allied military disaster on King Léopold of Belgium. "Had not this Ruler and his Government . . . sought refuge in what has proved to be a fatal neutrality," Churchill said, "the French and British Armies might well at the outset have saved, not only Belgium, but perhaps even Poland."

The Belgian king and government were foolhardy in believing that neutrality would save them from Hitler's wrath. They were even more foolish to wait until 6:30 A.M. on May 10, the day the Germans attacked, before allowing French and British troops to enter Belgian territory. However, Churchill did acknowledge that the Belgian Army "guarded our eastern flank and thus kept open our only line of retreat to the sea," but, he added, Léopold's decision to surrender also "exposed our whole flank and means of retreat." The fact is, Léopold did notify the British that his army was on the verge of collapse, but he did so only a short 24 hours before the surrender took effect.

After the surrender, Léopold remained under house arrest in Laeken Palace. His visit to Hitler's Berchtesgaden retreat in the Alps on November 19, 1940, left him open to the charge that he had remained in Belgium primarily to get more lenient terms from the Nazi dictator. According to Hubert Pierlot, "the King estimated that it was not on an improbable Allied victory that Belgium must pin hopes for independence, but on the moderation of the enemy." Whether or not this was in fact the king's primary motive for remaining in Belgium, it did Belgium little apparent good. Belgian independence was not restored until the country was liberated by the Allies in 1944. As for Léopold, after the Allies landed in

France in June 1944, the Nazi dictator deported him to Austria, where he remained until he was freed by soldiers of the U.S. 7th Army the following spring.

Before Léopold could return to Belgium, however, the Belgian Parliament passed a resolution demanding his abdication. Those who voted for the resolution believed that the king had committed treason by rejecting the government's demand that he go into exile following the surrender. But Léopold refused to abide by the parliamentary resolution unless less than 55 percent of the votes cast in a nationwide referendum wanted him to retain his throne. The referendum, which was held on March 12, 1950, supported the king by a vote of 57 percent, barely enough. But the French-speaking part of Belgium gave Léopold less than 50 percent of the vote. Paul-Henri Spaak, now premier, again demanded the king's abdication, but Léopold again refused to comply. Instead, he returned to Belgium and resumed his duties as king. However, anti-Léopold riots broke out in Belgium during the following year, prompting Léopold finally to accept abdication in favor of his son, Baudouin. Léopold died in 1983 of heart failure. He was eighty-one.

Perhaps the most important factor in explaining the French defeat was the absence of the United States at France's side. In 1940, no other nation had the economic resources or potential military might that could have saved France had they been available early enough. During World War I, the United States came to France's side late in the war (1917), but still in time to stem Germany's all-out offensive in the spring of 1918. Subsequently, the German army was forced to begin a retreat that would end only when its leaders requested an armistice the following November.

But American power was unavailable to France in 1940. After World War I, President Woodrow Wilson's stubborn opposition to compromise on the Versailles Treaty prompted the U.S. Senate to reject that agreement. In the wake of the treaty's demise, Senate support for a collateral Anglo-American treaty guaranteeing France's security evaporated. The United States withdrew into isolation and remained there until the Japanese attack on Pearl Harbor. America's absence (or limited participation) in European affairs during the interwar era contributed substantially to the continent's instability and ultimately to the defeat of France.

HITLER'S GREATEST TRIUMPH

Hitler, of course, was elated by his army's triumph over France. He ordered church bells in Germany to ring for three days. The German army had vanquished France in only six weeks, at the relatively small cost of 27,074 dead, 18,384 missing, and 111,034 wounded—an overall total not much

Hitler dances a jig before the signing of the French armistice, June 22, 1940.
(AP/Wide World Photos)

more than a third of Germany's casualties in one major World War I battle, Verdun.

To a considerable extent, Hitler was responsible for the great German victory. Very early he accepted the advantages offered by the blitzkrieg tactics introduced to him by Heinz Guderian, and he forced the Army high command to adopt them. Hitler also had appreciated the brilliance of the Manstein Plan and adopted it as his own. As a result, in June 1940, the Nazi warlord was master of Western Europe. His Wehrmacht seemed invincible.

Of course, other factors were important in explaining the German victory. One was luck. Hitler originally had wanted to strike against France in the late fall of 1939, following the conquest of Poland. But bad weather repeatedly forced him to postpone the offensive. Had the German attack taken place as originally planned, its spearhead would not have come through the Ardennes but, rather, through central Belgium, where it would have encountered the best Allied armies and likely stalemate.

The second piece of good fortune accorded Hitler was the crash of Reinberger's airplane in January 1940. The capture by the Belgians of the partially burned German invasion plans that Reinberger was carrying prompted Hitler to postpone the attack indefinitely until a new plan could be prepared. It was based primarily on Manstein's ideas, but Hitler also contributed his insights to its formulation. By calling for a strike through the Ardennes instead of central Belgium, the Manstein Plan assured that the spearhead of the German attack, seven panzer divisions, would confront one of the weakest armies in the French order of battle, General Corap's 9th Army, rather then the best Allied armies, which were rushing into Belgium. By the time the French high command understood what was happening, it was too late. Rigidly fixed to an obsolete strategy and doctrine, the French generals had no contingency plans for the massive German breakthrough on the upper Meuse. The best they could do was attempt to plug holes in their continuous front. They could no more envisage a rapid war of maneuver than they could believe that the Maginot Line might prove irrelevant.

The Germans were also granted the advantage of mostly dry, clear weather, which aided both their air arm and the wheeled transport of their ground forces. Moreover, Belgium and northern France were covered with a network of good roads and rails, conditions the Werhmacht would not find in Russia after Germany invaded that country the following year.

Although reluctant to attack France, the Army's General Staff, led by General Franz Halder, accepted the Manstein Plan once Hitler left them no alternative. Once accepted, they became the driving force behind its implementation. Led by Halder, the General Staff conducted the necessary theoretical, operational, and strategic planning that was required to make it work. Indeed, Halder proved to be much more aggressive than Hitler when it came to seeing the Manstein Plan through to a successful conclusion. Halder strongly opposed, and did what he could to subvert, Hitler's orders halting the panzers on May 17 and 24.

The army's organization and mode of operation also were responsible for the German victory. German field commanders and the Army General Staff formed a well-knit team. Halder was generally able to focus on a much broader scale than the individual commanders and had the prerogative of changing their orders. Yet German field commanders were permitted considerable freedom to alter operational directives to meet changed battlefield conditions. And the General Staff was still able to hold its field commanders to the overall plan of the campaign. The combination of tactical flexibility within a sound strategic framework proved to be a winning combination. Needless to say, Hitler, rather than the General Staff, got the lion's share of the credit for the army's triumph, although General von Brauchitsch and several other generals who participated in the campaign were given field marshal batons by the Führer.

※

The defeat of France represented the high point of Hitler's fortunes. But his triumph in the west was also the source of his ultimate defeat. His ability to foresee the potential of the Manstein Plan when the General Staff did not convinced him that he knew more about strategy than they did. His success in France subsequently reduced even more his willingness to listen to his military advisers and prompted him increasingly to interfere continually in their affairs.

Yet Hitler's limitations as a military leader were already displayed during the implementation of Plan Yellow. It was he, and not his panzer generals, who suffered from cold feet when the panzers struck out for the English Channel well in advance of their supporting infantry. He accepted the argument of an old-line general, von Rundstedt, to halt the panzers until infantry could be brought up to protect their flanks. Hitler's halt order on May 24, when Dunkirk was virtually undefended, prevented the panzers from giving him both a major strategic triumph as well as a stunning tactical victory. In so doing, Hitler short-circuited the Manstein Plan, which called for the destruction of the BEF as well as the French and Belgian armies. By letting the British army get away, Hitler allowed it to fight another day.

As a result of the BEF's escape, as well as other factors (including the superiority of the British navy and the RAF during that summer's Battle of Britain), Hitler was unable to conquer Britain. Stymied in the west, he turned his attention to the east and prepared for the invasion of Russia, an attack that was launched in June 1941. Had Britain not continued in the war, Hitler's armies might have succeeded in conquering Russia. However, Britain's continuation in the war would tie down in the west some 40 German divisions that otherwise might have seen action on the Russian front and possibly helped to defeat the Soviet Union. With both Russia and Britain out of the war, what fate would have awaited the United States?

However, the United States would enter the war, thanks to Japan's attack on Pearl Harbor on December 7, 1941. Then, four days later, Hitler would make another of his monumental blunders by declaring war on America. His action would ensure the creation of a "Grand Alliance" of the United States, Britain, and the Soviet Union that ultimately would defeat Germany.

※

Most of the German generals who fought in the Western campaign also played major roles in Russia. Among them were Brauchitsch, Halder,

Kleist, Manstein, Guderian, and Rundstedt. But all of them ultimately ran afoul of the Führer.

Brauchitsch was sacked in December 1941, after the army failed to take Moscow. In his place, Hitler named himself to head the army, thereby ending once and for all the independence of the German General Staff. Brauchitsch died in 1948, before he was to have been arraigned on war crimes charges. Franz Halder also lost his job in 1942, after yet another disagreement with Hitler. He was implicated in a 1944 bomb plot that very nearly killed Hitler and was sent to Dachau concentration camp, where he was found by American troops in 1945.

Kleist, promoted to field marshal after his success in the western campaign, led the 1st Panzer Army into the Ukraine in 1941. Manstein also rose to the rank of field marshal and, among other accomplishments in Russia, conducted a successful retreat of the German armies that were almost trapped in the Caucasus following the disastrous defeat of the German 6th Army at Stalingrad in February 1943. Manstein, who came to be regarded as Germany's best field commander, nevertheless was sacked by Hitler on the same day as Kleist, March 30, 1944.

In Russia, Guderian commanded the 2nd Panzer Group, which led the attack on Moscow during the autumn of 1941. After his failure to take the Soviet capital, however, he lost the Führer's favor and was transferred to the army reserve. Following the bomb plot against Hitler in 1944, Guderian was given Halder's old job, chief of the OKH General Staff. But in March 1945 he, too, was dismissed by Hitler. In poor health during his last years, he died at the age of sixty-six in 1954.

Rundstedt led Army Group South at the start of the Russian campaign. He subsequently went into forced retirement but was recalled to lead Hitler's armies in the west during 1944–45. After the war, he was imprisoned in England, but was released in 1949. He died, aged seventy-eight, in 1953.

Rommel, on the other hand, was sent to North Africa rather than Russia. There he gained fame as the "Desert Fox," leading Hitler's Afrika Korps against Montgomery's 8th Army. He then was placed in charge of planning the German defense of France in 1944. However, his implication in the attempt on Hitler's life that July cost Rommel his life. To spare his family, he accepted Hitler's order to commit suicide. He was awarded a hero's funeral.

Ultimately, Hitler also would be compelled to commit suicide. On April 30, 1945, he put a bullet in his head as Soviet troops advanced toward his Chancellery bunker, in the heart of bombed-out Berlin.

Notes

Prologue

The Frenchman with the brilliant war record: Adolphe Goutard, *The Battle of France: 1940,* trans. A. R. P. Burgess (London: Frederick Muller, 1958), 133.

Hitler, October 6, 1940: William L. Shirer, *The Collapse of the Third Republic: An Inquiry into the Fall of France in 1940* (New York: Simon and Schuster, 1969), 529.

Hitler, October 10, 1940: *Nazi Conspiracy and Aggression,* 10 vols. (Washington, D.C.: U.S. Government Printing Office, 1946), 6: 880–881.

Chapter One. The Reinberger Incident

The sources for the Reinberger incident are Karl Bartz's *Swastika in the Air: The Struggle and Defeat of the German Air Force 1933–1945* (London: W. Kimber, 1956), 9–13; Jean Vanwelkenhuyzen, "L'alerte du 10 Janvier 1940," *Revue d'histoire de la deuxième guerre mondiale,* 12 (Octobre 1953): 33–39; Hans-Adolf Jacobsen, "10 Januar 1940: Die Affaere Mechelen," *Wehrwissenschaftliche Rundschau,* 11 (April 1954): 497–513; Roger Keyes, *Outrageous Fortune: The Tragedy of Léopold III of the Belgians, 1901–1941* (London: Secker and Warburg, 1984), 134; Rémy (G. Renault-Roulier), *The Eighteenth Day: The Tragedy of King Léopold III of Belgium,* Stanley R. Rader, trans. (New York: Everest House, 1978), 75–76.

Chapter Two. The Dyle Plan

The Defense of Belgium: A translation of the unburned fragments of the Reinberger documents can be found in Belgian Ministry of Foreign Affairs, *Belgium: The Official Account of What Happened in 1939–1940* (New York: Evans Brothers, 1941): 85–91. **Belgian neutrality:** Keyes, 86. **Léopold:** Theodore Draper, *The Six Week's War: France, May 10–June 25, 1940* (New York: Viking Press, 1944), 12. **Van Overstraeten:** Vanwelkenhuyzen, 47–48; General Raoul Van Overstraeten, *Albert I–Léopold III: Vinqt ans de politique militaire belge, 1920–1940* (Bruges: Desclee de Brouwer, 1946), 451–452; Bartz, 14–15; Keyes, 134–135; Rémy, 73–74.

General Maurice Gamelin: Edward L. Spears, *Assignment to Catastrophe,* 2 vols. (New York: A. A. Wyn, Inc., 1954–1955), 1: 49; Alistair Horne, *To Lose a Battle: France, 1940* (Boston: Little, Brown, 1969), 116–122, Maurice Gustave Gamelin, *Servi,* 3 vols. (Paris: Plon, 1947), 3: 155–156. **Halder:** William L. Shirer, *The Collapse of the Third Republic: An Inquiry into the Fall of France in 1940* (New York: Simon and Schuster, 1969), 526. **Daladier and Reynaud:** Horne, 117–118; Charles de Gaulle, *War Memoirs,* 3 vols. (New York: Simon and Schuster, 1959), 1: 34. **"Notre Gamelin":** Martin S. Alexander, "Maurice Gamelin and the Defeat of France, 1939–1940," in Brian Bond, ed., *Fallen Stars: Eleven Studies of Twentieth Century Military Disasters* (London: Brassey's, 1991), 109; Jeffrey Gunsberg, *Divided and Conquered: The French High Command and the Defeat of the West* (Westport, Conn.: Greenwood Press, 1979), 111. **"Literally leaderless":** Jacques Benoist-Méchin, *Sixty Days that Shook the West: The Fall of France, 1940* (New York: G. P. Putnam's Sons, 1956), 79. **Fraser:** Alexander, 111. **Georges:** *Les Événements survenus en France de 1933 à 1945: Témoignages et documents recueillies par la Commission d'Enquête Parlementaire,* 9 vols. (Paris: Presses Universitaires, 1947), 3: 690–691. André Beaufre, *Le Drama de 1940* (Paris: 1965), 232. **Gamelin:** Adolphe Goutard, *The Battle of France: 1940,* trans. A. R. P. Burgess (London: Frederick Muller, 1958), 99. **"What a waste":** Shirer, *Collapse of the Third Republic,* 621; Jacques Minart, *P.C. Vincennes, Secteur 4,* 2 vols. (Paris: Le Nef, 1959), 2: 103.

The Phony War: Hitler: Shirer, *Collapse of the Third Republic,* 527. **Gamelin:** Goutard, 80. **Laffargue:** Ibid., 79. **Brooke:** Gregory Blaxland, *The Story of Gort's Army* (London: William Kimber, 1973), 28. **Ruby, Menu, and Grandsard:** Goutard, 132–133.

The Defense of France: Prewar France: Horne, 43–88; John Williams, *The Ides of May: The Defeat of France: May–June 1940* (London: Constable, 1968), 57–58, 62. **Economic statistics:** John J. Mearscheimer, *Conventional Deterrence* (Ithaca, N.Y.: Cornell University Press, 1983), 68–73. **Balance of forces:** Ernest R. May, *Strange Victory: Hitler's Conquest of France* (New York: Hill and Wang, 2000), 352; Mearscheimer, 91. Bernard Law Montgomery, *The Memoirs of Field Marshal the Viscount Montgomery of Alamein* (Cleveland: The World Publishing Company, 1958), 47. **Gort:** Draper, 31. **Corap's army:** Horne, 187–188.

The "Impenetrable" Ardennes: Liddell Hart: John Delaney, *Arms and Armour* (London; Sterling Publishing Co., 1996), 86. **Prételat:** Eugenia C. Kiesling, *Arming Against Hitler: France and the Limits of Military Planning* (Lawrence, Kan.: University of Kansas Press, 1996), 179.

The Breda Variant: Lord Gort: "Second Despatch," *London Gazette,* supplement, October 17, 1941, 5925. **Georges:** Pierre Lyet, *La Bataille de France: mai–juin 1940* (Paris: Payoy, 1947), 19, 22; Shirer, *Collapse of the Third Republic,* 586–589.

Allied Intelligence: Paillole: Eddy Bauer, *La Guerre des blindés,* 2 vols. (Paris: Payot, 1962), 1: 90–91. **Léopold:** Shirer, *Collapse of the Third Republic,* 589. **French military attaché in Berne:** Ibid. **"Enigma":** F. W. Winterbotham, *The Ultra Secret* (New York: Harper & Row, 1974), 31–32. For additional examples of Allied intelligence regarding German intentions, see May, 355–361.

The Unlearned Lessons of the Blitzkrieg in Poland: Rival tank strengths: Larry H. Addington, *The Blitzkrieg Era and the German General Staff, 1865–1911* (New Brunswick, N.J.: University of New Jersey Press, 1971), 101. **French secret service memorandum:** Goutard, 77. **Armengaud:** Horne, 132–133.

Charles de Gaulle: Prophet in the Wilderness: De Gaulle, 1: 29. **Gamelin:** Ibid., 1: 35, 37.

A False Start: Jean Vanwelkenhuyzen, "Die Krise von Januar 1940," *Wehrwissenschaftliche Rundshau,* 12 (February 1955), 66–90. **Oster:** Rémy, 73. **Delvoie and Gamelin:** Shirer, *Collapse of the Third Republic,* 575. **Spaak:** Paul-Henri Spaak, *The Continuing Battle: Memoirs of a European, 1936–1966* (Boston: Little, Brown, 1971), 24, 32; Minart, 1: 123–124; Shirer, *Collapse of the Third Republic,* 575–576. **Léopold:** Keyes, 79–80. **Daladier and Gamelin:** Gamelin, 3: 156–158; Shirer, *Collapse of the Third Republic,* 577–578; Minart, 1: 123, 133. **Brussels:** Shirer, *Collapse of the Third Republic,* 578. **Advised by the Belgians:** Minart, 1: 138. **Daladier and Gamelin:** Gamelin, 3: 159–160.

Chapter Three. The Manstein Plan

A Delayed Offensive: Hans-Adolf Jacobsen, *Fall Gelb: Der Kampf um den deutschen Operationsplan zur Westoffensive 1940* (Weisbaden: Franz Steiner, 1957), 90; Vanwelkenhuyzen, "L'alerte du 10 janvier, 1940," 52; Bartz, 14–15; Horne, 157; Telford Taylor, *The March of Conquest* (New York: Simon and Schuster, 1958), 60–61, 63. **Hitler's reaction:** Wilhelm Keitel, *The Memoirs of Field-Marshal Keitel,* Walter Gorlitz, ed., David Irving, trans. (New York: Stein and Day, 1966), 103. **Ilse Göring:** Ulrich von Hassell, *The Von Hassell Diaries, 1938–1944* (Garden City, N.Y.: Doubleday, 1947), 107–108. **Wenninger:** Keyes, 134; Bartz, 14–15; *Documents on German Foreign Policy, 1918–1945,* Series D, 1937–1945, 10 vols. (Washington: 1949–1956), 8: 658–666.

Hitler and His Generals: Percy Schramm, *Hitler: The Man and the Military Leader* (Chicago: Quadrangle Books, 1971), 17–23, 70–73, 104–107, 143–153; John Strawson, *Hitler's Battles for Europe* (Chicago: Charles Scribner, 1971), 51–54; Heinz Guderian, *Panzer Leader* (London: Michael Joseph, 1952), 131–132. **Halder:** Horne, 145–146; Eric von Manstein, *Lost Victories* (Chicago: Methuen, 1958), 29; Basil H. Liddell Hart, *The German Generals Talk* (New York: William Morrow, 1948), 33, 109; John W. Wheeler-Bennett, *The Nemesis of Power: The German Army in Politics, 1918–1945* (New York: Macmillan, 1953), 469; Barry A. Leach, "Colonel General Franz Halder," in Correlli Barnett, ed., *Hitler's Generals* (London: Weidenfeld and Nicolson, 1989), 101–128. **Brauchitsch:** Brian Bond, "Brauchitsch," in Barnett, 53. **Coup preparations:** Joachim Fest, *Plotting Hitler's Death: The Story of the German Resistance,* Bruce Little, trans. (New York: Metropolitan Books, 1996), 73–169; Wheeler-Bennett, 470–471. **Hitler, Brauchitsch, and Halder:** Goutard, 74; Wheeler Bennett, 470–471; Manstein, 85–86; Franz Halder, *The Halder War Diary, 1939–1942,* Charles Burdick and Hans-Adolf Jacobsen, eds. (Novato, Calf.: Presidio Press, 1988), 78; *Nazi Conspiracy and Aggression* (Washington: U.S. Government Printing Office, 1946), 3:

572–580; Samuel W. Mitcham Jr., *Hitler's Field Marshals and Their Battles* (Chelsea, Mich.: Scarborough House, 1990), 58; Fest, 127. **Hitler's November 5 address:** *Trials of War Criminals before the Nuremberg Military Tribunals* (Washington, D.C.: U.S. Government Printing Office, 1951), 10: 823–831.

Fall Gelb: Horne, 48–49, 141, 150–151, 157–168; Manstein, 103–105, 113–117, 119–122; Addington, 34–35, 90; Taylor, 168, 179; Jacobsen, *Fall Gelb*, 69–213; Keitel, 102–103; Shirer, *Collapse of the Third Republic*, 595–596; Draper, 51–53; R. T. Paget, *Manstein: His Campaigns and His Trial* (London: Collins, 1951), 1–13; Liddell Hart, 63–64.

Heinz Guderian: Heinz Guderian, *Achtung Panzer!* (Stuttgart: Deutsche Verlags-Anstalt, 1937); Guderian, *Panzer Leader*, 16–20, 26, 30, 89, 94–95; Horne, 48–49; Addington, 34–35. **Hitler:** Guderian, *Achtung Panzer!*, 30; Addington, 35. **Rival tank strength:** Kenneth Macksey, *Guderian: Creator of the Blitzkrieg* (London: Macmillan, 1975), Chapter 7.

Hitler Adopts the Manstein Plan: Guderian, *Panzer Leader*, 67–68; Manstein, 116–122; Horne, 141, 157–168; Draper, 51–53; Taylor, 168, 179; Jacobsen, *Fall Gelb*, 115–116; Kenneth Macksey, "Colonel-General Heinz Guderian," in Cormelli Barnett, ed. *Hitler's Generals* (London: Weidenfeld and Nicolson, 1989), 441–462; Mearscheimer, 124–129. **Hitler comment to Keitel:** Keitel, 102–103. **Schmundt:** Horne, 159. **Hitler, "cup of tea":** Shirer, *Collapse of the Third Republic*, 595. **"Drive a wedge":** Guderian, Panzer *Leader*, 90. **Guderian, Hitler and Busch:** Ibid., 91–93. *"Nicht kleckern, klotzen!":* Jacques Benoist-Méchin, 51–52.

Chapter Four. The Battle Begins, May 10–14

London: A Change of Government: Clare Boothe, *Europe in the Spring* (New York: Knopf, 1940), 126–127. **Chamberlain:** Henry H. Adams, *Years of Deadly Peril* (New York: McKay, 1969), 91–93, 95–98. **Amery:** Spears, 1: 120. **Churchill:** Great Britain, *Parliamentary Debates* (London: His Majesty's Stationary Office, 1941), Commons, 1939–1940, vol. 360, cols. 1348–1362.

Crisis in the French Cabinet, May 9: Shirer, *Collapse of the Third Republic*, 550–553; Pierre Cot, *Triumph of Treason* (Chicago: Ziff-Davis, 1944), 267–271. **Reynaud and Lamoureux:** Paul Baudouin, *The Private Diaries* (London: Eyre and Spottiswoode, 1948), 24. **Daladier and Reynaud:** James Vincent Sheean, *Between the Thunder and the Sun* (New York: Random House, 1943), 103; D. W. Brogan, *French Personalities and Problems* (London: Knopf, 1946), 175; Baudouin, 25–26; Reynaud, *In the Thick of the Fight, 1930–1945* (New York: Simon and Shuster, 1955), 285–286.

The German Offensive Begins, May 9–10: Keitel, 106–107.

The Fall of Eben Emael, May 10–11: James E. Mrazek, *The Fall of Eben Emael: Prelude to Dunkirk* (London: Hale, 1972), 28–33, 83–94, 116, 124–126, 145–146, 177–181, 183; Cajus Bekker, *The Luftwaffe War Diaries* (New York: Da Capo Press, 1994), 94–99; Horne, 220; Bartz, 31, 33; Taylor, 211–212.

War Comes to Belgium, May 9–10: Spaak, 33–36; *Belgium: The Official Account*, 27.

War Comes to Holland: Oster and Sas: Walter B. Maass, *The Netherlands At War: 1940–1945* (New York: Abelard-Schuman, 1970), 28–29. **Van Kleffens:** Ibid., 30–31. **German attack on Holland:** Bekker, 100–113; Taylor, 188–189, 192; Shirer, *Collapse of the Third Republic,* 721; Joseph Doumenc, *Histoire de la Neuvième armée* (Grenoble: B. Arthaud, 1945), 20–32. **Choltitz:** Bekker, 102.

The Allies Go to War, May 10: Shirer, *Collapse of the Third Republic,* 605–608. **Gamelin and Georges:** Gamelin, 3: 389; Beaufre, 180. **Reynaud:** Reynaud, *In the Thick of the Fight,* 287, 295; Baudouin, 27–28. **Churchill:** Laurence Thompson, *1940* (London: William Morrow, 1966), 93–94.

The Allied Advance to the Dyle, May 10: Brooke: Arthur Bryant, *The Turn of the Tide* (New York: Doubleday, 1957), 68–69. **Belgian people:** Ewan Butler and J. Selby Bradford, *The Story of Dunkirk* (London: Hutchinson, 1955), 81. **Montgomery:** Bryant, 74. Gamelin: Reynaud, *In the Thick of the Fight,* 295.

"Are They Leading Us into a Trap?": Reynaud and Daladier: Baudouin, 28. **Hitler:** Benoist-Méchin, 75. **Gamelin, May 12:** Horne, 243; François d' Astier de la Vigerie, *Le ciel n'était pas vide, 1940* (Paris: Julliard, 1952), 87–88.

The Attack on the Maas Bridges, May 12: Mansell: Charles Gardner, *First Blood for the R.A.F.: The Valorous Story of the Advanced Air Striking Force in France* (Philadelphia: David McKay, 1941), 213–216. **German interrogator:** Horne, 248.

The Battle of the Gembloux Gap, May 12–15: Goutard, 109–110; John Williams, *The Ides of May: The Defeat of France: May–June 1940* (London: Constable, 1986), 114–116; René Prioux, *Souvenirs de Guerre* (Paris: Flammarion, 1947), 69; Doumenc, 34–39. **Daladier:** Shirer, *Collapse of the Third Republic,* 626.

The Battle of the Ardennes Forest, May 10–12: Liddell Hart, 124–125; Erwin Rommel, *The Rommel Papers,* B. H. Liddell Hart, ed. (New York: Harcourt Brace, 1953), 6–7. **Blumentritt:** Horne, 211–212. **The German advance through the Ardennes:** Florian K. Rothbrust, *Guderian's XIXth Panzer Corps and the Battle of France: Breakthrough in the Ardennes, May 1940* (New York: Praeger, 1990), 54–65; Williams, 120; Horne, 251; Guderian, *Panzer Leader,* 98–99. **French forces:** Draper, 60–63. **Guderian in Bouillon:** Guderian, *Panzer Leader,* 101. **Doumenc's headquarters:** Beaufre, 181. **Gamelin:** Williams, 138–139.

The Bombing of Rotterdam, May 13–14: Maass, 38–42; Bekker, 107–113. **Kuechler:** Bekker, 107–108. **Schmidt:** Ibid., 108. **Kesselring:** Maass, 38; Bekker, 108. **Plutzar and Schmidt:** Bekker, 108. **Lackner:** Ibid., 109. **Schmidt and Choltitz:** Ibid., 109–110. **Lackner:** Ibid., 111. **Schmidt and Hoehne's bombardier:** Ibid., 111. **Dutch losses:** Maass, 40–42.

"Blood, Toil, Tears, and Sweat," May 13: Spears, 1: 138–139. **Churchill's speech:** *Parliamentary Debates,* Commons, 1939–1940, vol. 360, cols. 1501–1502.

Chapter Five. The Battle of the Meuse, May 12–15

The French Defenses on the Meuse River: Williams, 109–118; Gamelin, 1: 325; Doumenc, 75. **Corap's army:** Horne, 188–189; André Maurois, *The Battle of France* (London: The Right Book Co., 1940), 171.

Rommel Crosses the Meuse, May 12–15: Rommel, 8–13, 16. **Wipspelaere:** Horne, 258. **Rommel at Dinant:** Rommel, 8–10; Goutard, 159–160; Horne, 262. **Battle of Wastia Heights:** Goutard, 158–164; Horne, 277–281. **Battle of Onhaye:** Rommel, 11–13; Horne, 324–325. **22nd Division:** Goutard, 164. **Véron:** Goutard, 165; *Evénements,* 5: 1294.

The Counterattack of the French First Armored Division, May 15: **Billotte:** Goutard, 161. **Bruneau and Rommel:** Ibid., 165–169. **Tank battle:** Horne, 350–352. **Bruneau's losses:** Goutard, 168–169. **Battle of Philippeville:** Rommel, 15–16; Horne, 352–355.

Reinhardt Crosses the Meuse, May 13–14: Battle of Monthermé: Draper, 79–82. **Billotte and Georges:** Goutard, 167. Karl von Stackleberg, *Ich War Dabei, Ich Sah, Ich Schrieb* (Berlin: Schuetzenverlag, 1940), 122–124. Horne, 357.

The French 2nd Armored Division Dissolves, May 14–16: Shirer, *Collapse of the Third Republic,* 688–689; Horne, 367–368.

The Defense of Sedan: Robert Allan Doughty, *The Breaking Point: Sedan and the Fall of France, 1940* (Hamden, Conn.: Archon Books, 1990), 104–107; Williams, 110–115. **Taittinger-Frammond Report:** *Evénements,* 2: 359–360. **Huntziger:** Reynaud, 294; Doughty, 99. **Grandsard:** Goutard, 131–132; Charles L. Menu, *Lumière sur les Ruines* (Paris: Plon, 1953), 213.

Guderian's Plan of Attack, May 12: Guderian, *Panzer Leader,* 101.

The Attack Begins, May 13: Pruemers: Horne, 287; Guderian, *Panzer Leader,* 104. **Ruby:** Goutard, 133. **Loerzer:** Guderian, *Panzer Leader,* 98, 104. **Message to Barratt:** Horne, 288. *Grossdeutschland* **crossing:** Horne, 297–304.

The 1st Infantry Regiment Crosses, May 13: Doughty, 140–143; Guderian, *Panzer Leader,* 102.

The Collapse of the Frénois Line, May 13: Verron: Doughty, 145, 171–175. **Balck's advance:** Ibid., 185.

The Crossing of the 10th Panzer Division, May 13: Doughty, 155–157. **Rubarth:** Erhard Wittek, ed., *Die soldatische Tat: Berichte von Mitkämpfen des Heeres im Westfeldzug, 1940* (Berlin: Im Deutschen Verlag, 1940), 22–25; Feldwebel Schulze, "Erste Einfass vor Sedan," *Militar-Wochenblatt,* April 1941, 1291–1293.

The 2nd Panzer Division Crosses, May 13: French commander at Donchéry: Doughty, 172. **Keddig:** Horne, 303.

The Panic of the French 55th Infantry Division, May 13: Edmund Ruby, *Sedan: Terre d'Épreuve: Avec la IIème Armée, Mai-Juin 1940* (Paris: Flammarion, 1948), 132–135; Goutard, 136–137. **Lafontaine:** Doughty, 200.

The French High Command Awakens, May 13: Shirer, *Collapse of the Third Republic,* 650. **Huntziger's reports:** Minart, 2: 148.

Bridging the Meuse, May 13–14: First Lieutenant Grubnau, "Brückenschlag über die Maas westlich Sedan für den Übergang einer Panzer Division," *Militär-Wochenblatt,* January 3, 1941, cols. 1291–1293. **Nehring:** Doughty, 172. **Billotte:** D'Astier, 107; Graf Johann Adolf Kielmansegg, *Panzer zwischen Warschau und Atlantik* (Berlin: Verlag "Die Wehrmacht," 1941), 115. **Rundstedt:** Guderian, *Panzer Leader,* 106.

Lafontaine's Counterattack, May 14: Ruby, 133; Williams, 139–140; Doughty, 205–214, 245–265. **Labarthe:** Ruby, 149. **Georges and Doumenc:** Beaufre, 232–234. **Georges:** Shirer, *Collapse of the Third Republic,* 652.

The Panzers Attack, May 14: Doughty, 208–210, 255–260.

The French 71st Division Panics, May 14: Goutard, 136–137; Horne, 305–310, 329–330; Doughty, 191–197; Williams, 140–141; Menu, 226.

Guderian Turns West, May 14: Guderian, *Panzer Leader,* 106–107.

The French Third Armored Division's "Counterattack," May 14–15: Flavigny: Doughty, 279–286; Shirer, *Collapse of the Third Republic,* 653–657; Goutard, 140–141. **Flavigny's orders:** Ibid., 143–144. **Huntziger:** Shirer, *Collapse of the Third Republic,* 657. **Georges:** Gaston René Roton, *Années cruciales, 1939–1940* (Paris: Payot, 1947), 177; Minart, 2: 144; *Evénements,* 3: 694. **Flavigny's defense:** *Evénements,* 5: 1345, 1353. **Huntziger's defense:** Shirer, *Collapse of the Third Republic,* 655–656. **Georges's reaction:** *Evénements,* 3: 694.

Guderian Destroys Coraps's Right Wing, May 15: Rothbrust, 85–87. **Balck:** Ibid., 86; Guderian, *Panzer Leader,* 107–108.

Chapter Six. The German Drive to the English Channel, May 15–20

"We Have Been Defeated!": Churchill and Reynaud: Winston Churchill, *The Second World War,* 6 vols. (Boston: Houghton Mifflin, 1948–1954), vol. 2, *Their Finest Hour,* 42–43; Reynaud, *In the Thick of the Fight,* 320.

Gamelin's Eyes Are Finally Opened, May 15: Gamelin's telegram: Churchill, 2: 43. **Gamelin, "serious":** Shirer, 677. **Guillaut:** Minart 2: 152–153. **Bullitt's recollection of the Gamelin-Daladier phone conversation:** Orville H. Bullitt, ed., *For the President: Personal and Secret: Correspondence Between Franklin D. Roosevelt and William C. Bullitt* (Boston: Houghton Mifflin, 1972), 428. **Bullitt to FDR, May 16:** Ibid., 426. **Kennedy to FDR:** *Foreign Relations of the United States, 1940* (Washington, D.C.: G.P.O., 1941), 1: 225. **Roosevelt and Ickes:** John Lukacs, *The Duel* (New York: Ticknor and Fields, 1990), 73. **Churchill to Roosevelt:** Ibid., 76–77. **Roosevelt:** Norman Gelb, *Dunkirk: The Complete Story of the First Step in the Defeat of Hitler* (New York: William Morrow, 1989), 88.

Churchill in Paris, May 16: Churchill, 2: 46; Lord Ismay, *Memoirs* (London: Heinemann, 1960), 127. **Supreme War Council:** Churchill, 2: 45–61; Reynaud, *In the Thick* *of the Fight,* 321–327; Baudouin, 31–32; Horne, 397–398. **Churchill to War Cabinet:** Churchill, 2: 50. **Churchill, Reynaud and Daladier:** Ibid., 51. **Churchill:** Horne, 398.

Churchill and Roosevelt, May 17: *The Churchill War Papers,* vol. 2, *Never Surrender, May 1940–December 1940,* Martin Gilbert, ed. (New York: W. W. Norton, 1993), 65; John R. Colville, *Fringes of Power: 10 Downing Street Diaries, 1939–1955* (New York: W. W. Norton, 1985), 134. **Ismay:** Randolph Churchill and Martin Gilbert, *Winston S. Churchill,* 8 vols. (London: Macmillan, 1966–1985), vol. 6: *Their Finest Hour,* 354. **Roosevelt's telegram:** Ibid., 6: 55. Alexander Cadogan, *The Diaries of Sir Alexander Cadogan* (London: Cassell, 1971), 285. **Roosevelt:** Churchill and Gilbert, 6: 355. **Churchill's telegram:** Ibid., 6: 355–356. **Randolph Churchill's recollection:** Ibid., 6: 358.

King Léopold Decides to Stay in Belgium, May 15–18: Michiels: Rémy, 114. **Pierlot and Léopold:** Keyes, 232; Shirer, *Collapse of the Third Republic,* 695; *Rapport de la Commission d'Information instutée par S.M. Léopold III* (Brussels, 1947), 203. Reynaud, *In the Thick of the Fight,* 319. **Léopold, May 16:** Rémy, 116; Reynaud, *In the Thick of the Fight,* 318; Keyes, 237. **Pierlot's letter:** Keyes, 251–252.

Lord Gort's Growing Dismay, May 15–16: Gort: Brian Bond, "Gort," in John Keegan, ed., *Churchill's Generals* (New York: Grove Weidenfeld, 1991), 35. **Montgomery:** Nigel Hamilton, *Monty, The Making of a General* (New York: McGraw-Hill, 1981), 394. **Brooke:** Arthur Bryant, *The Turn of the Tide* (New York: Doubleday, 1957), 59–60. Henry Pownall, *Diaries,* Brian Bond, ed. (London: Leo Cooper, 1972), 314. **Churchill:** Nicholas Harman, *Dunkirk: The Patriotic Myth* (New York: Simon and Schuster, 1980), 74–75.

The Allied Retreat Begins, May 16: Pownall, 317. **Brooks:** Ronald Atkin, *Pillar of Fire: Dunkirk, 1940* (London: Sidgwick and Jackson, 1990), 94; René Balbaud, *Cette Drôle de Guerre* (London: Oxford University Press, 1941), 51. **German radio:** Rémy, 130.

The Race to the Channel Begins, May 16: Guderian, *Panzer Leader,* 108–109.

The Panzers Are Halted, May 16–17: Halder, 145. **Rundstedt:** Guenther Blumentritt, *Von Rundstedt: The Soldier and the Man* (London: Odhams Press, 1952), 71. **Hitler to Mussolini:** *Documents on German Foreign Policy, 1918–1945,* Series D, 1937–1945, 10 vols. (Washington: U.S. Department of State, 1949–1956), 9: 375. Lukacs, *Duel,* 63. **"The enemy has only six divisions":** Halder, 147–148. Guderian, *Panzer Leader,* 110–111. **Gretel Guderian:** Kenneth Macksey, *Guderian: Creator of the Blitzkrieg* (New York: Stein and Day, 1975), 112. Kielmansegg, 127.

De Gaulle's Counterattack, May 17: De Gaulle, 1: 37–40; Horne, 423–430. **Idée:** Ibid., 426, 428. Kielmansegg, 127–132. **Kleist:** Liddell Hart, 130.

Hitler Lifts the Panzer Halt Order, May 17: Halder, 149–151.

Pétain and Weygand Are Recalled to Paris, May 17: Reynaud: Shirer, *Collapse of the Third Republic,* 699, 702. **Pétain:** Pierre Héring, *La Vie exemplaire de Philippe Pétain*

(Paris: Paris-Livres, 1956), 77. **Gasser and Reynaud:** Rémy, 129–130. **Bullitt to FDR:** *Foreign Relations of the United States, 1940,* 1: 228–229. **Bullitt:** Gordon Wright, "Ambassador Bullitt and the Fall of France," *World Politics,* 1 (October 1957): 82. **Churchill:** John Lukacs, *Five Days in London, May 1940* (New Haven, Conn.: Yale University Press, 1999), 18. **Göring and Reynaud:** Reynaud, *Mémoires,* 2: 509.

Gamelin "Acts!", May 17: Gamelin's Order of the Day: Rémy, 122. **Gamelin and Doumenc:** Gamelin, 3: 415. **Gamelin and Daladier:** Ibid., 3: 416–419. **Reynaud and Gamelin:** Reynaud, *In the Thick of the Fight,* 344. **Pétain and Gamelin:** Gamelin, 3: 427. **Doumenc and Gamelin:** Minart, 2: 184–185. **Georges and Gamelin:** *Evénements,* 3: 689–691. **Gamelin's lunch:** Beaufre, 238–239.

Gort Decides to Withdraw to the Coast, May 19: O. J. Archdale, Diary, May 18, 1940 (unpublished, British Imperial War Museum); Pownall, 323; Gort, "Despatch," 5915. **Gort's liaison officer:** Eleanor M. Gates, *The End of an Affair: The Collapse of the Anglo-French Alliance* (London: George Allen and Unwin, 1981), 82. **Gort's withdrawal:** Keyes, 248.

The War Cabinet, May 19: Chartwell: John R. Colville, *Man of Valour: The Life of Field Marshal the Viscount Gort* (London: Collins, 1972), 204. **Ironside and Churchill:** Churchill and Gilbert, 6: 363–364. **Churchill's radio speech:** Ibid., 6: 364. **Eden and Colville:** Ibid. **Churchill to Roosevelt:** Ibid., 6: 368.

Weygand Takes Over, May 19–20: Pepin: Rémy, 131. **Notre Dame:** Horne, 476–478. Baudouin, 34–35. **Gamelin and Weygand:** Gamelin, 1: 5–8; 3: 432–437. **Weygand:** Beaufre, 240–241; Baudouin, 35, 37. **Gamelin:** Shirer, *Collapse of the Third Republic,* 709. **Buré:** Ibid., 712. **Madame Tabouis:** Keyes, 253. De Gaulle, 51. **Weygand:** Spears, 1: 201. Gamelin, 3: 434–435. Maxime Weygand, *Recalled to Service* (London: Heinemann, 1952), 51–52.

Ironside's Visit to Gort, May 20: Gort, "Despatch," 5921. **"Just jelly":** Atkin, 95. Edmund Ironside, *Time Unguarded: The Ironside Diaries, 1937–1940,* R. Macleod and D. Kelly, eds. (London: Constable, 1963), 321, 326.

Guderian Reaches the Channel, May 20: Guderian, *Panzer Leader,* 496, 112–115; Kielmansegg, 133; William L. Shirer, *Berlin Diary: The Journal of a Foreign Correspondent, 1934–1941* (Boston: Little, Brown, 1988), 379–380. **2nd Panzer Division:** Guderian, *Panzer Leader,* 113. **Attack by German planes:** Ibid. **"Today's battles":** Ibid., 500. Halder, 153. **Jodl:** Horne, 488. **Rundstedt:** Ibid., 508.

Chapter Seven. The Weygand Plan, May 20–26

Frankforce, May 20: L. F. Ellis, *The War in France and Flanders, 1939–1940* (London: H.M.S.O., 1953), 88; Harman, 92–95; Blaxland, 133–135; Horne, 499–500; Shirer, *Collapse of the Third Republic,* 718. **Franklyn:** Blaxland, 135–136. **Prioux:** Horne, 500. **Vautrin:** Ibid., 499. **Leese:** Blaxland, 136.

Rommel Advances Toward Arras, May 20: Halder, 157; Rommel, 31–33.

Martel's Attack, May 21: Ellis, 88–89; Blaxland, 138–146; Harman, 96–100; Draper, 187–189. **Diaries:** Harman, 98.

Rommel's Counterattack, Evening, May 21: Durham subaltern and Manley: Atkin, 97. Rommel, 33–35. Harman, 100. **Rundstedt:** Liddell Hart, 131.

The Ypres Conference, May 21: Keyes, 269–277, 290; Weygand, 59–64. **Weygand and Van Overstraeten:** Rémy, 157–158, 160. **Léopold, Van Overstraeten, and Pierlot:** Shirer, *Collapse of the Third Republic,* 715–716. **Pownall and Gort:** Rémy, 169. **Fagalde:** Blaxland, 172. **Gort's account of the meeting:** Gort, "Despatch," 5918. **"Dirty dogs":** Keyes, 284. **Léopold:** Ibid., 289–290.

Churchill Visits Paris, May 22: Churchill and Colville: *Churchill War Papers,* 2: 107. Ismay, 131. **Churchill's description of Weygand:** *Churchill War Papers,* 2: 110; Horne, 521; Churchill, 2: 64–65. **Churchill and Weygand:** Churchill and Gilbert, 6: 379–381. **Supreme Allied War Council:** *Churchill War Papers,* 2: 111–114. **Churchill to Gort:** Churchill, 2: 65. **Ironside and Churchill:** *Churchill War Papers,* 2: 116; Spears, 1: 166. **Munster:** Churchill and Gilbert, 6: 381. Pownall, 333. **Gort:** Gates, 94. **Weygand:** Jacques Weygand, *The Role of General Weygand* (London: Eyre and Spottiswoode, 1948), 65.

Léopold Decides to Stop on the Lys, May 22: Rémy, 180.

Guderian Resumes His Advance, May 21: Guderian, *Panzer Leader,* 113; Goutard, 226.

The Halt Order, May 24: Goutard, 227–228, 233–234; Horne, 533–535; Ellis, 138–139, 383; Blaxland, 109; Larry H. Addington, *The Blitzkrieg Era and the German General Staff, 1865–1941* (New Brunswick, N.J: Rutgers University Press, 1971), 115; Walter Goerlitz, *The German General Staff* (New York: Praeger, 1953), 376; Guderian, *Panzer Leader,* 117. **Rundstedt:** Liddell Hart, 72–73. **Göring:** Goutard, 232–233. **Rundstedt and Hitler:** James E. Duffy, *Hitler Slept Late* (New York: Praeger, 1991), 31, 35–37; Halder, 165. **Lossberg:** *Goutard, 229.* **Kesselring and Göring:** Bekker, 123. **Thoma:** Benoist-Méchin, 145. **Dietrich:** Guderian, *Panzer Leader,* 117. **Kleist:** Liddell Hart, 133–134. **Hitler:** Benoist-Méchin, 145. **Blumentritt and Hitler:** Liddell Hart, 134–136. **Rundstedt:** Ibid., 135. **Guderian:** Benoist-Méchin, 145.

Spears in Paris, May 25: Spears, 1: 181, 183–185, 188–191, 194. **Varillon:** Gates, 155. **Pétain:** Louis Marin, "Gouvernement et commandement (mai–juin 1940)," *Revue d' Histoire de la Deuxiéme Guerre Mondiale* 8 (October 1952), 5. **Mandel and Spears:** Spears, 1: 205–207.

The French War Committee, Evening, May 25: Weygand: *Evénements,* 6: 1694–1695. Reynaud, *In the Thick of the Fight,* 369. **Campinchi:** Baudouin, 54–55. **Pétain:** Ibid., 54. **Reynaud:** Ibid., 53. **Weygand:** Ibid., 55–56. Baudouin's account was challenged by Reynaud after the war. For more on this controversy, see Gates, 488, n. 11 and Reynaud, *In the Thick of the Fight,* 394–397.

Léopold Moves Toward Capitulation, May 25: Léopold's minutes of the May 25 meeting: Rémy, 210–211. **Léopold and Pierlot:** Ibid., 234–237, 240–244.

Gort Decides to Withdraw to the Coast, May 25: Churchill to Reynaud: *Churchill War Papers,* 2: 117. **Gort to Churchill:** Keyes, 326–327. **Churchill's phone call to Reynaud:** Churchill and Gilbert, 6: 385. **Reynaud and Weygand:** Ibid; Spears, 1: 167; Colville, *Man of Valour,* 213. **Colville:** Churchill and Gilbert, 6: 385; F. W. Winterbotham, The *Ultra Secret* (New York: Dell, 1975), 34–35; Ronald Lewin, *Ultra Goes to War: The Secret Story* (London: Hutchinson, 1978), 70. **King George:** Keyes, 299. **Archdale:** Blaxland, 114–115. **Gort's decision:** Shirer, *Collapse of the Third Republic,* 733. **Gort and Pownall:** David Divine, *The Nine Days of Dunkirk* (London: Faber and Faber, 1959), 55; Gort, "Despatch," 5923. **Eden's cable:** Blaxland, 254; Ellis, 173–174.

The British Defense Committee, Evening, May 25: Churchill, Dill, and Karslake: Churchill and Gilbert, 6: 398.

The Battle of Calais, May 24–27: Churchill: Atkin, 118. **War Office order:** Ellis, 165. **Churchill to Nicholson:** Churchill and Gilbert, 6: 395. **Nicholson:** Ellis, 167. **10th Panzer Division war diary:** Ibid. **Dinort:** Bekker, 123–124. "**Calais was the crux**": Churchill, 2: 82.

The Demise of the Weygand Plan, May 26: Blanchard's order: Ellis, 172. **Reynaud and Weygand:** Keyes, 299–300; Churchill, 2: 72. **Reynaud:** Baudouin, 47.

Chapter Eight. The Retreat to Dunkirk, May 26–28

London, May 26: Churchill: Churchill and Gilbert, 6: 403. **Churchill's letter to Chamberlain:** Ibid., 314. **Halifax:** Lukacs, *Five Days,* 126. **Bastianini and Halifax:** Ibid., 109. **Mussolini:** Benoist-Méchin, 166. **Churchill and Halifax:** War Cabinet, Minutes, 26 May 1940, 9 A.M., Cabinet Papers, 65/13. **Westminster Abbey prayer service:** Lukacs, *Five Days,* 105. **Churchill and Reynaud:** War Cabinet, Minutes, 26 May 1940, 2 P.M., Cabinet Papers, 65/13. **Churchill and Halifax:** Ibid. **Reynaud:** Baudouin, 57–58. **Eden to Gort:** Ellis, 174. **Admiralty order:** Ibid., 182. Cadogan, 290. Ismay, 12. Colville, *Diary,* 141.

Withdrawal to Dunkirk Begins, May 26–27: W. J. R. Gardner, ed., *The Evacuation from Dunkirk: Operation Dynamo, 26 May–4 June 1940* (Portland, Ore.: Frank Cass, 2000), 15. **Gort:** Churchill, 2: 84; Blaxland, 254. **Churchill to Gort:** Churchill, 2: 90. James M. Langley, *Fight Another Day* (London: Collins, 1974), 42–45.

The Dunkirk Perimeter: Ellis, 177–178; Harman, 140–141, 160; Gelb, 156–157; Spears, 1: 192.

Operation Dynamo Begins, May 26: Dudley: Gardner, *Evacuation from Dunkirk,* 15–16. **Ramsay to his wife:** W. S. Chalmers, *Full Cycle: The Biography of Admiral Sir Bertram Home Ramsay* (London: Hodder and Stoughton, 1959), 73. **Duggan:** Harman, 128. **Tennant arrives:** Ibid., 135–136. **May 27 total:** Garland, *Evacuation from Dunkirk,* 25. **Tennant:** Atkin, 150. Anthony Rhodes, *Sword of Bone* (London: Buchan and Enright, 1986), 215. "**During the first night**": Chalmers, 74. "**Please send**": Ibid. **Calcutta:** Ellis, 186. Basil Bartlett, *My First War* (New York: Macmillan, 1941), 117. Rhodes, 227. Bartlett, 120. **Mole:** Chalmers, 74; Atkin, 151.

Hitler Unleashes His Panzers, May 26: Halder, 167; Guderian, *Panzer Leader,* 119.

Defending the Allied Pocket: Megaw: Blaxland, 261–262. Rommel, 40. Pownall, 344. **Loveluck:** Atkin, 127–128.

The Massacre at Le Paradis, May 27: Atkin, 151–152. **Norfolks' officer:** Blaxland, 285. Leslie Aitken, *Massacre on the Road to Dunkirk: Wormhout, 1940* (London: William Kimber, 1977), 116. Pooley's story is told in Cyril Jolly, *The Vengeance of Private Pooley* (London: Heineman, 1956).

The Massacre at Wormhoudt, May 28: Aitken, 90–96. **Mohnke and Dietrich:** Patrick Wilson, *Dunkirk, 1940: From Disaster to Deliverance* (Barnesley, Eng.: Leo Cooper, 1999), 68–69.

Churchill vs. Halifax: Round 2, May 27–28: Text of "British Strategy in a Certain Eventuality": Churchill, 2: 87–89. **Greenwood, Churchill, Chamberlain, and Halifax:** War Cabinet, Minutes, 27 May 1940, 11 A.M., Cabinet Papers, 65/13; Lukacs, *Five Days,* 147–155; Churchill and Gilbert, 6: 411, 422. **Halifax diary:** Earl of Birkenhead, *Halifax: The Life of Lord Halifax* (London: Hamish Hamilton, 1955), 458. Cadogan, 291. Colville, *Diary,* 291. **FDR's fireside address:** Gelb, 152–153. **Army's Ordnance Division:** Ibid, 153. **Churchill, Westminster Abbey, Parliament and Cabinet meeting:** Churchill, 2: 99–100; *Churchill War Papers,* 2: 181, 182, 187; Ben Pimlott, ed., *'The Second World War Diary of Hugh Dalton, 1940–1945* (London: Jonathan Cape, 1986), 29. War Cabinet, Minutes, 28 May 1940, 7 P.M., Cabinet Papers, 65/13; P. M. H. Bell, *A Certain Eventuality: Britain and the Fall of France* (London: Saxon House, 1974), 48. **Attlee:** Churchill and Gilbert, 6: 411. **Churchill's order:** Churchill, 2: 91. **Churchill's phone call to Reynaud:** Churchill and Gilbert, 6: 422.

Léopold Surrenders, May 27–28: Van Overstraeten: Rémy, 270; Bond, *Britain, France and Belgium,* 86–87, 90, 93, 95–97. Pownall, 347–350. Anthony Eden, *Facing the Dictators* (London: Cassell, 1962), 111. **Churchill to Keyes:** Bond, *Britain, France and Belgium,* 3. Oscar Michiels, *Dix-Huit Jours de guerre en Belgique* (Paris: Berger-Levrault, 1947), 210–211. **Derousseaux:** Rémy, 303. **Léopold, Keyes, Elisabeth:** Ibid., 292. **Léopold and Reichenau:** Ibid., 309–311. **Gillon:** Ibid., 311. **Keyes and Davy:** *Churchill War Papers,* 2: 176–178. **Reynaud:** Spears, 1: 248. **Pierlot's address:** Rémy, 313–315. **Pierlot, Spaak, and Léopold:** Keyes, 412–444.

Chapter Nine. Operation Dynamo, May 28–June 4

Filling the Gap, May 28: Gort: Blaxland, 271–273. **Brooke:** Harman, 131–132. **Montgomery:** Alun Chalfont, *Montgomery of Alamein* (London: Atheneum, 1976), 114; **Battle of Nieuport:** Atkin, 183.

The French 1st Army, May 28–29: Gort: Ellis, 209; Pownall, 359. **Gort: "Despatch,"** 5927. **Blanchard:** Gates, 108. **De la Laurencie:** Robert Jackson, *Dunkirk: The British Evacuation* (New York: St. Martin's Press, 1976), 68. **French 1st Army surrenders:** Ellis, 210; Blaxland, 295. **Matthew, Brooks, and Loveluck:** Atkin, 145.

Gort's Predicament, May 28: Churchill to Gort: *Churchill War Papers,* 2: 190; Gort, "Despatch," 5929.

Operation Dynamo, May 28: Gardner, *Evacuation from Dunkirk,* 34. **Ramsay:** Chalmers, 76–77. **Rescued men:** Gelb, 234. **RAF:** Chalmers, 77. **Tennant:** Gardner, *Evacuation from Dunkirk,* 28.

Naval Losses, May 29: Gardner, *Evacuation from Dunkirk,* 36–38; Walter Lord, *The Miracle of Dunkirk* (New York: Viking Press, 1982), 120–124; Atkin, 170–171. **Zimmermann:** Lord, 120. Bartlett, 121–125.

The Attack on the East Mole, May 29: Gardner, *Evacuation from Dunkirk,* 38–45.

Back to the Beaches, May 29: Dove: Lord, 143.

The Panzers Are Withdrawn, May 29: Guderian: Ellis, 208. Halder, 169–170. **Battle of Furnes:** Lord, 151.

French Evacuation, May 29–30: Jean Beaux: Harman, 152–153. D. Barlone, *A French Officer's Diary (23 August 1939–1 October 1940)* (Cambridge: Cambridge University Press, 1942), 56–57. **Brooke:** Bryant, 115; Gelb, 224. **Hilton:** Lord, 174. **Abrial:** Atkin, 185–186. **Gort and Dill:** Ibid., 185. **Champon:** Ibid. **Churchill and Reynaud:** Churchill, 2: 106–107; Spears, 1: 279.

French Pleas for Assistance, May 29–30: Weygand: Benoist-Méchin, 186–187. **Bullitt to FDR:** Ibid., 189. **Purvis:** Churchill and Gilbert, 6: 426. **Hull to Bullitt:** Bullitt, 446–447. **Churchill:** War Cabinet, Minutes, 30 May 1940, Cabinet Papers, 65/13.

The Evacuation Continues, May 30: Wake-Walker: Harman, 174, 250; Chalmers, 83. **Tennant:** Harman, 175. **Pound:** Lord, 168. **May 30 evacuation total:** Harman, 250. Gort, "Despatch," 5931. Gardner, *Evacuation from Dunkirk,* 56.

Gort Is Ordered Home, May 30: Churchill to Gort: Churchill and Gilbert, 6: 432. **Montgomery:** Nigel Nicolson, *Alex: The Life and Times of Field Marshall Earl Alexander of Tunis* (London: Weidenfeld and Nicolson, 1973), 103–104. **Wake-Walker:** Lord, 172–173.

The Evacuation, May 31–June 1: "All tanks hostile": Lord, 208. **Coxswain:** Gelb, 255. **Dibbens:** Lord, 167. **Belgian fishing boats:** Gardner, *Evacuation from Dunkirk,* 73. **Brooke:** Lord, 277. **Galway:** *Manchester Guardian,* June 5, 1940; Gelb, 295.

Churchill in Paris, May 31: Lord, 180; Spears, 1: 295–318; Ismay, 134.

Gort Leaves, Alexander Takes Over, May 31: De la Laurencie: Lord, 181. **Gort:** Ellis, 234. **Alexander:** Gelb, 266–267. **Abrial:** Blaxland, 331. **Eden:** Gelb, 267. **Abrial to Weygand:** Lord, 183. **Alexander:** Ibid., 184.

The German Attack on the Perimeter, May 31: Halder, 172. **Kuechler:** Lord, 209–211. **Surreys:** Ibid., 199–200. **Duriez:** Patrick Wilson, *Dunkirk, 1940: From Disaster to Deliverance* (Barnsley, Eng.: Leo Cooper, 1999), 85; Langley, 46–47.

Evacuation from De Panne, May 31: Chalmers, 85; Gardner, *Evacuation from Dunkirk,* 70. "Off the streets!": Gelb, 268. Wake-Walker: Chalmers, 85–86. McClelland: Ibid, 86; Gardner, *Evacuation from Dunkirk,* 76–77. Ramsay: Gelb, 274. May 31 total: Gardner, *Evacuation from Dunkirk,* 65, 84. Tennant and Alexander: Chalmers, 88.

The Defense of the Perimeter, June 1: Langley, 47–54.

The Evacuation, June 1–2: Wake-Walker: Lord, 216. Ivanhoe's captain: Gelb, 277. RAF: Ibid., 278. Tennant: Chalmers, 89. Ramsay suspends daylight evacuations: Gardner, *Evacuation from Dunkirk,* 96–98.

Gort in London, June 1: War Cabinet, Minutes, 1 June 1940, Cabinet Papers, 65/7; Gelb, 279–280. Churchill and Reynaud: Spears, 2: 6–7. Dill and Tennant: Lord, 229–230. French soldiers: Ibid., 234.

The Evacuation, June 2–3: Blaxland, 343. Estimates: Gardner, *Evacuation from Dunkirk,* 105. Ramsay: Chalmers, 91–92. Kuechler's attack: Lord, 250. Tennant and Willy: Atkin, 227. Tennant: Lord, 248. Alexander: Gelb, 298. Wake-Walker: Lord, 248. *Vanquisher* and *Malcolm:* Gelb, 297. Wake-Walker: Lord, 252; Gardner, *Evacuation from Dunkirk,* 105. Darlan: Benoist-Méchin, 214. Weygand: Lord, 252. Churchill: Spears, 2: 23. Churchill to Reynaud and Weygand: Churchill and Gilbert, 6: 456.

The Last Evacuation, June 3–4: Ramsay: Chalmers, 91–93. Malcolm: Lord, 256–258. Lady of Mann: Harman, 223. Quai Félix Faure: Ibid., 223–224; Jacques Mordal, *La Bataille de Dunkerque* (Paris: Editions Self, 1948). Final evacuation totals: Ellis, 246; Gardner, *Evacuation from Dunkirk,* Table 3, ff. 211. Troup: Ellis, 245–246. Cameron: Lord, 261. Langley, 57–60.

The Surrender, June 4: Daily Intelligence Summary: Lord, 267. Cranz-Beaufrère: Ibid. Schmidt: Ibid., 268–269.

Chapter Ten. Aftermath

The Miracle of Dunkirk: Churchill's speech: *Parliamentary Debates,* Commons, vol. 360, cols. 787–796. Gates, 118–119, 481. Wedgwood, Sackville-West, Nicolson, and Cannon: Churchill and Gilbert, 6: 468. Weygand and Churchill: Atkin, 236.

The Defeat of France: French losses: Hans Umbreit, "The Battle for Hegemony in Western Europe," in Klaus A. Maier, Horst Rohde, and Bernd Stegemann, eds., *Germany and the Second World War,* 2 vols. (Oxford: Clarendon Press, 1990), 2: 317; Gates, 74, 119, 123. De Gaulle: Atkin, 233. Weygand: Baudouin, 76. De Gaulle: J. E. and H. W. Kaufmann, *Hitler's Blitzkrieg Campaigns: The Invasion and Defense of Western Europe, 1939–1940* (Conshohocken, Pa.: Combined Books, 1993), 308. French tanks: Addington, 101. French aircraft: Gates, 74–75. Pownall, 368. Spears, 1: 205. Pierlot: *Le Soir* (Brussels), July 19, 1947. Shirer, *Collapse of the Third Republic,* 742–743.

Hitler's Greatest Triumph: German losses: Atkin, 231.

Index

Numbers in *italics* indicate maps and photos.

Guderian, Heinz *(continued)*

panzer divisions attacked unopposed by
RAF and French naval air arm, 222

plan of attack in battle at the Meuse,
128–30

planning and organizing panzer divisions,
46–48

pushing troops to march to English
Channel, 175

reaching the Channel, 200–202

realizing disruption of French command
structure, 178

receiving order to halt on Canal Line, 223

refusal to accept notion of Hitler's
political reason for stopping panzers,
229

request to be relieved of command,
180–81

turning west, 151

unhappy with Hitler's adjustments to
Fall Gelb, 53

use of *Grossdeutschland* at the Meuse, 133

wanting to be in action at the Meuse, 135

watching aerial bombardment at the
Meuse, 131

watching approach of divisions to Meuse,
128

worried about counterattack, 143, 151

Guillaut (Col.), 160, 161

Gunsburg, Jeffrey, 12

Haig, Rudolph, 300

Halder, Franz, 11, 35–36, 48, *105,* 179–80,
202, 357, 358, 359

agreement to coup against Hitler, 37–40

anger at possibility of British escape,
269–70

anticipating next stage of assault on
France, 304

appointment of Kleist, 129

confident about panzers' advance, 178

continuing resentment of Hitler for
stopping panzer advance, 323

demanding freedom of panzers'
movement, 186

desire to kill Hitler, 36

development of *Fall Gelb,* 41, 43–45

disagreement with Guderian on timing of
Meuse crossing, 51

importance of seizing Arras, 205

livid over Hitler's order to halt panzers,
226

on Hitler's nervousness, 185

opposed to western offensive, 36

Halifax, Lord, 248–50

disagreement with Churchill's assessment
of Hitler's aims, 254

discussing Italian peace initiative with
Reynaud, 252

reporting on Italian-Allied peace feeler, 283

serving Churchill faithfully after
disagreements, 285

support for negotiations with Germans
and Italians, 279, 280–81, 283–84

Hall, George, 278

Hart, Basil Liddell, 22, 36, 45, 223, 229,
286

Haug (Sgt.), 71

Hautcoeur, Auguste, 10

Héring, Pierre, 161

Hilton, Bob, 306

Hirtschold, Hauptmann, 244–45

Hitler, Adolf

acknowledging Guderian's strategies, 47

adopting and adjusting Manstein Plan,
48, 50–54

agreeing with order to halt panzers on
Canal Line, 225

anxious about panzers' exposed flanks, 202

appointing Rommel to 7th Panzer
Division, 110

asserting no war aims against Britain and
France, 15

belief that British would not reenter war,
228

called meeting with field commanders, 179

celebrating success at Eben Emael, 75

commitment of armored strength to
battle of Ardennes Forest, 94–95

contempt for General Staff, 39–41

dancing a jig before signing of French
armistice, *356*

death of, 359

declaration of war against U.S., 162, 358

demanding unconditional cease-fire from
Belgium, 288

desire to conquer French army, 2

desire to defeat western powers, 40

desire for honorable peace with Britain,
228–29